THE ALAMO.

HISTORY

OF

T E X A S,

FROM ITS

DISCOVERY AND SETTLEMENT

WITH

A description of its principal Cities and Counties, and the Agricultural, Mineral, and Material Resources of the State.

BY

J. M. MORPHIS.

NEW YORK:
UNITED STATES PUBLISHING COMPANY,
13 University Place.

1875.

JOHN F. TROW & SON,
PRINTERS AND BOOKBINDERS,
205–213 *East 12th St.*,
NEW YORK.

DEDICATION.

To the people of Texas and the United States, this work is respectfully inscribed, with the fervent hope that it may, in some degree, lead to a better understanding of the past, and tend somewhat to the diminution of all unpleasant feelings engendered in their hearts by their mutual sufferings and calamities during the late contest between the Northern and Southern States.

In a history of Texas, it is impossible to omit the four long weary years of war, yet the writer has not treated these at any length, nor attempted a description of a single one of the many bloody engagements of the war, hoping that they may be remembered alone to prevent their recurrence.

The settlement of Anglo-Americans in Texas, and the causes which led to the Texas Revolution, and the establishment of the Republic of Texas, with a narrative of the principal events which occurred during its existence, constitute the main part of this volume, and vindicate the citizens of Texas as well as those of the United States from the unjust charge of Mexicans, that by might, not right, Texas was wrested from Mexico, and made one of the United States.

Although the Comanches and other Indians were in the peaceable occupation and enjoyment of most all of Texas in 1836, the writer has not investigated their title, but admits that of Spain and Mexico to have been good, and claims, through the latter, as the United States claim their soil through Great Britain, by the right of revolution and self-preservation.

In this volume, the author's intention has been to show plainly and clearly to the world, that Texans were not only right in throwing off the government of Mexicans (who had invited them to colonize their wild lands with the promise of equal rights with themselves, and after inducing them through empresarios, or colonial agents, to leave their homes in the United States and endure the hardships and privations incident to the settlement of a country bordering on warlike savages, and, afterwards faithless to their promises, attempted to enslave them), but that they deserve the praise of all good people for changing a wilderness into green fields and happy homes, founding prosperous cities in the whilom haunts of the cruel Comanches, and, after ten years' warfare against vastly superior numbers, adding a great State (more than five times larger than the State of New York, and containing more than a million inhabitants) to the American Union, which, may the great, wise, and most merciful God, forever shield, protect, and advance, in power, wisdom, and happiness!

PREFACE.

In the great arena of human life, whether in the cause of virtue and progress, or in that of vice and immorality, wise men have agreed that

"The pen is mightier than the sword."

Whenever a free and elevated press has attacked any public abuse, or any public policy in a government of the people, it will be observed that it has been changed.

"Thoughts that breathe and words that burn,"

are sent out by the press to eagerly waiting readers, who may be benefited or injured thereby.

The personification of a virtuous thought may arrest the hand of a would-be assassin, humble the proud heart of the monarch on his throne, and lead one who is far astray from the lovely paths of rectitude and happiness, to the worship of the pure, the beautiful and the good.

A story well told, of noble and generous action, may thrill the hard heart of an obdurate miser with admiration, and cause him to give his hoarded treasures to the relief of the distressed.

But while good thoughts come to us from the press as rain from heaven, causing us to be "gentle, mild and kind"—"to be wise as serpents but harmless as doves"—alas, it often happens that ugly, hateful and slanderous lies issue from the press and go forth on their mission of evil.

And a prostituted press is almost as powerful for evil in making the worse appear the better side, as the virtuous press is in the defence of truth.

The great poet of Avon says:

> "Slander,
> Whose edge is sharper than the sword; whose tongue
> Out-venoms all the worms of Nile; whose breath
> Rides on the passing winds, and doth belie
> All corners of the world, Kings, Queens and States,
> Maids, matrons, nay, the secrets of the grave
> This viperous slander enters."

Now, in view of the power of the press for good and evil, I do most earnestly pray the Almighty to aid and encourage, to comfort and cherish, particularly here in America, a truthful and virtuous press.

But a lying, slanderous one, let it not abide in our country! and may the eyes of those who support such a one be opened to the enormity of their offence!

May they see and understand that to buy and read a slanderous history is to give aid, comfort and encouragement to vice:

> "Which is a monster of so frightful mien,
> As to be hated needs but to be seen;
> Yet seen too oft, familiar with her face,
> We first endure, then pity, then embrace."

The historian should be found upon the watch-tower of freedom sounding the alarm and giving notice of the insidious approach of the enemies of liberty or working for the advancement of learning, the progress of science and art.

He should labor in the glorious cause of humanity for whatsoever things tend to produce the greatest happiness to the greatest number.

And his noble efforts thus directed to the happiness of mankind should receive the sympathy and encouragement of all good people. Such men live in the memory of a grateful posterity as benefactors of their race.

Magnanimous Hector will keep Homer fresh in the hearts of his readers so long as men continue to admire honor and bravery.

Shakspeare, Bacon and Addison will never die, while our own Franklin, Jefferson and Irving will forever live in the hearts of their countrymen.

If, in the following pages, the writer has prostituted his pen and thrown impediments in the way of his people and country to prosperity and happiness, in the impressive language of the poet:

> * * * "The wretch
> Living, shall forfeit fair renown,
> And, doubly dying, shall go down
> To the vile dust, from whence he sprung,
> Unwept, unhonored and unsung."

Even the doom of the traitor, pronounced by the author of "Lalla Rookh," that he should live in sight of the glorious and ineffable joys of paradise without being permitted to enter—

> "Beholding heaven and feeling hell,"

would not be too bad for him.

His object has been to amuse and interest, if not to instruct, and he closes the preface to his book with the presumptuous quotation from the poet:

> "My thoughts * are with the dead; anon
> My place with them will be,
> And I with them shall travel on
> Through all futurity.
> Yet leaving here a name, I trust,
> That will not perish in the dust.

* Occasionally.

HISTORY OF TEXAS.

CHAPTER I.

The Discovery of Texas claimed by France and Spain.—Its Settlement by the Spanish.—Origin of the Name.—Letters of Generals Jackson and Houston.—Mexican Troops expelled from Texas.

THE early history of Texas, like that of Greece, Rome, or the Oriental nations of the Old World, is somewhat involved in obscurity. For while distinguished French writers claim that La Salle took possession of the whole country from the Mississippi river to the Rio Grande in the year 1685, and made settlements therein for the glory and renown of their *grand monarque* Louis XIV., Spanish historians affirm that De Soto, so far back as 1544, took possession of all the country lying west, as well as east of the *Father of Waters*, in the name of his most Catholic majesty, the King of Spain.

But as the names given to all the principal rivers in Texas, such as Trinidad, Angelina, Brazos de Dios, Colorado, Neches, Nueces, Guadalupe, Salado, San

Marcos, Frio, Pecos and Rio Grande, are Spanish, we may reasonably conclude that Spain, rather than France, first settled Texas.

And yet even the name, Texas, is of doubtful origin, for while some say that it was the name of the capital village of the Nassonite Indians, others assert that it is derived from the Spanish word *tejer*, to weave, and applied to weaving the grass over and around their cottages; and others that it is from *tejas*, tiles, coverings, or cobwebs.

The latter say that at an early day some Spaniards travelling the Camino del Rey, between San Antonio and the Hondo, camped on the Neches, and their commander, in the morning, beholding many spider-webs between himself and the rising sun, all spangled with dew drops and glittering like diamonds, joyfully exclaimed: "*Mira las tejas!*"—that is to say, "Look at the spider webs!"—and named the land Texas.

The records of the famous mission of the Alamo show that it was founded in 1703 by the order of St. Francis.

Before that time, in 1691, the Spaniards had made small settlements on the Hondo, Neches, and Guadalupe, but on account of Indian hostilities they were abandoned.

Not until 1715 were missions permanently established and maintained at the Alamo, Concepcion, San

Jose, and among the Aes and Nacogdoches Indians, near the present cities of San Augustine and Nacogdoches.

From civil strife, troubles with the Indians, and other causes, the Spanish settlements did not flourish, for in 1765 the whole population of the province of Texas was estimated at 1,500—one-half European, the other half domiciliated Indians; while the sum total of its exports and imports were estimated at only ninety thousand dollars per annum.

Under Spanish despotism and priestcraft, immigration from other countries than Spain was prohibited, and Texas continued to languish until 1821, when Moses Austin, the father of S. F. Austin, was empowered to introduce colonists, who were to receive 640 acres of land each, provided they were Roman Catholics, of good character and habits, and would be faithful subjects of his Catholic majesty.

Moses Austin died in 1821, but his grant to found a colony in Texas was confirmed to his son, S. F. Austin on the 18th of February, 1823, by Iturbide, Emperor of Mexico, who, on the nineteenth of March thereafter, abdicated, and gave way for the Republic of Mexico, under which Austin's grant was confirmed on the fourteenth of April following, when he proceeded to locate and settle San Filipe, as the capital of his colony.

Soon after, Hayden Edwards, Sterling C. Robertson, Martin de Leon, Green De Witt, James Power, M'Mullen, and Gloine, were also made *empresarios*, as the leaders of colonies were called, and authorized to introduce immigrants; and made settlements at Gonzales, Victoria, Goliad, Refugio, Liberty, and at Nacogdoches.

Besides those introduced by the *empresarios*, many immigrants came on their own account, and after looking round, exercised the divine right of Popes, Kings, and American citizens, *squatter sovereignty;* they pitched their tents in the forest on streams of running water, built their rude houses, fenced in rich land, ploughed, planted, and—although often annoyed by Indians and thieves—made bountiful crops and happy homes.

In December, 1832, when General Sam Houston, an ex-member of Congress, and ex-governor of Tennessee, from his voluntary exile among savages—with whom

"Wrought upon, perplex'd in the extreme,"

he had sought relief—first came to Texas, he found but two houses between Jonesborough and Nacogdoches.

After visiting San Filipe, San Antonio, and Natchitoches, Louisiana, fascinated with the country, he settled in Nacogdoches.

His name fills the brightest pages of Texan history, and he is called *the Father of Texas.*

Yoakum says of him:

"Among the new-comers into Texas in the year 1832 was Sam Houston, late governor of the State of Tennessee, a man of extraordinary fortunes. By birth a Virginian, but brought up in Blount County, among the mountains of East Tennessee, he volunteered at an early age as a soldier in the army; was promoted to the rank of lieutenant; fought at the battle of the *Horse-shoe*, in which he was severely wounded; returned to Tennessee, where he attracted the attention of General Jackson, and was taken into his military family; was appointed Indian agent for the Cherokees; he afterward studied law, was elected attorney-general for Tennessee, and major-general of the state militia; represented the Nashville district in Congress, and was elected governor of the state. He was appointed second lieutenant in the 39th regiment of infantry, by President Madison, on the 20th of April, 1815, "to rank as such from the 20th of May, 1814;" and first lieutenant in the 1st regiment of infantry, by President Monroe, on the 5th of March, 1818, "to rank as such from the 1st of May, 1817." In November, 1817, he was appointed sub-agent of the Cherokee Indians. On the 14th of December, 1821, he was elected major-general of the middle division of Tennessee militia. In August of the years 1823 and 1825 he was elected a representative to Congress; and in August, 1827, he was chosen governor of the State of Tennessee; married—which soon proving unfortunate, he resigned his office of governor, and in April, 1829, went into voluntary exile among those Cherokee Indians, for whom he had been agent twelve years before. But they had been removed, and in 1829 were living on the Indian lands near Cantonment Gibson. He had been adopted by the chief, Oolooteka, and on the 21st of October of the above-mentioned year was admitted to the rights of citizenship by an official act of the authorities of the nation. Among these people he subsisted by trade, making an occasional trip to the older states.

In June 1829, President Jackson thus wrote to him about his exile and misfortunes:

"My affliction was great, and as much as I well could bear, when I parted with you on the 18th of January last. I then viewed you as on the brink of happiness, and rejoiced. About to be united in marriage to a beautiful young lady, of accomplished manners and of respectable connections, and of your own selection—you the governor of the state, and holding the affections of the people: these were your prospects when I shook you by the hand and *bade you farewell!* You can well judge of my astonishment and grief in receiving a letter from you, dated at Little Rock, A. T., 11th of May, conveying the sad intelligence that you were then a private citizen, '*an exile from your country!*' What reverse of fortune! How unstable are all human affairs!"

What a sad commentary on the emptiness of all earthly things?

The vanity of fame, ambition gratified, the possession of wealth, beauty, and power!

Gov. Houston had them all, and yet, being unhappy, resigned them and went into voluntary exile among savages!

But:

> "There's a divinity that shapes our ends,
> Rough-hew them how we will."

Soon becoming weary of his life with the Indians, he quit them and returned again to his people, after which, with his majestic person and excellent mind, he became *a Samson in the field and a Solomon in counsel.*

As an evidence of his masterly genius, which seemed then to foresee the glorious results of the Texas revolution, as it did later, the disastrous end of our late unhappy civil war, and in order to inform the reader what Texas then was under Mexican domination, and the brilliant future awaiting her, I here insert a genuine, *verbatim et literatim* letter, which speaks for itself, from the beloved "Father of Texas," to his life-long friend, the illustrious hero of Chalmette:

NACHITOCHES, La., *Feb.* 13, 1833.

TO PRESIDENT JACKSON:

Dear Sir—Having been as far as Bexar, in the province of Texas, where I had an interview with the Comanche Indians, I am in possession of some information that will doubtless be interesting to you, and may be calculated to forward your views, if you should entertain any, touching the acquisition of Texas by the United States. That such a measure is desirable by nineteen-twentieths of the population of the province, I cannot doubt. They are now without laws to govern or protect them. Mexico is involved in civil war. The Federal Constitution has never been in operation. The government is essentially despotic, and must be so for years to come. The rulers have not honesty, and the people have not *intelligence.*

The people of Texas are determined to form a State government, and to separate from Coahuila; and unless Mexico is soon restored to order, and the Constitution revived and re-enacted, the Province of Texas will remain separate from the confederacy of Mexico. She has already beaten and expelled all the troops of Mexico from her soil, nor will she permit them to return. She can defend herself against the whole power of Mexico; for really Mexico is powerless and penniless to all intents and purposes. Her want of money, taken in connection with the course which Texas *must and will adopt*, will render a transfer of Texas inevitable to some power; and if the United States does not press for it, England will most assuredly obtain it by some means. Now is a very important crisis for Texas, as relates to her future prosperity and safety, as well as the relation it is to bear toward the United States. If Texas is desirable to the United States, it is now in the most favorable attitude, perhaps, that it can be, to obtain it on fair terms. England is *pressing her suit* for it, but its citizens will resist if any transfer should be made of them to any other power but the United States.

I have travelled nearly five hundred miles across Texas, and am now enabled to judge pretty correctly of the soil and the resources of the country. And I have no hesitation in pronouncing it the finest country, to its extent, upon the globe; for the greater portion of it is richer and more healthy, in my opinion, than West Tennessee. There can be no doubt but the country east of the Rio Grande would sustain a population of ten millions of souls. My opinion is, that Texas will, by her members in convention, on the first of April, declare all that country as Texas proper, and form a State Constitution. I expect to be present at the convention, and will apprise you of the course adopted so soon as its members have taken a final action. It is probable I may make Texas my abiding place; in adopting this course, I will *never forget* the country of my birth.

From this point I will notify the commissioners of the Indians at Fort Gibson of my success, which will reach you through the War Department.

I have with much pride and inexpressible satisfaction seen your messages and proclamation touching the nullifiers of the South, and their "Peaceable remedies." God grant that you may save the Union! It does seem to me that it is reserved for you, and you alone, to render millions so great a blessing. I hear all voices commend your course, even in Texas—where is felt the liveliest interest for the preservation of the Republic.

Permit me to tender you my sincere felicitations, and most earnest solicitude for your health and happness—and your future glory, connected with the prosperity of the Union.

Your friend and obedient servant,

SAM HOUSTON.

Gen. Houston did make this *richer and more healthy country than West Tennessee his abiding place*, and was chairman of the committee on the Constitution in the convention which met at San Filipe on the first of April, 1833, but when he said in his letter to President Jackson:

"She has already beaten and expelled all the troops of Mexico from her soil, nor will she permit them to return"—he spoke of the past, which I will explain.

In June, 1832, Wm. B. Travis, and P. C. Jack, with other Texans, were arrested and imprisoned by Col. Bradburn, the commanding officer of Anahuac.

Bradburn was a tyrannical and an overbearing man, but Travis and Jack were popular, so their friends endeavored to release them.

They came on Bradburn unexpectedly, and he promised to release them, but asked time, in order to prepare for defence.

In the meantime, he prepared, mounted his cannon, and caused his assaulters to retire.

They demanded cannon of the commander of Fort Velasco, which he refused, and they took the cannon by force.

The commander, Capt. John Austin, the Alcalde of the 2d department of Austin colony, in reply to an official letter of Col. Mexia, who came with a fleet of five vessels and 400 men to the mouth of the Brazos, in order to find out and punish the offenders—thus briefly gives this portion of the history of Texas:

"We are farmers, and not soldiers; therefore desire that the military commandants shall not interfere with us at all. Since 1830, we have been pretty much governed militarily, and in such a despotic manner that we were finally driven to arms, to resist within their limits the military subalterns of the General Government. We have not insulted the flag of our adopted country, as had been surmised from our first movements; but, on the contrary, we have sustained its true dignity, and attacked those who had outraged it, by using it as a pretext for their encroachments upon the constitution and sovereignty of the State of Coahuila and Texas, and as a cover for their baseness and personal crimes.

"The commandant of Fort Velasco acted under the orders of the commandant of Anahuac, Col. Juan Davis Bradburn. An investigation of the conduct of that officer will inform you fully of the details of many despotic and arbitary acts. He was sustained by the commandant of Nacogdoches, Col. Piedras, and by that of Fort Velasco, Lieut.-Col. Ugartechea, and, consequently, we were *compelled* to oppose them all.

"Therefore we attacked Fort Velasco on the 26th of last month, with one hundred and twelve farmers, hastily collected, without discipline, and badly armed; and, after an obstinate and bloody engagement of eleven hours, it surrendered, on the terms expressed in the enclosed copy of the capitulation—every article of which has been strictly complied with on our part, besides furnishing the provisions needed for the troops."

Col. Mexia was received kindly by the Texans, and after professing himself satisfied with their explanations, returned with his fleet and the garrison of the dismantled fort at Velasco to Mexico, in order to aid Santa Anna in establishing the Plan of Vera Cruz.

The odious Bradburn after being forced to release his prisoners, escaped from the fort at Anahuac and fled to New Orleans.

Among the persons who took part in the release of Travis and Jack, were the venerable Edwin Waller, Wm. J. Russell, Frank W. Johnson, Judge Munson, Andrew Mills, Wm. H. Wharton, Henry Brown, the father of John Henry Brown, and T. Bennett.

The capture of Velasco took place on the 26th June, and was followed by that of Nacogdoches on the 2d August, 1832, which Kennedy thus describes:

Piedras, the commandant at Nacogdoches, declined Mexia's invitation to join the "Liberating Army" in Mexico, which afforded the inhabitants of that place a pretext for expelling him. Declaring in favor of the Vera Cruz Plan, the Nacogdoches settlers attacked the garrison in their "*quartel,*" and after protracted skirmishing, in which three Texans were killed and seven wounded, and eighteen Mexicans killed and twenty-two wounded, the latter evacuated their quarters during the night and retreated towards the river Angelina. Pursued by a party of mounted men, who killed two of their number and wounded several, their leader, Piedras, proposed a temporary cessation of hostilities; as it was late in the evening, he was allowed to occupy the house of an Anglo-American without molestation from the Texans. The next morning, the Mexicans, terrified by a deceptive report of the approach of a large hostile force, surrendered at discretion, and, after being disarmed, were permitted to continue their route to San Antonio de Bexar. Other garrisons withdrew into the interior about the same time. The citizens of Bexar and the governor of the State openly declared for the Plan of Vera Cruz; political unanimity generally prevailed, and in August, 1832, Texas was free from military domination and internal strife.

CHAPTER II.

The Convention of 1833, its members and action.—The Constitution and Memorial prepared by it.—Austin takes the Constitution and Memorial of the Convention of 1833 to Mexico.—His Arrest and Imprisonment.—Col. Almonte sent to Texas.—His Report on Texas.

THE convention of 1833, at San Filipe, was composed of the representative men of Texas, and its action will ever command the respect of all true lovers of liberty and self-government.

Yoakum says of it:

A body of more distinguished men had not met in Texas. Among them were Branch T. Archer, Stephen F. Austin, David G. Burnet, Sam Houston (one of the five delegates from Nacogdoches), J. B. Miller, and William H. Wharton. The latter was chosen President of the convention. The members entered upon their labors in earnest. The requisite committees were appointed: among them were the important committees on the constitution and on a memorial to the supreme government of Mexico. Sam Houston was appointed chairman of the first, and David G. Burnet of the second named committee. The constitution framed was a model of republicanism, with now and then an indication, however, that some clauses were inserted and some principles retained to please the Mexican ear. The right of trial by jury, the writ of *habeas corpus*, the right of petition, freedom of the press, direct and universal suffrage, and all those clauses usual in a bill of rights, were inserted. On the subject of religious liberty, however, they were silent.

The memorial throws so much light on the situation of Texas in 1833, explains so clearly the causes which led to the revolution, and is itself such a rare and excellent document, that it is here inserted:

TEXAN MEMORIAL.

Memorial of the Texan Convention of April, 1833, *to the General Congress of the United Mexican States.*

The inhabitants of Texas, by their representatives elect in convention assembled, would respectfully approach the national Congress, and present this their memorial, praying that the union which was established between Coahuila and Texas, whereby the two ancient provinces were incorporated into one free and independent state, under the name of "COAHUILA AND TEXAS," may be dissolved, abrogated, and perpetually cease; and that the inhabitants of Texas may be authorized to institute and establish a separate state government, which will be in accordance with the federal constitution and the constitutive act; and that the state so constituted shall be received and incorporated into the great confederation of Mexico, on terms of equality with the other states of the Union.

To explain the grounds of this application, your memorialists would respectfully invite the attention of the general Congress to the following considerations:—

The consolidation of the late provinces of Coahuila and Texas was, in its nature, provisional, and, in its intention, temporary. The decree of the sovereign constituent Congress, bearing date the 7th of May, 1824, contemplates a separation, and guarantees to Texas the right of having a state government whenever she may be in a condition to ask for the same. That decree provides that, "so soon as Texas shall be in a condition to figure as a state of itself, it shall inform Congress thereof, for its resolution." The implication conveyed by this clause is plain and imperative; and vests in Texas as perfect a right as language can convey, unless it can be presumed that the sovereign constituent Congress, composed of the venerable fathers of the republic, designed to amuse the good people of Texas by an illusory and disingenuous promise, clothed in all the solemnity of a legislative enactment. Your memorialists have too high a veneration for the memory of that illustrious body to entertain any apprehensions that such a construction will be given to their acts by their patriotic successors, the present Congress of Mexico.

The decree is dated anterior to the adoption of the federal constitution, and therefore, by a clear and fundamental principle of law and justice, it obviates the necessity of recurring to the correspondent provision in the fiftieth article of that instrument, which requires "the ratification of three-fourths of the other states" in order "to form a new state out of the limits of those that already exist." And it assures to Texas—by all the sanctity of a legislative promise, in which the good faith of the Mexican nation is pledged—an exemption from the delays and uncertainties that must result from such multiplied legislative discussion and resolution. To give to the federal constitution, which is the paramount law of the land, a retrospective operation, would establish a precedent that might prove disastrous to the whole system of the nation's jurisprudence, and subversive of the very foundations of the government.

The authority of precedents is decidedly in favor of the position which your memorialists would respectfully sustain before the general Congress. By the *Constitutive Act*, adopted on the 31st of January, 1824, Coahuila, New Leon, and Texas were joined together, and denominated THE INTERNAL EASTERN STATE. By a law passed by the constituent Congress on the 7th of May, 1824, that union was dissolved, and the province of New Leon was admitted into the confederacy as an independent state. It is on the *second* article of this law that the people of Texas now predicate their right to a similar admission. The constitutive act, above mentioned, consolidated the late provinces of Chihuahua, Durango, and New Mexico, under the style of "the internal northern state;" and on the 22d of May, 1824, a summary law decreed that "Durango should form a state of the Mexican Confederation," and she was admitted accordingly. The same privilege was extended to Chihuahua by a decree of the 6th of July of the same year. These conjunct provinces stood, at the period of their separation, in precisely the same relation to the federal government that Texas and Coahuila now occupy. They have been separated and erected into free and independent states in a summary manner; and the same right was guaranteed "whenever she should be in a condition to accept it." The other case, of Sonora and Sinaloa, is materially variant in matter of fact. Those provinces were originally incorporated into the confederation as one state, without any antecedent condition or guarantee; and, at the adoption of the present constitution, they justly became liable to all the forms and restrictions prescribed in that national pact.

We would further suggest to the honorable Congress that the present juncture is peculiarly felicitous for dispensing with interminable and vexatious forms.

The federal government is wisely employed in adopting important organic improvements, and aiming at a salutary renovation of the political system. The disasters of an eventful civil convulsion are yielding to the regenerating influences of domestic concord and improved experience; and every department of the confederacy is open to such needful modifications as the wisdom of the renewed Congress may designate. Texas solicits, as her portion in the general reformation, to be disenthralled from her unhappy connection with Coahuila; and she avails herself of this opportunity, by means of her chosen delegates, who are the authorized organs of the people, to communicate "to the general Congress" that she is now "in a situation to figure as a state by herself," and is profoundly solicitous that she may be permitted to do so.

The general Congress may possibly consider the mode of this communication as informal. To this suggestion we would, with great deference, reply, that the events of the past year have not only violated the established forms and etiquette of the government, but have suspended, at least, its vital functions; and it would appear exceedingly rigorous to exact from the inhabitants of Texas, living on a remote frontier of the republic, a minute conformity to unimportant punctilios. The ardent desire of the people is made known to the Congress through their select representatives, the most direct and unequivocal medium by which they can possibly be conveyed; and surely the enlightened Congress will readily concur with us in the sentiment that the wishes and wants of the people form the best rule for legislative guidance. The people of Texas consider it not only an absolute right, but a most sacred and imperative duty to themselves, and to the Mexican nation, to represent their wants in a respectful manner to the general government, and to solicit the best remedy of which the nature of their grievances will admit. Should they utterly fail in this duty, and great and irremediable evils ensue, the people would have reason to reproach themselves alone; and the general Congress, in whom the remedial power resides, would also have reason to censure their supineness and want of fidelity to the nation. Under this view, we trust the Congress will not regard with excessive severity any slight departure which the good people of Texas may in this instance have made from the ordinary formalities of the government.

And we would further suggest to the equitable consideration of the federal Congress that, independent of and anterior to the express guarantee contained in the decree of the 7th of May, 1824, the right of having a separate state government was vested in and belonged to Texas, by the fact that she participated as a distinct province in the toils and sufferings by which the glorious emancipation of Mexico was achieved, and the present happy form of government was established. The subsequent union with Coahuila was a temporary compact, induced by a supposed expediency, arising from an inadequate population on the part of Texas "to figure as a state of itself." This inducement was transient in its nature; and the compact, like all similar agreements, is subject to abrogation, at the will of either party, whenever the design of its creation is accomplished, or is ascertained to be impracticable. The obvious design of the union between Coahuila and Texas was, on the one part, at least, the more effectually to secure the peace, safety and happiness of Texas. That design has not been accomplished, and facts piled upon facts afford a melancholy evidence that it is utterly impracticable. Texas never has and never can derive from the connection benefits in any wise commensurate with the evils she has sustained, and which are daily increasing in number and in magnitude.

But our reasons for the proposed separation are more explicitly set forth in the subjoined remarks.

The history of Texas, from its earliest settlement to the present time, exhibits a series of practical neglect and indifference to all her peculiar interests on the part of each successive government which has had the control of her political destinies. The recollection of these things is calculated to excite the most pungent regrets for the past, and the most painful forebodings for the future. Under the several regal dominions Texas presented the gloomy spectacle of a province profusely endowed by nature, abandoned and consigned to desolation by the profligate avariciousness of a distant despot. The tyrants of Spain regarded her only as a convenient barrier to the mines of the adjacent provinces; and the more waste and depopulated she was, the more effectually she answered their selfish and unprincipled purpose. Her agricultural resources were either unknown, or esteemed of no value to a government anxious only to sustain its wasting magnificence by the silver and gold wrung from the prolific bosom of Mexico. To foster the agricultural interests of any portion of her splendid viceroyalty, or her circumjacent conquests, was never the favorite policy of Spain. To have done so, would have nurtured in her remote dominions a hardy and industrious population of yeomanry, who have ever proved the peculiar dread of tyrants, and the best assurance of a nation's independence.

It was natural, then, that the royal miscreants of Spain should regard Texas with indifference, if not with a decided and malignant aversion to her improvement. But it would be both unnatural and erroneous to attribute similar motives to the paternal government of independent, confederate, republican Mexico. She can have no interest averse to the common weal; can feel no desire to depress the agricultural faculties of any portion of her common territory; and can entertain no disquieting jealousies that should prompt her to dread the increase or to mar the prosperity of any portion of her agricultural population. These are the best, the broadest, and the most durable bases of her free institutions.

We must look to other causes, therefore, for the lamentable negligence that has hitherto been manifested toward the prosperity of Texas. The fact of such negligence is beyond controversy. The melancholy effects of it are apparent in both her past and present condition. The cause must exist somewhere. We believe it is principally to be found in her political annexation to Coahuila. That conjunction was, in its origin, unnatural and constrained; and the longer it is continued, the more disastrous it will prove. The two territories are disjunct in all their prominent respective relations. In point of locality, they approximate only by a strip of sterile and useless territory, which must long remain a comparative wilderness, and present many serious embarrassments to that facility of intercourse which should always exist between the seat of government and its remote population. In respect to commerce and its various intricate relations, there is no community of interests between them. The one is altogether *interior;* is consequently abstracted from all participation in maritime concerns; and is naturally indifferent, if not adverse, to any system of polity that is calculated to promote the diversified and momentous interests of commerce. The other is blest with many natural advantages for extensive commercial operations, which, if properly cultivated, would render many valuable accessions to the national marine, and a large increase to the national revenues. The importance of an efficient national marine is evinced, not only by the history of other and older governments, but by the rich halo of glory which encircles the brief annals of the Mexican navy. In point of climate and of natural productions, the two territories are equally dissimilar. Coahuila is a pastoral and a mining country: Texas is characteristically an agricultural district. The occupations incident to these various intrinsic properties are equally various and distinct; and a course of legislation that may be adapted to the encouragement of the habitual industry of the one district might present only embarrassment and perplexity, and prove fatally deleterious to the prosperity of the other.

It is not needful, therefore—neither do we desire

—to attribute any sinister or invidious design to the legislative enactments or to the domestic economical policy of Coahuila (whose ascendancy in the joint councils of the state gives her an uncontrolled and exclusive power of legislation), in order to ascertain the origin of the evils that affect Texas, and which, if permitted to exist, must protract her feeble and dependent pupilage to a period coeval with such existence. Neither is it important to Texas whether those evils have proceeded from a sinister policy in the predominant influences of Coahuila, or whether they are the natural results of a union that is naturally adverse to her interests. The effects are equally repugnant and injurious, whether emanating from the one or the other source.

Bexar, the ancient capital of Texas, presents a faithful but a gloomy picture of her general want of protection and encouragement. Situated in a fertile, picturesque, and healthful region, and established a century and a half ago (within which period populous and magnificent cities have sprung into existence), she exhibits only the decrepitude of age—sad testimonials of the absence of that political guardianship which a wise government should always bestow upon the feebleness of its exposed frontier settlements. A hundred and seventeen years have elapsed since Goliad and Nacogdoches assumed the distinctive name of towns, and they are still entitled only to the diminutive appellation of villages. Other military and missionary establishments have been attempted, but, from the same defect of protection and encouragement, they have been swept away, and scarcely a vestige remains to rescue their locations from oblivion.

We do not mean to attribute these specific disasters to the union with Coahuila, for we know they transpired long anterior to the consummation of that union. But we do maintain that the same political causes, the same want of protection and encouragement, the same mal-organization and impotency of the local and minor faculties of the government, the same improvident indifference to the peculiar and vital interests of Texas, exist *now* that operated then. Bexar is still exposed to the depredations of her ancient enemies, the insolent, vindictive, and faithless Comanches. Her citizens are still massacred, their cattle destroyed or driven away, and their very habitations threatened, by a tribe of erratic and undisciplined Indians, whose audacity has derived confidence from success, and whose long-continued aggressions have invested them with a fictitious and excessive terror. Her schools are neglected, her churches desolate, the sounds of human industry are almost hushed, and the voice of gladness and festivity is converted into wailing and lamentation, by the disheartening and multiplied evils which sur round her defenceless population. Goliad is still kept in constant trepidation; is paralyzed in all her efforts for improvement; and is harassed on all her borders by the predatory incursions of the Wacoes, and other insignificant bands of savages, whom a well-organized local government would soon subdue and exterminate.

These are facts, not of history merely, on which the imagination must dwell with an unwilling melancholy, but they are events of the present day, which the present generation feel in all their dreadful reality. And these facts, revolting as they are, are as a fraction only in the stupendous aggregate of our calamities. Our misfortunes do not proceed from Indian depredations alone; neither are they confined to a few isolated, impoverished, and almost tenantless towns. They pervade the whole territory—operate upon the whole population—and are as diversified in character as our public interests and necessities are various. Texas at large feels and deplores an utter destitution of the common benefits which have usually accrued from the worst system of internal government that the patience of mankind ever tolerated. She is virtually without a *government;* and if she is not precipitated into all the unspeakable horrors of anarchy, it is only because there is a redeeming spirit among the people, which still infuses some moral energy into the miserable fragments of authority that exist among us. We are perfectly sensible that a large portion of our population, usually denominated "the colonists," and composed of Anglo-Americans, have been greatly calumniated before the Mexican government. But could the honorable Congress scrutinize strictly into our real condition—could they see and understand the wretched confusion, in all the elements of government, which we daily feel and deplore—our ears would no longer be insulted, nor our feelings mortified, by the artful fictions of hireling emissaries from abroad, nor by the malignant aspersions of disappointed military commandants at home.

Our grievances do not so much result from any positive misfeasance on the part of the present state authorities, as from the total absence, or the very feeble and mutile dispensation, of those restrictive influences which it is the appropriate design of the social compact to exercise upon the people, and which are necessary to fulfil the ends of civil society. We complain more of the *want* of *all* the important attributes of government, than of the abuses of any. We are sensible that all human institutions are essentially imperfect. But there are relative degrees of perfection in modes of government as in other matters, and it is both natural and right to aspire to that mode which is most likely to accomplish its legitimate purpose. This is wisely declared in our present state constitution, to be "the happiness of those who compose it." It is equally obvious that the happiness of the people is more likely to be secured by a local than by a remote government. In the one case, the governors are partakers, in common with the governed, in all the political evils which result to the community, and have therefore a personal interest in so discharging their respective functions as will best secure the common welfare. In the other supposition, those vested with authority are measurably exempt from the calamities that ensue an abuse of power, and may very conveniently subserve their own interests and ambition, while they neglect or destroy "the welfare of the associated."

But, independent of these general truths, there are some impressive reasons why the peace and happiness of Texas demand a local government. Constituting a remote frontier of the republic, and bordering on a powerful nation, a portion of whose population, in juxtaposition to hers, is notoriously profligate and lawless, she requires, in a peculiar and emphatic sense, the vigorous application of such laws as are necessary, not only to the preservation of good order, the protection of property, and the redress of personal wrongs, but such also as are essential to the prevention of illicit commerce, to the security of the public revenues, and to the avoidance of serious collision with the authorities of the neighboring republic. That such a judicial administration is impracticable under the present arrangement, is too forcibly illustrated by the past to admit of any rational hope for the future.

It is an acknowledged principle in the science of jurisprudence, that the prompt and certain infliction of mild and humane punishment is more efficacious for the prevention of crime than a tardy and precarious administration of the most sanguinary penal code. Texas is virtually denied the benefit of this benevolent rule by the locality and the character of her present government. Crimes of the greatest atrocity may go unpunished, and hardened criminals triumph in their iniquity, because of the difficulties and delays which encumber her judicial system, and necessarily intervene a trial and conviction, and the sentence and the execution of the law. Our "supreme tribunal of justice" holds its sessions upward of seven hundred miles distant from our central population; and that distance is greatly enlarged, and sometimes made impassable, by the casualties incident to a "*mail*" conducted by a single horseman through a wilderness often infested by vagrant and murderous Indians. Before sentence can be pronounced by the local courts on persons charged with the most atrocious crimes, a copy of the process must be transmitted to an assessor, resident at Leona Vicario (Saltillo), who is too far removed from the scene of guilt to appreciate the importance of a speedy decision, and is too much estranged from our civil and domestic concerns to feel the miseries that result from a total want of legal protection in person and property. But our difficulties do not terminate here. After the assessor shall have found leisure to render his opinion, and final judgment is pronounced, it again becomes necessary to resort to the capital to submit the tardy sentence to the supreme tribunal for "approbation, revocation, or modification," before the judgment of the law can be executed. Here we have again to encounter the vexations and delays incident to all governments where those who exercise its most interesting functions are removed by distance from the people on whom they operate, and for whose benefit the social compact is created.

These repeated delays, resulting from the remoteness of our courts of judicature, are pernicious in many respects. They involve heavy expenses, which, in civil suits, are excessively onerous to litigants, and give to the rich and influential such manifold advantages over the poor as operate to an absolute exclusion of the latter from the remedial and protective benefits of the law. They offer seductive opportunities and incitements to bribery and corruption, and endanger the sacred purity of the judiciary, which, of all the branches of the government, is most intimately associated with the domestic and social happiness of man, and should therefore be not only sound and pure, but unsuspected of the venal infection. They present insuperable difficulties to the exercise of the corrective right of recusation, and virtually nullify the constitutional power of impeachment. In criminal actions they are no less injurious. They are equivalent to a license to iniquity, and exert a dangerous influence on the moral feelings at large. Before the tedious process of the law can be complied with, and the criminal—whose hands are perhaps imbrued in a brother's blood—be made to feel its retributive justice, the remembrance of his crime is partially effaced from the public mind; and the righteous arbitrament of the law, which, if promptly executed, would have received universal approbation, and been a salutary warning to evil-doers, is impugned as vin dictive and cruel. The popular feeling is changed from a just indignation of crime, into an amiable but mistaken sympathy for the criminal; and an easy and natural transition is converted into disgust and disaffection toward the government and its laws.

These are some of the evils that result from the

annexation of Texas to Coahuila, and the exercise of legislative and judicial powers by the citizens of Coahuila over the citizens of Texas. The catalogue might be greatly enlarged, but we forbear to trespass on the time of the honorable Congress (confiding to the worthy citizens who shall be charged with the high duty of presenting this memorial and the protocol of a constitution which the people of Texas have framed, as the basis of their future government, the more explicit enunciation of them). Those evils are not likely to be diminished, but they may be exceedingly aggravated by the fact that that political connection was formed without the cordial approbation of the people of Texas, and is daily becoming more odious to them. Although it may have received their reluctant acquiescence, in its inception, before its evil consequences were developed or foreseen, the arbitrary continuance of it now, after the experience of nine years has demonstrated its ruinous tendencies, would invest it with some of the most offensive features of usurpation. Your memorialists entertain an assured confidence that the enlightened Congress of Mexico will never give their high sanction to anything that wears the semblance of usurpation or of arbitrary coercion.

The idea may possibly occur, in the deliberations of the honorable Congress, that a territorial organization would cure our political maladies, and effectuate the great purposes which induce this application; and plausible reasons may be advanced in favor of it. But the wisdom of Congress will readily detect the fallacy of these reasons, and the mischief consequent to such vain sophistry. In this remote section of the republic, a territorial government must, of necessity, be divested of one essential and radical principle in all popular institutions—the immediate responsibility of public agents to the people whom they serve. The appointments to office would, in such case, be vested in the general government; and although such appointments should be made with the utmost circumspection, the persons appointed, when once arrayed in the habiliments of office, would be too far removed from the appointing power to feel the restraints of a vigilant supervision and a direct accountability. The dearest rights of the people might be violated, the public treasures squandered, and every variety of imposition and iniquity practised, under the specious pretext of political necessity, which the far-distant government could neither detect nor control.

And we would further present, with great deference, that the institution of a territorial government would confer upon us neither the form nor the substance of our high guarantee. It would, indeed, diversify our miseries, by opening new avenues to peculation and abuse of power; but it would neither remove our difficulties nor place us in the enjoyment of our equal and vested rights. The only and adequate remedy that your memorialists can devise, and which they ardently hope the collective wisdom of the nation will approve, is to be found in the establishment of a *local state government.* We believe that if Texas were endowed with the faculties of a state government, she would be competent to remedy the many evils that now depress her energies, and frustrate every effort to develop and bring into usefulness the natural resources which a beneficent Providence has conferred upon her. We believe that a local legislature, composed of citizens who feel and participate in all the calamities which encompass us, would be enabled to enact such conservative, remedial, and punitive laws, and so to organize and put into operation the municipal and inferior authorities of the country, as would inspire universal confidence; would encourage the immigration of virtuous foreigners—prevent the ingress of fugitives from the justice of other countries—check the alarming accumulations of ferocious Indians, whom the domestic policy of the United States of the North is rapidly translating to our borders; would give impulse and vigor to the industry of the people—secure a cheerful subordination and a faithful adhesion to the state and general governments; and would render Texas what she ought to be—a strong arm of the republic, a terror to foreign invaders, and an example of peace and prosperity—of advancement in the arts and sciences, and of devotion to the Union—to her sister states. We believe that an executive chosen from among ourselves would feel a more intense interest in our political welfare, would watch with more vigilance over our social concerns, and would contribute more effectually to the purposes of his appointment. We believe that a local judiciary, drawn from the bosom of our own peculiar society, would be enabled to administer the laws with more energy and promptitude—to punish the disobedient and refractory—to restrain the viciousness of the wicked—to impart confidence and security of both person and property to peaceable citizens—to conserve and perpetuate the general tranquillity of the state—and to render a more efficient aid to the co-ordinate powers of the government in carrying into effect the great objects of its institution. We believe that, if Texas were admitted to the Union as a separate state, she would soon "figure" as a brilliant star in the Mexican constellation, and would shed a new splendor around the illustrious city of Montezuma. We believe she would contribute largely to the national wealth and aggandizement—would furnish new staples for commerce, and new materials for manufactures. The cotton of Texas would give employment to the artisans of Mexico; and the precious metals, which are now flowing into the coffers of England, would be retained at home, to reward the industry and remunerate the ingenuity of native citizens.

The honorable Congress need not be informed that a large portion of the population of Texas is of foreign origin. They have been invited here by the munificent liberality and plighted faith of the Mexican government; and they stand pledged, by every moral and religious principle, and by every sentiment of honor, to requite that liberality, and to reciprocate the faithful performance of the guarantee to "protect their liberties, property, and civil rights," by a cheerful dedication of their moral and physical energies to the advancement of their adopted country. But it is also apparent to the intelligence of the honorable Congress that the best mode of securing the permanent attachment of such a population is, to incorporate them into the federal system, on such equitable terms as will redress every grievance, remove every cause of complaint, and insure, not only an identity of interests, but an eventual blending and assimilation of all that is now foreign and incongruous. The infancy of imperial Rome was carried to an early adolescence by the free and unrestricted admission of foreigners to her social compact. England never aspired to "the dominion of the seas" until she had united the hardiness of Scotland and the gallantry of Ireland to her native prowess. France derives her greatness from the early combination of the Salii, the Frank, and the Burgundian. And Mexico may yet realize the period when the descendants of Montezuma will rejoice that their coalition with the descendants of Fernando Cortez has been strengthened and embellished by the adoption into their national family of a people drawn by their own gratuitous hospitality from the land of Washington and of freedom.

For these and other considerations, your memorialists would solemnly invoke the magnanimous spirit of the Mexican nation, concentrated in the wisdom and patriotism of the federal Congress. And they would respectfully and ardently pray that the honorable Congress would extend their remedial power to this obscure section of the republic; would cast around it "the sovereign mantle of the nation," and adopt it into a free and plenary participation of that "constitutional *régime*" of equal sisterhood which alone can rescue it from the miseries of an ill-organized, inefficient, internal government, and can reclaim this fair and fertile region from the worthlessness of an untenanted waste, or the more fearful horrors of barbarian inundation.

Your memorialists, on behalf of their constituents, would, in conclusion, avail themselves of this opportunity to tender to the honorable Congress their cordial adhesion to the *plan of Zavaleta;* and to express their felicitations on the happy issue of the late unhappy conflict. They would also declare their gratitude to the patriot-chief and his illustrious associates whose propitious conquests have saved from profanation "the august temple in which we have deposited the holy ark of our federal constitution," and have secured the ultimate triumph of the liberal and enlightened principles of genuine republicanism. And they would unite their fervent aspirations with the prayers that must ascend from the hearts of all good Mexicans, that the Supreme Ruler of the universe, who "doeth his will in the army of heaven, and among the inhabitants of the earth," would vouchsafe to this glorious land the blessings of peace and tranquillity; would preserve it, in all future time, from the horrors of civil discord; and would shed down upon its extended population the increased and increasing effulgence of light and liberty which is fast irradiating the European continent, and extirpating the relics of feudal despotism of the antiquated errors of a barbarous age from the civilized world.

DAVID G. BURNET,
Chairman of the Committee.

But a feeling of distrust or jealousy of their Texan colonists seems at this time to have swayed the councils of Mexico, for when Stephen F. Austin presented this constitution and memorial to that government, then centralized under the entire control of Santa Anna, he was arrested and kept in Mexico, till September, 1835.

To the eloquent appeals of the memorial, the Mexican authorities, in imitation of the conduct of Great Britain just before the memorable contest for Independence, when petitions from her American colonists were presented—*turned a deaf ear*.

In the spring of 1834, while Stephen Austin was languishing in a Mexican prison, Colonel Joan Almonte was commissioned by the Supreme Government to visit Texas, and report his observations to the Executive, which are so pertinent that the following extracts are here inserted:

"This report," he observes, "although imperfect, will afford some idea of *what Texas is, and what it was.*

"What it will be, it is not difficult to anticipate. If we consider the extraordinary and rapid advances that industry has made; its advantageous geographical position, its harbors, the easy navigation of its rivers, the variety of its productions, the fertility of the soil, the climate, etc.,—the conclusion is, that

Texas must soon be the most flourishing section of the Republic. There is no difficulty in explaining the reason of this prosperity. In Texas, with the exception of some disturbers (*con ecepcion de algunos revoltosos*), they only think of growing the sugar-cane, cotton, maize, wheat, tobacco; the breeding of cattle, opening of roads, and rendering the rivers navigable. Moreover, the effects of our political commotions are not felt there, and often it is only by mere chance our dissensions are known. Situated as Texas is, some 450 leagues from the capital of the Federation, it is easy to conceive the rapidity of its progress in population and industry, for the reason that Texas is out of the reach of the civil wars that have unfortunately come upon us. The inhabitants of that country continue, without interruption, to devote themselves to industrious occupations, giving value to the lands with which they have been favored by the munificence of the Government.

"If, then, the position of Texas is so advantageous, why should not the Mexicans participate in its benefits? Are not they the owners of those valuable lands? Are they not capable of encountering dangers with firmness and courage? Let small companies be formed; enter into contracts with agricultural laborers; appoint to each of the companies its overseer, agent, or colonial director; and I will be the surety that, in less than one or two years, by the concession of eleven-league grants of land, which will not cost perhaps more than a trifle for the stamped paper on which the title is made out, the grants will be converted into a property worth more than from fifteen to twenty thousand dollars. Let those who wish to test the worth of this assurance visit the plantations of the colonists, and they will perceive I am no dreamer."

"If, as is possible," he proceeds to say, "I return to Texas as colonial director, I shall have great pleasure in affording to purchasers of land and Mexcan Empresarios all the information in my power for the better colonization of the country. I do not hesitate particularly to assure retired officers and invalids, that the best way to provide for their families is to solicit permission of the Government to capitalize their pay, and go and colonize Texas. There they will find peace and industry, and obtain rest in their old age, which, in all probability, will not be found in the centre of the Republic."

The report opens with a general notice of Texas, and then enters upon separate statistical details respecting the three departments—Bexar, the Brazos, and Nacogdoches. My object being to adduce the Commissioner's authority as Mexican evidence to fact, I shall refer to his testimony in the order of his own arrangement. The investigation commenced in the spring, and terminated in the autumn of 1834.

"The population of Texas," states the report, "extends from Bexar to the Sabine River, and in that direction there are not more than 25 leagues of unoccupied territory to occasion some inconvenience to the traveller. The most difficult part of the journey to Texas is the space between the Rio Grande and Bexar, which extends a little more than 50 leagues by what is called the Upper Road, and above 65 leagues by the way of Loredo. These difficulties do not arise from the badness of the road itself, but from the absence of population, rendering it necessary to carry provisions and even water during summer, when it is scarce in this district. This tract is so flat and rich in pasturage that it may be travelled with sufficient relays, and at a suitable speed, without the fear of wanting forage.

"In 1806 the department of Bexar contained two municipalities: San Antonio de Bexar, with a population of 5,000 souls, and Goliad, with 1,400; total, 6,400. In 1834 there were four municipalities, with the following population respectively:—San Antonio de Bexar, 2,400; Goliad, 700; Victoria, 300; San Patricio, 600; total 4,000. Deducting 600 for the municipality of San Patricio (an Irish settlement), the Mexican population had declined from 6,400 to 3,400 between 1806 and 1834. This is the only district of Texas in which there are no negro laborers. Of the various colonies introduced into it, only two have prospered; one of Mexicans, on the river Guadalupe, by the road which leads from Goliad to San Felipe; the other of Irish, on the river Nueces, on the road from Matamoras to Goliad. With the exception of San Patricio, the entire district of Bexar is peopled by Mexicans. *The greater part of the lands of Bexar can easily be irrigated*, and there is no doubt that so soon as the Government, compassionating the lot of Texas, shall send a respectable force to chastise the savages, the Mexicans will gladly hasten to colonize those valuable lands which court their labor.

"Extensive undertakings cannot be entered on in Bexar, as there is no individual capital exceeding 10,000 dollars. All the provisions raised by the inhabitants are consumed in the district. The wild horse is common, so as rarely to be valued at more than 20 rials (about 10 shillings British) when caught. Cattle are cheap; a cow and a calf not being worth more than 10 dollars, and a young bull or heifer from 4 to 5 dollars. Sheep are scarce, not exceeding 5,000 head. The whole export trade is confined to from 8,000 to 10,000 skins of various kinds, and the imports to a few articles from New

Orleans, which are exchanged in San Antonio for peltry or currency.

"There is one school in the capital of the Department supported by the municipality, but apparently the funds are so reduced as to render the maintenance of even this useful establishment impossible. What is to be the fate of those unhappy Mexicans who dwell in the midst of savages without hope of civilization? Goliad, Victoria, and even San Patricio, are similarly situated, and it is not difficult to foresee the consequences of such a state of things. In the whole department there is but one curate, the vicar died of cholera morbus in September last.

"The capital of the Department of the Brazos is San Felipe de Austin, and its principal towns are the said San Felipe, Brazoria, Matagorda, Gonzalez, Harrisburg, Mina, and Velasco. The district containing these towns is that which is generally called 'Austin's Colony.'

"The following are the municipalities and towns of the Department, with the population: San Felipe, 2,500; Columbia, 2,100; Matagorda, 1,400; Gonzalez, 900; Mina, 1,100; total, 8,000. Towns: Brazoria, Harrisburg, Velasco, Bolivar. In the population are included 1,000 negroes, introduced under certain conditions guaranteed by the State Government (*introducidos bajo ciertas condiciones, garanti-*

zadas por el gobierno del estado); and although it is true that a few African slaves have been imported into Texas, yet it has been done contrary to the opinion of the respectable settlers, who were unable to prevent it. It is to be hoped that this traffic has already been stopped; and it is desirable that a law of the General Congress and of the State should fix a *maximum* period for the introduction of negroes into Texas, as servants to the empresarios, which period ought not, in my opinion, to exceed ten or twelve years, at the end of which time they should enjoy absolute liberty.

"The most prosperous colonies of this Department are those of Austin and Dewitt. Towards the north-west of San Felipe there is now a new colony under the direction of Robertson; the same that was formerly under the charge of Austin.

"In 1833, upwards of 2,000 bales of cotton, weighing from 400 to 500 lbs. each, were exported from the Brazos; and it is said that in 1832 not less than 5,000 bales were exported. The maize is all consumed in the country, though the annual crop exceeds 50,000 barrels. The cattle, of which there may be about 25,000 head in the district, are usually driven for sale to Natchitoches. The cotton is exported regularly from Brazoria to New Orleans, where it pays 2½ per cent. duty, and realizes from 10 to 10½ cents per lb. for the exporter, after paying cost of trans port, etc. The price of cattle varies but little throughout Texas, and is the same in the Brazos as in Bexar. There are no sheep in this district; herds of swine are numerous, and may be reckoned at 50,000 head.

"The trade of the Department of the Brazos has reached 600,000 dollars. Taking the estimate for 1832 (the settlements having been ravaged by the cholera in 1833), the exports and imports are estimated thus: 5,000 bales of cotton, weighing 2,250,000 lbs., sold in New Orleans, and producing, at 10 cents per lb., 225,000 dollars net; 50,000 skins, at an average of 8 rials each, 50,000 dollars. Value of exports, 275,000 dollars (exclusive of the sale of live stock). The imports are estimated at 325,000 dollars.

"In this Department there is but one school, near Brazoria, erected by subscription, and containing from thirty to forty pupils. The wealthier colonists prefer sending their children to the United States; and those who have not the advantages of fortune care little for the education of their sons, provided they can wield the axe and cut down a tree, or kill a deer with dexterity.

"The Department of Nacogdoches contains four municipalities and four towns. Nacogdoches municipality has a population of 3,500; that of San Augustine, 2,500; Liberty, 1,000; Johnsburg, 2,000; the town of Anahuac, 50; Bevil, 140; Teran, 10; Tanaha, 100; total population, 9,900, in which is included about 1,000 negroes, introduced under special arrangements.

"Until now it appears that the New York Company are only beginning to interest themselves in settling their lands, bought or obtained by contract with Messrs. Zavala, Burnet, and Vehlein, empresarios, who first undertook the colonization of the immense tracts which they obtained of the State of Coahuila and Texas, and which are laid down in the maps of the North as lands of the 'Galveston Bay Company.' In consequence of that transaction, the Company are proprietors of nearly three-fourths of the Department of Nacogdoches, including the twenty leagues of boundary from that town to the Sabine. Of the contracts of Zavala, Burnet, and Vehlein, some expired last year, and others will expire during the present year. The Supreme Government, if at all anxious to do away with a system of jobbing so ruinous to the lands of the nation, at the hands of a few Mexicans and foreigners, ought, without loss of time, to adopt means to obviate the confusion daily arising out of contracts with the speculators, which create a feeling of disgust among the colonists, who are dissatisfied with the monopoly enjoyed by com-

3*

panies or contractors that have acquired the lands with the sole object of speculating in them.

"The settlements of this district have not prospered, because speculators have not fulfilled their contracts, and the scattered population is composed of individuals who have obtained one or more leagues of land from the state, and of others who, in virtue of the law of colonization inviting strangers, have established themselves wherever it appeared most convenient. But the latter have not even the titles to their properties, which it would be only fair to extend for them, in order to relieve them from that cruel state of uncertainty in which some have been placed for several years, as to whether they appertain to the United States or to Mexico. And as these colonists have emigrated at their own expense, it seems just that the contractors on whose lands they have settled, and who were not instrumental to the introduction of their families, should not receive the premium allowed by law. In stipulating with those contractors (*empresarios*) both the General and State Government have hitherto acted with too much negligence, and it would be well that they should now seriously turn their attention to a matter so deeply important.

"There are three common schools in this department; one in Nacogdoches, very badly supported, another at San Augustine, and the third at Johnsburg.

Texas wants a good establishment for public instruction, where the Spanish language may be taught; otherwise the language will be lost: even at present, English is almost the only language spoken in this section of the Republic.

"The trade of this Department amounts for the year to 470,000 dollars. The exports consist of cotton, skins of the deer, otter, beaver, etc., Indian corn, and cattle. There will be exported during this year about 2,000 bales of cotton, 90,000 skins, and 50,000 head of cattle, equal in value to 205,000 dollars. The imports are estimated at 265,000 dollars; the excess in the amount of imports is occasioned by the stock which remains on hand in the stores of the dealers.

"There are about 50,000 head of cattle in the whole Department, and prices are on a level with those in the Brazos. There are no sheep, nor pasturage adapted to them. There are above 60,000 head of swine, which will soon form another article of export.

"There are machines for cleaning and pressing cotton in the Departments of Nacogdoches and the Brazos. There are also a number of saw-mills. A steamboat is plying on the Brazos River, and the arrival of two more is expected; one for the Neches, the other for the Trinity.

"The amount of the whole trade of Texas for the year 1834 may be estimated at 1,400,000 dollars.

DEPARTMENTS.	IMPORTS.	EXPORTS.	TOTAL.
Bexar............	$40,000	$20,000	$60,000
Brazos...........	325,000	275,000	600,000
Nacogdoches......	265,000	205,000	470,000
Approximate valuation of contraband trade with the interior, through the ports of Brazoria, Matagorda and Copano......			270,000
Total..................................			$1,400,000

"Money is very scarce in Texas; not one in ten sales are made for cash. Purchases are made on credit, or by barter; which gives the country, in its trading relations, the appearance of a continued fair. Trade is daily increasing, owing to the large crops of cotton, and the internal consumption, caused by the constant influx of emigrants from the United States."

The Commissioner estimates the whole population of Texas proper at 36,300; of which 21,000 are civilized inhabitants, and 15,300 Indians. The number of hostile Indians is estimated at 10,800, and of friendly tribes 4,500; of the former, 9,900 are appropriated to the Department of Bexar, and the remaining 900 to the Brazos.

CHAPTER III.

A Letter from Austin.—Santa Anna.—The State of Mexico.—Travis attacks Anahuac.—Capture of the *Correo*.—War and peace parties.—Letter of Travis.—Travis, Zavala and others proscribed.—Judge Williamson and General Cos.—Austin's return and speech at Columbia.—Committees of Safety formed.—A Consultation suggested.—Zavala, Delegation to Indians.—Cos arrives in Texas.—Battle of Gonzales and capture of Goliad.—Benj. Milam.—Austin elected Commander-in-chief.

THE refusal of the Mexican Government to grant Texans the right *to figure as a state*, and the imprisonment of their commissioner vexed and troubled them.

From his prison the patriot Austin wrote to his people on the 25th of August, 1834:

"I do not know as yet what court is to investigate my case. I have long since requested to be delivered to the authorities of the State of Coahuila and Texas; and I presume I shall finally be sent to the district court (Federal Judge) of that state. The President, Santa Anna, is friendly to Texas and to me (of this I have no doubt), would have set me at liberty long since, and in fact issued an order to that effect in June, had not some statements arrived about that time from the State Government of Coahuila and Texas against me, which I understand have contributed to keep me in prison so long. It is said the report of the State Government on the subject is founded solely on the statements of some influential persons who live in Texas. Who those persons are I know not. It is affirmed that they are North Americans by birth, and I am told that if I am not imprisoned for life, and totally ruined in property and reputation, it will not be for the want of exertion and industry on the part of some of my countrymen who live in Texas. Whether all this be true or not, I know I am unwilling to believe it. I am also told that no efforts were left untried, during the last winter and spring, to prejudice the members of the legislature and State Government against me at Monclova." He warned the colonists against interfering in "the political family quarrels" of the Republic, they "having everything to lose and nothing to gain." He called upon the settlers to obey Santa Anna, who professed to be friendly to Texas and himself, and cautioned the farmers against "inflammatory politicians," he having begun to lose confidence in all persons except those who sought their living between the "handles of the plough."

This letter was no doubt seen by Santa Anna, and Mr. Austin perhaps wrote thus of him in order to gain his liberty.

According to Yoakum, Santa Anna, on the 5th October, 1834, "convoked a meeting composed of his four secretaries of state, the three representatives from Coahuila and Texas, three of his confidential generals, Lorenzo de Zavala, and Stephen F. Austin. The session was opened at eleven o'clock in the morning. The president having stated the topics to which the discussion was limited, Austin laid before the meeting the object of his mission, and the grounds of his petition. After a discussion which lasted three hours, embracing every head of the question, and in which several of the members participated, Austin urged lastly the separation of Texas from Coahuila, and its formation into an independent state. This was opposed by the representatives of the state in the national Congress, and particularly by Victor Blanco, who spoke last on the subject. Santa Anna then resolved—

"1. That he would meditate maturely the decree repealing the 11th article of the law of the 6th of April, 1830, and, if no objections were presented, would give it his sanction.

"2. That a corps, composed of cavalry, infantry, and artillery, four thousand strong, should be stationed at Bexar, for the protection of the *coast* and frontier of the country, to be under the command of General Mexia.

"3. That proper steps should be taken to have regular mails, and to remove all obstacles to the agricul tural and other industry of the inhabitants, 'who are viewed with the greatest regard.'

"4. That Texas must necessarily remain united with Coahuila, because it had not the elements warranting a separation, nor would it be convenient. And though it might be allowed to form a territory, if the inhabitants called for it, yet the dismembering of a state was unknown to Mexican laws, and he would be at a loss how to proceed."

From this extract, which is doubtless correct, it appears that at this time Santa Anna was *the State* of Mexico as clearly as ever Louis the 14th was *the State* of France.

He was jealous and distrustful of the Texans, refused to release Austin, but still kept him under his eye, nor did he release him until nearly a year after this time.

It might have been that he feared his presence in Texas until after sending thither troops to keep them in subjection, for he knew Austin's popularity and influence with his people.

And then, again, Santa Anna had heard of the restlessness of the Texans and their aspirations for self-government, and perhaps doubted whether they would support his despotism if left free to act for themselves.

In the meantime the wily Mexican sent troops to San Antonio, to Goliad and to Anahuac. Capt.

Tenorio, with twenty men, was stationed at the latter place in order to collect duties and imposts on foreign goods entering the port of Galveston.

Early in 1835, Col. Wm. B. Travis, with some Texans, captured Tenorio and his men, disarmed them and sent them away, thus showing their contempt for the Mexican Government, which had invited them to immigrate and become citizens, but afterwards failed to do justice and protect them.

To avenge this insult the Mexican Government sent a man-of-war to Galveston, which, according to Kennedy, failed to accomplish its mission. He says:

"An exaggerated account of the proceedings at Anahuac having reached General Cos, he despatched Captain Thompson, a naturalized citizen of Mexico, in the war schooner *Correo*, to Galveston, to inquire into the circumstances of the affair, and report as soon as possible the result of his investigation at Matamoros. Thompson proved himself altogether unfit for his mission. Instead of instituting an inquiry into the facts of the alleged outrage, he assumed the character of a blustering dictator, exceeded his orders, and, under the pretext of protecting the revenue, attacked and captured a vessel in the Texan trade. This had the effect of irritating the public mind against both Thompson and the Government, and the former having continued to linger on the coast, a merchant vessel, the *San Felipe*, fitted out with cannon at New Orleans, and commanded by Captain Hurd, captured the *Correo*, and sent it with its commander to New Orleans, on a charge of piratically interrupting the trade of Mexico and the United States. The insolent assumption of authority by Thompson, on the one side, and the insulting seizure of a Mexican vessel of war, on the other, operated injuriously on the relations subsisting between the General Government and Texas, and imparted greater boldness to the section of Anglo-Americans who desired to bring on an open rupture."

At this time there was a party openly for peace and willing to submit to Mexican domination on any terms, rather than take up arms, while at the same time there was another party composed of such men as Cols. Frank W. Johnson, James Bowie, Judge R. M. Williamson, Wm. B. Travis, P. H. Jack, John A. Wharton, Edwin Waller, and others of the same kind of mettle, who wore the galling chains of despotic rule mightily against their wills, and were desirous of *an open rupture.*

On the 30th July, 1835, Col. Travis wrote from *San Felipe*, to Bowie, who was then in Nacogdoches: "The people are much divided here. The *peace party*, as they style themselves, I believe, are the strongest, and make much the most noise. Unless we could be united, had we not better be quiet, and settle down for a while? There is now no doubt but that a central government will be established. What will Texas do in that case? Dr. J. H. C. Miller, and Chambers, from Gonzales, are, I believe, for unqualified submission. I do not know the minds of the people upon the subject; but if they had a bold and determined leader, I am inclined to think they would kick against it. . . . . General Cos writes that he wants to be at peace with us; and he appears to be disposed to cajole and soothe us. Ugartechea does the same. . . . God knows what we are to do! I am determined, for one, to go with my countrymen: right or wrong, 'sink or swim, live or die, survive or perish,' I am with them!"

Five days before Travis wrote this letter, one of the peace party, Dr. J. H. C. Miller, wrote from San Felipe, to John W. Smith, of San Antonio:

"All here is in a train for peace. The war and speculating parties are entirely put down, and are preparing to leave the country. They should *now* be demanded of their respective chiefs, a few at a time. First, Johnson, Williamson, Travis and Williams, and perhaps that is enough. Captain Martin, once so revolutionary, is now, thank God, where he should be, in favor of peace and his duty; and by his influence, in a good degree, has peace been restored. But now they should be demanded. The moment is auspicious.

The people are up. Say so, and oblige one who will never forget his true allegiance to the supreme authorities of the nation, and who knows that, till they are dealt with, Texas will never be quiet. Travis is in a peck of troubles. Dr. J. B. Miller disclaims his act in taking Anahuac, and he feels the breach. Don Lorenzo de Zavala is now in Columbia, attempting to arouse, etc. Have him called for, and he also will be delivered up. Williams, Baker and Johnson are now on a visit to him, and no doubt conspiring against the Government. Fail not to move in this matter, and that *quickly*, as now is the time."

On the 31st July, the day after Travis wrote his letter to his friend Bowie, Ugartechia, the Mexican commandant of San Antonio, on the information given by Dr. Miller's letter, issued an order for the immediate arrest of Travis, Johnson, Williamson, Williams, Baker, Moore, Zavala, Corvajal, and Zembrana.

Buck Travis and Three-legged Willie as Col. Travis and Judge Williamson were familiarly called by their associates, were even then old Texans—so were Sam Williams, Frank Johnson and Moseley Baker, but Zavala was a refugee from the city of Mexico, of which he had been governor—he had also been Mexican minister to France, but was a republican and an opponent of the usurpation and despotism of Santa Anna. Says Yoakum:

"Santa Anna was extremely solicitous to obtain possession of the person of Zavala. The latter had been his friend, and had sustained him in a trying hour. But the aid was given for the cause of liberty! Santa Anna had deserted that cause, and now wished to sacrifice an ancient friend, who might live to reproach him for his perfidy. 'I give this supreme order,' says Tornel to Cos, 'having the honor to direct it to you, requiring you to provide and bring into action all your ingenuity and activity in arranging energetic plans for success in the apprehension of Don Lorenzo Zavala, which person, in the actual circumstances of Texas, must be very pernicious. To this end I particularly recommend that you spare no means to secure his person, and place it at the disposition of the Supreme Government.'

"Cos, in transmitting this order to Ugartechea, on the 8th of August, directed him, if Zavala was not given up, to proceed at the head of all his cavalry to execute the command, and to give to the local authorities on the route information as to his sole object. General Cos also approved of Colonel Ugartechea's requisition upon the alcaldes for the other obnoxious individuals previously mentioned, and especially Travis, whose arrest he ordered, that he might be conducted to Bexar, to be tried by a military court."

Judge Williamson, on the 4th of July, had delivered a powerful oration on the situation and "the importance of our country, our property, our liberty, and our lives, which are all involved in the present contest between the states and the military." Again, on the 22d June, he had spoken of Cos, at San Filipe, "as capable of as much hypocrisy as he deemed necessary to conceal his designs and ensnare the Texan patriots. He did not, however, deceive them long. He sent them a circular, dated the 12th of June, 1835, full of the paternal views of the national government. At the same time he despatched a message to the commandant at Anahuac, informing him that the two companies of New Leon and the battalion of Morales would sail immediately for Texas; and that they would be followed by another strong force, which he had solicited the government to send. With this despatch also went another, from Ugartechea, giving the information that the force which had conquered Zacatecas, and which was then at Saltillo, had likewise been ordered to Texas, and would soon regulate matters!"

The order for the arrest of these popular patriots was never executed, but fired the hearts of Texans with a spirit of resistance. Even the officers of the Mexican Government became enthused. Henry Rueg, the political chief of Nacogdoches, took side with the war party, and addressed a circular to his department, prating of the constitution of 1824, and his adherence to the federal form of government.

In answer to this circular, General Cos, the brother-in-law of Santa Anna, wrote to him:

"You are made responsible for the consequences which such a document may produce; for it is your duty to give to your subordinates an example of submission and respect to the laws of the country. You have invited and conducted them toward rebellion and open resistance to its superior dispositions. The plans of the revolutionists of Texas are well known to this commandancy; and it is quite useless and vain to cover them with a hypocritical adherence to the Federal Constitution. The constitution by which all Mexicans may be governed is the constitution which the colonists of Texas *must obey*, no matter on what *principles* it may be formed."

Before this time, in order to defend themselves against the Indians, the inhabitants of Mina (now Bastrop), had organized a *Committee of Safety*, of which Edward Burleson, J. W. Bunton, Sam Wolfenburger, and John McGee were distinguished members.

The first meeting at Bastrop was on May 17th, 1835, after which the municipalities of San Filipe, Columbia, Nacogdoches and San Augustine also formed committees of safety and vigilance, which proved of great good in communicating information and forming concerted action beween the different sections of the state.

On the 8th of September, 1835, at a public meeting in Brazoria, Mr. Austin thus gives an account of his mission to the city of Mexico, his treatment while there, and the ultimate design of Mexican politicians to overthrow the state governments and establish on their ruins a centralized despotism:

"I left Texas," said Mr. Austin, "in April, 1833, as the public agent of the people, for the purpose of applying for the admission of this country into the Mexican Confederation as a state separate from Coahuila. This application was based upon the constitutional and vested rights of Texas, and was sustained by me in the city of Mexico to the utmost of my abilities. No honorable means were spared to effect the objects of my mission, and to oppose the forming of Texas into a Territory, which was attempted. I rigidly adhered to the instructions and wishes of my constituents, so far as they were communicated to me. My efforts to serve Texas involved me in the labyrinth of Mexican politics. I was arrested, and have suffered a long persecution and imprisonment. I consider it to be my duty to give an account of these events to my constituents, and will therefore at this time merely observe that I have never, in any manner, agreed to anything, or admitted anything, that would compromise the constitutional or vested rights of Texas. These rights belong to the people, and can only be surrendered by them.

"I fully hoped to have found Texas at peace and in tranquillity, but regret to find it in commotion; all disorganized, all in anarchy, and threatened with immediate hostilities. This state of things is deeply to be lamented; it is a great misfortune, but it is one which has not been produced by any acts of the people of this country; on the contrary, it is the natural and inevitable consequence of the revolution that has spread all over Mexico, and of the imprudent and impolitic measures both of the general and state governments with respect to Texas. The people here are not to blame, and cannot be justly censured. They are farmers, cultivators of the soil, and are pacific from interest, from occupation, and from inclination. They have uniformly endeavored to sustain the constitution and the public peace, and have never deviated from their duty as Mexican citizens. If any acts of imprudence have been committed by individuals, they evidently resulted from the revolutionary state of the whole nation, the imprudent and censurable conduct of the state authorities, and the total want of a local government in Texas. It is, indeed, a source of surprise and creditable congratulation, that so few acts of this description have occurred under the peculiar circumstances of the times. It is, however, to be remembered that acts of this nature were not the acts of the people, nor is Texas responsible for them. They were, as I before observed, the natural consequences of the revolutionary state of the Mexican nation; and Texas certainly did not originate that revolution, neither have the people, as a people, participated in it. The consciences and hands of the Texans are free from censure, and clean.

"The revolution in Mexico is drawing to a close. The object is to change the form of government, destroy the Federal Constitution of 1824, and establish a central or consolidated government. The states are to be converted into provinces.

"Whether the people of Texas ought or ought not to agree to this change, and relinquish all or a part of their constitutional and vested rights under the Constitution of 1824, is a question of the most vital importance, one that calls for the deliberate consideration of the people, and can only be decided by them, fairly convened for the purpose. As a citizen of Texas I have a right to an opinion on so important a matter—I have no other right, and pretend to no other. In the report which I consider it my duty to make to my constituents, I intend to give my views on the present situation of the country, and especially as to the constitutional and natural rights of Texas, and will, therefore, at this time, merely touch this subject.

"Under the Spanish Government, Texas was a separate and distinct province. As such it had a separate and distinct local organization. It was one of the unities that composed the general mass of the nation, and as such participated in the war of the revolution, and was represented in the Constituent Congress of Mexico that formed the Constitution of 1824. This Constituent Congress, so far from destroying this unity, expressly recognized and confirmed it by the law of May 7th, 1824, which united Texas with Coahuila *provisionally*, under the especial guarantee of being made a State of the Mexican Confederation as soon as it possessed the necessary elements. That law and the Federal Constitution gave to Texas a specific political existence, and vested in its inhabitants special and defined rights, which can only be relinquished by the people of Texas, acting for themselves as a unity, and not as a part of Coahuila, for the reason that the union with Coahuila was *limited*, and only gave power to the State of Coahuila and Texas to govern Texas for the time being, *but always subject to the vested rights of Texas.* The State, therefore, cannot relinquish those vested rights, by agreeing to the change of government; or by any other act, unless expressly authorized by the people of Texas to do so; neither can the General Government of Mexico legally deprive Texas of them without the consent of this people. These are my opinions.

"An important question now presents itself to the people of this country.

"The Federal Constitution of 1824 is about to be destroyed, the system of government changed, and a central or consolidated one established. Will this act annihilate all the rights of Texas, and subject this country to the uncontrolled and unlimited dictation of the new government?

"This is a subject of the most vital importance. I have no doubt the Federal Constitution will be destroyed, and a central government established, and that the people will soon be called upon to say whether they agree to this change or not. This matter requires the most calm discussion, the most mature deliberation, and the most perfect union. How is this to be had? I see but one way, and that is by a General Consultation of the people by means of delegates elected for that purpose, with full powers to give such an answer, in the name of Texas, to this question, as they may deem best, and to adopt such measures as the tranquillity and salvation of the country may require.

"It is my duty to state that General Santa Anna

verbally and expressly authorized me to say to the people of Texas that he was their friend, that he wished for their prosperity, and would do all he could to promote it; and that, in the new Constitution, he would use his influence to give to the people of Texas a special organization, suited to their education, habits, and situation. Several of the most intelligent and influential men in Mexico, and especially the Ministers of Relations and War, expressed themselves in the same manner. These declarations afford another and more urgent necessity for a General Consultation of all Texas, in order to inform the General Government, and especially General Santa Anna, what kind of organization will suit the education, habits, and situation of this people.

"It is also proper for me to state that, in all my conversation with the President, and ministers, and men of influence, I advised that no troops should be sent to Texas, and no cruisers along the coast. I gave it as my decided opinion, that the inevitable consequence of sending an armed force to this country would be war. I stated that there was a sound and correct moral principle in the people of Texas that was abundantly sufficient to restrain or put down all turbulent or seditious movements, but that this moral principle could not and would not unite with any armed force sent against this country; on the contrary, it would resist and repel it, and ought to do so. This point presents another strong reason why the people of Texas should meet in General Consultation. This country is now in anarchy, threatened with hostilities; armed vessels are capturing everything they can catch on the coast, and acts of piracy are said to be committed under cover of the Mexican flag. Can this state of things exist without precipitating the country into a war? I think it cannot, and therefore believe that it is our bounden and solemn duty, as Mexicans and as Texans, to represent the evils that are likely to result from this mistaken and most impolitic policy in the military movements.

"My friends, I can truly say that no one has been, or is now, more anxious than myself to keep trouble away from this country. No one has been, or now is, more faithful to his duty as a Mexican citizen, and no one has personally sacrificed or suffered more in the discharge of his duty. I have uniformly been opposed to have anything to do with the family political quarrels of the Mexicans. Texas needs peace and a local government; its inhabitants are farmers, and they need a calm and quiet life. But how can I, or any one, remain indifferent when our rights, our all, appear to be in jeopardy, and when it is our duty, as well as our obligation, as good Mexican citizens, to express our opinions on the present state of things, and to represent our situation to the government? It is impossible. The crisis is such as to bring it home to the judgment of every man that something must be done, and that without delay. The question will perhaps be asked, What are we to do? I have already indicated my opinion. Let all personalities, or divisions, or excitements, or passion, or violence, be banished from among us. Let a General Consultation of the people of Texas be convened as speedily as possible, to be composed of the best, and most calm, and intelligent, and firm men in the country, and let them decide what representations ought to be made to the General Government, and what ought to be done in future."

The amiable manners, good sense, sterling integrity, and sufferings of Stephen F. Austin had endeared him to his people, who listened to his advice as children to the admonitions of a parent.

Immediately after his return from Mexico, he was chosen chairman of the Committee of Vigilance of the municipality of San Filipe. Pearson, in his "Life of Hon. Edwin Waller," says:

"Up to the time of his arrival, our people were divided on the question of submission or resistance. Austin's arrival and declared opinion that we had no choice but resistance, reconciled all former conflict of opinion. Up to this time some of our best citizens were so far deceived and misled by the asurances of

Colonel Ugartechea, commandant at San Antonio, and General Cos, commander of the Eastern Department, that they were not only disposed to await events, but denounced those in favor of resistance in no measured terms."

The municipality of Columbia has the honor of putting the ball in motion for a CONSULTATION, for as early as June 23d, 1835, its citizens approved it, and on the 15th of August following at a public meeting instructed its Committee of Safety to prepare an address to the people of Texas, requesting union and concert of action for a General Consultation of all the municipalities.

The committee appointed at the meeting of the 15th of August, consisting of John A. Wharton, W. D. C. Hall, Henry Smith, Silas Dinsmore, James F. Perry, John G. McNeil, Robert H. Williams, W. H. Jack, F. A. Bingham, John Hodge, Wade H. Bynum, Branch T. Archer, William T. Austin, and others, issued an address on the 20th of the same month, and expressed it to all the jurisdictions in which an election of five delegates was suggested, to take place on the 5th of October in each municipality, to represent the same in the Consultation to meet at Washington, ten days thereafter.

It is reported that Don Lorenzo Zavala, in an address made by him on the 7th of August, 1835, at

Harrisburg, said that "Coahuila and Texas formed a state of the republic, and, as one part of it is occupied by an invading force, the free part of it should proceed to organize a power which would restore harmony, and establish uniformity in all the branches of the public administration, which would be a rallying-point for the citizens, whose hearts now tremble for liberty. But as this power can only be organized by means of a convention, which should represent the free will of the citizens of Texas, it is my opinion that this step should be taken, and I suggest the 15th day of October as a time sufficient to allow all the departments to send their representatives."

On the 19th of September, 1835, the Committee of Safety of San Filipe, of which Stephen F. Austin was chairman, issued a circular, signed by himself, advising as follows:

"That the people should maintain the position taken by them at their primary meetings—to insist on their rights under the Federal Constitution of 1824, and the law of the 7th of May of that year, and union with the Mexican Confederation.

"That every district should send members to the General Consultation, with full powers to do whatever may be necessary for the good of the country.

"That every district should organize its militia,

where it is not already done, and hold frequent musters; and that the captains of companies make a return, without delay, to the chief of this department, of the force of his company, and of its arms and ammunition, in order that he may lay the same before the General Consultation of Texas. Volun teer companies are also recommended.

"This committee deem it to be their duty to say that, in its opinion, all kind of conciliatory measures with General Cos and the military at Bexar are hopeless, and that nothing but the RUIN of Texas can be expected from any such measures. They have already, and very properly, been resorted to without effect. WAR is our only resource. There is no other remedy. We must defend our rights, ourselves, and our country, by force of arms. To do this we must unite—and in order to unite, the delegates of the people must meet in General Consultation and arrange a system of defence, and give organization to the country, so as to produce concert. Until some competent authority is established to direct, all that can be done is to recommend this subject to the people, and to advise every man in Texas to prepare for war, and lay aside all hope of conciliation."

The people of San Augustine and Nacogdoches also, led on by the eloquent appeals of Rusk and Houston, held meetings and passed resolutions providing for organizing the militia and negotiating with the Indians, of whom Yoakum says: "There were more than a thousand warriors among the different tribes that had emigrated from the United States, and almost surrounded the frontier of eastern Texas."

Houston and Rusk were members of a delegation sent to conciliate them.

They informed the Indians that "they had ordered all their surveyors to keep away from their lands, and not to make any marks on them; that they did not intend that any white man should interrupt them on their lands."

On the 12th of September, the Safety Committee of San Filipe issued a circular to the Indians, promising them all their just and legal rights.

About this time General Cos landed at Copano with 400 men, and marched by way of Goliad to San Antonio, he and his soldiers openly proclaiming the object of his mission—*General Cos with his troops intended to overrun Texas, and establish custom-houses and detachments of his army where he thought proper. To disarm the people, drive out all Americans who had come into Texas since* 1830, *and to punish those who had insulted the Supreme Government of Mexico and refused obedience to its laws.*

The first battle of the Texan revolution took place at Gonzales, on the 2d of October, 1835.

Commencing to disarm the Texans, Captain Castonado was sent from San Antonio by its commandant, Ugartechea, with two hundred men to Gonzales for a brass six-pounder cannon at that place.

The people of Gonzales refused to deliver it up, sent for assistance to Bastrop, San Filipe, and other places, whose people flew to their aid, and they attacked and drove off Castonado and his men. The following account of the affair is taken from Kennedy, vol. 2, pages 108, 109:

"The Texan force at Gonzales had been increased by volunteers from the Guadalupe, La Baca, and Colorado, to 168 men, of whom fifty were mounted. In an election for field-officers, they chose John H. Moore, colonel, and J. W. E. Wallace, lieutenant colonel. About seven o'clock in the evening of the 1st, they crossed the river Guadalupe. The line of march was formed by 'placing the cavalry in advance of the cannon (the brass six-pounder claimed by Ugartechea), two companies of flankers in open column on each side, with a company of infantry in the rear.' They moved regularly and in silence, until the Mexicans, alarmed by a shot from one of their piquets, formed in order of battle on a high mound. This was about four o'clock in the morning, during the prevalence of a thick fog, under cover of which the Texans advanced on the open prairie until they were within about three hundred and fifty yards of the enemy. The scouts in front having discharged their rifles, retired into the main body, closely pursued by a small detachment of Mexicans. The six-pounder was now brought to bear upon the entire force of the enemy, who fell back to a position distant between three and four hundred yards. The Texans advanced in good order, when Castonado, the Mexican commander, conveyed, through a prisoner, his desire for a conference, which was granted. Having inquired the reason of the attack by the colonists, he was referred to his orders, which commanded him to take by force the cannon that had been presented to the citizens of Gonzales, for the defence of the Constitution, by the constituted authorities under the Confederation, who alone were entitled to their obedience. He, they said, was the instrument of Santa Anna, who had overturned the rights of all the states except Texas, for whose constitutional privileges they were determined to fight to the last. The conference terminated without an adjustment, and the commanders joined their respective ranks. The Gonzales six-pounder resumed its fire, and the Texans advanced in double-quick time until within about two hundred yards of the enemy, when the latter retreated precipitately on the road to San Antonio de Bexar, having sustained a considerable loss in killed and wounded. The Texans, of whom not a man was injured, remained masters of the field, and having collected the spoils of victory, returned in triumph to Gonzales."

Thus commenced the memorable contest for liberty and struggle for independence in Texas, which in its development will call for a tear of sympathy from the generous for the misfortunes and calamities of those who suffered and died in it, and a word of applause and admiration for its victorious survivors, who in the end so wisely and heroically constructed upon the ruins of Mexican misrule and domination, the beautiful fabric of Anglo-American Republicanism.

After the return of Castonado to San Antonio, Ugartechia wrote to Austin, in explanation of the Correo matter saying: "I know you are right to complain of Thompson's proceedings, which I still less approve, as they were arbitrary, he having no authority to act in such a manner." That he would himself set out the next day (the 5th), "with the knowledge of Cos, with a force composed of every description of arms, sufficient to prove that the Mexicans would never suffer themselves to be insulted." He stated, however, in conclusion, that if Austin "would use his influence with the political chief *to have the gun delivered up to the writer, wherever it might meet him, from that spot he would immediately return;* if not, he would act militarily, and the consequence would be a war declared by the colonists, which should be maintained by the nation with corresponding dignity."

But the ball of revolution had been put in motion and *increased by going.* News of the battle of Gonzales sped like lightning through the settlements. Houston and Rusk, Austin and Johnson, Bowie and Travis, hastened to the scene of conflict, while Capt. George Collingsworth, with about forty planters from Old Caney and Matagorda, marched to attack Goliad, where he arrived at midnight on the 9th, sent two or three men into the town to reconnoitre, while he waited for his command to come up.

"The latter," says Yoakum, "having got lost, were detained; but on their route they fell in with the gallant Milam, who, having escaped from prison in Monterey, had rode night and day to reach Texas. He had stopped in a musquit-thicket to rest, when the Texans discovered and recognized him. A nobler volunteer could not have joined the ranks. Their number now being forty-eight, they advanced upon the town, guided by pioneers acquainted with the localities. They first attacked the quarters of Lieutenant-Colonel Sandoval, the commandant. The sentinel having fired was shot down; the door of the commandant was then broken open with axes, and he was taken prisoner. The Mexicans were completely surprised, and surrendered unconditionally. Of the enemy there was one killed and three wounded; the Texans had one slightly wounded, and they took about twenty-five prisoners—the balance escaped."

Kennedy, in his account of the capture of Goliad, differs with Yoakum as to date and numbers, but is so complimentary to the lamented Milam and the farmers of Old Caney and Matagorda, that it is here inserted:

"The colonists in the west, nothwithstanding their paucity of numbers and limited resources, acted boldly on the offensive. On the 8th, a detachment of fifty men, under Captain Collingsworth, attacked and captured the post of Goliad, containing stores to the amount of 10,000 dollars, with two brass cannon and 300 stand of arms. The garrison, which was commanded by Lieutenant-Colonel Sandoval, surrendered after a slight resistance. One Mexican soldier was killed and three wounded, and one Texan slightly wounded. A most valuable addition was made to the military councils of the colonists at Goliad, in the person of Colonel Milam, who unexpectedly appeared at this critical period.

"Benjamin R. Milam, whose name will long be held in grateful and honored remembrance by the people of Texas, was born of humble parents in the State of Kentucky, and received but a very imperfect education. 'Endowed by nature with a strength of mind and spirit of enterprise almost peculiar to the inhabitants of the Western States,' fortified by habits of independence, he associated with the Indian tribes, in order to explore the more southerly parts of Texas. In the war with Great Britain, in 1812–15, he acquired a high reputation among his countrymen; but, dissatisfied with the prospects that awaited him in his native state at the close of that contest, he engaged in the struggle for Mexican liberation, and was quickly distinguished for courage, activity, zeal, and love of freedom. Opposed to the usurpation of Iturbide, he was arrested and imprisoned; but eventually released by a rising of the people. Having assisted in the expulsion and punishment of the military emperor, he obtained, in 1828, a government grant of land in Texas. Having been arrested by the usurper Santa Anna, he had recently escaped. Shunning the habitations of the Mexican, and trasversing unfrequented paths for a distance of 600 miles, with a few scanty articles of food provided at the place of his confinement, he had arrived near the town of Goliad, and threw himself, faint, and almost exhausted, among the tall grass of the prairie. The approach of armed men arrested his attention, and presuming them to be his Mexican pursuers, he determined to defend himself to the last, and only surrender liberty with life. To his astonishment and joy, he discovered the advancing force to be his fellow-colonists of Texas, who were marching against Goliad. He entered the ranks of the volunteers as a private soldier, although accustomed and well qualified to command, and was foremost in the assault on Goliad—remaining with the army after the capture of the fort, in the same humble grade, as an example to those who might aspire to lead before they had learned to obey."

There being *no head to the Texans*, at the suggestion of the Safety Committee of San Filipe, made by circular on the 4th of October, a GENERAL COUNCIL was formed of one member from each committee of safety of the various municipalities, on the 11th of October, which was to serve as a government until the people had time to make a better one.

THE CONSULTATION met on the 16th, but Austin, with a majority of the members-elect, having joined the army of Gonzales, there was no quorum, and it adjourned to meet on the 1st November, when most of its members, at the invitation of Austin, who had been elected commander-in-chief of the Texans on the evening of the 10th, joined the army, while some of them remained to assist the General Council in organizing victory out of the slender resources of the state.

Never were a people more united; *the peace party*

had been swallowed up or totally absorbed by the war party, and "it required more patriotism to keep men at home than to get them into the service!"—San Filipe Safety Committee, October 13th, 1835, Circular.

CHAPTER IV.

Austin goes to *San Antonio.*—Battle of *Concepcion.*—Report of Colonel Bowie.—Lipantitlan taken by *Westover.*—*The Consultation.*—*Provisional Government.*—Austin's Report to Provisional Government.—*Decree of October 3d.*—The army before San Antonio ordered to raise the siege.—Colonel B. R. Milam calls for volunteers.—Attack on San Antonio, death of Colonel Milam, capture of the city, surrender of Cos, etc.

ON the 13th of October, 1835, having organized his little army, variously estimated at from three to five hundred men, Gen. Austin set out for San Antonio de Bexar, which he proposed to attack, and drive away its commandant, Gen. Cos, with the Mexican army under his command.

Before starting, however, he wrote to Zavala, who had succeeded him as chairman of the Committee of Safety at San Filipe, begging him to urge the eastern volunteers "to hurry on by forced marches" to join him, and "not to stay for cannon or for anything." He also solicited supplies of ammunition, with provisions and other necessaries for the troops.

Upon arriving at the Salado about five miles east of San Antonio on the 20th, he sent in a flag of truce to Gen. Cos, who refused to receive it or to acknowledge

Austin's military capacity, and threatened to fire on a second flag if sent.

From the Salado, Austin moved to the mission of Espada, ten or twelve miles below the city on the San Antonio River, and there for a few days awaited re-inforcements.

On the 27th, he sent Colonels Fannin and Bowie with ninety-two men to select, nearer the enemy, some eligible situation for camping, who, after inspecting the old missions of San José and San Juan, approached the mission of Concepcion, and encamped for the night in a bend of the river, with level prairie in front, and the densely timbered bank of the river forming an angle on both flanks and in their rear—about a mile and a half from San Antonio. The next morning was foggy, notwithstanding which, the cunning Mexicans came slyly from the city and unbeknowenst to the Texans, surrounded and commenced firing at them.

Colonel James Bowie's official report as to the subsequent details of the action which followed, being very full and complete, is here inserted:

"The men were called to arms, but were for some time unable to discover their foes, who had entirely surrounded the position, and kept up a constant firing at a distance, with no other effect than a waste of ammunition. When the fog rose it was apparent to all that we were surrounded, and that a desperate fight was inevitable, all communication with the main army having been cut off. Immediate preparation was made by extending our right flank (first division) to the south, and placing the second division on the left, on the same side; so that they might be prepared for the enemy should they charge into the angle, and avoid the effect of a cross-fire of our own men, and likewise form a compact body, so that either might reinforce the other at the shortest notice without crossing the angle—an exposed ground, which would have occasioned certain loss. The men, in the meantime, were ordered to clear away bushes and vines under the eminence in the rear, and along the margin of the river, and at the steepest places to cut steps for foothold, in order to afford them space to form and pass, and at suitable places ascend the 'bluff,' discharge their rifles, and fall back to reload. The work was not completed to our wish before the Mexican infantry were seen to advance, with arms trailed, to the right of the first division, and form the line of battle about two hundred yards distance from the right flank. Five companies of cavalry supported them, covering our whole front and flank.

"The engagement commenced at about eight o'clock, A.M., by the deadly crack of a rifle from the extreme right. The action was immediately general. The discharge from the enemy was one continued blaze of fire, whilst that from our lines was more slowly delivered, but with good aim and deadly effect, each man retiring under cover of the hill and timber, to give place to others until he reloaded. The battle had not lasted more than ten minutes, when a brass six-pounder was opened on our line at the distance of about eighty yards from the right flank of the first division, and a charge sounded. But the cannon was cleared, as if by magic, and a check put to the charge. The same experiment was resorted to with like success three times, the division advancing under cover of the hill at each fire, and thus approximating near the cannon and victory. 'The cannon and victory,' was truly the war-cry; the enemy only fired it five times, and it had been three times cleared, and their charge as often broken, when a disorderly and precipitate retreat was sounded and most readily obeyed, leaving the cannon to the victors. Thus a detachment of ninety-two men gained a complete victory over part of the main army of the Central Government, being at least four to one, with only the loss of one brave soldier (Richard Andrews), and none wounded.*

---

* Colonel Bowie estimated the Mexican loss at about sixty killed and forty wounded, the list of killed including many officers. None of the artillerymen escaped unhurt. There was no accurate return of the Mexican loss.

"No invidious distinction can be drawn between any officer or private on this occasion. Every man was a soldier, and did his duty agreeably to the situation and circumstances under which he was placed. At the close of the engagement a piece of heavy artillery was brought up and fired thrice, but at a distance, and by a reinforcement of another company of cavalry, aided by six mules ready harnessed, they got it off. The main army (of Texas) reached us in about an hour after the enemy's retreat. Had it been possible to communicate with you (General Austin) and bring you up earlier, the victory would have been conclusive, and Bexar ours before twelve o'clock."

At noon on the next day General Cos sent a flag of truce to General Austin, requesting permission to bury the dead, which was granted.

After the battle of Concepcion, Austin encamped with his army on the field of battle until the 2d of November. He then moved up north of the city, and camped on the river near its source.

Occasional skirmishes took place, in one of which, the GRASS FIGHT, about fifty Mexicans were killed and several wounded, while the Texans lost two wounded and one missing.

In the meantime, Captain Westover, of the command stationed at Goliad, after its capture by the gallant Collingsworth, with thirty-six men attacked and took Lipantitlan, above San Patricio, its garrison of twenty-one men and two pieces of artillery.

While returning to Goliad after paroling their prisoners, they were attacked while crossing the Nueces by about seventy Mexicans, of whom they killed and wounded about twenty, with a loss of one wounded, when the Mexicans retired.

"News of these successes," says Yoakum, "spread over the country through the agency of the committees of safety, and cheered the Texans in their struggle. The same intelligence, reaching the United States, kindled a flame of sympathy everywhere. At New York, Cincinnati, Louisville, Nashville, Macon, Huntsville, Natchitoches, Mobile, New Orleans, and other places, funds were raised, and *emigrants* fitted out in squads, companies, and battalions. True, there were, in all these places, icy spirits, who had no sympathy, and who condemned Texas for not submitting to Santa Anna. Such men, if they really knew the wrongs inflicted on Texas, and those greater wrongs with which she was threatened—had they lived in the time of the American Revolution, would have opposed it also. It ill became a country like the United States, still red with the blood of her rebellion against George III., to blame Texas for going into the contest with Mexican despotism. The former revolted because of *taxation without represen tation.* The wrongs of Texas were so much greater that she did not even complain of the absence of that right! Mexico complained to the United States that the revolted Texans were 'daily obtaining from New Orleans assistance of all kinds, in men, munitions, and arms, in silver and soldiers, who publicly enlist in that city, and carry with them arms against a friendly nation.' There was no law in the United States to prevent public meetings, or to prohibit the transmission of funds or arms to other countries; nor was there any law to prevent persons from leaving the United States, provided they did not organize and array their forces within her limits. President Jackson was not the man to shrink from any official duty, however painful; but, as an individual, he could not but feel an interest in a struggle like that in which Texas was engaged; and what he thought, he spoke. It cannot be denied that in some instances the law was violated, and that organized bodies of men did leave the United States; but the sympathy for the cause of the Texans was almost universal, and no one made it his business to advise prosecuting officers of these movements. They came—they aided Texas; she gave them a home, and many of them remained within her limits. The Lafayettes, the Pulaskis, and the Kosciuskos of Texas will be kindly remembered, not only throughout her borders, but wherever liberty has friends."

But to return to the CONSULTATION, which met in San Filipe November 1st, 1835, and organized on the 3d. Gen. Houston and other members, by the advice of Gen. Austin, left the army while it was encamped at the mission of Espada, to attend it. The municipalities were represented as follows:

Municipality of *Bevil:* John Bevil, S. H. Everitt, Wyatt Hanks.

San Augustine: William N. Sigler, A. Houston, A. E. C. Johnson, Henry Augustin, A. Horton, A. G. Kellogg.

Nacogdoches: Sam Houston, James W. Robinson, Daniel Parker, William Whitaker.

Columbia: John A. Wharton, J. S. D. Byrom, Edwin Waller, Henry Smith.

Austin: Wylie Martin, Randal Jones, Thomas Barnett, Jesse Burnham, William Menefee.

Liberty: Henry Millard, Claiborne West, George M. Patrick, J. B. Woods, A. B. Hardin.

Harrisburg: Lorenzo D. Zavala, M. W. Smith, William P. Harris, John W. Moore, C. C. Dyer, David B. Macomb.

Matagorda: R. R. Royal, Charles Wilson.

Mina: D. C. Barrett, R. M. Williamson, J. S. Lester.

Washington: Asa Mitchell, Elijah Collard, Jesse Grimes, Philip Coe, Asa Hoxey.

Gonzales: W. S. Fisher, J. D. Clements, George W. Davis, James Hodges, William W. Arrington, Benjamin Fuqua.

Viesca: S. T. Allen, A. G. Perry, J. G. W. Pierson, Alexander Thompson, J. W. Parker.

Tenehaw: Martin Parmer.

The Consultation superseded the council, and after thirteen days' labor organized a Provisional Government, republic in form, and elected Henry Smith, Governor; J. W. Robertson, Lieutenant-Governor; Sam Houston, Commander-in-Chief of the Army, and a council of twelve to co-operate with the Governor.

Branch T. Archer, William H. Wharton, and Stephen F. Austin, were duly chosen commissioners to the United States. Messrs. A. Houston, Daniel Parker, Jesse Grimes, A. G. Perry, D. C. Barrett, Henry Millard, Martin Parmer, J. D. Clements, R. R. Royal, W. P. Harris, E. Waller, and W. Hanks, were the counsel elected out of the Consultation, to remain and co-operate with Governor Smith in carrying out the organic law.

On the 25th of the same month, Gen Austin, having been notified of his new appointment, turned over the command of the army before San Antonio, to Col. Edward Burleson, who had just been elected to suc-

S. F. Austin.

ceed him, and on the 30th, in person, made in substance the following excellent Report to the Provisional Government:

"I have the satisfaction to say that the patriotism which drew together the gallant volunteers now in service before Bexar and Fort Goliad is unabated. They left all the comforts and endearments of home to defend their constitutional rights, and the republican principles of the Federal System and Constitution of 1824, and the vested rights of Texas under the law of the 7th of May of that year. Their basis is the Constitution and the Federal System. But should these be destroyed in Mexico, and the decree of the 3d of October last, passed by the Central party (a copy of which is herewith presented), be carried into effect, and a Central and despotic government established, where all the authority is to be concentrated in one person, or in a few persons, in the city of Mexico, sustained by military and ecclesiastical power; the volunteer army will also, in that event, do their duty to their country, to the cause of liberty, and to them selves—as honor, patriotism, and the first law of nature may require.

"That every people have the right to change their government, is unquestionable; but it is equally certain and true, that this change, to be morally or politically obligatory, must be effected by the free expression of the will of the community, and by legal and consti tutional means; for otherwise the stability of governments and the rights of the people would be at the mercy of fortunate revolutionists—of violence or faction.

"Admitting, therefore, that a Central and despotic or *strong* government is best adapted to the education and habits of a portion of the Mexican people, and that they wish it; this does not, and cannot, give to them the right to dictate by unconstitutional means and force to the other portion, who have equal rights, and differ in opinion.

"Had the change been effected by constitutional means, or had a National Convention been convened, and every member of the Confederacy been fairly represented, and a majority agreed to the change, it would have placed the matter on different ground; but, even then, it would be monstrous to admit the principle, that the majority have the right to destroy the minority, for the reason that self-preservation is superior to all political obligations. That such a government as is contemplated by the before-mentioned decree of the 3d of October would destroy the people of Texas must be evident to all, when they consider its geographical situation, so remote from the contemplated centre of legislation and power; populated as it is by a people who are so different in education, habits, customs, language, and local wants, from all the rest of the nation; and, especially, when a portion of the Central party have manifested violent religious and other prejudices and jealousies against them. But no National Convention was convened, and the Constitution has been, and now is, violated and disregarded.

"The constitutional authorities of the State of Coahuila and Texas solemnly protested against the change of government, for which act they were driven by military force from office and imprisoned. The people of Texas protested against it, as they had a right to do, for which they have been declared rebels by the Government in Mexico.

"However necessary, then, the basis established by the decree of the 3d of October may be to prevent civil wars and anarchy in other parts of Mexico, it is attempted to be effected by force and unconstitutional means. However beneficial it may be to some parts of Mexico, it would be ruinous to Texas. This view presents the whole subject to the people. If they submit to a forcible and unconstitutional destruction of the social compact which they have sworn to support, they violate their oaths. If they submit to be tamely destroyed, they disregard their duty to themselves, and violate the first law which God has stamped upon the heart of man, civilized or savage—which is the law or the right of self-preservation.

"The decree of the 3d of October, therefore, if carried into effect, evidently leaves no remedy for Texas but resistance, secession from Mexico, and a direct resort to natural rights.

"Such I believe to be the view which the volunteer army, lately under my command, has taken of this subject; and such, in substance, the principles it is defending, and will defend. That they are sound and just, and merit the approbation of all nations, I sincerely and conscientiously believe.

"It may be out of place to speak of myself in such a communication as this, but I deem it right to say that I have faithfully labored for years to unite Texas permanently to the Mexican Confederation, by separating its local government and internal administration, so far as practicable, from every other part of Mexico, and placing it in the hands of the people of Texas, who are certainly best acquainted with their local wants, and could best harmonize in legislating for them. There was but one way to effect this union, with any hope of permanency or harmony, which was by erecting Texas into a State of the Mexican Confederation. Sound policy, and the true interest of the Mexican Republic, evidently required that this should be done.

"The people of Texas desired it; and if proofs were wanting (but they are not) of their fidelity to their obligations as Mexican citizens, this effort to erect Texas into a state affords one which is conclusive to every man of judgment who knows anything about this country; for all such are convinced that Texas could not, and would not, remain united to Mexico without the right of self-government as a separate state.

"The object of the Texans, therefore, in wishing a separation from Coahuila, and the erection of their country into a state, was to avoid a total separation from Mexico by a revolution. Neither Coahuila, nor any other portion of the Mexican nation, can legislate on the internal affairs of Texas: it is impossible. This country must either be a state of the Mexican Confederation, or must separate *in toto*, as an independent community, or seek protection from some power that recognizes the principles of self-government. I can see no remedy between one of these three positions and total ruin.

"I must particularly call the attention of the Provisional Government to the Volunteer Army now in the field. That their services have been, and now are, in the highest degree useful and important to Texas, is very evident. Had this army never crossed the Guadalupe—a movement which some have condemned—the war would have been carried by the Centralists into the colonies, and the settlements on the Guadalupe and La Baca would probably have suffered, and perhaps have been broken up. The town of Gonzales had already been attacked, and many of the settlers were about to remove.

"What effect such a state of things would have had upon the moral standing and prospects of the country, although a matter of opinion, is worthy of mature consideration, more especially when it is considered that, at the time, the opinions of many were vacillating and unsettled, and much division prevailed. The Volunteer Army have also paralyzed the force of General Cos, so that it is shut up within the fortifications of Bexar, incapable of any hostile movements whatever outside of the walls, and must shortly surrender or be annihilated. The enemy has been beaten in every contest and skirmish, which has proved the superiority of the volunteers, and given confidence to every one. Our undisciplined volunteers, but few of whom were ever in the field before, have acquired some experience, and much confidence in each other and in themselves, and are much better prepared for organization, and to meet a formidable attack than they were before.

"The post of Goliad has been taken by the volunteers, and the enemy deprived of large supplies which were at that place, and of the facilities of procuring others by water, through the port of Copano, which is also closed upon them by the occupation of Goliad. The enemy has been driven from the river Nueces by a detachment of the volunteers who garrison Goliad, and by the patriotic sons of Ireland from Power's colony. More than one hundred of the enemy, including many officers, have been killed; a great many have been wounded, others have deserted, and a valuable piece of brass cannon, a six-pounder, has been taken, and another preserved (the one that was at Gonzales) from falling into the hands of the enemy. Three hundred head of horses have been taken, and the resources for sustaining an army in Bexar are all destroyed or exhausted, so that an enemy in that place is at this time more than three hundred miles from any supplies of bread-stuff, and many other necessary articles. All this has been effected by the Volunteer Army in a little more than one month, and with the loss of only one man killed in battle, and one wounded (who has nearly recovered) before Bexar; one wounded at Goliad, and one at Lipantitlan, on the Nueces. In short, the moral and political influence of the campaign is equally beneficial to Texas and to the sacred cause of the Constitution and of liberty, and honorable to the Volunteer Army. This army is composed, principally, of the most intelligent, respectable, and wealthy citizens of the country; and of volunteers from

Louisiana and Alabama—men who have taken up arms from principle, from a sense of duty, and from the purest motives of patriotism and philanthropy. They have bravely sustained the rights of Texas and the cause of Mexican liberty, and patiently borne the exposure and fatigue of a winter's campaign during the most inclement, wet, and cold spell of weather known in this country for many years. The most of them are men of families, whose loss would have made a fearful void in our thin community. They might have been precipitated upon the fortifications of Bexar, which were defended by seven or eight hundred men and a number of cannon, and taken the place by storm against superior numbers; and Texas might, and in all probability would, have been covered with mourning in the hour of victory. On consultation with the officers in council of war, it was deemed most prudent not to hazard so much in the commencement of the contest, when a disaster would have been so materially injurious; and the system was adopted of wasting away the resources, and spirits, and numbers of the enemy by a siege, the ultimate success of which appeared to be certain, without any serious hazard on our part. That the fall of Bexar within a short time, and with a very little loss, will be the result, I have no doubt.

"I consider the Volunteer Army to be the main

hope of Texas at this time, and until a regular army can be organized; and I recommend that it be sustained and provided for in the most effectual and efficient manner.

"Before closing this communication, I deem it to be my duty to recommend to the consideration of the Provisional Government the situation of the inhabitants of Bexar and Goliad. The necessary and indispensable operations of the war have compelled the army to make use of a considerable amount of their property, particularly corn and beef cattle. So soon as circumstances will permit, I respectfully recommend that some system be adopted to ascertain the amount of property thus used, and to provide for a just compensation. This recommendation also extends to horses or other property lost by the Volunteers.

"I will present to government another report on a special subject of importance."

"In the other report of Mr. Austin alluded to, he advised the calling of a convention, with plenary powers, and is as follows:

"At the time of the former elections, the people did not and could not fully understand their true situation; for it was not known then, to a certainty, what changes would take place in Mexico, what kind of government would be established, or what course would be pursued towards Texas. It was only known then that the Central party was in power, that all its measures tended to the destruction of the Federal system, and that preparations were making to invade Texas.

"But, at the present time, the people know that the government is changed—that Centralism is established by the decree of the 3d of October last, and that they are threatened with annihilation. In short, the whole picture is now clearly before their view, and they see the dangers that are hanging over them. Can these dangers be averted by a provisional organization which is based upon a declaration that is equivocal and liable to different constructions? Does not the situation of the country require a more fixed and stable state of things? In short, is it not necessary that Texas should now say in plain, and positive, and unequivocal lauguage, what is the position she occupies, and will occupy; and can such a declaration be made without a new and direct resort to the people, by calling, as speedily as possible, a convention with plenary powers, based upon the principle of equal representation in proportion to the population?

"These are questions of the most vital importance. I respectfully submit them to the calm deliberation of the Provisional Government, in the full confidence that all the attention will be given to the subject which its importance merits.

"Without expressing any individual opinion of my own as to the time or day when the new elections ought to take place, which would, perhaps, be indecorous in such a communication as this, the object of which is to lay facts before the Provisional Government, I deem it to be my duty to say, that so far as I could judge of the opinions and wishes of the citizens who were in the Volunteer Army when I left them on the 25th ult., they were in favor of an *immediate* election of a convention with plenary power."

In all probability, had the *Consultation* made a *declaration of independence*, *framed a Constitution*, and ordered an election for officers under it, Mr. Austin would have been satisfied. The decree so often alluded to in the foregoing pages is as follows:

[Decree of the 3d of October, 1835.]

"*Office of the First Secretary of State,*
Interior Department.

"His Excellency the President, *pro tem.*, of the Mexican United States to the Inhabitants of the Republic. Know ye, that the General Congress has decreed the following:

"ART. 1. The present governors of the states shall continue, notwithstanding the time fixed by the Constitution may have expired; but shall be dependent for their continuance in the exercise of their attributes upon the Supreme Government of the nation.

"ART. 2. The legislatures shall immediately cease to exercise their legislative functions: but before dissolving (and those which may be in recess meeting for the purpose), they shall appoint a Department Council, composed, for the present, of five individuals, chosen either within or without their own body, to act as a council to the governor; and in case of a vacancy in that office, they shall propose to the Supreme General Government three persons possessing the qualifications hitherto required: and until an appointment be made, the gubernatorial powers shall be exercised by the first on the list who is not an ecclesiastic.

"ART. 3. In those states where the legislature cannot be assembled within eight days, the Ayuntamiento of the capital shall act in his place, only for the purpose of electing the five individuals of the Department Council.

"ART. 4. All the judges and tribunals of the states, and the administration of justice, shall continue as hitherto, until the organic law relative to this branch be formed. The responsibilities of the functionaries which could only be investigated before Congress, shall be referred to, and concluded before the Supreme Court of the nation.

"ART. 5. All the subaltern officers of the state shall also continue for the present (the places which are vacant, or which may be vacated, not to be filled), but they, as well as the officers, revenues, and branches under their charge, remain subject to, and at the disposal of, the Supreme Government of the nation, by means of the respective governors.

"Palace of the Federal Government in Mexico, October 3d, 1835.

"MAGUIL BARRAGAN,

"A. D. MANUEL DIEZ DE BONILLA."

General Austin gained but little glory as a military man. His great, big heart was too tender to see men bleed and die without pain; and then each one of the volunteer army was his dear friend.

"I am afraid," he wrote to Captain Dimit, on the 2d of November, "that our future operations will be tedious and prolonged, owing to the strength of the fortifications at this place, of which we have certain information. Whether the army can be kept together long enough to await the arrival of reinforcements, and the necessary supply of heavy battering-cannon and ammunition, I am sorry to say, is somewhat uncertain."

At one time he had 1,000 men before San Antonio, after this he was joined by *the New Orleans Grays* and English's company from Eastern Texas, so that had all remained he would have had 1,300 men with which to have taken the place by assault. But he felt sure of it in the end, and would not order an assault for fear of losing a few precious lives, so the men became impatient of camp life and wanted to go home. Rusk and Travis would enthuse them occasionally by dashing up with them near the fortifications, but the cold weather and rains set in and *they went home.* They were mostly farmers with families, and had joined the army in a hurry, with their summer clothes on—it had turned cold, so they went home to see their families and to get winter clothes.

"The men," says Kennedy, "wearied with idly gazing at the walls of the beleaguered town, importuned the general to order an immediate assault. One day, and then another, were successively named for indulging their ardor, but nothing was done; and on the evening of the 4th of December, the order was given to break up the camp and retire into winter quarters."

This order was received by the majority of the 500 remaining troops with regret and chagrin.

Yoakum writes: "It was then," says an eye-witness, "that the scene was wholly indescribable, and serious apprehensions were entertained that our camp would become the theatre of blood."

Some wished to obey the order and raise the siege, while others were eager for an attack.

At the height of the excitement *glorious old Ben Milam* cried out, at the top of his voice: "*Who will go with old Ben Milam into San Antonio?*"

This inquiry was answered joyously and instantly by 300 volunteers, whom, with the approbation of the commanding general, Burleson, he organized into two divisions, one of which he commanded in person, while the other was led by Colonel Frank Johnson, one of the *proscribed.*

General Cos had about 800 men in the Alamo and the *Plazas*—an oblong square surrounded by stone houses and separated by the church and houses north and south of it. Solidad, Acequia, and Flores Streets run into the Plazas from the north, and were fortified by cannon and barricades where they entered the Plazas—named Main and Military, the latter west, the former east of the church.

Having sent Colonel J. C. Neill with a party to make a feint attack upon the Àlamo, Colonel Milam and Johnson with 300 men and two cannon, before day on the morning of the 5th, entered the city and made lodgments in two famous buildings known as the Veramandi and Garza houses, about one hundred yards apart, the former east of Solidad, the latter east of Acequia Streets. The following despatch, signed by B. R. Milam and Edward Burleson, and dated 6th December, 1835, was sent to the Provisional Government at San Filipe:

"Yesterday morning, at daylight, or rather some twenty minutes before, Colonel Milam, with a party of about 300 volunteers, made an assault upon the town of Bexar. His party he distributed in two divisions, which, on entering the town, took possession of two buildings near each other—near the place where they have been ever since battling with the enemy. They have so far had a fierce contest, the enemy offering a strong and obstinate resistance. The houses occupied by us command some of the cannon in the place, or have silenced them entirely, as it is reported to us. *The issue is doubtful, of course* Ugartechea is on the way, with considerable reinforcements; how near has not yet been exactly ascertained; but certainly he is not more than from fifty to sixty miles off. This express has been despatched for an immediate supply of ammunition, as much powder and lead as can possibly be sent instantly. Of the first-mentioned article, there is none beyond the cannon cartridges already made up. I hope that good mules, or horses, will be procured to send on these articles with the greatest possible speed, travelling night and day, for there is not a moment to be lost. Reinforcements of men are, perhaps, indispensable to our salvation. I hope every exertion will be made to force them to our relief immediately."

In his official report of the storming of San Antonio, Colonel Johnson says:

"At seven o'clock a heavy cannonading from the town was seconded by a well-directed fire from the Alamo, which for a time prevented the possibility of covering our lines, or effecting a safe communication between the two divisions. In consequence of the twelve-pounder having been dismounted, and the want of proper cover for the other gun, little execution was done by our artillery during the day. We were, therefore, reduced to a close and well-directed fire from our rifles, which, notwithstanding the advantageous position of the enemy, obliged them to slacken their fire, and several times to abandon their artillery within range of our shot. Our loss during the day was one private killed; one colonel and one first-lieutenant severely wounded; one colonel slightly, three privates dangerously, six severely, and three slightly. During the whole of the night (of the 5th) the two divisions were occupied in strengthening their positions, opening trenches, and effecting a safe communication, although exposed to a heavy cross-fire from the enemy, which slackened towards morning. I may remark that the want of proper tools rendered this undertaking doubly arduous.

"At daylight of the 6th the enemy were observed to have occupied the tops of the houses in our front, where, under cover of breast-works, they opened through loop-holes a very brisk fire of small arms on our whole line, followed by a steady cannonading from the town, in front, and from the Alamo on the left flank, with few interruptions during the day. A detachment of Captain Crane's company, under Lieutenant W. McDonald, followed by others, gallantly possessed themselves, under a severe fire, of the house to the right, and in advance of the first division, which considerably extended our line; while the rest of the army was occupied in returning the enemy's fire and strengthening our trenches, which enabled our artillery to do some execution, and complete a safe communication from right to left. Our loss this day amounted to three privates severely wounded and two slightly.* During the night the fire from the enemy was inconsiderable, and our people were occupied in making and filling sand-bags, and otherwise strengthening our lines.

"At daylight on the 7th it was discovered that the enemy had, during the night previous, opened a trench on the Alamo side of the river, and on the left flank,

* The late Thomas W. Ward lost a leg here, and was afterwards nick-named *Old Peg-Leg.* Hon. Sam. A. Maverick and J. W. Smith did good service in this *storming party.*

as well as strengthened their battery on the cross street leading to the Alamo. From the first, they opened a brisk fire of small arms; from the last, a heavy cannonade, as well as small arms, which was kept up until eleven o'clock, when they were silenced by our superior fire. About twelve o'clock, Henry Karnes,* of Capt. York's company, exposed to a heavy fire from the enemy, gallantly advanced to a house in front of the first division; and, with a crow-bar, forced an entrance, through which the whole company immediately followed him, and made a secure lodgment. In the evening, the enemy renewed a heavy fire from all the

---

* Henry Karnes was one of those remarkable characters whose true history is a romance. He was raised in Tennessee. At an early age he joined a company of Arkansas trappers, who turned their attention to attacks on the Pawnee villages on the head-branches of Red River; but, having disagreed, they separated. Karnes, with three or four others, proceeded across to the head of the Trinity. Here, having their horses stolen, they obtained a canoe, and floated down the river to Robbins's Ferry. Karnes procured employment at Groce's Retreat, where the war found him. He entered the Texan service, and fought with a hearty good-will. One who was often with him, and by his side at Concepcion, says he never knew him to swear before or since that day. But when he came into the lines, after being shot at so often, and began to load his rifle, he exclaimed with some wrath, "The d———d rascals have shot out the bottom of my powder-horn!" Karnes rose to the rank of colonel in Texas. He was of low stature, and weighed about one hundred and sixty pounds; was quiet, sober, and temperate, and had an effeminate voice. He was wholly illiterate, yet he had remarkable gentleness and delicacy of feeling, and was otherwise amiable in private life. He died at San Antonio, in August, 1840, surrounded by his numerous friends.—*Yoakum.*

positions which could bear upon us, and at about half-past three o'clock, as our gallant commander, Colonel Milam, was passing into the yard of my position (the house of Berimendi) he received a rifle shot in the head, which caused his instant death—an irreparable loss at so critical a moment. Our casualties otherwise, during the day, were only two privates slightly wounded.

"At a meeting of officers, held at seven o'clock, I was invested with the chief command, with Major Morris as my second. Captains Llewellyn, English, Crane, and Landrum, with their respective companies, forced their way into, and took possession of the house of Don J. Antonio Navarro, an advanced and important position close to the square. The fire of the enemy became interrupted and slack during the whole night, and the weather exceedingly cold and wet.

"The morning of the 8th continued cold and wet, and but little firing on either side. At nine o'clock, the same companies who took possession of Don J. Antonio Navarro's house, aided by a detachment of the Grays, advanced and occupied the Zambrano Row, leading to the Square, without any accident. The brave conduct on this occasion of William Graham, of Cook's company of Grays, merits mention. A heavy fire of artillery and small arms was opened on this position by the enemy, who disputed every inch of ground, and after suffering a severe loss in officers and men, were obliged to retire from to room to room, until they evacuated the whole building. During this time, our men were reinforced by a detachment from York's company, under the command of Lieutenant Gill. The cannonading was exceedingly heavy from all quarters during the day, but did no essential damage. Our loss consisted of one captain seriously wounded and two privates severely. At seven o'clock, P.M., the party in Zambrano's Row were reinforced by Captains Swisher, Alley, Edwards, and Duncan, and their respective companies.

"This evening we had undoubted information of the arrival of a strong reinforcement to the enemy, under Colonel Ugartechea. At half-past ten o'clock, P.M., Captains Cook and Patton, with the company of New Orleans Grays * and a company of Brazoria Volunteers, forced their way into the priest's house in the square, although exposed to the fire of a battery

---

* "The appearance of the Grays at Nacogdoches on their way to San Antonia," says the late Adolphus Sterne, "had a fine effect on the Cherokee Indians, a large number of whom were then in town. Their fine uniform caps and coats attracted the notice of the chief, Bolles. He inquired if they were *Jackson's* men. 'Certainly they are,' said Sterne. 'Are there more coming?'—'Yes,' was the reply. 'How many more?' asked Bolles. Sterne told him to count the hairs on his head, and he would know. In twenty minutes the Indians had all left the town!"

of three guns and a large body of musqueteers. Before this, however, the division was reinforced from the reserve by Captains Cheshire, Lewis, and Sutherland, and their companies.

"Immediately after we got possession of the priest's house, the enemy opened a furious cannonade from all their batteries, accompanied by incessant volleys of small arms, against every house in our possession, and every part of our lines, which continued unceasingly until half-past six o'clock A.M. of the 9th, when they sent a flag of truce, with an intimation that they desired to capitulate. Our loss in this night's attack, consisted of one man only, dangerously wounded, while in the act of spiking a cannon."

On the morning of the 10th, Gen. Cos surrendered, and on the 14th set out for the Rio Grande, with 1,105 troops, the remainder of his army, which amounted to about 1,400, having concluded to remain in San Antonio.

Thus by the heroism of Milam and his comrades was the stronghold of the Mexicans in Texas taken, but at the loss of that gallant soldier, the brave Milam.

Often have I entered the Old Veramandi and asked: "*Where is Milam's grave?*" but no one ever answered the question, and unless some of his comrades in this brilliant achievement shall return to the place of his glory, and mark the "*grave where our hero they buried*," it will be unknown to future generations.

With the capture of San Antonio ended the campaign of 1835. In a little more than two months every hostile Mexican had been driven from the soil of Texas, with but very slight loss. Col. Johnson, with a small garrison, remained at San Antonio, while the majority of the little army went home. In the language of the English historian of Texas: "They had toiled, and suffered, and fought, like men to whom the fairest fields and the brightest skies are valueless and cheerless, without the invigorating exercise of their constitutional rights. With the degenerate races of the South, liberty was but a poetical abstraction—the catch-word of the intriguing demagogue—the war-cry of the ambitious soldier: with the Anglo-Americans it was a substantial inheritance—dear to them as the memory of their ancestors—essential to their social progress as the air of heaven to their physical existence. It was the spirit of independence that stimulated the Northern husbandmen to turn their faces toward the sun of the tropic, and sustained them amidst trials of which the pampered inhabitants of the cities of the old world can form no conception. The charter which had hitherto protected and encouraged the settlers—the Mexican Constitution of 1824—had been violated; the armed partisan had usurped the seat of the judge; drum-head decisions had been substituted for the awards of law, and the colonists were left to choose between resistance, with its danger, and submission, with its disgrace. They made their election with a full perception of the consequences it might involve, and staked life and land in defence of their chartered liberties. Their first essay in the field was astonishingly successful; and the storming of Bexar will rank among the most remarkable feats of chivalrous daring. To what did they owe their success? Not to the arts of professional soldiership, for of these they were ignorant; not to numerical strength, for they were comparatively few—ill-armed, ill-clad, and ill-fed. In their moral organization—in the proud sense of their superiority, as instructed freemen, over the puppets of ignorant and intolerant misrule, lay the secret of their triumphs."

CHAPTER V.

The PROVISIONAL GOVERNMENT and the GENERAL COUNCIL.—Gen. Houston's Proclamation.—Dr. James Grant and the Matamoras *fever*.—Gen. Mexia's Expedition to Tampico.—Cols. Fannin and Johnson made *Agents* and supersede Gen. Houston.—*His Report*.—Treaty with the Indians.—Capture of the *Hannah Elizabeth* by the *William Robbins*.—Col. Tom McKinney.—Austin borrows $250,000.—The Convention at Washington.—Declaration of Independence, and Government *ad interim*.

THE Provisional Government of Texas, which existed only about four months, was not a success. The governor and Council soon fell out, and the Council passed a resolution deposing Gov. Smith and placing in his stead the lieut.-governor.

In less than a month after its inauguration it was openly declared that "the existing authorities were not equal to the crisis; that the officers and the members of the council were worthless and imbecile; and that it was necessary forthwith to reorganize the government and give it a more energetic administration, in order to save the country from ruin."

Gen. Houston sided with the governor, but gave his powerful aid on the stump and in *the Council* for the support and continuance of the administration.

Before the news of the storming of San Antonio arrived, in his official capacity he issued the following.

Proclamation of Sam Houston, Commander-in-Chief of the Army of Texas.

HEADQUARTERS, WASHINGTON, TEXAS, *December* 12, 1835.

CITIZENS OF TEXAS: Your situation is peculiarly calculated to call forth all your manly energies. Under the republican constitution of Mexico you were invited to Texas, then a wilderness. You have reclaimed and rendered it a cultivated country. You solemnly swore to support the constitution and its laws. Your oaths are yet inviolate. In accordance therewith you have fought with the liberals against those who sought to overthrow the constitution in 1832, when the present usurper was the champion of liberal principles in Mexico. Your obedience has manifested your integrity. You have witnessed with pain the convulsions of the interior, and a succession of usurpations. You have experienced in silent grief the expulsion of your members elect from the State Congress.

You have realized the horrors of anarchy and the dictation of military rule. The promises made to you have not been fulfilled. Your memorials for the redress of grievances have been disregarded; and the agents you have sent to Mexico have been imprisoned for years, without enjoying the rights of trial agreeably to law. Your constitutional executive has been deposed by the bayonets of a mercenary soldiery, while your Congress has been dissolved by violence, and its members either fled or were arrested by the military force of the country. The federation has been dissolved, the constitution declared at an end, and centralism has been established. Amid all these trying vicissitudes, you remained loyal to the duty of citizens, with a hope that liberty would not perish in the Republic of Mexico. But while you were fondly cherishing this hope, the dictator required the surrender of the arms of the civic militia, that he might be enabled to establish on the ruins of the constitution, a system of policy which would forever enslave the people of Mexico. Zacatecas, unwilling to yield her sovereignty to the demand which struck at the root of all liberty, refused to disarm her citizens of their private arms. Ill-fated state! Her power as well as her wealth aroused the ambition of Santa Anna, and excited his cupidity. Her citizens became the first victims of his cruelty, while her wealth was sacrificed in payment for the butchery of her citizens. The success of the usurper determined him in exacting from the people of Texas submission to the central form of government; and, to enforce his plan of despotism, he dispatched a military force to invade the colonies, and exact the arms of the inhabitants. The citizens refused the demand, and the invading force was increased. The question then was, "Shall we resist the oppression and live free, or violate our oaths and bear a despot's stripes?" The citizens of Texas rallied to the defence of their rights. They have met four to one, and, by their chivalry and courage, have vanquished the enemy with a gallantry and spirit which is characteristic of the justice of our cause.

The army of the people is now before Bexar, besieging the central army within its wall. Though called together at the moment, the citizens of Texas, unprovided as they were in the necessary munitions of war and supplies for an army, have maintained a siege for months. Always patient and untiring in their patriotism and zeal in the cause of liberty, they have borne every vicissitude of season and every incident of the soldier with a contempt of peril which reflects immortal honor on the members of the army of the people.

Since our army has been in the field, a consultation of the people by their representatives, has met, and established a provisional government. This course has grown out of the emergencies of the country; the army has claimed its peculiar care. We are without law, and without a constitutional head. The provisional executive and the general council of Texas are earnestly engaged in the discharge of their respective duties, preparing for every exigency of the country; and I am satisfied, from their zeal, ability, and patriotism, that Texas will have everything to hope, from their exer tions in behalf of the principles which we have avowed.

A regular army has been created, and liberal encouragement has been given by the government. To all who will enlist for two years, or during the war, a bounty of twenty-four dollars and eight hundred acres of land will be given. Provision has also been made for raising an auxiliary volunteer corps, to constitute part of the army of Texas, which will be placed under the command, and subject to the orders of the commander-in-chief. The field for promotion will be open. The terms of service will be various. To those who tender their services for, or during the war, will be given a bounty of six hundred and forty acres of land; an equal bounty will be given to those who volunteer their services for two years; if for one year, a bounty of three hundred and twenty acres; and to those who may volunteer for a shorter period, no bounty of land will be given, but the same liberal pay, rations, etc., will be allowed them as other members of the army. The rights of citizenship are extended to all who will unite with us in defending the republican principles of the constitution of 1824.

Citizens of Texas, your rights must be defended. The oppressors must be driven from our soil. Submission to the laws and union among ourselves will render us invincible; subordination and discipline in our army will guarantee to us victory and renown. Our invader has sworn to exterminate us, or sweep us from the soil of Texas. He is vigilant in his work of oppression, and has ordered to Texas ten thousand men to enforce the unhallowed purposes of his ambition. His letters to his subalterns in Texas have been intercepted, and his plans for our destruction are disclosed. Departing from the chivalric principles of civilized warfare, he has ordered arms to be distributed to *a portion of our population*, for the purpose of creating in the midst of us a *servile* war. The hopes of the usurper were inspired by a belief that the citizens of Texas were disunited and divided in opinion; that alone has been the cause of the present invasion of our rights. He shall realize the fallacy of his hopes in the union of her citizens, and their ETERNAL RESISTANCE to his plans against constitutional liberty. We will enjoy our birthright, or *perish in its defence.*

The services of five thousand volunteers will be accepted. By the first of March next we must meet the enemy with an army worthy of our cause, and which will reflect honor upon freemen. Our habitations must be defended; the sanctity of our hearths and firesides must be preserved from pollution. Liberal Mexicans will unite with us. Our countrymen in the field have presented an example worthy of imitation.

Generous and brave hearts from a land of freedom have joined our standard before Bexar. They have, by their heroism and valor, called forth the admiration of their comrades in arms, and have reflected additional honor on the land of their birth. Let the brave rally to our standard.

SAM HOUSTON,
Commander-in-Chief of the Army.

But notiwthstanding his efforts the governor and the Council kept on at war, one great cause of which was a plan for the capture of Matamoras, which originated with one Dr. Grant, who was one of the storming party that entered San Antonio on the 8th December, and was wounded seriously on the first day of the contest.

Grant was a man of wealth, and lived in the interior of Mexico, and was very plausible in representing the facility with which Matamoras, with all its wealth, might be taken, "and thence," according to Yoakum, carrying the war "into the interior of Mexico, that he might return to his princely domains at Parras. Among the volunteers and adventurers at San Antonio he was incessantly painting in lively colors the rich spoils of Tamaulipas, New Leon, Coahuila, and San Luis Potosi, the facility of the descent, the cowardly nature of the inhabitants, and the charming beauties of the valleys of the San Juan, the Sabinas, and the Santander.

"This was enough: the bold and fiery spirits who had just driven twice their number from the strong walls of Bexar and the Alamo, were ready to go. They wanted but a leader and a cause. The authority of Texas was invoked. The governor was prudent, and preferred to follow the landmarks laid down by the Consultation. The Council was otherwise. This body, changing almost daily, contained but few of the original members, and the change had not been for the better, in either wisdom or integrity. They had ceased to feel any responsibility for their official conduct."

Dr. Grant, as did also the Mexican General Mexia, declared that the inhabitants of Matamoras and the interior of Mexico were opposed to the centralism of Santa Anna as much as Texans were, and, as a matter of course, would join hands and hearts with them on their approach, and was so successful that he not only made followers in the army at San Antonio, but also carried with him the Council and many good Texans.

Gen. Houston opposed this movement, and in order to counteract it sent the following order to Colonel James Bowie:

"[Army Orders.] HEADQUARTERS, SAN FELIPE, *December* 17, 1835.

"SIR: In obedience to the order of his Excellency Henry Smith, Governor of Texas, of this date, I have the honor to direct that, in the event you can obtain the services of a sufficient number of men for the purpose, you will forthwith proceed on the route to Matamoras, and, if possible, reduce the place and retain possession until further orders. Should you not find it within your power to attain an object so desirable as the reduction of Matamoras, you will, by all possible means, conformably to the rules of civilized warfare, annoy the troops of the central army; and reduce and keep possession of the most eligible position on the frontier, using the precaution which characterizes your mode of warfare. You will conduct the campaign. Much is referred to your discretion. Should you commence the campaign, you will, from time to time, keep the government advised of your operations, through the commander-in-chief of the army. Under any circumstances, the port of Copano is important.

"If any officers or men, who have at any time been released on *parole*, should be taken in arms, they will be proper subjects for the consideration of a court-martial. Great caution is necessary in the country of an enemy.

"SAM HOUSTON,

"*Commander-in-Chief.*"

On the 14th December, twenty-eight surviving members of the ill-fated expedition fitted out at New Orleans, under the auspices of General Mexia, numbering 130 men, which sailed to Tampico in November, having been deserted by their God-and-Liberty-loving-Greaser-commander, after a drum-head trial and conviction, were shot to death.

On the 7th of January the Council created Col. J. W. Fannin *agent*, with plenary powers to organize a force and reduce Matamoras, with liberty to report to the commanding general, the governor, or the Council.

Soon after this, Col. F. W. Johnson was also commissioned for the same purpose.

On the 6th, Gov. Smith ordered Gen. Houston "to repair to Bexar, or such other point on the frontier as he might deem most eligible, and establish his head-quarters; also to establish such subordination, and place the army in such situation, as to commence active operations by the earliest day possible; and in the meantime, to annoy and injure the enemy as much as circumstances would permit."

Starting on the 8th, Gen. Houston arrived at Goliad on the 16th. From thence he went to Refugio, where, on the 21st, Col. F. W. Johnson exhibited to him his powers from the Council, and also made him acquainted with those of Col. Fannin, whereupon, considering him self superseded, he returned through Goliad to Wash-

Sam Houston

ington, and on the 30th made the following report to Gov. Smith:

" *To Governor Henry Smith.*

"MUNICIPALITY OF WASHINGTON, *January* 30, 1836.

"SIR: I have the honor to report to you that, in obedience to your order under date of the 6th inst., I left Washington on the 8th, and reached Goliad on the night of the 14th. On the morning of that day I met Captain Dimit, on his return home with his command, who reported to me the fact that his *caballada* of horses (the most of them private property) had been pressed by Dr. Grant, who styled himself acting commander-in-chief of the federal army, and that he had under his command about two hundred men. Captain Dimit had been relieved by Captain P. S. Wyatt, of the volunteers from Huntsville, Alabama. I was also informed by Major R. C. Morris that bread-stuff was wanted in camp; and he suggested his wish to remove the volunteers farther west. By express, I had advised the stay of the troops at Goliad until I could reach that point.

"On my arrival at that post, I found them destitute of many supplies necessary to their comfort on a campaign. An express reached me from Lieutenant-Colonel Neill, of Bexar, of an expected attack from the enemy in force. I immediately requested Colonel

James Bowie to march with a detachment of volunteers to his relief. He met the request with his usual promptitude and manliness. This intelligence I forwarded to your excellency, for the action of government. With a hope that supplies had or would immediately reach the port of Copano, I ordered the troops, through Major R. C. Morris, to proceed to Refugio mission, where it was reported there would be an abundance of beef—leaving Captain Wyatt and his command, for the present, in possession of Goliad, or until he could be relieved by a detachment of regulars under the command of Lieutenant Thornton, and some recruits that had been enlisted by Captain Ira Westover. On the arrival of the troops at Refugio, I ascertained that no breadstuffs could be obtained, nor was there any intelligence of supplies reaching Copano, agreeably to my expectations, and in accordance with my orders of the 30th of December and 6th of January inst., directing the landing and concentrating of all the volunteers at Copano. I had also advised Colonel A. Houston, the quartermaster-general, to forward the supplies he might obtain at New Orleans to the same point. Not meeting the command of Major Ward, as I had hoped from the early advice I had sent him by Major George W. Poe, I determined to await his arrival and the command of Captain Wyatt With a view to be in a state of readiness to march tc the scene of active operations at the first moment that my force, and the supplies necessary, could reach me, I ordered Lieutenant Thornton with his command (total twenty-nine) to Goliad, to relieve Captain Wyatt; at the same time ordering the latter to join the volunteers at Refugio. I found much difficulty in prevailing on the regulars to march until they had received either money or clothing; and their situation was truly destitute. Had I not succeeded, the station at Goliad must have been left without any defence, and abandoned to the enemy, whatever importance its occupation may be to the security of the frontier. Should Bexar remain a military post, Goliad must be maintained, or the former will be cut off from all supplies arriving by sea at the port of Copano.

"On the evening of the 20th, F. W. Johnson, Esq., arrived at Refugio, and it was understood that he was empowered by the General Council of Texas to interfere in my command. On the 21st, and previous to receiving notice of his arrival, I issued an order to organize the troops so soon as they might arrive at that place, agreeably to the 'ordinance for raising an auxiliary corps' to the army. A copy of the order I have the honor to enclose herewith. Mr. Johnson then called on me, previous to the circulation of the order, and showed me the resolutions of the General

Council, dated 14th of January, a copy of which I forward for the perusal of your excellency.

"So soon as I was made acquainted with the nature of his mission, and the powers granted to J. W. Fannin, Jr., I could not remain mistaken as to the object of the Council, or the wishes of individuals. I had but one course left for me to pursue (the report of your being deposed had also reached me), which was, to return, and report myself to you in person—inasmuch as the objects intended by your order were, by the *extraordinary* conduct of the Council, rendered useless to the country; and, by remaining with the army, the Council would have had the pleasure of ascribing to me the evils which their own conduct and acts will, in all probability, produce. I do consider the acts of the Council calculated to protract the war for years to come; and the field which they have opened to insubordination, and to *agencies* without limit (unknown to military usage), will cost the country more useless expenditure than the necessary expense of the whole war would have been had they not transcended their proper duties. Without integrity of purpose, and well-devised measures, our whole frontier must be exposed to the enemy. All the available resources of Texas are directed through *special* as well as *general agencies*, against Matamoras; and must, in all probability, prove as unavailing to the interest as they will to the honor of Texas. The regulars at Goliad cannot long be detained at that station, unless they should get supplies; and now all the resources of Texas are placed in the hands of *agents* unknown to the government in its formation, and existing by the mere will of the Council; and will leave all other objects, necessary for the defence of the country, neglected, for the want of means, until the meeting of the convention in March next.

"It was my wish, if it had been possible, to avoid for the present the expression of any opinion which might be suppressed in the present crisis. But since I reported to your excellency, having had leisure to peruse all the documents of a controversial nature growing out of the relative duties of yourself and the General Council to the people of Texas, are solution of the Council, requiring of me an act of insubordination and disobedience to your orders, demands of me that I should inquire into the nature of that authority which would stimulate me to an act of treason, or an attempt to subvert the government which I have sworn to support. The only constitution which Texas has is the 'organic law.' Then any violation of that law, which would destroy the basis of government, must be treason. Has treason been committed? if so, by whom, and for what purpose? The history of the last few weeks will be the best answer that can be rendered.

"After the capitulation of Bexar, it was understood at head-quarters that there was much discontent with the troops then at that point, and that it might be necessary to employ them in some active enterprise, or the force would dissolve. With this information was suggested the expediency of an attack on Matamoras. For the purpose of improving whatever advantages might have been gained at Bexar, I applied to your excellency for orders, which I obtained, directing the adoption of such measures as might be deemed best for the protection of the frontier and the reduction of Matamoras. This order was dated 17th of December; and on the same date I wrote to Colonel James Bowie, directing him, in the event he could obtain a sufficient number of volunteers for the purpose, to make a descent on Matamoras; and, if his force would not justify that measure, he was directed to occupy the most advanced post, so as to check the enemy, and by all means to place himself in a situation to command Copano. Colonel Bowie did not receive the order: having left Goliad for Bexar, he was not apprised of it until his arrival at San Felipe, about the 1st of January instant. My reason for ordering Colonel Bowie on the service was, his familiar acquaintance with the country, as well as the nature of the population through which troops must pass, as also their resources; and to this I freely add that there is no man on whose forecast, prudence, and valor, I place a higher estimate than Colonel Bowie.

"Previous to this time, the General Council had adopted a resolution requiring the governor to direct the removal of the head-quarters of the army, and I had been ordered to Washington, for their establishment, until further orders. I had been detained, awaiting copies of the ordinances relative to the army. Their design was manifest, nor could their objects be misapprehended, though the extent to which they were then carrying them was not known. Messrs. Hanks and Clements were engaged in writing letters to individuals at Bexar, urging and authorizing a campaign against Matamoras; and, that their recommendation might bear the stamp of authority, and mislead those who were unwilling to embark in an expedition not sanctioned by government, and led by private individuals, they took the liberty of signing themselves members of the military committee; thereby deceiving the volunteers, and assuming a character which they could only use or employ in the General Council, in proposing business for the action of that body. They could not be altogether ignorant of the impropriety of such conduct, but doubtless could easily find a solid justification in the bullion of their patriotism and the ore of their integrity. Be their motive whatever it might, many brave and honorable men were deluded by it, and the campaign was commenced upon Matamoras, under Dr. Grant, as 'acting' commander-in-chief of the volunteer army—a title and designation unknown to the world. But the General Council, in their address to the people of Texas, dated January 11th, state that 'they never recognized in Dr. Grant any authority whatever as an officer of the government, or army, at the time.' They will not, I presume, deny that they did acknowledge a draft, or order, drawn by him, as *acting commander-in-chief*, amounting to seven hundred and fifty dollars. But this they will doubtless justify, on the ground that your excellency commissioned General Burleson, and, of course, the appointment of Dr. Grant, as his aid-de-camp, would authorize him to act in the absence of General Burleson. It is an established principle in all armies that a staff-officer can claim no command in the line of the army, nor exercise any command in the absence of the general, unless he holds a commission in the line. In the absence of General Burleson, the senior colonel—or, in the absence of the colonel, the major—or, in his absence, the senior captain—would have the command; but in no event can the *aide*, or staff-officer, unless he holds a commission in the line of the army, have any command; and his existence must cease, unless he should be continued or reappointed by the officer of the line who succeeds to the command in the absence of his superior. When General Burleson left the army, his aide had no command, but the field officer next in rank to himself. Then, who is Dr Grant? Is he not a Scotchman, who has resided in Mexico for the last ten years? does he not own large possessions in the interior? has he ever taken the oath to support the organic law? is he not deeply interested in the hundred-league claims of land which hang like a murky cloud over the people of Texas? is he not the man who impressed the property of the people of Bexar? is he not the man who took from Bexar, without authority, or knowledge of the government, cannon and other munitions of war, together with supplies necessary for the troops at that station, leaving the wounded and the sick destitute of needful comforts? Yet this is the man whose outrages and oppressions upon the rights of the people of Texas are sustained and justified by the acts and conduct of the General Council.

"Several members of that body are aware that the interests and feelings of Dr. Grant are opposed to the independence and true interests of the people of Texas. While every facility has been afforded to the meditated campaign against Matamoras, no aid has been rendered for raising a regular force for the defence of the country, nor one cent advanced to an officer or soldier of the regular army, but every hindrance thrown in the way. The Council had no right to project a campaign against any point or place. It was the province of the governor, by his proper officers, to do so. The Council had the right of consenting or objecting, but not of projecting. The means ought to be placed at the disposition of the governor; and if he, by himself, or his officers, failed in their application, while he would be responsible for the success of the armies of Texas, he could be held responsible to the government, and punishable; but what recourse has the country upon agents who have taken no oath, and given no bonds to comply with the powers granted by the Council?

"The organic law declares, in article third, that 'the governor and General Council have power to organize, reduce, or increase the regular forces;' but it delegates no power to create army-agents, to supersede the commander-in-chief, as will be seen by reference to the second article of the 'military' basis of that law. After declaring that there shall be a regular army for the protection of Texas during the present war, in the first article, it proceeds in the second to state the constituents of that army: 'The regular army of Texas shall consist of one major-general, who shall be commander-in-chief of all the forces called into public service during the war.' This, it will be remembered, is a law from which the Council derive their powers; and, of course, all troops in service since the adoption of this law, and all that have been accepted, or to be accepted during my continuance in office, are under my command. Consequently, the Council could not create an *agency* that could assume any command of troops, so as to supersede my powers, without a plain and palpable violation of their oaths. New names given could not change the nature of their obligations: they had violated the 'organic law.'

"I will now advert to an ordinance of their own body, entitled 'an ordinance and decree to organize and establish an auxiliary volunteer corps of the army of Texas,' etc., passed December 5, 1835. The ordinance throughout recognizes the competency of the governor and commander-in-chief as the only persons authorized to accept the services of the volunteers, and makes it their especial duty to do so. It also gives the discretion to the commander-in-chief to accept the services of the volunteers for such term as 'he shall think the defence of the country and the good of the service require.' It is specified that muster-rolls shall accompany the reports of volunteers, and, when reported by the commander-in-chief to the governor, that commissions shall issue accordingly. Where elections take place in the volunteer corps, the ordinance declares that they shall be certified to the commander-in-chief, and by him forwarded to the governor. The third section of the law declares that when controversies arise in relation to the rank of officers of the same grade, they shall be be determined 'by drawing numbers, which shall be done by order of the commander-in-chief of the army.' This law was enacted by the General Council, and they cannot allege that any misconstruction could arise out of it; for it plainly points out the duties of the governor and commander-in-chief, as defined by themselves. Yet, without the repeal of this law, they have proceeded to appoint agents to exercise the very powers declared by them to belong to the governor and commander-in-chief! This they have done, under the impression that a *change of names* would enable them to put down the governor and the commander-in-chief, not subject to them for their places, but created by the Consultation, and both of whom are as independent of the Council as the Council is of them—the commander-in-chief being subject to the organic law, and all laws conformable thereto, under the orders of the governor. I have obeyed the orders of your excellency as promptly as they have met my knowledge; and had not the Council, by acts as outrageous to my feelings as they are manifestly against law, adopted a course that must destroy all hopes of an army, I should yet have been on the frontier, and, by all possible means, I would at least have sought to place it in a state of defence.

"It now becomes my duty to advert to the subject of the powers granted by the General Council to J. W. Fannin, Jr., on the 7th of January, 1836; and at a time when two members of the military committee, and other members of the Council, were advised that I had received orders from your excellency to repair forthwith to the frontier of Texas, and to concentrate the troops for the very purpose avowed in the resolutions referred to. The powers are as clearly illegal as they were unnecessary. By reference to the resolutions, it will be perceived that the powers given to J. W. Fannin, Jr., are as comprehensive in their nature, and as much at variance with the organic law and the decrees of the General Council, as the decrees of the General Congress of Mexico are at variance with the Federal Constitution of 1824, and really delegate to J. W. Fannin, Jr., as extensive powers as those conferred by the Congress on General Santa Anna. Yet the cant is kept up, even by J. W. Fannin, Jr., against the *danger* of a regular army; while he is exercising powers which he must be satisfied are in open violation of the organic law. J. W. Fannin, Jr., is a colonel in the regular army, and was sworn in and received his commission on the very day that the resolutions were adopted by the Council. By his oath he was subject to the orders of the commander-in-chief, and, as a subaltern, could not, without an act of mutiny, interfere with the general command of the forces of Texas; yet I find, in the *Telegraph* of the 9th inst., a proclamation of his, dated on the 8th, addressed: 'Attention, volunteers,' and requiring them to rendezvous at San Patricio. No official character is pretended by him, as his signature is private. This he did with a knowledge that I had ordered the troops from the mouth of the Brazos to Copano, and had repaired to that point to concentrate them. On the 10th inst., F. W. Johnson issued a similar proclamation, announcing Matamoras as the point of attack. The powers of both these gentlemen were derived, if derived at all, from the General Council, in opposition to the will of the governor; because certain purposes were to be answered, or the safety and harmony of Texas should be destroyed.

"Colonel Fannin, in a letter addressd to the General Council, dated on the 21st of January, at Velasco, and to which he subscribes himself, 'J. W. Fannin, Jr., Agent Provisional Government,' when speaking of anticipated difficulties with the commander-in-chief, allays the fears of the Council by assuring them that, 'I shall never make any myself;' and he then adds: 'The object in view will be the governing principle, and should General Houston be ready and willing to take command, and march direct ahead, and execute your orders, and the volunteers to submit to it, or a reasonable part of them, I shall not say nay, but will do all in my power to produce harmony.' How was I to become acquainted with the orders of the Council? Was it through my subaltern? It must have been so designed—as the Council have not, up to the present moment, given me any official notice of the orders to which Colonel Fannin refers. This modesty and subordination on his part is truly commendable in a subaltern, and would imply that he had the right to 'say nay.' If he has this power, whence is it derived? Not from any law,—and contrary to his sworn duty as my subaltern, whose duty is obedience to my lawful commands, agreeably to the rules and regulations of the United States army, adopted by the Consultation of all Texas. If he accepted any appointment incompatible with his *obligation* as a colonel in the regular army, it certainly increases his moral responsibilities to an extent which is truly to be regretted.

"In another paragraph of his letter, he states: 'You will allow that we have too much division, and one cause of complaint is this very expedition, and that it is intended to remove General Houston.' He then assures the Council that no blame shall attach to him, but most dutifully says to them, 'I will go where you have sent me, and will do what you have ordered me, if possible.' The order of the Council, as set forth in the resolutions appointing Colonel Fannin agent, and authorizing him to appoint as many agents as he might think proper, did most certainly place him above the governor and the commander-in-chief of the army—nor is he responsible to the Council, or the people of Texas. He is required to report, but he is not required to obey the Council. His powers are as unlimited and absolute as Cromwell's ever were. I regard the expedition, as now ordered, an individual, and not a national measure. The resolutions passed in favor of J. W. Fannin, Jr., and F. W. Johnson, and their proclamations, with its original start—Dr. Grant—absolve the country from all responsibility for its consequences. If I had any doubt on the subject, previous to having seen, at Goliad, a proclamation of J. W. Fannin, Jr., sent by him to the volunteers, I could no longer entertain one, as to the campaign, so far as certain persons are interested in forwarding it. After appealing to the volunteers, he concluded with the assurance that '*the troops should be paid out of the first spoils taken from the enemy.*' This, in my opinion, connected with the extraordinary powers granted to him, by the Council, divests the campaign of any character save that of a piratical or predatory war.

"The people of Texas have declared to the world, that the war in which they are now engaged, is a war of principle, in defence of their civil and political rights. What effect will the declaration above referred to have on the civilized world, when they learn that the individual who made it has since been clothed with absolute powers by the General Council of Texas; and that, because you refuse to ratify their acts, they have declared you no longer the governor of Texas? It was stated by way of inducement to the advance on Matamoras, that the citizens of that place were friendly to the advance of the troops of Texas upon that city. They, no doubt, ere this, have J. W. Fannin's proclamation (though it was in manuscript), and if originally true, what will now be their feelings toward men who 'are to be paid out of the first spoils taken from the enemy'? The idea which must present itself to the enemy, will be, if the city is taken it will be given up to pillage; and when the spoils are collected, a division will take place. In war, when spoil is the object, friends and enemies share one common destiny. This rule will govern the citizens of Matamoras in their conclusions, and render their resistance desperate. A city containing twelve thousand souls will not be taken by a handful of men who have marched twenty-two days without breadstuffs, or necessary supplies for an army. If there ever was a time when Matamoras could have been taken by a few men, that time has passed by. The people of that place are not aware of the high-minded and honorable men who fill the ranks of the Texan army. They will look upon them as they would look upon Mexican mercenaries, and resist them as such. They too will hear of the impressment of the property of the citizens of Bexar, as reported to your excellency, by Lieutenant-Colonel Neill, when Dr. Grant left that place for Matamoras, in command of the volunteer army.

"If the troops advance upon Matamoras, there ought to be a co-operation by sea, with the land forces, or all will be lost; and the brave men who have come to toil with us in our marches, and mingle in our battles for liberty, will fall a sacrifice to the selfishness of some who have individual purposes to answer, and whose influence with the Council has been such as to impose upon the honest part of its members; while those who were otherwise, availed themselves of every artifice which they could devise, to shield themselves from detection.

"The evil is now done, and I trust sincerely that the 1st of March may establish a government on some permanent foundation, where honest functionaries will regard and execute the known and established laws of the country, agreeably to their oaths. If this state of things cannot be achieved, the country must be lost. I feel, in the station which I hold, that every effort of the Council has been to mortify me individually, and, if possible, to compel me to do some act which would enable them to pursue the same measures toward me, which they have illegally done toward your excellency, and thereby remove another obstacle to the accomplishment of their plans. In their attempts to embarrass me, they were reckless of all prejudice which might result to the public service from their lawless course.

"While the Council was passing resolutions affecting the army of Texas, and transferring to J. W. Fannin, Jr., and F. W. Johnson the whole control of the army and resources of Texas, they could order them to be furnished with copies of the several resolutions passed by that body, but did not think proper even to notify the major-general of the army of their adoption; nor have they yet caused him to be furnished with the acts of the Council relative to the army. True it is, that they passed a resolution to that effect, but it never was complied with. Their object must have been to conceal, and not to promulgate their acts. 'They have loved darkness rather than light, because their deeds are evil.'

"I do not consider the Council as a constitutional body, nor their acts lawful. They have no quorum agreeably to the organic law, and therefore I am compelled to regard all their acts as void. The body has been composed of seventeen members, and I perceive that the act of 'suspension,' passed against your excellency, was by only ten members present; the president *pro tem.* having no vote. Only ten members remain, when less than twelve members could not form a quorum agreeably to the organic law, which required two-thirds of the whole body. I am not prepared to violate either my duty or my oath, by yielding obedience to an act manifestly unlawful, as it is, in my opinion, prejudicial to the welfare of Texas.

"The lieutenant-governor, and several members of the Council, I believe to be patriotic and just men; but there have been, and when I left San Felipe there were, others in that body on whose honesty and integrity the foregoing facts will be the best commentary. They must also abide the judgment of the people.

"I have the honor to be,

"Your excellency's obedient servant,

"SAM HOUSTON,

"*Commander-in-Chief of the Army.*"

Without doubt General Houston's indignation was great against *the General Council!* Indeed, he was sorely vexed. He even called the gallant Colonel Johnson, who distinguished himself so highly in the reduction of San Antonio, *Mr. Johnson*, and the heroic Colonel Fannin, who with the immortal Bowie had gained such great glory at Concepcion, he styles *Mr. J. W. Fannin, Jr.*

What could he do, by staying longer with the troops at Refugio, when *the Matamoras fever* was raging so fiercely?

He wisely concluded to go for *the enemy in his rear;* so he returned to Washington, aided all he could the movement for a convention with *plenary powers*:—thus to wipe out the detestable GENERAL COUNCIL, the impotent governor, Henry Smith, and the execrable PROVISIONAL GOVERNMENT generally, and from the government established upon their overthrow, have his commission as commander-in-chief of the Texan forces reissued or confirmed, then he would take command and lead the gallant patriots of Texas to victory and independence. At any rate he did not stay to be in the way of the gallant gentlemen who had fought so nobly at La Purisima Concepcion and San Antonio de Bexar.

Austin had requested him to command the army in his stead when it first approached San Antonio in the preceding year, but he refused, because Austin, not himself, had been *elected* by the men. General Austin insisted that he (Houston) had been elected to command the troops from the municipality of Nacogdoches and San Augustine—but Houston peremptorily refused to supersede him.

On the return of General Houston to San Felipe, Governor Smith granted him a furlough till the 1st March, in which he stated:

"Your absence is permitted in part by the illegal acts of the Council, in superseding you, by the unauthorized appointment of agents to organize and control the army, contrary to the organic law, and the ordinances of their own body. In the meantime, you will conform to your instructions, and treat with the Indians."

On the 23d of February, 1836, General Houston and Mr. Forbes, as commissioners for Texas, made a treaty with the Indians, which in contemplation of the next campaign with the Mexicans was of incalculable importance.

Communication about this time between Texas and New Orleans was much interrupted by two Mexican vessels of war, the *Bravo* and *Montezuma.*

"The *Hannah Elizabeth,*" says Yoakum, "freighted with cannon, arms, and ammunition, intended for the Texan service, and an adventure of goods and provisions belonging in part to Peter Kerr, sailed from New Orleans for Matagorda. Kerr was himself on board, as were likewise José M. J. Carbajal and Fernando de Leon, the latter two having charge of the other freight. She was discovered, pursued, and run aground, at Pass Cavallo, by the *Bravo.* In the chase she had thrown overboard her cannon and ammunition. She was boarded by a prize-crew, consisting of Lieutenant Mateo and eleven men from the *Bravo;* and Carbajal, De Leon, and some others were transferred as prisoners to that vessel. Shortly after, the *Bravo* was driven off by a *norther.* In a day or two afterward, the citizens of Matagorda having received notice of the wreck, purchased and armed the schooner *William Robbins,* placed her under the command of Captain Hurd, and, with a small force on board, commanded by Captain S. Rhoads Fisher, retook the stranded vessel and made the prize-crew prisoners. This was all very well; but they went further, and appropriated to themselves the goods and provisions, allowing Kerr to retain his part on payment of half their value! But Kerr being unable to do this, got none. Governor Smith being duly advised of these proceedings, took occasion in a special message to reprehend them severely."

Now the *William Robbins* happened to belong to the firm of *McKinney* & Williams, and when Colonel

Tom heard this reprehension of Governor Smith, he vowed that he would punish him, but respecting the officer, he waited until Smith ceased to be chief magistrate, when he coolly and calmly proceeded to whip his excellency until he hollowed: "*Oh, don't! don't! don't!*" Colonel Tom McKinney was a rare old Texan —was agent and creditor of Texas for many years. After a contest with Dr. G. A. Feris, of Richmond, many years ago, the doctor said: "Why, Tom McKinney is the best man in Texas! he can whip anybody!" Indeed he was a brave, liberal, and gentle man—loved by his friends and respected even by his enemies.

On the 11th of January, Mr. Austin and his associate commissioners negotiated a loan of $200,000, and on the 18th another for $50,000, which enabled the Texan agents to send supplies to the troops at a time when they were much needed.

On the 1st February an election was held by order of the Council for delegates to a convention with *plenary powers*, which assembled at Washington, March 1st, and on the next day made and signed the following:

"DECLARATION OF INDEPENDENCE.

"When a government has ceased to protect the lives, liberty, and property of the people, from whom its legitimate powers are derived, and for the advancement of whose happiness it was instituted; and so far from being a guarantee for their inestimable and inalienable rights, becomes an instrument in the hands of evil rulers for their oppression—When the Federal Republican Constitution of their country, which they have sworn to support, no longer has a substantial existence, and the whole nature of their government has been forcibly changed, without their consent, from a restricted Federative Republic, composed of Sovereign States, to a consolidated central military despotism, in which every interest is disregarded but that of the army and the priesthood, both the eternal enemies of civil liberty, the ever-ready minions of power, and the usual instruments of tyrants—When, long after the spirit of the constitution has departed, moderation is at length so far lost by those in power, that even the semblance of freedom is removed, and the forms themselves of the constitution discontinued, and so far from their petitions and remonstrances being regarded, the agents who bear them are thrown into dungeons, and mercenary armies sent forth to enforce a new government upon them at the point of the bayonet—

"When, in consequence of such acts of malfeasance and abduction on the part of the government, anarchy prevails, and civil society is dissolved into its original elements—in such a crisis, the first law of nature, the right of self-preservation, the inherent and inalienable right of the people to appeal to first principles, and take their political affairs into their own hands in extreme cases, enjoins it as a right towards themselves, and a sacred obligation to their posterity, to abolish such government, and create another in its stead, calculated to rescue them from impending dangers, and to secure their welfare and happiness.

"Nations, as well as individuals, are amenable for their acts to the general opinion of mankind. A statement of a part of our grievances is therefore submitted to an impartial world, in justification of the hazardous but unavoidable step now taken, of severing our political connection with the Mexican people, and assuming an independent attitude among the nations of the earth.

"The Mexican Government, by its colonization laws, invited and induced the Anglo-American population of Texas to colonize its wilderness under the pledged faith of a written constitution, and that they should continue to enjoy that constitutional liberty and republican government to which they had been habituated in the land of their birth—the United States of America.

"In this expectation they have been cruelly disappointed, inasmuch as the Mexican nation has acquiesced in the late changes made in the government by

General Antonio Lopez de Santa Anna, who, having overturned the constitution of his country, now offers to us the cruel alternatives, either to abandon our homes, acquired by so many privations, or submit to the most intolerable of all tyranny, the combined despotism of the sword and the priesthood.

"It has sacrificed our welfare to the State of Coahuila, by which our interests have been continually depressed through a jealous and partial course of legislation, carried on at a far-distant seat of government, by a hostile majority, in an unknown tongue, and this too nothwithstanding we have petitioned, in the humblest terms, for the establishment of a separate state government, and have, in accordance with the provisions of the National Constitution, presented to the General Congress a republican constitution, which was, without just cause, contemptuously rejected.

"It incarcerated in a dungeon, for a long time, one of our citizens, for no other cause but a zealous endeavor to procure the acceptance of our Constitution, and the establishment of a State Government.

"It has failed and refused to secure, on a firm basis, the right of trial by jury, that palladium of civil liberty, and only safe guarantee for the life, liberty, and property of the citizen.

"It has failed to establish any public system of education, although possessed of almost boundless resources (the public domain), and although it is an axiom in political science, that unless a people are educated and enlightened, it is idle to expect the continuance of civil liberty, or the capacity for self-government.

"It has suffered the military commandants, stationed among us, to exercise arbitrary acts of oppression and tyranny, thus trampling upon the most sacred rights of the citizen, and rendering the military superior to the civil power.

"It has dissolved, by force of arms, the State Congress of Coahuila and Texas, and obliged our representatives to fly for their lives from the seat of government, thus depriving us of the fundamental political right of representation.

"It has demanded the surrender of a number of our citizens, and ordered military detachments to seize and carry them into the interior for trial, in contempt of the civil authorities, and in defiance of the laws and the constitution.

"It has made piratical attacks upon our commerce, by commissioning foreign desperadoes, and authorizing them to seize our vessels, and convey the property of our citizens to far-distant parts for confiscation.

"It denies us the right of worshipping the Almighty according to the dictates of our own conscience, by the support of a national religion calculated to promote the temporal interest of its human functionaries, rather than the glory of the true and living God.

"It has demanded us to deliver up our arms, which are essential to our defence—the rightful property of freemen—and formidable only to tyrannical governments.

"It has invaded our country both by sea and by land, with the intent to lay waste our territory, and drive us from our homes; and has now a large mercenary army advancing to carry on against us a war of extermination.

"It has, through its emissaries, incited the merciless savage, with the tomahawk and scalping-knife, to massacre the inhabitants of our defenceless frontiers.

"It has been, during the whole time of our connection with it, the contemptible sport and victim of successive military revolutions, and hath continually exhibited every characteristic of a weak, corrupt, and tyrannical government.

"These, and other grievances, were patiently borne by the people of Texas, until they reached that point at which forbearance ceases to be a virtue. We then took up arms in defence of the National Constitution. We appealed to our Mexican brethren for assistance; our appeal has been made in vain; though months have elapsed, no sympathetic response has yet been heard from the interior. We are, therefore, forced to the melancholy conclusion, that the Mexican people have acquiesced in the destruction of their liberty, and the substitution therefor of a military government; that they are unfit to be free, and incapable of self-government.

"The necessity of self-preservation, therefore, now decrees our eternal political separation.

"WE, *therefore, the delegates, with plenary powers, of the people of Texas, in solemn convention assembled, appealing to a candid world for the necessities of our condition, do hereby resolve and declare, that our political connection with the Mexican nation has forever ended, and that the people of Texas do now constitute a* FREE, SOVEREIGN, and INDEPENDENT REPUBLIC, *and are fully invested with all the rights and attributes which properly belong to independent nations; and, conscious of the rectitude of our intentions, we fearlessly and confidently commit the issue to the Supreme Arbiter of the destinies of nations.*

"In witness whereof we have hereunto subscribed our names.

NAMES.	AGE.	PLACE OF BIRTH.	FORMER RESIDENCE.
Richard Ellis	54	Virginia	Alabama.
C. B. Stewart	30	South Carolina	Louisiana.
James Collingsworth	30	Tennessee	Tennessee.
Edwin Waller	35	Virginia	Missouri.
Asa Brigham	46	Massachusetts	Louisiana.
J. S. D. Byron	38	Georgia	Florida.
Fras. Ruis	54	Bexar, Texas	———
J. Anto. Navarro	41	Bexar, Texas	———

NAMES.	AGE.	PLACE OF BIRTH.	FORMER RESIDENCE.
J. B. Badgett..........	29	North Carolina........	Arkansas Territory.
W. D. Lacy............	28	Kentucky..............	Tennessee.
William Menifee.......	40	Tennessee.............	Alabama.
John Fisher...........	36	Virginia..............	Virginia.
M. Coldwell...........	38	Kentucky..............	Missouri.
W. Motley.............	24	Virginia..............	Kentucky.
L. D. Zavala..........	47	Yucatan...............	Mexico.
George W. Smyth.......	33	North Carolina........	Alabama.
S. H. Everitt.........	29	New York..............	New York.
E. Stapp..............	53	Virginia..............	Missouri.
Cla^{e}. West.............	36	Tennessee.............	Louisiana.
W. B. Scates..........	30	Virginia..............	Kentucky.
M. B. Menard..........	31	Canada................	Illinois.
A. B. Hardin..........	38	Georgia...............	Tennessee.
J. W. Bunton..........	28	Tennessee.............	Tennessee.
Thomas G. Gazeley....	35	New York..............	Louisiana.
R. M. Coleman.........	37	Kentucky..............	Kentucky.
S. C. Robertson........	50	North Carolina........	Tennessee.
George C. Childress....	32	Tennessee.............	Tennessee.
B. Hardiman..........	41	Tennessee.............	Tennessee.
R. Potter.............	36	North Carolina........	North Carolina.
Thomas J. Rusk.......	29	South Carolina........	Georgia.
Charles S. Taylor......	28	England...............	New York.
John S. Roberts.......	40	Virginia..............	Louisiana.
R. Hamilton..........	53	Scotland..............	North Carolina.
C. M. Kinney.........	70	New Jersey............	Kentucky.
A. H. Lattimer........	27	Tennessee.............	Tennessee.
James Power..........	48	Ireland...............	Louisiana.
Sam Houston..........	43	Virginia..............	Tennessee.
David Thomas.........	35	Tennessee.............	Tennessee.
E. Conrad.............	26	Pennsylvania..........	Pennsylvania.
Martin Parmer........	58	Virginia..............	Missouri.
E. O. Legrand.........	33	North Carolina........	Alabama.
S. W. Blount..........	28	Georgia...............	Georgia.
James Gaines..........	60	Virginia..............	Louisiana.
W. Clark, Jr..........	37	North Carolina........	Georgia.
S. O. Pennington......	27	Kentucky..............	Arkansas Territory.
W. C. Crawford.......	31	North Carolina........	Alabama.
John Turner..........	34	North Carolina........	Tennessee.
B. B. Goodrich........	37	Virginia..............	Alabama.
G. W. Barnett.........	43	South Carolina........	Mississippi.
J. G. Swisher..........	41	Tennessee.............	Tennessee.
Jesse Grimes..........	48	North Carolina........	Alabama.
S. Rhoads Fisher......	41	Pennsylvania..........	Pennsylvania.
Samuel A. Maverick....	29	South Carolina........	South Carolina.
John White Bower.....	27	Georgia...............	Arkansas Territory.
James B. Woods.......	34	Kentucky..............	Kentucky.
Andrew Briscoe........	—	——————.........	————
John W. Moore........	—	——————.........	————
Thomas Barnett.......	—	——————.........	————

On the 4th of March, 1836, the Convention made General Sam Houston commander-in-chief of the land forces of the Texan army, "with all the rights, privileges, and powers due to a commander-in-chief in the United States of America," and on the 6th ordered him to proceed to the frontier, to establish his headquarters and organize the army.

On the 16th, the Convention adopted the Constitution of the Republic, and on the same day, as a government *ad interim*, made David G. Burnet, President; Lorenzo de Zavala, Vice-President; S. P. Carson, Secretary of State; Baily Hardiman, Secretary of the Treasury; Thomas J. Rusk, Secretary of War; Robert Potter, Secretary of the Navy; and David Thomas, Adjutant-General—and then adjourned.

CHAPTER VI.

Santa Anna resolves on the Conquest of Texas.—His Army.—Invests the Alamo.—The Defence of that place.—Letters of Colonel Travis.—An Escape from and *the Fall of the Alamo.*

NEWS of the storming of San Antonio and the capture of his brother-in-law, General Cos, coming to the ears of the President-General, Santa Anna, he forthwith determined to raise and lead in person an army to the subjugation of the rebellious Texans.

Santa Anna was the most popular man in all Mexico, and upon the question of retaking Texas, Mexicans were almost a unit, so he had but little trouble in soon collecting an army of 8,000 men, "composed of the best troops in Mexico, and commanded by the most experienced officers" of the Republic.

General Vicente Filisola, a veteran revolutionist, was the second in command to Santa Anna, who was aided by Colonel Almonte, and supported by Generals Urrea, Sesma, Gaona, Tolsa, Andrade, Woll, and *Cos*, the last of whom, according to Kennedy, "violated the conditions of the first article of his capitulation at Bexar, by which he and his officers were permitted to retire with their arms and private property into the interior of the republic, "under parole of honor that they would not in any way oppose the re-establishment of the Federal Constitution of 1824."

Colonel Ampudia, afterwards General Ampudia, was in command of the artillery, of which there was a considerable train, including mortars, while Colonel Louis Tola acted as engineer.

Says Kennedy:

"There was an immense mass of baggage, with several thousand mules and horses for its transport; indeed all the preparations were on a scale of grandeur that contrasted strangely with the contemptuous terms in which the heads and promoters of the expedition spoke of the people whose destruction it was intended to accomplish."

General Filisola, in his account of the campaign, says there was also *an immense number of women* who followed in the wake of the army, which information called from *the innocent* Yoakum the following *astute* comment: "*But for what purpose they were permitted, unless to take care of the plunder, we are not informed.*"

On the 23d of February, 1836, Santa Anna, crossing the *Alazan*, where, in 1813, the Republicans under the gallant Perry gained a signal victory over the forces of the viceroy under Elisondo, entered San Antonio without opposition, and having demanded the surrender of the *Alamo*, which was refused, commenced a furious bombardment of that *devoted* place! When it was invested, the Alamo was defended by one hundred and fifty-six men, commanded by the gallant captor of Anahuac, Colonel W. B. Travis, and included Colonel James Bowie, the hero of *Concepcion*, Colonel Davy Crockett, the celebrated ex-member of Congress from Tennessee, Colonels J. B. Bonham and J. Washington, with others less famous.

On the 24th, Colonel Travis sent the following letter by express to his people:

"COMMANDANCY OF THE ALAMO, BEXAR, *February* 24, 1836.

"FELLOW-CITIZENS AND COMPATRIOTS: I am besieged by a thousand or more of the Mexicans under Santa Anna. I have sustained a continued bombardment for twenty-four hours, and have not lost a man. The enemy have demanded a surrender at discretion; otherwise the garrison is to be put to the sword, if the place is taken. I have answered the summons with a cannon-shot, and our flag still waves proudly from the walls. *I shall never surrender or retreat.* Then I call on you, in the name of liberty, of patriotism, and of everything dear to the American character, to come to our aid with all despatch. The enemy are receiving reinforcements daily, and will no doubt increase to three or four thousand in four or five days. Though this call may be neglected, I am determined to sustain myself as long as possible, and die like a soldier who never forgets what is due to his own honor and that of his country. Victory or death!

"W. BARRET TRAVIS,

"*Lieutenant-Colonel commanding.*

"*P. S.*—The Lord is on our side. When the enemy appeared in sight, we had not three bushels of corn. We have since found, in deserted houses, eighty or ninety bushels, and got into the walls twenty or thirty head of beeves. "T."

On the 1st of March he was joined by thirty-two men from Gonzales, who increased his force to 188 soldiers. On the 3d of March he wrote to the President of the Convention at Washington:

"From the 25th to the present date the enemy have kept up a bombardment from two howitzers (one a five-and-a-half inch, and the other an eight-inch), and a heavy cannonade from two long nine-pounders mounted on a battery on the opposite side of the river, at the distance of four hundred yards from our walls. During this period the enemy have been busily employed in encircling us with entrenched encampments at the following distances: In Bexar, 400 yards west; in Lavilleta, 300 yards south; at the powder-house, 1,000 yards east by south; on the ditch,

800 yards northeast; and at the old mill, 800 yards north. Notwithstanding all this, a company of thirty-two men from Gonzales made their way to us on the morning of the 1st instant, at three o'clock, and Colonel J. B. Bonham (a courier from the same place) got in this morning at 11 o'clock.

"I have so fortified the place that the walls are generally proof against cannon balls, and I still continue to intrench in the inside, and strengthen the walls by throwing up the earth. At least 200 shells have fallen inside our walls without having injured a single man; indeed we have been so fortunate as not to lose a man from any cause, and we have killed many of the enemy. The spirits of my men are still high, although they have had much to depress them. . . . .

"Colonel Fannin is said to be on the march to this place with reinforcements; but I fear it is not true, as I have repeatedly sent to him for aid without receiving any. Colonel Bonham, my special messenger, arrived at La Bahia (Goliad) fourteen days ago, with a request for aid; and on the arrival of the enemy in Bexar, I sent an express to Colonel Fannin, which reached Goliad on the next day, urging him to send on reinforcements. *None have yet arrived.* I look to the *colonies alone* for aid; unless it arrive soon, I shall have to fight the enemy on his own terms. I will, however, do the best I can under the circumstances; and I feel confident that the deter mined spirit and desperate courage heretofore evinced by my men will not fail them in the last struggle; and although they may be sacrificed to the vengeance of a Gothic enemy, the victory will cost that enemy so dear that it will be worse than a defeat.

"I hope your honorable body will hasten on reinforcements, ammunition, and provisions to our aid as soon as possible. We have provisions for twenty days for the men we have: our supply of ammunition is limited. At least 500 lbs. of cannon powder, and 200 rounds of six, nine, twelve, and eighteen pound balls, ten kegs of rifle powder, and a supply of lead should be sent to this place without delay under a sufficient guard. If these things are promptly sent, and large reinforcements are hastened to this frontier, this neighborhood will be the great and decisive battle-ground. The power of Santa Anna is to be met here or in the colonies: we had better meet it here than to suffer a war of desolation to rage in our settlements. A blood-red banner waves from the church of Bexar, and in the camp above us, in token that the war is one of vengeance against rebels: they have declared us such, and demanded that we should surrender at discretion, or this garrison should be put to the sword. Their threats have had no influence on me or my men, but to make all fight with desperation, and with that high-souled courage which characterizes the patriot, who is willing to die in defence of his country's liberty and his own honor.

'The citizens of this municipality are all our enemies, except those who joined us heretofore; we have but three Mexicans in the fort. Those who have not joined us in this extremity should be declared public enemies, and their property should aid in defraying the expenses of the war.

"The bearer of this will give your honorable body a statement more in detail, should he escape through the enemy's lines.—*God and Texas! Victory or Death!*"

In one of his last letters he says: "I am still here, in fine spirits, and well to do. With one hundred and forty-five men, I have held this place ten days against a force variously estimated from fifteen hundred to six thousand; and I shall continue to hold it till I get relief from my countrymen, or I will perish in its defence. We have had a shower of bombs and cannon-balls continually falling among us the whole time, yet none of us have fallen. We have been miraculously preserved."

He then closes by saying: "Take care of my little boy. If the country should be saved, I may make him a splendid fortune; but if the country should be lost, and I should perish, he will have nothing but the proud recollection that he is the son of a man who died for his country."

I will now describe the memorable FALL OF THE ALAMO as related to me by Mrs. Susan Hannig, formerly Mrs. Dickinson, who witnessed it.

"On February 23d, 1836, Santa Anna, having captured the pickets sent out by Col Travis to guard the post from surprise, charged into San Antonio with his troops, variously estimated at from six to ten thousand, only a few moments after the bells of the city rang the alarm.

"Capt. Dickinson galloped up to our dwelling and hurriedly exclaimed: "The Mexicans are upon us, give me the babe, and jump up behind me." I did so, and as the Mexicans already occupied Commerce street, we galloped across the river at the ford south of it, and entered the fort at the southern gate, when the enemy commenced firing shot and shell into the fort, but with little or no effect, only wounding one horse.

"There were eighteen guns mounted on the fortifications, and these, with our riflemen, repulsed with great slaughter two assaults made upon them before the final one.

"I knew Colonels Crockett, Bowie and Travis well. Col. Crockett was a performer on the violin, and often during the siege took it up and played his favorite tunes.

"I heard him say several times during the eleven days of the siege: 'I think we had better march out and die in the open air. I don't like to be hemmed up.'

"There were provisions and forage enough in the fort to have subsisted men and horses for a month longer.

"A few days before the final assault three Texans entered the fort during the night and inspired us with sanguine hopes of speedy relief, and thus animated the men to contend to the last.

"A Mexican woman deserted us one night, and going over to the enemy informed them of our very inferior numbers, which Col. Travis said made them confident of success and emboldened them to make the final assault, which they did at early dawn on the morning of the 6th of March.

"Under the cover of darkness they approached the fortifications, and planting their scaling ladders against our walls just as light was approaching, they climbed up to the tops of our walls and jumped down within, many of them to immediate death.

"As fast as the front ranks were slain, they were filled up again by fresh troops.

"The Mexicans numbered several thousands while there were only one hundred and eighty-two Texans.

"The struggle lasted more than two hours when my husband rushed into the church where I was with my child, and exclaimed: 'Great God, Sue, the Mexicans are inside our walls! All is lost! If they spare you, save my child.'

"Then, with a parting kiss, he drew his sword and plunged into the strife, then raging in different portions of the fortifications.

"Soon after he left me, three unarmed gunners who abandoned their then useless guns came into the church where I was, and were shot down by my side. One of them was from Nacogdoches and named Walker. He spoke to me several times during the siege about his wife and four children with anxious tenderness. I saw four Mexicans toss him up in the air (as you would a bundle of fodder) with their bayonets, and then shoot him. At this moment a Mexican officer came into the room, and, addressing me in English, asked: 'Are you Mrs. Dickinson?' I answered 'Yes.' Then said he, 'If you wish to save your life, follow me.' I followed him, and although shot at and wounded, was spared.

"As we passed through the enclosed ground in front of the church, I saw heaps of dead and dying. The Texans on an average killed between eight and nine Mexicans each—182 Texans and 1,600 Mexicans were killed.

"I recognized Col. Crockett lying dead and mutilated between the church and the two story barrack building, and even remember seeing his peculiar cap lying by his side.

"Col. Bowie was sick in bed and not expected to live, but as the victorious Mexicans entered his room, he killed two of them with his pistols before they pierced him through with their sabres.

"Cols. Travis and Bonham were killed while working the cannon, the body of the former lay on the top of the church.

"In the evening the Mexicans brought wood from the neighboring forest and burned the bodies of all the Texans, but their own dead they buried in the city cemetery across the San Pedro."

Thus perished the heroes of the Alamo! of whom the poet says:

"Gashed with honorable scars,
Low in Glory's lap they lie;
Though they fell, they fell like stars,
Streaming splendor through thesky.'

Remembrance of their devoted patriotism has no doubt inspired Texans with generous emulation on many occasions besides that of San Jacinto, where their victorious charge was made with the memorable battle-cry:

"*Remember the Alamo!*"

To Texans these words should speak volumes, and not only remind them of the plains of San Jacinto, but of Mansfield, Sabine Pass, Pleasant Hill, Gains' Mill, and an hundred other fields of glory and death on which their soldiers rushed

> "Where the battle wreck lay thickest,
> And death's brief pang was quickest."

They should say to the youth of Texas:

> "*Dulce et decorum est pro patria mori.*"

They should picture to their young minds, in glowing colors, the contest between Leonidas and his three hundred Spartans with the myriad hosts of Persia at Thermopylæ.

They should say to them: "If we fall, we will fall in a blaze of glory, but if we are victorious, the Union will redound with our praise."

They should point the slow moving finger of scorn at the coward and exclaim:

> "Cowards die many deaths, the brave but once."

They should cause them to remember the beautiful lines of the poet:

> "The muffled drum's sad roll has beat
> The soldier's last tattoo;
> No more on life's parade shall meet
> That brave and gallant few.

"On fame's eternal camping ground
Their silent tents are spread,
And Glory guards with ceaseless round
The bivouac of the dead."

The following account of *an escape from the Alamo* is from a late Texas publication, and may throw more light upon the last hours of its immortal defenders:

"About two hours before sunset, on the third day of March, 1836, the bombardment suddenly ceased, and the enemy withdrew an unusual distance. Taking advantage of that opportunity, Col. Travis paraded all of his effective men in a single file; and, taking his position in front of the centre, he stood for some moments, apparently speechless from emotion. Then, nerving himself for the occasion, he addressed them substantially as follows:

"'My Brave Companions: Stern necessity compels me to employ the few moments afforded by this probably brief cessation of conflict in making known to you the most interesting, yet the most solemn, melancholy, and unwelcome fact that perishing humanity can realize. But how shall I find language to prepare you for its reception? I cannot do so. All that I can say to this purpose is, be prepared for the worst. I must come to the point. Our fate is sealed. Within a very few days—perhaps a very few hours—we must all be in eternity. This is our destiny, and we cannot avoid it. This is our *certain* doom.

"'I have deceived you long by the promise of help. But I crave your pardon, hoping that after hearing my explanation, you will not only regard my conduct as pardonable, but heartily sympathize with me in my extreme necessity. In deceiving you, I also deceived myself, having been first deceived by others.

"'I have continually received the strongest assurances of help from home. Every letter from the Council, and every one that I have seen from individuals at home, has teemed with assurances that our people were ready, willing, and anxious to come to our relief; and that within a very short time we might confidently expect recruits enough to repel any force that would be brought against us. These assurances I received as facts. They inspired me with the greatest confidence that our little band would be made the nucleus of an army of sufficient magnitude to repel our foes, and to enforce peace on our own terms. In the honest and simple confidence of my heart, I have transmitted to you these promises of help, and my confident hopes of success. But the promised help has not come, and our hopes are not to be realized.

"'I have evidently confided too much in the promises of our friends. But let us not be in haste to censure them. The enemy has invaded our territory much earlier than we anticipated; and their present approach is a matter of surprise. Our friends were evidently not informed of our perilous condition in time to save us. Doubtless they would have been here by the time they expected any considerable force of the enemy. When they find a Mexican army in their midst, I hope they will show themselves true to their cause.

"'My calls on Col. Fannin remain unanswered, and my messengers have not returned. The probabilities are that his whole command has fallen into the hands of the enemy, or been cut to pieces, and that our couriers have been cut off.

"'I trust that I have now explained my conduct to your satisfaction, and that you do not censure me for my course.

"'I must again refer to the assurances of help from home. *They are what deceived me, and caused me to deceive you.* Relying upon these assurances, I determined to remain within these walls until the promised help should arrive, stoutly resisting all assaults from without. Upon the same reliance, I retained you here, regarding the increasing force of our assailants with contempt, till they outnumbered us more than twenty to one, and escape became impossible. For the same reason, I scorned their demand for a surrender at discretion, and defied their threat to put every one of us to the sword, if the fort should be taken by storm.

"'I must now speak of our present situation. Here we are, surrounded by an army that could almost eat us for a breakfast, from whose arms our lives are for the present protected by the stone walls. We have no hope of help, for no force that we could ever reasonably have expected could cut its way through the strong ranks of these Mexicans. We dare not surrender; for, should we do so, that black flag,now waving in our sight, as well as the merciless character of our enemies, admonishes us of what would be our doom. We cannot cut our way out through the enemy's ranks; for, in attempting that, we should all be slain in less than ten minutes. Nothing remains then, but to stay within this fort and fight to the last moment. In this case, we must, sooner or later, all be slain; for I am sure that Santa Anna is determined to storm the fort and take it, even at the greatest cost of the lives of his own men.

"Then we must die! Our speedy dissolution is a fixed and inevitable fact. Our business is, not to make a fruitless effort to save our lives, but to choose the manner of our death. But three modes are presented to us. Let us choose that by which we may best serve our country. Shall we surrender, and be deliberately shot, without taking the life of a single enemy? Shall we try to cut our way out through the Mexican ranks, and be butchered before we can kill twenty of our adversaries? I am opposed to either method; for, in either case, we could but lose our lives without benefiting our friends at home—our fathers and mothers, our brothers and sisters, our wives and little ones. The Mexican army is strong enough to march through the country, and exterminate its inhabitants, and our countrymen are not able to oppose them in open field. My choice, then, is to remain in this fort, to resist every assault, and to sell our lives as dearly as possible.

"'Then let us band together as brothers, and vow to die together. Let us resolve to withstand our adversaries to the last; and, at each advance, to kill as many of them as possible. And when, at last, they shall storm our fortress, let us kill them as they come! kill them as they scale our wall! kill them as they leap within! kill them as they raise their weapons, and as they use them! kill them as they kill our companions! and continue to kill them as long as one of us shall remain alive!

"'By this policy, I trust that we shall so weaken our enemies that our countrymen at home can meet them on fair terms, cut them up, expel them from the country, and thus establish our own independence, and secure prosperity and happiness to our families and our country. And, *be assured*, our memory will be gratefully cherished by posterity, till all history shall be erased, and all noble deeds shall be forgotten.

"'But I leave every man to his own choice. Should any man prefer to surrender, and be tied and shot; or to attempt an escape through the Mexican ranks, and be killed before he can run a hundred yards, he is at liberty to do so.

"'My own choice is to stay in this fort, and die for my country, fighting as long as breath shall remain in my body. *This will I do, even if you leave me alone.* Do as you think best—but no man can die with me without affording me comfort in the moment of death.'

"Col. Travis then drew his sword, and with its point traced a line upon the ground, extending from the right to the left of the file. Then, resuming his position in front of the centre, he said, 'I now want every man who is determined to stay here and die with me to come across this line. Who will be first? March!'

"The first respondent was Tapley Holland, who leaped the line at a bound, exclaiming, 'I am ready to die for my country!' His example was instantly followed by every man in the file, with the exception of Rose. Manifest enthusiasm was universal and tremendous. Every sick man that could walk arose from his bunk and tottered across the line. Col. Bowie, who could not leave his bed, said, 'Boys, I am not able to come to you, but I wish some of you would be so kind as to remove my cot over there.' Four men instantly ran to the cot, and, each lifting a corner, carried it across the line. Then every sick man that could not walk made the same request, and had his bunk removed in like manner.

"Rose, too, was deeply affected, but differently from his companions. He stood till every man but himself had crossed the line. A consciousness of the real situation overpowered him. He sank upon the ground, covered his face, and yielded to his own reflections. For a time he was unconscious of what was transpiring around him. A bright idea came to his relief; he spoke the Mexican dialect very fluently, and could he once get safely out of the fort, he might easily pass for a Mexican and effect an escape. Thus encouraged, he suddenly aroused as if from sleep. He looked over the area of the fort; every sick man's berth was at its wonted place; every effective soldier was at his post, as if awaiting orders; he felt as if dreaming.

"He directed a searching glance at the cot of Colonel Bowie. There lay his gallant friend. Colonel David Crockett was leaning over the cot, conversing with its occupant in an undertone. After a few seconds Bowie looked at Rose and said, 'You seem not to be willing to die with us, Rose.' 'No,' said

Rose, 'I am not prepared to die, and shall not do so if I can avoid it.' Then Crockett also looked at him, and said, 'You may as well conclude to die with us, old man, for escape is impossible.'

"Rose made no reply, but looked up at the top of the wall. 'I have often done worse than to climb that wall,' thought he. Suiting the action to the thought he sprang up, seized his wallet of unwashed clothes, and ascended the wall. Standing on its top, he looked down within to take a last view of his dying friends. They were all now in motion, but what they were doing he heeded not. Overpowered by his feelings he looked away and saw them no more.

"Looking down without he was amazed at the scene of death that met his gaze. From the wall to a considerable distance beyond, the ground was literally covered with slaughtered Mexicans and pools of blood.

"He viewed this horrid scene but a moment. He threw down his wallet and leaped after it. He alighted on his feet, but the momentum of the spring threw him sprawling upon his stomach in a puddle of blood. After several seconds he recovered his breath; he arose and took up his wallet; it had fallen open and several garments had rolled out upon the blood. He hurriedly thrust them back, without trying to cleanse them of the coagulated blood which adhered to them. Then, throwing the wallet across his shoulders, he walked rapidly away.

"He took the road which led down the river around a bend to the ford, and through the town by the church. He waded the river at the ford and passed through the town. He saw no person in town, but the doors were all closed, and San Antonio appeared as a deserted city.

"After passing through the town he turned down the river. A stillness as of death prevailed. When he had gone about a quarter of a mile below the town his ears were saluted by the thunder of the bombardment, which was then renewed. That thunder continued to remind him that his friends were true to their cause, by a continual roar, with but slight intervals, until a little before sunrise on the morning of the sixth, when it ceased and he heard it no more.

"At twilight he recrossed the river on a foot-log, about three miles below the town. He then directed his course eastwardly towards the Guadalupe River, carefully bearing to the right to avoid the Gonzales road."

The writer takes this account of Mr. Rose, *cum grano salis*, but it may be true.

The poet sayeth:

'Tis strange—but true; for truth is always strange;
Stranger than fiction.

The fondness of the writer for localities made famous by the heroic achievements of the founders of our glorious republic, has carried him to the Alamo with as much zeal as the Mohammedan visits the tomb of his prophet.

Indeed, the Alamo has peculiar interest for every Texan who loves his country and is proud of his State. But I have stood on Bunker's Hill, Brooklyn Heights, and from the deck of a floating palace on the bosom of the Father of Waters, viewing the plains of Chalmette, revolved in my mind the virtue and heroism displayed by American valor and patriotism.

Even on Plymouth Rock and the field of Lexington I have wandered and meditated, comparing the illustrious founders and warriors of the nations of the Old World with the distinguished heroes and statesmen of America.

At the graves of Washington, Franklin, and Hamilton I have often pondered upon the lasting fame with which their patriotic devotion has caused a grateful posterity to stamp their names:

"First in war, first in peace, and first in the hearts of their countrymen."

Their memory will be cherished with veneration by future generations, when the names of Alexander, Cæsar, and Napoleon will be forgotten.

The following sketch from Kennedy may interest the reader:

"Among the slain there was one who, surrounded by a heap of the fallen enemy, displayed even in death the freshness of the hunter's aspect, and whose eccentricities, real or reputed, have familiarized England with his name—David Crockett, of Tennessee, a character such as could only have been produced and perfected within the limits of his own country.

"The whole man, physical and mental, was of frontier growth. His playthings from infancy were the axe and the rifle. Few among his youthful companions displayed more activity and strength; none aimed his piece with a steadier hand or truer eye. In the metaphorical eulogy of the western woodsmen, he was more than 'a horse,'—he was 'a steamboat.' During the war of 1812, David took up arms for his country, and fought bravely, though no admirer of parade or drill. After the war, he turned to industrial pursuits, and was a successful hunter and thriving planter. Hospitality kept cheerful watch at his door, and the wayfarer was ever welcome to a plentiful meal, and a glass of 'old Monongahela.'

"The ambition to be politically distinguished, which

prevails wherever free institutions are established, is, perhaps, a more active passion in new states than in old. Crockett did not escape the general mania for public life. His conscience told him that he was an honest man, and rumor and the newspapers strangely lied if there were many of the same stamp in the great house at Washington. Reforms were wanting—there was no question of that—but means were essential to an end, and sound reforms demanded clean-handed legislators. David felt that he had a call. He had mastered the 'varmint' of the woods—'coon,' bear, and panther—and why should he not 'use up' the prowlers that preyed upon the commonwealth? The great Tennessee hunter determined to 'run for Congress.'

"The stump of a tree is frequently the rostrum of a western orator; hence the name of 'stump speeches' has been given in the States to those morsels of eloquence which are seasoned and sauced exclusively for the popular palate. Possessed of robust health and powerful lungs, backed by never-faltering perseverance, Crockett was a giant on the stump. If poor in classical lore, he was affluent in the figures and phraseology of life in the West. After a long and arduous struggle, he was chosen a member of Congress for Tennessee.

"His career as a patriotic legislator disappointed his

hopes, and fell far short of his electioneering promises. When he entered Congress he imagined that his prowess as a hunter and a wrestler would inspire his opponents with awe, and enable him to shoulder the state wagon out of the ruts by a few prompt and dexterous heaves; but he found difficulties at Washington which he never contemplated when an aspirant for representative honors. The first thing, he said, that 'bothered' him were the Congressional rules and orders, and 'what those rascally things were made for he could not reckon, for they did no good.' If he happened to damage these rules and orders, and then got in a 'fair track,' his tongue did not wag so glibly as it used to do on the stump, and he frequently found himself short of breath and his knees weak when he attempted to harangue the House. He could not understand this, but he found it was so day after day. He often looked round to see if there was any man bigger and stronger than himself to produce this quaking, for, until then, none but a stronger man than himself could shake his nerve. His visions of reform, one after another, vanished, for he could not make the members listen to his reasoning. He began to suspect that he had different work to do than when he used to go 'a gunning.' Often as he might hit a political wild cat, the 'crittur' held out, as if it had nine times the nine lives attributed to grimalkin.

"Many an odd saying and grotesque story was fathered on 'Colonel Crockett,' whose raciness of speech and manners was, however, spoiled by mixing in political society. He lost the wild originality of the frontier, without acquiring the polish or sprightliness of city life. Still, Washington had its attractions, and he was anxious to retain his place in the legislature; but he must have his own way, and would not submit to be trammelled; the consequence of which was that his constituents chose a more pliable candidate. This was a heavy blow to David, who had been for years a 'lion,' and to whom excitement of some kind was indispensable. Disgusted with politics, and irritated by public ingratitude, military renown acquired fresh attractions in his eyes. At this time Texas had raised the standard of resistance against military usurpation. To the cause of Texan liberty he resolved to devote himself, and, shouldering his rifle, he started for the Sabine, and arrived at Nacogdoches, accompanied by several volunteers, in the commencement of the war. Having determined to become a citizen of Texas, he proceeded with his companions to the office of Mr. Forbes (then first judge of the municipality), to take the oath of allegiance, which was tendered to him in the following form:

"'I do solemnly swear that I will bear true allegiance to the Provisional Government of Texas, or any future Government that may be hereafter declared; and that I will serve her honestly and faithfully against all her enemies and oppressors whatsoever, and observe and obey the orders of the Governor of Texas, the orders and decrees of the present or future authorities, and the orders of the officers appointed over me according to the rules and articles for the government of Texas—so help me God.'

"Crockett was not the man to make a solemn declaration without scrutinizing its import. He refused to take the oath as tendered, stating that although he was willing to swear to support any future *Republican* Government, he could not subscribe his name to this form, as the 'future' government might be despotic. Mr. Forbes then inserted the word 'republican' between the words 'future' and 'government;' and the instrument was signed. The original, deposited in the office of the War Department of Texas, exhibits the interlineation and the autograph of David Crockett.

"Biography is the handmaid of History, and frequently a more agreeable companion than her mistress; I therefore offer no apology for this brief notice of one of 'the heroes of the Alamo.' Poor David! thy simple uprightness merited a happier end! Yet, to borrow a phrase of thine own coinage, thou didst 'go a-head for the right;' and thy blood was shed upon a holy altar, and from thy smouldering ashes arose a flame which streamed from the San Antonio to the Mississippi and Ohio, lighting up, in many a generous heart, a fire not to be extinguished, so long as those who dishonored thy manly form continued to tread the soil in which their barbarian vindictiveness denied thee and thy gallant comrades the humble privilege of a soldier's grave!"

CHAPTER VII.

The Capture of San Patricio, Refugio, and GOLIAD.—*The Massacres of Col. Grant's, Capt. King's, Col. Ward's, and Fannin's commands.*

WHILE Santa Anna was marching from the Rio Grande upon San Antonio, another division of his army, under Gen. Jose Urrea, was advancing by the coast route upon San Patricio, Refugio and Goliad.

San Patricio was first attacked, and after an obstinate defence by some forty or fifty troops under Col. F. W. Johnson, was taken by assault, and all its defenders killed, except Col. Johnson and four others who made their escape. Dr. or Col. Grant, who was associated in the command with Col. Johnson, and fought gallantly with him at the storming of San Antonio, in December, 1835, was out scouting with about sixty men at the time of the attack on San Patricio, and was ambuscaded at Agua Dulce on the 2d of March, four days before the fall of the Alamo, and his whole party put to death.

Yoakum says Grant was wounded and taken prisoner; that his life was spared that the enemy might have the benefit of his services in attending their numerous wounded, and thus describes his tragic end:

"While Dr. Grant was in San Patricio, curing his own wound, and carefully ministering to the wants of the wounded of the enemy, he was promised that, so soon as he recovered, and those under his care were convalescent, he should have a passport to leave the country without molestation. The captain left in command of the town, after the departure of Urrea, secretly despatched eight men in search of a wild horse. The animal was captured about three weeks after the battle of the 2d of March. Grant was now brought forth, and, by order of the captain, his feet were strongly bound to those of the horse, and his hands to the tail. "Now," said the captain, "you have your passport—go!" At the same moment the cords by which the *mustang* was tied were severed. The fierce animal, finding his limbs unfettered, sprang away with great violence, leaving behind him, in a short distance, the mangled remains of poor Grant! Nothing can be added to this simple statement of facts."

The following autograph letter of Colonel Fannin to his friend Mr. Joseph Mims, of Brazoria, corroborates the murder of his prisoners by General Urrea at San Patricio, and gives an account of his own resources, embarrassments, and vexatious surroundings:

"GOLIAD, *February 28th*, 1836.

"MR. JOSEPH MIMS:

"The advice I gave you a few days back is *too true*—the enemy have the town of Bexar, with a large force, and I fear will soon have our brave countrymen in the Alamo.

"Another force is near me, and crossed the Neuces yesterday morning, and attacked a party by surprise, under Colonel Johnson, and routed them, killing Captain Raison, and *several others, after* they had surrendered. I have about four hundred and twenty men here, and if I can get provisions in to-morrow or next day, can maintain myself against any force. I will never give up the ship whilst there is a pea in the dish. If I am *whipped*, it will be *well done*, and you may never expect to see me.

"I hope to see *all Texas in arms soon;* if not, we lose our homes, and must go east of the Trinity for a while. Look to our property—save it for my family, whatever may be my fate.

"I expect some in about this time, by Cogley, and wish you to receive and take care of it. I now tell you, be *always ready;* I have not as much confidence in the people of Texas as I once had; they have been called on and entreated to fly to arms and prevent what has now been done. I have but *three* citizens in the ranks, and though I have called on them for *six weeks*, *not one* yet arrived, and no assistance in bringing me provisions—even teams refused me. I feel too indignant to say more about them. If I was honorably out of their service, I would never re-enter it.

"But I must now play a bold game; I will go the *whole hog*. If I am lost, be the censure on the right heads, and may my wife and children, and children's children, curse the sluggards *forever*. I am too mad, and too much to do—anything—but *fight*.

"If my family arrive, send my wife this letter. Enquire of McKinney.

"Hoping for the best, being prepared for the worst, I am in a devil of a bad humor.

"Farewell.

"J. W. FANNIN, JR."

On the morning of the 14th of March, Fannin received an order from General Houston to evacuate Goliad and fall back on Victoria, when he immediately despatched a courier to Ward to return immediately. The courier not returning in time, he sent a second, and then a third, neither of whom ever returned.

On the 12th of March, the advance of Urrea's army reached Refugio, and found there twenty men commanded by Captain King, who, with *the mission* as a fortification, resolved to defend the place, and sent for assistance to Colonel Fannin, then in command of

Goliad with about four hundred men. Colonel Ward, with about one hundred troops, was sent by Colonel Fannin to the relief of Captain King, and at daylight on the morning of the 14th, entered *the mission*, when Captain King with thirteen men were sent out to reconnoitre, soon after which General Urrea surrounded and attacked *the mission* on all sides, but, after repeated assaults, was repulsed with a loss of two hundred in killed and wounded, while the Texans lost only three severely wounded.

General Urrea, in giving an account of his attack and defeat at Refugio, says:

"The enemy, though at first confounded by the movement, opened a lively fire upon our infantry, the greater part of whom, being recruits from Yucatan, could not sustain it, and fell back, nor could my exertions avail to bring them forward again; and their native officers, who, a few moments before, had been all boasting and arrogance, disappeared in the most critical moment! These soldiers, with few exceptions, do not understand Spanish; and the officers, unacquainted with their *patois*, found it difficult to make them understand the word of command. The infantry having fallen back upon a house and court-yard situated at fifteen or twenty paces from the church, I ordered a part of the cavalry to alight, in order to inspirit them by their example, but all would not do.

The cavalry alone were unequal to carry the place. The moment was urgent; and I ordered a retreat, which, however, could not be effected with the order that disciplined troops would have maintained."

After fighting gallantly all day long, and having almost entirely exhausted their ammunition, at night the Texans left their three wounded comrades in *the mission*, and retreated towards Victoria. On the morning of the 15th, Urrea took possession of the mission, despatched and cast out the dead bodies of the wounded Texans, placed therein his own wounded, and followed in pursuit of Ward's and King's commands, which had separated the day before; King having left the fortifications to reconnoitre, and thereafter having been unable to re-enter. On the morning of the 16th, the cavalry of Urrea came up with Captain King and the thirteen soldiers under his command, surrounded them in the open prairie, with their powder wet, and forced their surrender, in six hours after which they killed every one of them!

On the 17th, Urrea approached Goliad, which was occupied by Colonel Fannin with about three hundred men, who, after slight skirmishing on the 18th, on the morning of the 19th dismantled the fortifications, burned the buildings, and with his little army commenced his retreat towards Victoria, and after marching nine miles from Goliad, stopped to rest in the open prairie, five miles from the Coleta, where there was abundance of water, *not believing that the Mexicans would dare follow him!*

After a halt of about an hour, Colonel Fannin resumed his retreat towards Victoria, but soon found that while he rested the Mexicans had completely surrounded him in a depression of the plain, six or seven feet below the surrounding surface!

But notwithstanding such a disadvantageous position, and such an egregious blunder, he formed his three hundred Texans into a hollow square, and repulsed the repeated assaults of the twelve hundred infantry and seven hundred cavalry of the enemy.

The conflict lasted from 1 o'clock P.M. till dark, when Urrea drew off his troops with a loss of about fifty killed and about one hundred and fifty wounded, while the Texan loss was seven killed and ninty-seven wounded.

Colonel A. C. Horton, with twenty-eight horsemen from Matagorda, who joined Colonel Fannin on the 16th, took no part in this action. He had been sent forward to examine the crossing of the Coleta, but hearing the noise of battle, galloped back, and seeing Fannin surrounded, retreated to Victoria.

In explanation of this retreat, Captain Shackleford says:

"I candidly believe, even with *the whole* of his force,

he never could have cut his way through such an immense number of Mexican cavalry."

Yoakum says:

"They had a full view of the engagement; and, seeing the Texans very nearly surrounded by so large a force of the enemy, Horton's lieutenant, *Moore*, objected to any attempt to reach their comrades by penetrating the Mexican lines, alleging that they would all be cut to pieces. Immediately he dashed off in another direction, taking with him nearly all the party."

During the night, which the Texans passed without water, they dug trenches, and threw up breastworks, preparing to renew the conflict in the morning, while the Mexican cavalry sounded their bugles all around them until morning.

No effort was made to retreat or get water during the night, and in the morning Col. Fannin, who had been shot through the thigh during the battle, and with the other wounded was suffering agonies for want of water, after a consultation with his officers, surrendered himself and his command as prisoners of war to Gen. Jose Urrea, the commander of the Mexican army, and were marched and transported back to Goliad and incarcerated in the *old mission* of La Bahia, opposite the present town of Goliad.

Santa Anna upon receiving information of their

capture immediately ordered their execution, and on Palm Sunday, March 27th, 1836, the gallant Col. Fannin with his command, and Col. Ward, who, with his command, was overtaken and captured the day after the surrender of Fannin, were marched out of the mission on the pretence of getting provisions, and all, to the number of three hundred and thirty, shot down in cold blood, their bodies denied sepulture, and, after partial cremation, left on the open plain as food for dogs and vultures!

Twenty-seven escaped from the slaughter by running to the San Antonio River and evading their pursuers. Of this number was the amiable and accomplished John C. Duval, whose companion or fileman on this march to death was a large powerful fellow, who received several balls in his body at the same time, and falling down upon John, covered his body so that the lancers who rode along the line of the dead and wounded in order to dispatch all, passed John without running him through, when he took to his heels, gained the river, plunged in, while a shower of bullets followed him, swam for dear life, and gained the opposite bank and safety.

After five days' fasting, thirsting, and walking, he, with two companions, got to the Guadalupe River, found it swollen by recent rains, when, weary and hungry, they laid themselves down on the bank for the night, but before sleeping they heard a pig squeal near by them. All were up in a moment and went for the pig, when they found an old sow with five pigs, three of which with great difficulty they captured, and, after building a fire, roasted with the hair on and ate greedily but joyfully.

I have heard John Duval say that never before nor since had he ate such a delicious supper as he did on this occasion!

John Duval's account of his escape is corroborated by S. T. Brown's, of the Georgia battalion, which says:

"Soon after I made my escape, I was joined by John Duval and —— Holliday, of the Kentucky volunteers, both of whom were with me at the massacre, but not until I had swam across the San Antonio, about half a mile from the butchery.

"For five days we had nothing to eat except wild onions, which abound in the country; when, reaching the Gaudalupe, we found a nest of young pigs, and these lasted us several days. In the course of a few days, wandering at random in the open country, often wide off of our supposed direction, we saw fresh signs of cavalry, and withdrew to the swamp, but had been perceived going there, and were taken by two Mexicans armed with guns and swords; that is, Duval and myself were captured; Holliday lay close and was not discovered. One of the men seized me and held on; Duval was placed between them to follow on. He sprang off, and one man threw down his gun and ran after him in vain. Duval made his escape, and I have not seen him since."

Another poor fellow, who was not shot to death, when the Mexican lancers passed along after the infantry had done their work feigned to be dead, but not looking like a corpse, a Mexican plunged his lance through his breast in order to finish him.

The wounded Texan, knowing that death would surely follow such a rash act, moved not a limb of his body nor a muscle of his face, but preserved his *feigned* but not lifeless appearance, to the best of his ability, and after the Mexicans retired from this field of slaughter, although shot and then thrust through the body, he crawled to the San Antonio River, made his escape, recovered from his wounds, and attended the Houston Fair in 1874, where he divided honors with the surviving veterans of the Texas revolution on that memorable occasion.

To justify the murder of their prisoners taken at San Patricio, Refugio and Goliad, the Mexicans plead a law of their Supreme Government, *to take no prisoners, to treat the rebels as pirates, and kill all Texans found with arms in their hands.* But civilization and refinement

> "Will plead like angels, trumpet-tongued, against
> The deep damnation of their taking-off."

The Goliad massacre thrilled the American heart with horror and astonishment, and was the death-knell of Mexican power in Texas. No more success attended the victorious murderers, and in less than one month from the date of their atrocities at Goliad, they cried for mercy to the heroes of San Jacinto, piteously exclaiming: "Me no Alamo! me no Goliad!" and to the imperishable honor and glory of these same heroes, their lives were spared.

The severe lesson taught by the disasters of San Patricio, Refugio and Goliad should have learned Texans obedience to orders, endurance and fortitude in their marches, prudence in the selection of their camps, and watchfulness all the time.

Had Col. Fannin obeyed the order of his commanding officer to fall back to Gonzales, or had he marched from Goliad to the Coleta without stopping *to rest*, or had he selected a commanding position for his camp, instead of the lowest place in the prairie, his deplorable defeat and sacrifice might have been avoided.

San Patricio *was surprised*, Col. Grant with his command *was ambuscaded*, while King and Ward *lost the way* from Refugio to Goliad, only thirty miles over the prairie!

After contrasting the sad results of Texan blunders

at San Patricio, Refugio, and Goliad with the astuteness displayed by the heroes of San Jacinto in charging the Mexicans while napping, we can say with truth: *Success attends the vigilant, the active, and the brave—not careless, sleeping warriors!*

About three months after the massacre, the *bones* and other remains of Col. Fannin and his comrades were gathered together by some Texan troops commanded by Gen. T. J. Rusk and buried in one common grave about 300 yards south of the *old mission*, but no monument marks the spot; however, the present town of Goliad, north of the river, but in sight of *the old mission*, with its beautiful mansions, gardens and groves, will forever remind Texans of the Goliad massacre and the cruel, savage, bloodthirsty, prisoner-murdering, priest-ridden Mexicans, who there murdered their brethren.

This brings to mind the address of the General Council, 23d October, 1835.

"Like our fathers of the Revolution"—said the address—"we have sworn to live free or die: like our fathers of 1776, we have pledged to each other our lives, fortunes, and sacred honors, and have vowed to drive every Mexican soldier beyond the Rio Grande, or whiten the plains with our bones."

It is said that in anticipation of returning home soon, on the very evening before the execution, the prisoners, who were mostly planters and sons of planters from Georgia and Alabama, were singing and playing on flutes and other musical instruments, "Home, sweet home!"

The veil which hides the future from the present and enables poor frail, *erring* mortals to bear up under present misfortunes and sufferings, with the hope, in the end, of arriving at the goal of success—has been called *the mercy veil!*

This *mercy veil* shut out the impending horrors of the morrow from the poor prisoners! Little did they dream of Mexican treachery and cruelty!

Jack and Travis had been prisoners at Anahuac in 1831, but they were not killed—the odious Bradburn did not murder his prisoners!

Even Austin had returned from Mexico after an imprisonment of years—the Mexicans did not murder their prisoners!

The general condemnation of the President General, Santa Anna, for the sacrifice of so many noble and gallant spirits caused that distinguished butcher to make the following defence, which clearly accounts for his hating the Texans and his ordering them to be put to death.

He says: "This last event [the surrender of Fannin and his followers] has been productive of much evil to myself, and it is therefore necessary that I should make a short digression respecting it. To avoid repetition, I make this observation once for all—the war of Texas was not only just on the part of Mexico, but imperatively called for by the undisguised character of the hostility which provoked it. It is notorious that the soldiers of Travis in the Alamo, those of Fannin at Coleta, the riflemen of Dr. Grant, and Houston himself and the troops of San Jacinto, with very few exceptions, came from New Orleans and other points of the neighboring republic, exclusively to support the rebellion in Texas, having had no previous relation with the colonists or their enterprises.

"This country was soon invaded, not by a nation recognized as such, coming to vindicate rights positive or supposed; nor yet by Mexicans, led away by a political fanaticism to defend or attack the public administration of their country; no, it was invaded by men hurried on by the lust of conquest, with rights far less apparent and plausible than Cortes and Pizarro. As for those who raised the standard of revolt throughout the immense territory which Mexico possesses, from Bexar to the Sabine, what name shall I give them, or how treat them? The laws, ever in vigor, and whose strict observance the government earnestly enforces, term them pirates and banditti; and the nations of the world would never have forgiven Mexico had she treated such men with the respect which is due only to the honorable, the upright, the respecters of the rights of nations. Till then [the massacre at Goliad], I had enjoyed among my fellow citizens the reputation—preferable in my mind to that of a brave man—the reputation of being humane after victories won. So completely unfortunate was I destined to become, that even the solitary virtue, which my bitterest enemies never denied me, is now disputed. I am represented as more ferocious than the tiger; I who was ambitious to be distinguished for nothing so much as my clemency, in a country that yields to no other in humane and generous feeling. The execution of Fannin and his followers is the ground on which they accuse me of having been barbarous and sanguinary. . . . The prisoners at Goliad stood condemned by the law, by a universal law, by the right of self-protection, which every nation and every individual enjoys. They did not surrender under the form of capitulation, as General Urrea has shown; how, then, could I turn the sword of justice from their heads without directing it against my own? Let it be said (though I confess that such is not my opinion) that the law is unjust; yet to impute the homicide to the mere instrument, and not to the hand that directs it, can there be greater blindness? The prisoners were in the highest degree embarrassing to the commandant at Goliad; before taking to flight they had set fire to the place; and nothing was left us but the church to house the sick and wounded. The sole security of the garrison consisted of perpetual vigilance, being greatly inferior in number to the prisoners; our provisions were barely sufficient for our own people; we were without cavalry to conduct them as far as Metamoras. All these considerations, *urged by the commandant of the place*, weighed heavily on my mind, and tended to bias my resolution.

"It has been said that a capitulation was made; and although the conduct of General Urrea contradicts the assertion, I addressed the Supreme Government on the subject, begging that an inquiry might be instituted, to show that neither officially nor confidentially was any knowledge of the same communicated to me; that had such been the case, though General Urrea had no power to grant it, I should have been induced, on the score of humanity, to appeal to the sovereign pity of Congress to deliver Fannin and his soldiers from death. With less motive, and taking advantage of their medical skill, several doctors were saved from death, as well as forty prisoners who were employed in the construction of different useful things. In fine, eighty-six men taken in Copano were saved, I having drawn up a statement that it appeared certain that they never made use of their arms, nor had committed any depredation, though taken with arms in their hands; and having submitted the same to Congress, I entreated their clemency."

Dr. John Shackleford, a gentlemen of truth and integrity says:

"We then raised a white flag, which was responded to by the enemy. Major Wallace was then sent out, together with one or two others who spoke the Mexican language. They shortly returned, and reported that the Mexican general could capitulate with the commanding officer only. Colonel Fannin, although quite lame, then went out with the flag. When he was about to leave our lines, the emotions of my mind were intense, and I felt some anxiety to hear the determination of the men. I remarked to him that I would not oppose a surrender, provided we could obtain an *honorable capitulation*—one on which he could rely; that, if he could not obtain such 'come back—our graves are already dug—let us all be buried together!' To these remarks the men responded in a firm and determined manner, and the colonel assured us that he never would surrender on any other terms. He returned in a short time thereafter, and communicated the substance of an agreement entered into by General Urrea and himself. Colonel Holzinger, a German, and an engineer in the Mexican service, together with several other officers, then came into our lines to consummate the arrangement. The first words Colonel Holzinger uttered, after a very polite bow, were, '*Well, gentlemen, in eight days, liberty and home!*' I heard this distinctly. The terms of the capitulation were then written in both the English and Mexican languages, and read two or three times by officers who could speak and read both languages. The instruments which embodied the terms of capitulation as agreed on were then signed and interchanged in the most formal and solemn manner, and were in substance as follows:

"1. That we should be received and treated as prisoners of war, according to the usages of the most civilized nations.

"2. That private property should be respected and restored; that the side-arms of the officers should be given up.

"3. That the men should be sent to Copano, and thence to the United States in eight days, or so soon thereafter as vessels could be procured to take them.

"4. That the officers should be paroled, and return to the United States in like manner.

"I assert most positively that this capitulation was entered into, without which a surrender never would have been made."

"Here let me remark that I have read General Urrea's pamphlet. . . . . . On this point, as well as his denial of any capitulation, I never read a more villainous *falsehood* from the pen of any man who aspired to the rank of general."—*Ib.*

"On passing from one part of the wounded to another, I made it convenient to see Fannin, and stated to him how badly we were treated.

"He immediately wrote to Gen. Urrea adverting to the terms of our capitulation. Urrea wrote to Portilla in answer: 'Treat the prisoners with consideration, and particularly their leader, Fannin.'"

Gen. Urrea's pamphlet, referred to by Dr. Shackleford, contains the following extracts from his campaign diary: "All the assurance I could make him, Fannin, was, that I would interpose in his behalf with the general-in-chief, which I accordingly did, in a letter from Victoria.

"After my ultimatum, the leaders of the enemy's forces conferred together, and the result of their deliberations was to surrender upon the terms proposed. They at the same time gave orders to those under their command to come forth and pile their arms. Nine pieces of artillery, three standards, more than a thousand muskets, a quantity of pistols, rifles, and dirks, of superior quality, a number of wagons, and a considerable quantity of provisions, together with about *four hundred* prisoners, remained in the hands of the army, among whom were ninty-seven wounded, Fannin and others of the leading men being among the number. I gave orders that the whole of them, with their baggage, should march to Goliad, guarded by two hundred infantry, and that such of the wounded as were unable to proceed should be conveyed in carts, wagons, and other vehicles found in the enemy's camp. Twenty-seven of their dead, of the day previous, were interred, together with *eleven* of our own. We had *forty-nine* soldiers wounded, and *five* officers, among whom was Captain Ballasteros, severely."

"*March* 21.—At daybreak I continued my march, and at seven o'clock took possession of Victoria.

"*March* 22.—I marched, with two hundred foot and fifty horse, to a mountain pass called *Las Juntas*. Here I met with four men from Ward's company, who were in search of provisions, and from them I learned that the whole band *was in ambush* in a neighboring wood. I immediately surrounded it, and sent in one of the prisoners to announce to his leader and companions, that unless they surrendered at discretion they would be cut to pieces. Mr. Ward, known under the title of their colonel, desired to speak with me; and after a few minutes' conversation, he with his troop of *one hundred* men surrendered at discretion.

"*March* 23.—In this place I received advice that

eighty-two of the enemy had surrendered in Copano, with all their arms, ammunition, and provisions."

But Santa Anna's order to Urrea convicts him. It is as follows:

"*To* GENERAL URREA, *Commander, etc.:*

[Official.] "In respect to the prisoners of whom you speak in your last communication, you must not fail to bear in mind the circular of the Supreme Government, in which it is decreed, that foreigners invading the republic, and taken with arms in their hands, shall be judged and treated as pirates; and as, in my view of the matter, every Mexican guilty of the crime of joining these adventurers loses the rights of a citizen by his unnatural conduct, the five Mexican prisoners whom you have taken ought also to suffer as traitors."

[Unofficial.] "In regard to foreigners who make war, and those unnatural Mexicans who have joined their cause, you will remark that what I have stated to you officially is in accordance with the former provisions of the Supreme Government. An example is necessary, in order that those adventurers may be duly warned, and the nation be delivered from the ills she is daily doomed to suffer.

"ANTONIO LOPEZ DE SANTA ANNA.

"GENERAL QUARTERS, BEXAR, *March* 23, 1836."

SANTA ANNA.

"*To* General Urrea, *etc.:*

"Under date of the present, I have stated to the commandant of the post of Goliad, as follows:

"By a communication made to me by Colonel D. F. Garay, of that place, I am informed that there have been sent to you by General Urrea, *two hundred and thirty-four* prisoners, taken in the action of *Encinal del Perdido* (Coleta), on the 19th and 20th of the present month; and as the Supreme Government has ordered that all foreigners taken with arms in their hands, making war upon the nation, shall be treated as pirates, I have been surprised that the circular of the said Supreme Government has not been fully complied with in this particular. *I therefore order that you should give immediate effect to the said ordinance in respect to all those foreigners* who have yielded to the force of arms, having had the audacity to come and insult the republic, to devastate with fire and sword, as has been the case in Goliad, causing vast detriment to our citizens; in a word, shedding the precious blood of Mexican citizens, whose only crime has been their fidelity to their country. I trust that, in *reply* to this, you will inform me that *public vengeance has been satisfied* by the punishment of such detestable delinquents. I transcribe the said decree of the Government for your guidance, and that you may strictly fulfil the same, in the zealous hope that, for the future, the provisions of the Supreme Government may not, for a moment, be infringed.

"ANTONIO LOPEZ DE SANTA ANNA.

"HEADQUARTERS, BEXAR, *March* 23, 1836."

If any other proof should be necessary to convict him, the reader is supplied with the following:

"*From the Commandant at Goliad to General Urrea.*

"In compliance with the definitive orders of his excellency the general-in-chief, which I received direct, at four o'clock to-morrow morning the prisoners sent by you to this fortress will be shot. I have not ventured to execute the same sentence on those who surrendered to Colonel Vara, at Copano, being unacquainted with the particular circumstances of their surrender; and I trust you will be pleased to take upon yourself to save my responsibility in this regard, by informing me what I am to do with them.

"J. N. DE PORTILLA.

"GOLIAD, *March* 26, 1836."

Further from the Diary of General Urrea.

"*March* 24–27.—These days were passed in necessary regulations, in refitting the troops, and in the care of the sick and wounded. On the 25th I sent Ward and his companions to Goliad. On the 27th, between nine and ten o'clock in the morning, I received a communication from Lieutenant-Colonel Portilla, military commandant of Goliad, informing me that he had received an order from his excellency the commander-in-chief, to shoot all the prisoners there, and that he had resolved to comply with the same. The order in question was received by Portilla at seven o'clock on the evening of the 26th; he communicated it to me the same date, but necessarily it only came to my knowledge after the execution had taken place. Every soldier in my division was confounded at the news; *all was amazement and consternation.* I was no less struck to the heart than my companions in arms, who stood there the witnesses of my sorrow; let one of those present at that painful moment deny the fact. More than *a hundred and fifty* of those who fortunately remained with me escaped this catastrophe, consisting of those who had surrendered at Copano, together with the surgeons and young men whom I had placed to tend on the hospitals, whose services, as well as those of many of the prisoners, were very important to the army.

"The melancholy event of which I here speak has caused a more than ordinary sensation, not only among my own countrymen, but among strangers the most distant from us. Nor have those been wanting who would fix the fearful responsibility on me, although nothing could be more clear and unequivocal than my conduct in regard to this horrid transaction.

"Nothing could be more painful to me than the idea of sacrificing so many gallant men, and particularly the amiable, spirited, and soldier-like Fannin. They certainly surrendered in the full confidence that Mexican generosity would not be sterile in their regard; they assuredly did so, or otherwise they would have resisted to the last, and sold their lives as dearly as possible."

The conclusion is plain, Urrea tried to save his prisoners, but Gen. Santa Anna refused, and ordered their execution—he alone is responsible for THE GOLIAD MASSACRE.

CHAPTER VIII.

The Retreat of Gen. Houston from Gonzales to the Navidad; thence to the Colorado and the Brazos.—Santa Anna passes him.—The *Twin Sisters*.—The Panic.—Address of the Secretary of War.—Houston pursues Santa Anna.—The two encamp on the plains of *San Jacinto*.

WE will now turn from the sad and mournful details of the fate of the noble and gallant gentlemen who perished at Goliad, to the operations of General Houston and his army at Gonzales. On the 6th of March, the memorable date of the fall of the Alamo, he set out from San Felipe for Gonzales, and arrived there just in time to hear its mothers, widows, and orphans weeping and agonizing over the loss of their sons, husbands, and fathers, who, after fighting like heroes against overwhelming numbers, died as the bravest of the brave at the Thermopylæ of Texas. As Capt. R. E. Handy wrote to J. J. R. Pease: "For four-and-twenty hours after the news reached us, not a sound was heard, save the wild shrieks of women, and the heart-rending screams of their fatherless children. Little groups of men might be seen in various corners of the town, brooding over the past, and speculating of the future; but they scarcely spoke above a whisper. The public and private grief were alike heavy. It sank deep into the heart of the rudest soldier."

Gen. Houston at first did not believe the report, and wrote to the chairman of the military committee on the 13th March: "I am using all my endeavors to get a company to send in view of the Alamo; and, if possible, arrive at the *certainty* of what all believe—its fall. The scarcity of horses, and the repulse of a party of twenty-eight men, the other day, within eighteen miles of Bexar, will, I apprehend, prevent the expedition.

"This moment, Deaf Smith and Henry Karnes have assured me that they will proceed in sight of Bexar; and return within three days. The persons, whose statement is enclosed for your information, are in custody; and I will detain them, for the present, as spies.

"I beg leave to suggest the great importance of fortifications on Live-Oak Point and Copano, and the defence of Matagorda and Lavaca Bays.

"You may rest assured that I shall adopt and pursue such course of conduct as the present emergencies of the country require, and as the means placed at my disposal may enable me to do, for the defence of the country and the protection of its inhabitants.

"The projected expedition to Matamoras, under the

agency of the Council has already cost us over two hundred and thirty-seven lives; and where the effects are to end, none can foresee. Dr. Grant's party, as well as Colonel Johnson's, have been murdered. Major Morris, as reported, was struck down with a lance while gallantly fighting. Dr. Grant surrendered, and was tied by the enemy. Be pleased to send all possible aids to the army; and keep an eye to the coast.

"Intelligence from the seat of government, if favorable, has a most happy effect upon the spirits of the men. Frequent expresses sent to me, may be highly beneficial to the army."

"On the night of the same day, after burning Gonzales to the ground, he retreated eastward, before the victorious Mexicans, attended by the panic-stricken inhabitants of Gonzales and the surrounding country."

The following official letter explains the cause and gives an account of his situation:

"CAMP AT NAVIDAD, *March* 15, 1836.

"TO JAMES COLLINGSWORTH,

"*Chairman of Military Committee.*

"SIR: Since I had the honor to address you from Gonzales, the lady of Lieutenant Dickinson, who fell at the Alamo, has arrived, and confirms the fall of that place, and the circumstances, pretty much as my express detailed them. She returned in company with two negroes—one the servant of Colonel Travis, the other a servant of Colonel Almonte. They both corroborate the statement first made and forwarded to you. Other important intelligence arrived at Gonzales—that the army of Santa Anna had encamped at the Cibolo on the night of the 11th inst., after a march of twenty-four miles that day. The army was to encamp on the 12th at Sandy, and proceed direct to Gonzales. The number of the enemy could not be ascertained, but was represented as exceeding two thousand infantry. Upon this statement of facts, I deemed it proper to fall back and take post on the Colorado, near Burnham's, which is fifteen miles distant from this point. My morning report, on my arrival in camp, showed three hundred and seventy four effective men, without two days' provisions, many without arms, and others without any ammunition. We could have met the enemy, and avenged some of our wrongs; but, detached as we were, without supplies for the men in camp, of either provisions, ammunition, or artillery, and remote from succor, it would have been madness to hazard a contest. I had been in camp two days only, and had succeeded in organizing the troops. But they had not been taught the first principles of the drill. If starved out, and the camp once broken up, there was no hope for the future. By falling back, Texas can rally, and defeat any force that can come against her.

"I received the intelligence of the enemy's advance between eight and nine o'clock at night; and, before twelve, we were on the march in good order, leaving a number of spies, who remained and were reinforced next morning by a number of volunteers and brave spirits from Peach Creek. H. Karnes, R. E. Handy, and Captain Chenowith, have been very active. Only about twenty persons deserted the camp (from the first *sensation* produced by the intelligence) up to this time. I intend desertion shall not be frequent; and I regret to say that I am compelled to regard as deserters all who have left camp without leave; to demand their apprehension; and that, whenever arrested, they be sent to me at head-quarters for trial. They have disseminated throughout the frontier such exaggerated reports that they have produced dismay and consternation among the people to a most distressing extent.

"I do not apprehend the immediate approach of the enemy upon the present settlements; I mean those on the Colorado, for the country west of it is an uninhabited waste. This season the grass refuses to grow on the prairies.

"When the approach of the enemy was known, there were but two public wagons and two yoke of oxen in camp, and the few horses we had were very poor. I hope to reach the Colorado on to-morrow, and collect an army in a short time. I sent my aide-de-camp, Major William T. Austin, to Columbia this morning, for munitions and supplies, to be sent me immediately; and to order the troops now at Velasco to join me, provided they had not been previously ordered by you to fortify Copano and Dimit's Landing. I am fearful Goliad is besieged by the enemy. My order to Colonel Fannin, directing the place to be blown up, the cannon to be sunk in the river, and to fall back on Victoria, would reach him before the enemy could advance. That they have advanced upon the place in strong force, I have no doubt; and when I heard of the fall of the Alamo, and the number of the enemy, I knew it must be the case.

"Our forces must not be shut up in forts, where they can neither be supplied with men nor provisions. Long aware of this fact, I directed, on the 16th of January last, that the artillery should be removed, and the Alamo blown up; but it was prevented by the expedition upon Matamoras, the author of all our misfortunes.

"I hope that our cruisers on the gulf will be active, and that Hawkins and —— may meet the notice of the Government. Let the men of Texas rally to the Colorado!

"Enclosed you will receive the address of General Santa Anna, sent by a negro, to the citizens. It is in Almonté's handwriting. Santa Anna was in Bexar when the Alamo was taken. His force in all, in Texas, is, I think, only five or six thousand men—though some say thirty thousand! This cannot be true. Encourage volunteers from the United States—but I am satisfied we can save the country. Had it not been for the Council, we would have had no reverses. We must have the friendship of the Comanches and other Indians.

"Gonzales is reduced to ashes!

"I have the honor, etc.,

"SAM HOUSTON,

"*Commanding General.*'

From the Navidad he fell back to Burnham's, on the Colorado, and on the 17th of March wrote to Collingsworth:

"To-day, at half-past four in the afternoon, I reached this point with about six hundred men, including my rear-guard, which is a few miles behind with the families, which were not known to be on the route as the army marched, and for which the guard were sent back.

"It pains my heart that such consternation should have been spread by the deserters from camp. We are here; and, if only three hundred men remain on this side of the Brazos, I will die with them, or conquer our enemies. I would most respectfully suggest the assemblage of the troops at this point. It covers more of the country than any other known to me. When they are assembled, I will detach suitable numbers to each point as I may deem best."

On the 23d, says Yoakum, the government informed him that "orders were in execution for the mustering into service of two-thirds of the militia of the country. 'These,' said the Secretary of War, 'with the aid from the United States, will, if you can hold the enemy in check long enough for their concentration, present an insurmountable barrier to the progress of the enemy into the country.' 'One great object should be,' observes the Secretary of War, in a letter of the same date, 'to hold him in check until reinforcements and supplies can reach you. Every means has been put into requisition for the purpose of forwarding on both.'"

On the same day he wrote to the Secretary of War, unofficially:

"Dear Colonel: To-day I had the pleasure to receive your two letters by Mr. Walker. I thank you for them, and snatch a moment from the press of business to say a few things in compliance with your request, as well as to gratify my personal feelings. I have had no aid or assistance but my friend Hockley, who now fills your former station. By-the-by, I offer you my gratulations on your advancement. I trust you will find in me a worthy subaltern. You know I am not easily depressed, but, before my God, since we parted, I have found the darkest hours of my past life! My excitement has been so great, that, for forty-eight hours, I have not eaten an ounce, nor have I slept. I was in constant apprehension of a rout; a constant panic existed in the lines: yet I managed so well, or such was my good luck, that not a gun was fired in or near the camp, or on the march (except to kill beef), from the Guadalupe to the Colorado. All would have been well, and all at peace on this side of the Colorado, if I could only have had a moment to start an express in advance of the deserters; but they went first, and, being panic-struck, it was contagious, and all who saw them breathed the poison and fled. It was a poor compliment to me to suppose that I would not advise the Convention of any necessity which might arise for their removal. I sent word and advices, the first moment of leisure, to the Convention; and all was calm in my communications to Mr. Collingsworth. I had to advise troops and persons of my falling back, and had to send one guard thirty miles for a poor blind widow (and six children), whose husband was killed in the Alamo.

The families are now all on this side of the Guadalupe. These things pained me infinitely, and, with the responsibility of my command, weighed upon me to an agonizing extent.

"This moment an express has arrived, and states that Fannin took up his retreat on Saturday last (19th), and, a few miles from La Bahia, he was attacked by the Mexican army and surrounded about an hour and a half before sundown. The battle continued in the night, and the result is not known. The express states that Colonel Ward's command had not returned. I am at a loss to know how matters stand. I will try and make a good report for the future. The Matamoras policy, I hope, is now run out; and the evils, growing out of the conduct of the Council, ended.

"Changing this from a familiar to an official character, I must say that, if we are to meet an accession of force, which must be the case if Fannin is cut off, we must have the strength of the country. Arms and ammunition have just reached camp, and I hope what men we have will be well armed and supplied with fighting materials.

"Two spies have been taken to-day, and they report the force of the enemy in this quarter less than I had before heard it. Let the Mexican force be what it may, if the country will turn out, we can beat them. The retreat of the government will have a bad effect on the troops, and I am half-provoked at it myself. The Mexicans cannot fight us upon anything like fair terms. . . . I will get any advantage I can if I fight. If what I have heard from Fannin be true, I deplore it, and can only attribute the ill luck to his attempting to retreat in daylight in the face of a superior force. He is an ill-fated man.

"Do all you can. The troops are in fine spirits, but how this news will affect them I know not. Our spies have taken two of the enemy to-day, but I have not yet had time to examine them. I will in a few moments.

"*24th.*—I have examined the spies, and they represent the enemy much weaker than all former reports. They say Sesma has not more than seven hundred men, and one says six hundred."

Reinforcements came in very slowly, yet by the 25th the Texan army had increased to seven hundred men, and General Houston was making preparations to attack the advancing enemy, when the sad news of the defeat and surrender of Fannin and his army at the Coleta, on the 20th, and the capitulation of Ward and King's commands on the 16th and 20th of March, 1836, threw a damper over the cause of Texan independence, his troops and himself, causing the retreat of the Texans from the Colorado to San Felipe, where they arrived on the 28th.

The next day he wrote to the Secretary of War, Col. T. J. Rusk:

"CAMP NEAR MILL CREEK, *March* 29, 1836.

"SIR: On my arrival on the Brazos, had I consulted the wishes of all, I should have been like the ass between two stacks of hay. Many wished me to go below, others above. I consulted none. I held no councils of war. If I err, the blame is mine. I find Colonel Hockley, of my staff, a sage counsellor and true friend. My staff are all worthy, and merit well of me.

"There was on yesterday, as I understood, much discontent in the lines, because I would not fall down the river. If it should be wise for me to do so, I can cross over at any time, and fall down to greater advantage and safety. I apprehend, in consequence of my falling back, that the enemy may change their route to Matagorda. I ordered all the men residing on the coast, and those arriving from the United States at or south of Velasco, to remain and fortify at some safe point; and, on yesterday, I sent Colonel Harcourt, as principal engineer of the army, down to the coast, to erect fortifications at the most eligible point of defence. I placed at his disposal the resources of the lower country for its defence and protection.

"I pray God that you would get aid, speedy aid, from

the United States; or, after all inducements, we must suffer. I hope to-day to receive ninety men from the Red-lands. I cannot now tell my force, but will soon be able. The enemy must be crippled by the fights they have had with our men. I have ordered D. C. Barrett and E. Gritton to be arrested and held subject to the future order of the government. I do think they ought to be detained and tried as traitors and spies.

"For Heaven's sake, do not drop back again with the seat of government! Your removal to Harrisburg has done more to increase the panic in the country than anything else that has occurred in Texas, except the fall of the Alamo. Send fifty agents, if need be, to the United States. Wharton writes me, from Nashville, that the ladies of that place have fitted out, at their own expense, no less than two hundred men. . . .

"If matters press upon us, for God's sake let the troops land at Galveston bay, and by land reach the Brazos! Let no troops march with baggage-wagons, or wagons of any kind.

"Truly, etc., SAM HOUSTON."

"To-day I send Captain Smith to you, agreeably to your order. Great prosperity to you and the country, etc."

After writing this letter to the Secretary of War, on *the same day* he wrote to his friend, William Christy, *a noble and valuable friend to Texas*, the fol lowing patriotic appeal:

"HEAD-QUARTERS, CAMP MILL CREEK, *March* 29, 1836.

"*To* WILLIAM CHRISTY, *New Orleans.*

"DEAR SIR: I have ordered Captain David N. Burke and Edward Conrad to New Orleans, to procure men for the army of Texas. The present is probably the most important moment we have to experience. We now stand before the world as a nation, and stand almost alone. But for the assistance upon which we confidently rely from our brethren in the United States, we shall not be enabled to maintain the position we have assumed. With equal confidence I look to *you* for the immediate use of all the influence in your power to sustain our cause. I look to you as the most efficient and zealous agent of our country. Do exert all the talent and means you can command, for now is the time of need. Captain Burke and Mr. Conrad will bear this letter to you, with my orders: be good enough to render them all the assistance in your power.

"I have the honor, etc.,

"SAM HOUSTON."

The Government on the 22d of March, was moved, or rather moved from Washington on the Brazos to Harrisburg.

The effect of this move was to increase the panic, and cause soldiers to leave the army for the protection of their families. Says Yoakum:

"The voice of sorrow and despondency that came from the flying inhabitants touched the hearts of the small band who had ventured everything in this last effort for life and liberty. It did more—it prevented volunteers from coming from the east. The panic, as it travelled in that direction, had greatly increased. Citizens east of the Neches believed their danger more imminent than those west of the Trinity. Hence, able-bodied men were retained to defend families and neighborhoods. To add to the terror and distress, particularly in eastern Texas, there were some bad men who spread false alarms for the sake of plunder. It was understood, and perhaps with some truth, that all Americans, whether combatants or not, were to be driven from the country."

The gallant John W. Smith, who rode in and out of the Alamo while it was invested, wrote: "I find many wagons and carts with lone families, and three or four men with them, and many of them single men. If possible, an arrangement should be made, and the Committees of Safety or some other authority should stop and compel to return to the army all persons not having a passport."

"The extent of alarm and confusion arising from the flight of the citizens was at this time most distressing. Samuel P. Carson, the Secretary of the Navy, writing to President Burnet from Liberty, says: "I have issued orders to two different persons—one for Trinity and one for the Neches—to press boats, etc., to aid the people in crossing. The panic has reached this place, and the people are all leaving Trinity from the opposite (west) side, and preparations making by many on this. The river is rising rapidly, and I fear by to-night it will be impassable for any kind of carriage. The 'slues' on this side are belly-deep. There must be three hundred families—I know not the number of wagons, carts, carriages, etc. Destruction pervades the whole country. I must speak plainly—the relations existing between us, and the responsibility which rests on us, make it my duty. Never till I reached Trinity have I *desponded*—I will not say, *despaired*. If Houston has retreated, or been whipped, nothing can save the people from *themselves*: their *own* conduct has brought this calamity on them! If Houston retreats, the flying people may be covered in their escape. He must be advised of the state of the waters, and the impossibility of the people crossing."

"In fact, on every road leading eastward in Texas, were found men, women, and children, moving through the country over swollen streams and muddy roads, strewing the way with their property, crying for aid, and exposed to the fierce *northers* and rains of spring. The scene was distressing indeed; and, being witnessed by the small but faithful army of Texans, whose wives and families they were, thus exposed and suffering, nerved their arms and hearts for the contest then not distant." (Yoakum 2d, 118, 119.)

On the 31st of March, Gen. Houston wrote to Col. Rusk, Secretary of War, from camp west of Brazos:

"Sir: I have the honor to report to you my arrival at this point, with a view to receive reinforcements and supplies. It is the best and nearest route to Harrisburg, or the Bay, at which I could have struck the Brazos, and it will prevent the whole country passing the Trinity. The force of the enemy has been greatly exaggerated, I have no doubt. But the deserters have spread universal alarm throughout the country.

"I wish you to send flour, sugar, and coffee, on pack-horses, to this point, as soon as possible. Don't send by wagons; and let the pack-horses be well hobbled at night. My horses and baggage-wagons in camp give me all the care I have, except my general solicitude. One of my spies has just returned from a scout, and reports that he went ten miles beyond St. Bernard, on the road to Beason's, and saw nothing of the enemy. Two others went on, and said they would see the enemy if they had to cross the Colorado. Mr. E. Smith (Deaf) is out, and, if living, I will hear the truth and all important news.

"For Heaven's sake, do allay the fever and chill which prevails in the country, and let the people from the east march to the camp! Supplies are needed on the route from Nacogdoches to this point. The enemy would have been beaten at the Colorado. My intention was to have attacked him on the second night after the day on which the news of Fannin's destruction was reported by Kerr—but for that news, and the march of strong reinforcements, probably arriving that night, to the enemy. Previous to that, the troops were in fine spirits, and keen for action.

"The reinforcements promised to our army never arriving, has kept us in a mood not so enviable as could be wished for. Send daily expresses to me, and do let me know what to rely upon. I must let the camp know something, and I want everything promised to be realized by them. I hope I can keep them together; I have, thus far, succeeded beyond my hopes. I will do the best I can; but, be assured, the fame of Jackson could never compensate me for my anxiety and mental pain.

"I have the honor, etc.,

"SAM HOUSTON."

"P.S.—I have somewhere between seven and eight hundred effective men. Two nights since, when it was reported that the enemy were on this side of the Colorado, the citizens of San Felipe reduced it to ashes. There was no order from me for it.* I am glad of it, should the enemy march there. Our troops have suffered from heavy rains and dreadful roads."

General Houston has been severely censured for his retreat from the Colorado to the Brazos. Mr. Richardson, in his "History of Texas," says:

"That an extensive and, in some instances, intense excitement had been produced by the fall of the Alamo and its sequents, is both natural and true. But it is equally true that many brave men in the west, whose property and families were most exposed to the ravages of war, repaired with alacrity to the army. The panic and its effects have been exaggerated for selfish purposes. The army at Beason's received daily

---

* "It has been said you ordered the burning of San Felipe. I have contradicted it. I would like to be fully satisfied on the subject."—*David Thomas, Acting Secretary of War, to General Houston, April* 8, 1836.

accessions of men, who came to fight the enemy, and preserve their family hearths from desecration. How far the people of eastern Texas yielded to the panic we have no reliable authority to assert. But Mr. Yoakum had a *case* to make out, and he found it expedient to resort to quirks and quibbles.

"Almost simultaneous with Houston's arrival at Beason's, the Mexican General Sesma, with a force variously estimated at 600 to 800 men (60 or 70 being cavalry), and two field-pieces, took position on the right bank of the Colorado. On the 20th, Capt. Karnes crossed the river on a spying trip, with five men. He met twelve Mexicans, and dispersed them, killing one, and capturing one and three horses. Another passage of the river was made by 150 men, but resulted in nothing. The enemy had placed himself in a bend of the river, about midway between the two fords—Beason's and Dewees'. From the Texan camp to Dewees', around the bend, was six to seven miles: on a straight line crossing the river, not more than two miles. To prevent Sesma's crossing at Dewees', Capt. Patton was detailed, with some fifty men, to that point; and soon afterwards, Col. Sherman was despatched, with 100 men, to command that interesting position. Sherman's division was soon enlarged by volunteers from outside, to 350 or 400. Large additions were also made to the camp at head-quarters. There is no one matter of fact connected with this campaign that has been more controverted and misstated than the number of men composing the army at the Colorado. We trust the subjoined statements, by gentlemen who were present, and of unimpeachable veracity, will put an end to the strife. They are excerpts from manuscripts, which will be left at the office of *The Galveston News* for inspection.

"Col. Ben. F. Smith, acting Quartermaster and Adjt.-General, says: 'The number of men mustered in the army under Gen. Houston, at the time of the retreat from the Colorado, mentioned above, was about 1,360; and the men, to a man, were ready and eager for battle.' This was sworn to. Ex-President Anson Jones, who was with the army, says: 'On the morning we retreated from the Colorado, we had, by the official report of the day, over 1,500 effective men (I think 1,570). I assisted Col. John A. Wharton, the Adjt.-General, in making up his report. On the same morning, there were at least 100 men in camp who had not enrolled themselves in any company, but were ready and willing to fight. On the same morning, there were many on the way to join the army, enough to have increased the number to 2,000 or more in ten days. On the same day we were opposed by General Sesma, with only 600 to 700 men.'

"Major William I. E. Heard—his communication being signed by Eli Mercer—says: 'Our numerical force was from 1,500 to 1,600 men, the morning the army left the Colorado. I believe this because the issuing commissary told me that morning that there were 1,600 drew rations. The Mexican forces were reported by our spies to be between seven and eight hundred men, at the time our army left the Colorado. Our men were more anxious to engage the Mexicans than I ever saw one set of men to engage another, except at San Jacinto.'

"Col. Amasa Turner, then commanding a company of regulars, who joined the army on the morning of the retreat, and who now lives on the La Vaca, says: 'In relation to the number of men which composed the army at the time Gen. Houston left the Colorado, I am confident I am not mistaken. The morning report, including Sherman's command, was 1,464, rank and file. Roman's and Fisher's companies joined at the first camp (after the retreat), five miles from the Colorado. These would swell the number to 1,568, at the five-mile camp.' We have a printed handbill, issued by Capt. John Sharp, and dated Brazoria, March 27, 1836, in which the following occurs: 'Our army, now encamped at or near Beason's, on the Colorado, consists of 1,000 to 1,200 men, and reinforcements coming in hourly. They are all well armed with plenty of provisions, ammunition, etc., and are in good spirits. On my way down, I met several small companies pushing on for our camp; and those that came from the eastward, report from 300 to 500 men on their way from that quarter.' Capt. Sharp had been forty hours from the camp.

"Gen. Houston, with at least 1,500 to 1,600 Texans, and as brave a band as ever drew a trigger, fled from the Colorado! Peter Kerr, a worthy citizen, now residing in Burnet County, then a prisoner at the ranch of Martin de Leon, hearing of the defeat of Fannin, escaped from the enemy, and hastened to Houston's camp with the intelligence. He urged the commander-in-chief to attack Sesma forthwith, assuring him that Sesma had but about 700 men at that time. But on the next day Houston—retreated!! He fell back about five miles, on the pretence of seeking fresh grass. In order to mystify the true cause of his falling back, which was the beginning of his retreat, he put Kerr in arrest, alleging that he was a spy. The veil was too transparent to deceive any but the wilfully blind; but the pretext of seeking grass had a brief tranquillizing effect.

"From the moment the retreat was plainly begun, the indignant army dissolved away like the untimely snow of the hill-top before a vertical sun. The citizens of western Texas, whose families had been left at home, in the hope that the enemy would be met and defeated, were compelled, by the first and holiest promptings of nature, to abandon their dishonored flag draggling in the dust, and provide for the imminently exposed ones of their own households.

"On the morning of the 27th the retreat was resumed, and on the 28th the army arrived at San Felipe on the Brazos; and the beautiful West was given up to the ravages of an enemy as barbarian as the hordes of Attila."

The venerable editor of *The Galveston News*, besides this, made other strictures on Gen. Houston's errors during this campaign, in retaliation for which Gen. Houston said in the U. S. Senate:

"The *author* of this Almanac, Willard Richardson—I must immortalize him—if reports be true, and I have no reason to doubt them, had he been assigned to his proper place, would have been dignified by a penitentiary residence before this time, owing to the peccadilloes with which he was charged. Although they have been smothered and done away with, his character is not vindicated to the world. He still goes on from sin to sin, from abuse to slander. Sir, I have no disposition to animadvert more: but could the characters of these individuals, and the motives which prompted them, be known, it would not have been necessary for me to occupy the time of the Senate on this occasion, or to give a thought to what has transpired, in relation to the commander-in-chief of the army of Texas. I find, however, that bitter, that undying hostility to him, that will not perish even with his life; and I have no doubt the very creatures that are hunting him now would hunt him, if they could, beyond the grave."

Kennedy says: "The army under Houston, which mustered about 1,300 men, impatient for action, occupied a position at Beason's Ferry, on the Colorado, until the 26th of March. Having learned that there was a division of the enemy above and another below him, and that large reinforcements had joined them, Houston determined, on the 26th, to fall back upon the Brazos, apprehensive of being surrounded along with an army that was the main hope of Texas, being composed almost exclusively of the settlers themselves. Foreseeing that if the enemy should move to his rear, he would have to starve on the left bank of the Colorado, leaving the country unprotected, or share the fate of Fannin in his attempt to cross the prairies, he ordered a retreat to San Felipe, which he reached without molestation on the 27th. Leaving a detachment at San Felipe, and forwarding another to Ford Bend (half-way between Columbia and San Felipe), he moved with the main body to Groce's Ferry. This was the best and easiest crossing-place on the Brazos, and therefore the point most likely to be aimed at by the Mexicans. By securing the steamboat *Yellowstone*, lying at this point, Houston obtained the means of transporting his troops to any part of the river where the enemy should appear.

"On the evening of the 29th, some scouts, detached by Captain Baker, who commanded at San Felipe, made an erroneous report of the appearance of the Mexicans within a few miles of the town. The inhabitants, after hastily removing a part of their property beyond the Brazos, set fire to the town and destroyed with it goods to the amount of several thousand dollars, which might have been saved, had not the scouts mistaken a drove of cattle for a squadron of cavalry.

"General Santa Anna arrived at Gonzales on the 2d of April; and, the river being swollen, it was necessary to pass it on a raft. Anxious to advance, he proceeded on the 3d, with his staff and picket, to join General Sesma, on the Colorado, leaving to Filisola the charge of conducting the troops across the Guadalupe. On the 5th, he arrived at Paso del Atascosito, and on the 6th marched with the divisions of Sesma and Tolsa to San Felipe, which he reached on the 7th. General Woll was left at Atascosito, with a battalion and a picket of cavalry, for the purpose of constructing a raft to transport the artillery, wagons, and am munition, that were coming up with Filisola, across the Colorado.

"The swell of the Brazos, and the opposition of the detachment under Captain Baker, prevented Santa Anna from crossing the river at San Felipe. On the 9th of April, he took the choice companies and proceeded down the river, to select a suitable crossing-place. On the 11th, he arrived at the Old Fort, and despatched orders to Sesma and Filisola to join him there. He was joined by the former on the 13th, and without waiting for additional reinforcments, crossed the river and marched to Harrisburg, which he reached in the afternoon of the 16th. *Almonte's Journal* contains the following record of the march from San Felipe:

"'*Saturday, 9th.*—At 5 A.M. we left San Felipe with the choice companies of Guerreros, Metamoros, Mexico, and Toluca, and fifty cavalry of the regiment of Tampico and Dolores. At half-past twelve o'clock we arrived at the farm of Colls, and another a mile beyond—in all six and a half leagues. Three Americans were seen who took the road to Marion, or Orozimbo (Old Fort), and leading to Thompson's Ferry. We found at the farm a family from La Baca, who came by the way of the Brazos. Various articles were also found. The husband of the woman was a mulatto, the woman white. We sent Wilson (the mulatto) to reconnoitre at Marion, that is, at the ferry. He did not return. It rained some in the night, and the wind changed to the north.

"*Sunday*, 10*th*.—We remained at Coll's farm, waiting for our scout. The farm is on the left bank of the river San Bernardo. At a house seven leagues from the farm, on the road leading to the Colorado, there were 500 fanegas of corn and twenty barrels of sugar. In the afternoon the scout returned, and confirmed the accounts we had received of the position of the enemy. At a quarter before four o'clock, P.M., we took up our march for Marion, or Old Fort, on the road from Brazoria. At half-past five o'clock we made a short halt at the farm of the Widow Powell, or rather at a stream called Guajolota; from thence leaving the road from Brazoria on our right, we took the left, following the wagon tracks to Marion. We marched until half-past nine at night, and made another short halt. Night dark. At two in the morning we commenced the march on foot, from the President down to the soldier, leaving the baggage and cavalry, for the purpose of surprising the enemy, who defended the crossing place, before daylight. We did not succeed, as we found the distance double what we supposed it to be. Day broke upon us at a quarter of a league from the ferry and frustrated our plan. We then placed the men in ambush. The stream of Guajolota is seven and a half leagues from Marion, road level, with some miry places.

"'*Monday*, 11*th*.—Still in ambush. A negro passed at a short distance and was taken. He conducted us to the place he had crossed at, and having obtained a canoe we crossed without being perceived, a little below the principal crossing place. In the meantime the cavalry arrived at Marion and took possession of the houses. The enemy retired on the other side, and kept up a fire for a long time, until the Cazadores under command of Bringas crossed at the lower ford, and, ascending the river, were about to take them in the rear, when they abandoned Marion, and we remained in possession of the ferry, one canoe, and a flat-boat. A courier was despatched to General Sesma, with orders that he should come up with the whole division. The Cazadores slept on the other side of the river. Rain during the night.

"'*Tuesday*, 12*th*.—Day clear and fine. Was occupied in procuring the canoes and going up in the flat-boat to Thompson's Ferry. A Mexican and a Prussian came in. The Mexican is the son of Delgardo. In the afternoon the boat was injured. A courier came in from Guadalupe and from General Sesma. Wrote to Urrea at Matagorda.

"'*Wednesday*, 13*th*.—The boat was repaired. The division of General Sesma arrived. Many articles were found. General Urrea and F. V. Fernandez were written to. Despatches arrived from Urrea and Filisola.

"'*Thursday*, 14*th*.—We crossed the river early, with our beds only and provisions for the road. At three in the afternoon we started from Thompson's Ferry.

"'*Friday*, 15*th*.—At Harrisburg. [In pencil.]

"'*Saturday*, 16*th*.—At Lynchburg.' [In pencil.]"

But to return to the Texan CAMP WEST OF BRAZOS. On the 3d of April Gen. Houston wrote to Col. Rusk:

"I arrived at this place the 1st inst., and pitched my encampment in a secure position, in hopes that I should receive supplies, and more so, that I would be enabled to meet the enemy at any time, and under any circumstances which propriety might dictate. Since my location rains have fallen; and it is possible the water may invade my encampment, and compel me to remove, either back to the prairie, or to pass over the river to the east side. If I do pass, it will only be to make my camp on a healthy site, secure from water, and to defend our horses from the enemy; for I find that no care whatever will be taken of horses, and if they fall into the enemy's hands it would add to his facilities.

"My spies return and report the enemy only

about 1,000 strong on the Colorado, without pickets, and only a small camp-ground. My opinion is, that a detachment I sent to reconnoitre the enemy will attack him to-night. The detachment was twenty in number, under the command of Major Patton, my aide-de-camp. They are among the best hearts of the army.

"If I should pass the river, my design will be, should I quit a position opposite to this point, to drop down opposite Fort Bend, or some point below. The enemy would not have it in their power to pass the river for at least a month to come; and we could only cross with the aid of a steamboat, which I have pressed, and will retain till I can dispense with it.

"If I should pass the river, I will leave my most effective cavalry on this side. I sent you, in charge of Mr. Este, two prisoners, Peter Kerr, and Beregardo, a Mexican. I have nothing pointed against them; but suspicion has fallen upon them, and they are to be secured. You may rest easy at Harrisburg; the enemy will never cross the Brazos, and I hope the panic will soon subside. People are planting corn on the east side of this river.

"Mr. Zavala has arrived and reported for duty. I am glad of it. He informed me that I should have the pleasure of seeing you; and indeed it would give me pleasure to do so. I have ordered the troops below to occupy some defensible positions below on the river, or coast, and check the enemy. Rumors from the Mexican interior of wars, or difficulty in passing the Colorado, have caused them to delay; and at this time it is almost impossible for them to pass the prairies, owing to the rains that have fallen since we passed—then it was only possible for us to pass with our wagons. If they come, their artillery must come. They must raft it over the Colorado, which is very high, as I am informed. It must be out of its banks.

"I have looked for an express from you for several days. Eighty Redlanders have arrived, and are on the opposite bank. The arrival of others is daily expected.

"I have the honor, etc.,

"SAM HOUSTON."

The last letter of Gen. Houston to Col. Thomas J. Rusk, Secretary of War, gives an account of news from Goliad, etc., it is as follows:

"HEAD-QUARTERS, CAMP WEST OF BRAZOS, *April* 4, 1836.

"SIR: I have the honor to inform you that, by an express which reached me last night, I received intelligence that Colonel Fannin and his command had been attacked by a large body of Mexican cavalry and infantry, in the prairie, about eight miles east of San Antonio River, on his march from La Bahia to Victoria. The enemy were several times repulsed; the battle lasting until far in the night. On the next morning the enemy fired several cannon-shots and hoisted a flag of truce, which was met by a corresponding signal from Colonel Fannin. The commanders met, and stipulated that the Americans, on condition of a surrender, should be treated as prisoners of war, and in eight days sent to New Orleans on parole. On the eighth day the prisoners were marched out under a guard (after having been kept in close confinement), a file of soldiers on each side of the prisoners. The guard then doubled files on the right of the prisoners, killing all but one, who made his escape. The enemy are said to have lost 1,000 men in the action. . . . . . .

"Will not our friends rush to the conflict, and at once avenge the wrongs which have been inflicted on our dauntless comrades? The day of just retribution ought not to be deferred. Send expresses to the coast and to the United States. The army is just organizing, and will soon be prepared. The last advices report that the enemy cannot cross the Colorado—except a part of it—on account of high waters. Their delay is said, by others, to be owing to some difficulties in the interior, and a want of supplies.

"San Felipe was reduced to ashes, but not by my order.

"I have the honor, etc.,

"SAM HOUSTON."

"P.S.—It was reported in camp that you were coming to the army. As it is so reported, you had best come if possible. It will inspirit the troops. No express has reached me for some five days from Harrisburg. The army is in good spirits."

The Secretary of War, Col. Thos. J. Rusk, arrived in camp on the night of the 4th. He was from Georgia, and had settled in Nacogdoches before the war commenced: was a lawyer, of fine personal appearance, most agreeable manners, and solid sense, made a good speech, and told a funny story with splendid effect. He subsequently became commander-in-chief of the Texan army, and served many years as senator from Texas in the U. S. Congress. His arrival in camp no doubt did much good, for *things looked gloomy*. The Mexicans had already killed in battle or butchered, within less than one month, more Texans than now constituted their army under Gen. Houston.

Another battle might end as disastrous and bloody as the first, yet, after resting a few days and recuperating their physical abilities, hope revived their drooping spirits, and on the 7th of April their general issued the following order:

"HEAD-QUARTERS OF THE ARMY,
"CAMP WEST OF BRAZOS, *April* 7, 1836.

"*Army Orders.*—The advance of the enemy is at San Felipe. The moment for which we have waited with anxiety and interest is fast approaching. The victims of the Alamo, and the manes of those who were murdered at Goliad, call for *cool, deliberate* vengeance. Strict discipline, order and subordination will insure us the victory.

"The army will be in readiness for action at a moment's warning. The field officers have the immediate execution of this order in charge for their respective commands.

"SAM HOUSTON,
Commander-in-Chief."

"GEO. W. HOCKLEY, Inspector-General."

The enemy left San Felipe without giving him battle, and on the 12th of April, the acting Secretary of War wrote to Gen. Houston from Harrisburg:

"There are a number of families here, and in the neighborhood, who came here under the belief that they would be safe, who are now exposed to the attack of the enemy. . . . .

"You have assured the government that the enemy

should never cross the Brazos: they have relied on your assurance, but they find your pledges not verified, and numberless families exposed to the ravages of the enemy.

"The country expects something from you; the government looks to you for action.

"The time has now arrived to determine whether we are to give up the country, and make the best of our way out of it, or to meet the enemy and make at least one struggle for our boasted independence."

On the 13th of April Gen. Houston answered the Secretary of War, stating:

"At Gonzales I had 374 efficient men, without supplies, even powder, balls, or arms. At the Colorado, with 700 men, without discipline or time to organize the army. Two days since, my effective force in camp was 530 men (aggregate). . . . .

"I had reason to expect the attack would be made, and an effort made to cross the river at San Felipe, or at the point at which I was, as the prairie, at the latter point, approached nearer to the river, and the bottom was better than at any other point on the river. The cannonade was kept up at San Felipe until yesterday morning; and as the river was very high, and it was reported to me that the enemy were preparing rafts at that point, I had every reason to suppose that they intended to cross there, if possible.

"On the previous night, in consultation with the Secretary of War, we concluded to pass the river to this side. At ten o'clock, A.M., yesterday, I commenced crossing the river, and from that time till the present (noon) the steamboat and yawl (having no ferry-boat) have been engaged. We have eight or ten wagons, ox teams, and about two hundred horses, belonging to the army; and these have to pass on board the steamboat, besides the troops, baggage, etc. This requires time; but I hope in one hour to be enabled to be in preparation. I had sent an express evening before last to all the troops of Washington and above this point to meet me here by a rapid march. On yesterday morning I ordered all the command below to unite with the main body, so as to act promptly and efficiently when most necessary. It was impossible to guard all river passes for one hundred miles, and at once concentrate the force so as to guard any one point effectually, unless where the main body might be stationed. An invading army marches with everything necessary to conquest. I would at once have fallen back on Harrisburg, but a wish to allay the panic that prevailed, induced me to stop at the Brazos, contrary to my views of military operations. I had assurances of reinforcements by remaining on the Brazos. . . . . . .

"When I assured the department that the enemy

should not pass the Brazos, I did not intend to convey the idea that either the army or myself possessed powers of ubiquity; but that they should not pass through my encampment. . . . . .

"I beg leave to assure you that I will omit no opportunity to serve the country, and to serve it for the love of it, without ambition, or ulterior views into which selfishness can enter. I have, under the most disadvantageous circumstances, kept an army together, and where there has not been even murmuring or insubordination; but I cannot perform impossibilities. These remarks are not in anger, nor are they intended to be in the least personal to you, but arise out of the pressure of difficulties which you cannot appreciate, because they are unexplained to you."

Having crossed the Brazos and having received the famous *twin sisters*, two six-pounders, the generous donation of the good people of Cincinnati, after concentrating his forces, Gen. Houston resolves to pursue the enemy and give them battle.

After a very unpleasant march over very bad roads, which required many times the unloading of the wagons at boggy places, so that they could cross over empty, and then reloading, the Texan army arrived at Harrisburg on the 18th, when the notable spy Deaf Smith, Karnes, and others were sent out.

Smith* returned with two captive Mexicans from whom information was gained of the number and whereabouts of Santa Anna, and his army, which numbered between 700 and 800 men and was separated from the divisions of Gaona, Sesma, and Filisola.

Upon receiving this information General Houston crossed his army over Buffalo Bayou on the 19th, and threw himself in the way of Santa Anna. On the same day, Colonel Rusk issued the following address: to which General Houston added the subjoined:

"WAR DEPARTMENT, HEAD-QUARTERS OF THE ARMY,
"HARRISBURG, *April* 19, 1836.

"TO THE PEOPLE OF TEXAS—*Fellow Citizens:* Let me make one more appeal to you to turn out, and rally to the standard of your country. The army

---

* Deaf Smith was a member of that distinguished family as the following story taken from *Yoakum* will show: "It is given as related by the general himself. Smith came in, greatly fatigued, and somewhat exasperated. He repaired to the general's quarters, and said he wished to have a little talk with him. Said he: 'General, you are very kind to these Mexicans; I like kindness, but you are too kind—you won't allow me to kill any of them! If a man meets two of the enemy, and is not allowed to kill either, by the time he takes one and ties him, the other gets off so far that it is very fatiguing on a horse to catch him; and I wish you would let me manage things in my own way.' Houston told him not to be cruel, but that he must be his own judge of the necessity of securing such of the enemy as might be taken by him. Smith nodded his head—for he was a man of few words—and retired."

reached here yesterday late in the day. Our scouts arrested three of the Mexicans—one captain, one a *corréo* [express rider], direct from Mexico, and another, a servant. From the prisoners we learn many interesting facts. Santa Anna himself is just below us, and within the sound of the drum—has, we understand, only 500 men. We are parading our forces for the purpose of marching upon him. He has a reinforcement of about 1,000 men upon the Brazos, about forty miles from here. A few hours more will decide the fate of our army: and what an astonishing fact it is, that, at the very moment when the fate of your wives, your children, your homes, your country, and all that is dear to a freeman, are suspended upon the issue of one battle, not one-fourth of the people [men] of Texas are in the army! Are you Americans? are you freemen? If you are, prove your blood and birth by rallying at once to your country's standard! Your general is at the head of a brave and chivalrous band, and throws himself, sword in hand, into the breach, to save his country, and vindicate her rights. Enthusiasm prevails in the army; but I look around and see that many, very many, whom I anticipated would be first in the field, are not here.

"Rise up at once, concentrate, and march to the field!–a vigorous effort, and the country is safe! A different course disgraces and ruins you; and what is life worth with the loss of liberty? May I never survive it!

"Your fellow-citizen,

"THOMAS J. RUSK,

"*Secretary of War.*"

"*April* 19, 1836.

"We view ourselves on the eve of battle. We are nerved for the contest, and must conquer or perish. It is vain to look for present aid: none is at hand. We must now act or abandon all hope! Rally to the standard, and be no longer the scoff of mercenary tongues! Be men, be freemen, that your children may bless their fathers' names!

"Colonel Rusk is with me, and I am rejoiced at it. The country will be the gainer, and myself the beneficiary. Liberty and our country!

"SAM HOUSTON,

"*Commander-in-Chief.*"

On the 20th, the Texan army, marching down the bayou, met the Mexican army marching up, opposite Lynch's Ferry, just below the junction of the *San Jacinto* River with Buffalo Bayou, when, after slight skirmishing with little loss on either side, both armies encamped on the plains about three-fourths of a mile apart and reposed for the night.

The long wished for moment is at hand! There is

the army of Santa Anna, the captor of the Alamo! There stand those Mexicans who stormed the Thermopylæ of Texas, and put to death Travis, Bowie, Crockett, Bonham, and their immortal comrades!

There stand the murderers of the brave but unfortunate Red Rovers, the Duval Rifles, and the Georgia Battalion, who left all the comforts of home, the sweet society of dear friends, and from the lap of luxury and security leaped into the foremost ranks of a people struggling for liberty!

Why do the Texans hesitate? Why not sound the charge, and avenge the sacrifice of their dear comrades?

Providence orders the murderers' sleep, and their last night to be like Richard's, who said, in the language of the poet:

> "Oh, I have passed a miserable night,
> So full of fearful dreams, of ugly sights,
> That, as I am a Christian, faithful man,
> I would not spend another such a night,
> Though 'twere to buy a world of happy days."

CHAPTER IX.

The Battle of San Jacinto—The Mexican Army entirely defeated.—Santa Anna captured.—J. A. Sylvester, *Milt Swisher*, and Santa Anna.—The Armistice.—Texas Cabinet come to San Jacinto.—Division of the Cabinet as to treating with Santa Anna.—Lamar's letter to the Cabinet.—The Treaties of Velasco.

THE 21st of April, 1836, was a clear and beautiful day. Neither the sun of Bannockburn nor Austerlitz shone more lovely or more brilliantly.

The Texans seemed loath to commence the battle, while the Mexicans, although they received some reinforcements under General Cos, amounting to 520 men, appeared to be fearful and apprehensive of the coming strife, for they threw up breastworks and fortified their camp.

The evening sun was declining, when, after a council of war at three o'clock in the afternoon, the joyful order was given: Prepare for battle!

All were eager for the fray, and to the tune of "*Will you come to my bower?*" they charged forth to victory and renown. But as the reports of Gens. Houston and Rusk are very interesting, they are here inserted:

"HEAD-QUARTERS OF THE ARMY, SAN JACINTO,
"*April 25th*, 1836.

"*To* DAVID G. BURNET, *President of the Republic of Texas.*

"SIR: I regret extremely that my situation, since the battle of the 21st, has been such as to prevent my rendering you my official report of the same previous to this time.

"I have the honor to inform you that, on the evening of the 18th inst., after a forced march of fifty-five miles, which was effected in two days and a half, the army arrived opposite Harrisburg. That evening a courier of the enemy was taken, from which I learned that General Santa Anna, with one division of his choice troops, had marched in the direction of Lynch's Ferry, on the San Jacinto, burning Harrisburg as he passed down.

"The army was ordered to be in readiness to march early on the next morning. The main body effected a crossing over Buffalo Bayou, below Harrisburg, on the morning of the 19th, having left the baggage, the sick, and a sufficient camp-guard, in the rear. We continued to march throughout the night, making but one halt in the prairie for a short time, and without refreshments. At daylight we resumed the line of march, and in a short distance our scouts encountered those of the enemy, and we received information that General Santa Anna was at New Washington, and

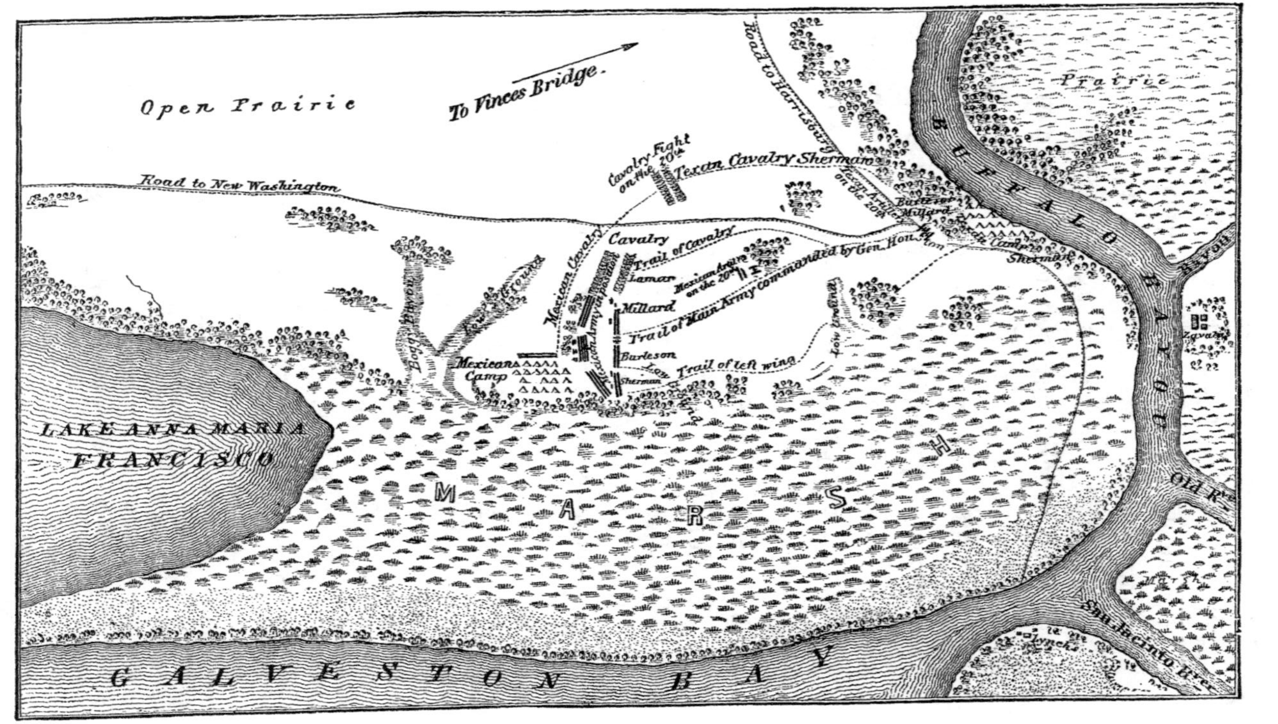

SAN JACINTO BATTLE GROUND.

would that day take up the line of march for Anahuac, crossing at Lynch's Ferry. The Texan army halted within half a mile of the ferry, in some timber, and were engaged in slaughtering beeves when the army of Santa Anna was discovered to be approaching in battle array, having been encamped at Clopper's Point, eight miles below. Disposition was immediately made of our forces, and preparation for his reception. He took a position with his infantry and artillery in the centre, occupying an island of timber, his cavalry covering the left flank. The artillery, consisting of one double-fortified medium brass twelve-pounder, then opened on our encampment. The infantry, in column, advanced with the design of charging our lines, but were repulsed by a discharge of grape and canister from our artillery, consisting of two six-pounders. The enemy had occupied a piece of timber within rifle-shot of the left wing of our army, from which an occasional interchange of small-arms took place between the troops, until the enemy withdrew to a position on the bank of the San Jacinto, about three-quarters of a mile from our encampment, and commenced fortification.

"A short time before sunset, our mounted men, about eighty-five in number, under the special command of Colonel Sherman, marched out for the purpose of reconnoitring the enemy. While advancing, they received a volley from the left of the enemy's infantry, and, after a sharp rencounter with their cavalry, in which ours acted extremely well, and performed some feats of daring chivalry, they retired in good order, having had two men severely wounded, and several horses killed. In the meantime, the infantry under the command of Lieutenant-Colonel Millard, and Colonel Burleson's regiment, with the artillery, had marched out for the purpose of covering the retreat of the cavalry, if necessary. All then fell back in good order to our encampment about sunset, and remained without ostensible action until the 21st, at half-past three o'clock, taking the first refreshment which they had enjoyed for two days. The enemy in the meantime extended the right flank of their infantry, so as to occupy the extreme point of a skirt of timber on the bank of the San Jacinto, and secured their left by a fortification about five feet high, constructed of packs and baggage, leaving an opening in the centre of the breastwork, in which their artillery was placed, their cavalry upon their left wing.

"About nine o'clock on the morning of the 21st, the enemy were reinforced by 500 choice troops, under the command of General Cos, increasing their effective force to upward of 1,500 men, while our aggregate force for the field numbered 783. At half-past three o'clock in the evening, I ordered the officers of the Texan army to parade their respective commands, having in the meantime ordered the bridge on the only road communicating with the Brazos, distant eight miles from our encampment, to be destroyed—thus cutting off all possibility of escape. Our troops paraded with alacrity and spirit, and were anxious for the contest. Their conscious disparity in numbers seemed only to increase their enthusiasm and confidence, and heightened their anxiety for the conflict. Our situation afforded me an opportunity of making the arrangements preparatory to the attack without exposing our designs to the enemy. The *first* regiment, commanded by Colonel Burleson, was assigned to the centre. The *second* regiment, under the command of Colonel Sherman, formed the left wing of the army. The artillery, under the special command of Colonel George W. Hockley, inspector-general, was placed on the right of the first regiment; and four companies of infantry, under the command of Lieutenant-Colonel Henry Millard, sustained the artillery upon the right. Our cavalry, sixty-one in number, commanded by Colonel Mirabeau B. Lamar (whose gallant and daring conduct on the previous day had attracted the admiration of his comrades, and called him to that station), placed on our extreme right, completed our line. Our cavalry was first despatched to the front of the enemy's left, for the purposes of attracting their notice, while an extensive island of timber afforded us an opportunity of concentrating our forces, and deploying from that point, agreeably to the previous design of the troops. Every evolution was performed with alacrity, the whole advancing rapidly in line, through an open prairie, without any protection whatever for our men. The artillery advanced and took station within two hundred yards of the enemy's breastwork, and commenced an effective fire with grape and canister.

"Colonel Sherman, with his regiment, having commenced the action upon our left wing, the whole line, at the centre and on the right, advancing in double-quick time, raised the war-cry, "*Remember the Alamo!*" received the enemy's fire, and advanced within point-blank shot, before a piece was discharged from our lines. Our line advanced without a halt, until they were in possession of the woodland and the enemy's breastwork—the right wing of Burleson's and the left of Millard's taking possession of the breastwork; our artillery having gallantly charged up within seventy yards of the enemy's cannon, when it was taken by our troops.

"The conflict lasted about eighteen minutes from the time of close action until we were in possession of the enemy's encampment, taking one piece of cannon (loaded), four stand of colors, all their camp-equipage, stores, and baggage. Our cavalry had charged and routed that of the enemy upon the right, and given pursuit to the fugitives, which did not cease until they arrived at the bridge which I have mentioned before—Captain Karnes, always among the foremost in danger, commanding the pursuers. The conflict in the breastwork lasted but a few moments; many of the troops encountered hand to hand, and, not having the advantage of bayonets on our side, our riflemen used their pieces as war-clubs, breaking many of them off at the breech. The rout commenced at half-past four, and the pursuit by the main army continued until twilight. A guard was then left in charge of the enemy's encampment, and our army returned with their killed and wounded. In the battle, our loss was two killed and twenty-three wounded, six of them mortally. The enemy's loss was six hundred and thirty killed, among whom was one general officer, four colonels, two lieutenant-colonels, five captains, twelve lieutenants; wounded two hundred and eight, of which were five colonels, three lieutenant-colonels, two second lieutenant-colonels, seven captains, one cadet; prisoners seven hundred and thirty—President-General Santa Anna, General Cos, four colonels, aides to General Santa Anna, and the colonel of the Guerrero battalion, are included in the number.

General Santa Anna was not taken until the 22d, and General Cos yesterday, very few having escaped. About six hundred muskets, three hundred sabres, and two hundred pistols, have been collected since the action. Several hundred mules and horses were taken, and nearly twelve thousand dollars in specie.

"For several days previous to the action, our troops were engaged in forced marches, exposed to excessive rains, and the additional inconvenience of extremely bad roads, badly supplied with rations and clothing; yet, amid every difficulty, they bore up with cheerfulness and fortitude, and performed their marches with spirit and alacrity—there was no murmuring.

"Previous to and during the action, my staff evinced every disposition to be useful, and were actively engaged in their duties. In the conflict I am assured that they demeaned themselves in such a manner as proved them worthy members of the army of San Jacinto. Colonel T. J. Rusk, Secretary of War, was on the field. For weeks his services had been highly beneficial to the army. In the battle, he was on the left wing, where Colonel Sherman's command first encountered and drove in the enemy: he bore himself gallantly, and continued his efforts and activity, remaining with the pursuers until resistance ceased.

"I have the honor of transmitting herewith a list of all the officers and men who were engaged in the action, which I respectfully request may be published, as an act of justice to the individuals. For the commanding general to attempt discrimination as to the conduct of those who commanded in the action, or those who were commanded, would be impossible. Our success in the action is conclusive proof of their daring intrepidity and courage; every officer and man proved himself worthy of the cause in which he battled, while the triumph received a lustre from the humanity which characterized their conduct after victory, and richly entitles them to the admiration and gratitude of their general. Nor should we withhold the tribute of our grateful thanks from that Being who rules the destinies of nations, and has, in the time of greatest need, enabled us to arrest a powerful invader while devastating our country.

"I have the honor, etc.,

"SAM HOUSTON,

"*Commander-in-Chief.*"

Report of THOMAS J. RUSK, *Secretary of War.*

"WAR DEPARTMENT, HEADQUARTERS, ARMY OF TEXAS,
"SAN JACINTO RIVER, *April* 22, 1836.

"*To His Excellency* DAVID G. BURNET, *President of Texas.*

"SIR: I have the honor to communicate to your excellency a brief account of a general engagement with the army of Santa Anna, at this place on the 21st instant.

"Our army, under the command of General Houston, arrived here on the 20th instant. The enemy, a few miles off at New Washington, apprised of our arrival, committed some depredations upon private property, and commenced their line of march to this point. They were unconscious of our approach until our standard was planted on the banks of the San Jacinto. Our position was a favorable one for battle. On the noon of the 20th, the appearance of our foe was hailed by our soldiers with enthusiasm. The enemy marched in good order, took a position in front of our encampment, on an eminence, within cannon-shot, where they planted their only piece of artillery, a brass nine-pounder; and then arrayed their cavalry and infantry a short distance on the right, under the shelter of a skirt of woods. In a short time, they commenced firing upon us; their cannon in front, their infantry on our left, and their cavalry changing their position on the right. A charge was made on the left of our camp by their infantry, which was promptly repelled by a few shots from our artillery, which forced them to retire. I have the satisfaction of stating that only two of our men were wounded, one very slightly, the other (Colonel Neill, of the artillery) not fatally.

"The attack ceased; the enemy retired and formed in two skirts of timber, and remained in that position, occasionally opening their cannon upon us, until just before sunset, when they attempted to draw off their forces. Their artillery and cavalry were removed to other points. Colonel Sherman, with sixty of our cavalry, charged upon theirs, consisting of upward of 100, killing and wounding several. Their infantry came to the assistance of their cavalry, and opened upon us an incessant fire for ten or fifteen minutes, which our men sustained with surprising firmness. Too much praise cannot be bestowed upon those who were engaged in this charge, for never was one of equal peril made with more courage, and terminated with less loss. Two of our men were severely wounded, but none killed. This terminated the movements of the day.

"Early next morning, about nine o'clock, the enemy received a reinforcement of 500 men, under the command of General Martin Prefecto de Cos, which increased their strength to 1,400 or 1,500 men. It was supposed that an attack upon our encampment would now be made; and having a good position, we stationed our artillery, and disposed of the forces, so as to receive the enemy to the best advantage. At three o'clock, however, the foe, instead of showing signs of attack, was evidently engaged in fortifying. We determined, therefore, immediately to assail him; and in half an hour we were formed in four divisions: the first, intended as our right wing, composed of the regulars under Colonel Millard, and the second division, under command of Colonel Sydney Sherman, formed our left wing. A division, commanded by Colonel Burleson, formed our centre. Our two six-pounders, under the command of Colonel Hockley, Captains Isaac N. Moreland and Stillwell, were drawn up on the right of the centre division. The cavalry, under command of Colonel Mirabeau B. Lamar, formed upon the right. At the command to move forward, all the divisions advanced in good order and high spirits. On arriving within reach of the enemy, a heavy fire was opened, first with their artillery on our cavalry. A general conflict now ensued. Orders were given to charge. Colonel Sherman's division moved up, and drove the enemy from the woods occupied by them on their right wing. At the same moment, Colonel Burleson's division, together with the regulars, charged upon and mounted the breastwork of the enemy, and drove them from their cannon; our artillery, the meanwhile, charging up and firing upon them with great effect. The cavalry, under Colonel Lamar, at the same time fell on them with great fury and great slaughter. Major-General Houston acted with great gallantry, encouraging his men to the attack, and heroically charged, in front of the infantry, within a few yards of the enemy, receiving at the same time a wound in his leg. The enemy soon took to flight, officers and all, some on foot and some on horseback. In ten minutes after the firing of the first gun, we were charging through the camp, and driving them before us. They fled in confusion and dismay down the river, followed closely by our troops for four miles. Some of them took the prairie, and were pursued by our cavalry; others were shot in attempting to swim the river; and in a short period the sanguinary conflict was terminated by the surrender of nearly all who were not slain in the combat. One-half of their army perished; the other half are prisoners, among whom are General Santa Anna himself, Colonel Almonté, and many other prominent officers of their army. The loss of the enemy is computed at over six hundred slain, and above six hundred prisoners; together with a *caballada* of several hundred mules taken, with much valuable baggage. Our loss, in point of numbers, is small, it being seven slain and fifteen wounded.

"This glorious achievement is attributed, not to superior force, but to the valor of our soldiers and the sanctity of our cause. Our army consisted of 750 effective men. This brave band achieved a victory as glorious as any on the records of history, and the happy consequences will be felt in Texas by succeeding generations. It has saved the country from the yoke of bondage; and all who mingled in it are entitled to the special munificence of government, and the heartfelt gratitude of every lover of liberty. The sun was sinking in the horizon as the battle commenced, but, at the close of the conflict, the sun of liberty and independence rose in Texas, never, it is to be hoped, to be obscured by the clouds of despotism. We have read of deeds of chivalry, and perused with ardor the annals of war; we have contemplated, with the highest emotions of sublimity, the loud-roaring thunder, the desolating tornado, and the withering simoom of the desert; but neither of these, nor all, inspired us with emotions like those felt on this occasion! The officers and men seemed to be actuated by a like enthusiasm. There was a general cry which pervaded the ranks—"*Remember the Alamo! remember La Bahia!*" These words electrified all. "Onward!" was the cry. The unerring aim and irresistible energy of the Texan army could not be withstood. It was freemen fighting against the minions of tyranny, and the result proved the inequality of such a contest.

"In a battle where every individual performed his duty, it might seem invidious to draw distinctions; but, while I do justice to all in expressing my high admiration of the bravery and gallant conduct of both officers and men, I hope I may be indulged in the expression of my highest approbation of the chivalrous conduct of Major James Collingsworth in almost every part of the engagement. Col. James Hockley, with his command of artillery, Col. Wharton, the adjutant-general, Major Cook, and, in fact, all the staff-officers, Col. Burleson and Col. Somervell on the right, Col. Millard in the centre, and Col. Sherman, Col. Bennett, and Major Wells on the left, and Col. Lamar on the extreme right with the cavalry—led on the charge and followed in the pursuit with dauntless bravery. All have my highest approbation. With such men, sustained as we shall be by the patriots and lovers of liberty in our mother-country, hateful Despotism cannot find a resting-place for the sole of her foot on the beautiful plains of Texas! A volume would not contain the deeds of individual daring and bravery. Each captain has been required to make report, and I hope justice will be done to all the brave spirits who mingled in the glorious achievement of yesterday.* My aide-de-camp, Dr. Motley, of Kentucky, fell near me, mortally wounded, and soon after

---

* Notwithstanding the fulness and many details given in these reports, neither contains the slightest allusion to Bob L——, who always looms foremost in my mind's eye when contemplating or reflecting upon the incidents of the battle of San Jacinto.

Bob L—— was a large, fine looking young volunteer from Georgia, who *did not hear the order* given to his company or regiment before the charge, to fall flat down on the ground, when they should see the flash of the enemy's cannon, and after the deadly missiles had passed harmlessly over their heads, to rise and continue the charge.

So when the charge was made and at the flash of the enemy's cannon, all his comrades fell down flat on the ground, Bob supposed they were all killed,

his spirit took its flight to join the immortal Milam and others in a better world.

"I have the honor to be, very respectfully, yours,

"THOMAS J. RUSK,

"*Secretary of War.*

"P. S.—Since writing the above, Gen. Cos has been brought in a prisoner by our cavalry.

"T. J. RUSK."

James A. Sylvester has the honor of capturing Santa Anna, but did not know his distinguished captive until he arrived in camp and was passing by the other prisoners (Col. John Milton Swisher, of Austin, familiarly known as *Milt. Swisher*, being on guard at the time), when *they* recognized him and exclaimed: "El Presidente! el Presidente!"

When taken, he said he was a private and then an aid to Santa Anna. He shed tears and kissed the hand of his captor, no doubt fearing that the mercy which he had shown to others would be meted out to him.

When brought to Gen. Houston, who was confined

---

and quickly concluding not to wait for another discharge, he broke like a quarter horse to the rear.

Poor Bob never could explain the matter to Gen. Houston's satisfaction, who sent for him after the battle, and advised him to marry into a brave family and cross the breed.

Thomas J Rusk

by his wound, he first acknowledged who he was. "I am Gen. Antonio Lopez de Santa Anna, and place myself at your disposition as a prisoner of war!"

Gen. Houston seated him on a tool chest, when Rusk, Almonté, and others joined them.

At his request, Santa Anna was given some opium, which he swallowed, after which he expressed a desire for peace between Texas and Mexico.

Gen. Houston granted an armistice, but declined to enter into negotiations for permanent peace, since, Texas having a government, he had no right to make peace. After some conversation about his treatment of Texans at the Alamo and Goliad, which Santa Anna tried to justify, the former by the rules of war, that, "when a fortress, insufficient to defend itself, was summoned to surrender, and refused, and caused the effusion of human blood, the vanquished, when it was taken, were devoted to execution," the latter, by the decrees of the Mexican Government making them *pirates.* Gen. Houston obtained from him the following order to his second in command:

"ARMY OF OPERATIONS.

"EXCELLENT SIR: Having yesterday evening, with the small division under my immediate command, had an encounter with the enemy, which notwithstanding I had previously taken all possible precautions, proved unfortunate, I am, in consequence, a prisoner in the hands of the enemy. Under these circumstances, your excellency will order General Gaona with his division to countermarch to Bexar, and wait for orders. Your excellency will also, with the division under your immediate command, march to the same place. The division under command of General Urrea will retire to Guadalupe Victoria. I have agreed with General Houston for an armistice, until matters can be so regulated that the war will cease forever.

"Your excellency will take the proper steps for the support of the army, which from this time remains under your command, using the moneys lately arrived from Metamoras, the provisions on hand there, as well as those at Victoria, and also the twenty thousand dollars withdrawn from Bexar, and which are now in that treasury.

"I hope your excellency will, without failure, comply with these dispositions—advising me, by return of the courier, that you have already commenced their execution. God and liberty!

"CAMP AT SAN JACINTO, *April 2d*, 1839.

"ANTONIO LOPEZ DE SANTA ANNA.

"TO HIS EXCELLENCY DON VICENTE FILISOLA,
"*General of Division.*"

After receiving this document, General Houston caused Santa Anna's tent to be placed near him, gave him his baggage, sent him his servants, staff officers, and treated him generally as kindly as a prisoner could be treated.

To the victors belong the spoils: so, after the commissary-general had sold all the captured property, which did not amount to $20,000, he distributed their shares to men and officers, who voted $3,000 to the *Navy*.

The President and his Cabinet at the approach of the enemy at Harrisburg left that place and reassembled at Galveston, from whence the following order was issued:

"DEPARTMENT OF WAR, GALVESTON, *April* 26, 1836.

"TO GENERAL SAM HOUSTON: If you consider it inexpedient to risk an engagement with the enemy, and consider a retreat *inevitable* from the position you now occupy, you are hereby ordered to march with the army under your command to the nearest and most convenient point to this island, giving information of the same to this department, when transports will be sent forthwith to cross the troops to this island.

"WARREN D. C. HALL,
"*Acting Secretary of War.*"

Soon after this the government learned of the change of things and the Cabinet came to San Jacinto, and entered into negotiations with their illustrious prisoner for a treaty of peace.

Upon this question the Cabinet divided. The President, D. G. Burnet—who, says Kennedy, "was a man of unblemished reputation, courteous manners, and intellectual attainments, the son of a physician in Newark, New Jersey, ... who, in the affairs of Texas, had always been distinguished by calmness and moderation, and had not unfrequently been exposed to censure for declining to keep pace with popular impatience. Whose prudence and forbearance, united with firmness and perseverance, well qualified him to fill the difficult post to which he had been called by the Convention,"—also Zavala, the Vice-President, the Secretary of State, James Collingsworth, the successor of S. P. Carson, and Peter W. Grayson, who succeeded David Thomas as Attorney-General, were in favor of making a treaty; while Mirabeau B. Lamar, who succeeded General Rusk as Secretary of War, who succeeded General Houston, disabled, as commander-in-chief, and *Robert Potter*, the Secretary of the Navy, were opposed to treating with Santa Anna at all, but were in favor of trying and punishing him.

In a letter to the Cabinet, Secretary Lamar eloquently said that "*he rather considered him as an apprehended murderer than as a prisoner of war.*

"The conduct of General Santa Anna will not permit me to view him in any other light. A chieftain battling for what he conceives to be the rights of his country, however mistaken in his views, may be privileged to make hot and vigorous war upon the foe; but when, in violation of all the principles of civilized conflict, he avows and acts upon the revolting policy of extermination and rapine, slaying the surrendered, and plundering whom he slays, he forfeits the commiseration of mankind, by sinking the character of the hero into that of an abhorred murderer. The President of Mexico has pursued such a war upon the citizens of this republic. He has caused to be published to the world a decree, denouncing as pirates beyond the reach of his clemency all who shall be found rallying around the standard of our independence. In accordance with this decree, he has turned over to the sword the bravest and best of our friends and fellow-citizens after they had grounded their arms, under the most solemn pledge that their lives should be spared. He has fired our dwellings, laid waste our luxuriant fields, excited servile and insurrectionary war, violated plighted faith, and inhumanly ordered the cold-blooded butchery of prisoners who had been betrayed into capitulation by heartless professions. I humbly conceive that the proclamation of such principles, and the perpetration of such crimes, place the offender out of the pale of negotiation, and demand at our hands other treatment than what is due to a mere prisoner of war. Instinct condemns him as a murderer, and reason justifies the verdict. Nor should the ends of justice be averted because of the exalted station of the criminal, or be made to give way to the suggestions of interest, or any cold considerations of policy. He who sacrifices human life at the shrine of ambition is a murderer, and deserves the punishment and infamy of one; the higher the offender, the greater reason for its infliction. I am, therefore, of opinion that our prisoner, General Santa Anna, has forfeited his life by the highest of all crimes, and is not a suitable object for the exercise of our pardoning prerogative.

"I still feel that strict justice requires this course; that it is sustained by reason, and will receive the sanction of the present generation, as well as the approving voice of posterity. If the Cabinet could concur with me in this view of the subject, and march boldly up to what I conceive to be the line of right, it would form a bright page in the history of this infant nation. It would read well in the future annals of the present period, that the first act of this young republic was to teach the Caligula of the age that, in the administration of public justice, the vengeance of the law falls alike impartially on the prince and the peasant. It is time such a lesson should be taught the despots of the earth: they have too long enjoyed an exemption from the common punishment of crime. Throned in power, they banquet on the life of man, and then purchase security by the dispensation of favors. We have it in our power now to give an impulse to a salutary change in this order of things. We are sitting in judgment upon the life of a stupendous villain, who, like all others of his race, hopes to escape the blow of merited vengeance by the strong appeals which his exalted station enables him to make to the weak or selfish principles of nature. Shall he be permitted to realize his hopes or not? Shall our resentment be propitiated by promises, or shall we move sternly onward, regardless of favor or affection, to the infliction of a righteous punishment? My voice is '*Fiat justitia ruat cœlum.*'"

"Let the same punishment be awarded him which we would feel bound in honor and conscience to inflict on a subaltern charged and convicted of a like offence: this is all that justice can require. If he have committed no act which would bring condemnation on a private individual, then let him be protected; but if he have perpetrated crimes which a man in humble life would have to expiate upon the scaffold, then why shield him from the just operations of a law to which another is held amenable? The exalted criminal finds security in negotiation, whilst the subaltern offender is given over to the sword of the executioner. Surely no considerations of interest or policy can atone for such a violation of principle. View the matter in every possible light, and Santa Anna is still a murderer.

"It will be useless to talk to a soldier of San Jacinto about national independence and national domain, so long as the bones of his murdered brethren lie bleaching on the prairies unrevenged. Treble the blessings proposed to be gained by this negotiation will be considered as poor and valueless, when weighed against that proud and high resentment which the soldier feels for wrongs received. In the day of battle the animating cry was 'ALAMO!' And why? Because it was known that the slaughterer of the Alamo was then in the field: it was him that was sought. It was not against the poor and degraded instruments of his tyranny that we warred; they fell, it is true, before our avenging strokes like grass before the reaper's sickle.

"The great difficulty in dealing with our prisoner as his crimes deserve arises, as I have already intimated, from the fact that education will not permit us to strip him of his ill-gotten honors, and view him in the attitude of a private individual. We are taught, by what we see around us in early childhood, to reverence wealth and power, and it is almost impossible in after-life to emancipate the mind from the slavish thraldom; so that when we approach the guilty lords of creation, there is an involuntary shrinking back, as if we deemed them privileged in enormity, and not amenable to us for their outrages. We feel that we should not deal with them as we would with ordinary men. If a peasant, convicted of murder, shall offer a bribe for the preservation of his life, it meets with prompt and indignant repulsion; but if a prince, under like circumstances, shall, in the fulness of his power, propose some lordly favor, it is accepted with avidity, as if it were upon our part a virtuous performance of duty. Besides this, we flatter ourselves that there is nothing wrong in the transaction, because we are not personally and privately the beneficiaries of the bargain; but certainly the right or wrong doth not depend upon who are the recipients, whether the public or an individual. If we have a right thus to act for the good of the nation, we can do the same for the good of a community; and if for a community, we can for a family; and if for a family, why may not that family be our own? This mode of reasoning will readily exhibit the fallacy, if not the immorality, of that doctrine which draws a distinction between a high and a low offender, and justifies a negotiation with the one which would be odious and criminal with the other.

"Never did the broad eye of day look upon a fouler murder; never were a better or a braver people sacrificed to a tyrant's ferocity. The most of them were youthful heroes.

"I have always thought, and still believe, that our sole reliance should be upon our swords, and not upon the faith of Santa Anna. If the armies now on the retreat shall dare a countermarch, there will not be in the next battle a Mexican left to tell the tale of their defeat; and if another expedition against us shall be gotten up in the fall or the spring, there will come into our country such a cavalcade of heroes as will make their chivalry skip. The very first army that turns its face to the East will awaken a war which will move onward and onward over the broad prairies of the West, knowing no termination until it reaches the walls of Mexico, where we shall plant the standard of the Single Star, and send forth our decrees in the voice of our artillery.

"That my feelings and opinions may not be misapprehended, I beg leave, by way of recapitulation, to state, that, toward the common soldiers among our Mexican prisoners I cherish no malice or resentment looking upon the most of them in the light of unwilling instruments in the hands of tyranny; neither can I perceive in the conduct of the officers any particular act which might not be considered as legitimate in a soldier devoted to his profession, or in a patriot enlisted in the cause of his country. These, after an exchange of prisoners, I would retain in the custody of the Government until the conclusion of the war; but, viewing General Santa Anna altogether in a different attitude, I would adopt the course in reference to him which I have already urged. His crimes being sanguinary, I would read his punishment from the Code of Draco."

But notwithstanding this eloquent appeal a majority of the Cabinet, imbued with the merciful sentiment of Him who commanded sinful mortals to do good for evil, to pray for their enemies—and while expiring upon the cross appealingly said in behalf of his murderers: "*Father, forgive them; they know not what they do*,"—voted for peace, and made the following treaties with the Mexican president:

TREATY OF VELASCO, MAY 14, 1836.

PUBLIC AGREEMENT.

Articles of Agreement entered into between His Excellency DAVID G. BURNET, *President of the Republic of Texas, of the one part, and His Excellency General* ANTONIO LOPEZ DE SANTA ANNA, *President-General-in-Chief of the Mexican Army, of the other part:—*

ARTICLE 1. General Antonio Lopez de Santa Anna agrees that he will not take up arms, nor will he exercise his influence to cause them to be taken up, against the people of Texas, during the present war of independence.

ARTICLE 2. All hostilities between the Mexican and Texan troops will cease immediately, both on land and water.

ARTICLE 3. The Mexican troops will evacuate the territory of Texas, passing to the other side of the Rio Grande del Norte.

ARTICLE 4. The Mexican army, in its retreat, shall not take the property of any person without his consent and just indemnification, using only such articles as may be necessary for its subsistence in cases where the owners may not be present, and remitting to the commander of the army of Texas, or to the commissioners to be appointed for the adjustment of such matters, an account of the value of the property consumed, the place where taken, and the name of the owner, if it can be ascertained.

ARTICLE 5. That all private property, including horses, cattle, negro slaves, or indentured persons of whatever denomination, that may have been captured by any portion of the Mexican army, or may have taken refuge in the said army, since the commencement of the late invasion, shall be restored to the commander of the Texan army, or to such other persons as may be appointed by the Government of Texas to receive them.

ARTICLE 6. The troops of both armies will refrain from coming into contact with each other; and, to this end, the commander of the army of Texas will be careful not to approach within a shorter distance of the Mexican army than five leagues.*

ARTICLE 7. The Mexican army shall not make any other delay on its march than that which is necessary to take up their hospitals, baggage, etc., and to cross the rivers. Any delay, not necessary to these purposes, to be considered an infraction of this agreement.

ARTICLE 8. By express, to be immediately despatched, this agreement shall be sent to General Filisola, and to General T. J. Rusk, commander of the Texan

---

* Nearly thirteen and one-sixth miles.

army, in order that they may be apprised of its stipulations; and, to this end, they will exchange engagements to comply with the same.

ARTICLE 9. That all Texan prisoners now in possession of the Mexican army, or its authorities, be forthwith released, and furnished with free passports to return to their homes; in consideration of which a corresponding number of Mexican prisoners, rank and file, now in possession of the Government of Texas, shall be immediately released. The remainder of the Mexican prisoners that continue in possession of the Government of Texas, to be treated with due humanity: any extraordinary comforts that may be furnished them to be at the charge of the Government of Mexico.

ARTICLE 10. General Antonio Lopez de Santa Anna will be sent to Vera Cruz, as soon as it shall be deemed proper.

The contracting parties sign this instrument for the above-mentioned purposes, by duplicate, at the port of Velasco, this the 14th day of May, 1836.

DAVID G. BURNET,
ANT°. LOPEZ DE SANTA ANNA.

JAMES COLLINGSWORTH, *Secretary of State.*
BAILEY HARDEMAN, *Secretary of the Treasury.*
P. H. GRAYSON, *Attorney-General.*

SECRET AGREEMENT.

ANTONIO LOPEZ DE SANTA ANNA, *General-in-Chief of the Army of Operations, and President of the Republic of Mexico, before the Government established in Texas, solemnly pledges himself to fulfil the Stipulations contained in the following Articles, so far as concerns himself:—*

ARTICLE 1. He will not take up arms, nor cause them to be taken up, against the people of Texas, during the present war for independence.

ARTICLE 2. He will give his orders that, in the shortest time, the Mexican troops may leave the territory of Texas.

ARTICLE 3. He will so prepare matters in the Cabinet of Mexico, that the mission that may be sent thither by the Government of Texas may be well received, and that by means of negotiations all differences may be settled, and the independence that has been declared by the Convention may be acknowledged.

ARTICLE 4. A treaty of commerce, amity, and limits, will be established between Mexico and Texas, the territory of the latter not to extend beyond the Rio Bravo del Norte.

ARTICLE 5. The present return of General Santa Anna to Vera Cruz being indispensable for the purpose of effecting his solemn engagements, the Government of Texas will provide for his immediate embarkation for said port.

ARTICLE 6. This instrument, being obligatory on one part as well as on the other, will be signed in duplicate, remaining folded and sealed until the negotiations shall have been concluded, when it will be restored to his excellency General Santa Anna; no use of it to be made before that time, unless there should be an infraction by either of the contracting parties.

PORT OF VELASCO, *May the 14th*, 1836.

ANTO. LOPEZ DE SANTA ANNA.
DAVID G BURNET.

JAMES COLLINGSWORTH, *Secretary of State.*
BAILEY HARDEMAN, *Secretary of the Treasury.*
P. H. GRAYSON, *Attorney-General.*

The ratification by General Filisola of the *public agreement*, in accordance with the provision of the 8th article, took place on the 26th May, 1836, more than a month after the battle of San Jacinto.

CHAPTER X.

Retreat of the Mexican Army under Filisola.—General Woll taken prisoner.—Houston, his wound, retirement, etc.—Santa Anna and the Texas Cabinet at Velasco.—His *protest* and the President's answer, etc.

WHEN news of the defeat and capture of Santa Anna reached Gen. Filisola, he was at the Brazos. "On the afternoon of the 23d," says Filisola, "I was concluding the operation of sending across the river the section with which General Gaona was to march to Nacogdoches, when a soldier of the frontier dragoons presented to me a small piece of paper, written with a pencil, by Colonel Mariano Garcia, first aid of Guerrero, in which he informed me of the unfortunate occurrence of the afternoon of the 21st. A short time after, some fugitives arrived, and among them Captain Miguel Aguirre, of the Tampico regiment, wounded in the action in the thigh, by a rifle-ball, who said that the defeat had been perfect, and the existence of the President quite doubtful. Such news made me immediately suspend the passage of the river by the force that was to have gone with Gaona, and to send a picket of cavalry in the direction of the battle-ground, as much to acquire correct information of the actual fate of the President as to protect the fugitives who might have escaped. But the enemy had burnt the bridge, which was the only road for retreating; and consequently the picket accomplished little or nothing in either respect, for all had been killed or made prisoners. Alarm and discouragement was general among all classes, for it was believed that all the prisoners, the President included, would have been shot, as a reprisal for the conduct observed with theirs at Bexar and Goliad."

Soon this *alarm and discouragement* turned to *a panic* and *a flight*—the road from the ferry over the Brazos to Victoria, was strewn with wagons, baggage, artillery, kettles, blankets and broken-down horses. The streams were all swollen, the roads all miry, and the commissary of the unfortunate Mexicans empty. A quart of corn sold for a dollar, and a loaf of bread for three dollars. Even officers went days without bread to eat.

On the 28th, *Deaf Smith* caught up with the fugitives and handed to Filisola the order of Santa Anna to retreat, but he didn't stop; he kept on retreating, yet sent Gen. Woll back to see about things with a flag of truce. Gen. Houston, who still commanded, fearing that if tidings went back through Gen. Woll of the paucity of the Texan army, that possibly Filisola, who yet commanded more than four thousand men, might again advance and try *his* luck in another battle—put Gen. Woll under arrest.

Gen. Woll, wishing to return to Filisola, appealed to the flag of truce which he bore into the Texans' camp, but it was not of any use. Gen. Houston thought he had found out too much, and detained him.

On the 5th May, 1836, he turned over the command of the army to Gen. Rusk, and on taking leave of *the heroes of San Jacinto* issued the following very complimentary address:

"Comrades: Circumstances connected with the battle of the 21st render our separation for the present unavoidable. I need not express to you the many painful sensations which that necessity inflicts upon me. I am solaced, however, by the hope that we will soon be reunited in the great cause of liberty. Brigadier-General Rusk is appointed to the command of the army for the present. I confide in his valor, his patriotism, and his wisdom. His conduct in the battle of San Jacinto was sufficient to insure your confidence and regard. The enemy, though retreating, are still within the limits of Texas. Their situation being known to you, you cannot be taken by surprise. . . . . In taking leave of my brave comrades in arms, I cannot suppress the expression of that pride which I so justly feel in having had the honor to command them in person; nor will I with hold the tribute of my warmest admiration and gratitude for the promptness with which my orders were executed, and union maintained through the army."

It has been said that Gen. Houston did not wish to fight Santa Anna at San Jacinto, but wished to retreat towards Nacogdoches and the Red lands.

Gen. M. B. Lamar says (*Galveston News*, June 23d, 1855): "Some time after the council of war, I met Gen. Houston, and expressed to him the strong desire of the army to make battle. He replied nearly as follows: 'Sir, can I whip Santa Anna and his whole army by myself?' Would you have me attack them alone? The officers are all opposed to fighting, and so are the men. I have always been ready to fight, but the army has not, and how can I battle?' This language astonished me much, because it was so directly opposed to my knowledge of facts; but being a stranger in the army, and scarcely acquainted with Gen. Houston, I dropped the subject. Soon after this, I saw Col. John A. Wharton, and repeated to him what Gen. Houston had said. Wharton inquired: 'Do you think he will fight?' My reply was: 'He says he will.' Taking leave of me, the Colonel repaired immediately to Gen. Houston, and asked him if he would order a battle provided the army was ready to make the attack. Houston said he would.

This I got from Wharton, immediately after his leaving Houston. In a short time there was a general rejoicing through the camp: and Wharton was dashing from point to point, ordering a general parade, and *marshalling the troops for battle!* . . . At the moment we were all preparing for battle, and the lines were actually forming, Houston came to me, and said, in a whining and despairing tone: 'Col. Lamar, do you really think we ought to fight?' My reply was: 'Gen. Houston, your question comes too late. What did we come here for, but to fight?'"

Gen. Houston after speaking of Sherman's charge on the 20th, says:

"Things remained without any change until about twelve o'clock, when the general was asked to call a council of war. No council of war had ever been solicited before. It seemed strange to him. What indications had appeared he did not know. The council was called, however, consisting of six field officers and the Secretary of War. The proposition was put to the council, 'Shall we attack the enemy in position, or receive their attack in ours?' The two junior officers—for such is the way of taking the sense of courts in the army—were in favor of attacking the enemy in position. The four seniors, and the Secretary of War, who spoke, said, that 'to attack veteran troops with raw militia is a thing unheard of; to charge upon the enemy without bayonets in an open prairie, had never been known; our situation is strong; in it we can whip all Mexico.'" Understanding this as the sense of the council, the general dismissed them. They went to their respective places.

"In the morning the sun had risen brightly, and he determined with this omen, 'To-day the battle shall take place.'"

But overlooking the fact that a challenge passed between Gens. Lamar and Houston, that they were enemies—that the Secretary of State, S. P. Carson, wrote to Gen. Houston on the 14th of April, 1836: "My view is, that you should fall back, if *necessary*, to the Sabine. I am warranted in saying that volunteer troops will come on in numbers, from the United States. . . . . . You must fall back, and hold out, and let nothing goad or provoke you to a battle, unless you can, *without doubt*, whip them, or unless you are compelled to fight."

Overlooking also the following letter to Henry Raguet, of Nacogdoches:

"CAMP AT HARRISBURG, *April* 19*th*, 1836.

"This morning we are in preparation to meet Santa Anna. It is the only chance of saving Texas. From time to time I have looked for reinforcements, in vain. The Convention adjourning to Harrisburg struck panic throughout the country. Texas could have started at least 4,000 men; we have only about 700 to march with, besides the camp guard. We go to conquer. *It is wisdom growing out of necessity to meet and fight the enemy now. Every consideration enforces it. No previous occasion would justify it. The troops are in fine spirits, and now is the time for action.*

"Adjutant-General Wharton, Ins. Gen. Hockley, aide-de-camp Horton, aides-de-camp W. H. Patton, Collingsworth.

"Volunteer aids, Perry, Perry.

"Maj. Cook, Assistant Inspector-General will be with me.

"We shall use our best efforts to fight the enemy, to such advantage as will insure victory though the odds are greatly against us. I leave the result in the hands of a wise God, and rely upon His providence.

"My country will do justice to those who serve her. The rights for which we fight will be secured, and Texas free.

"Sam Houston,

"*Commander-in-Chief.*

"Col. Rusk is in the field.

"Houston."

Yet it is consonant to Gen. Houston's character,

that he made it appear that he wished to retreat rather than fight.

It is said that he was very anxious for his oldest son to be named after him, yet he insisted on Mrs. Houston's naming the boy herself, saying *he would have nothing to do in the matter whatever.*

Mrs. Houston begged him to name the child! No, *he would have no hand in it.* Finally she asked him to *suggest* a name.

"Well, madam," said he, "my mother named me Sam, and I'm not ashamed of it. Suppose *you* name the boy Sam!" And the child was named *Sam.*

So he may have acted with regard to the battle of San Jacinto—appearing not to desire it, yet really anxious for it.

After issuing the address as stated, in consequence of his wounded ankle, Gen. Houston went to New Orleans for medical treatment, where more than twenty pieces of fractured bone were taken out.

In the meantime the Texan Cabinet had moved to Velasco, where the treaties with Santa Anna were made, and on the 1st of June, in pursuance of *the public agreement,* placed Santa Anna, Cols. Almonté and Nunez, with Caro, his private secretary, on board the *Invincible,* J. Brown, commander, with the intention of sending him to Vera Cruz.

Santa Anna, with the approbation of the Cabinet,

issued the following short farewell to the Texan army:

"My Friends: I have been a witness of your courage in the field of battle, and know you to be generous. Rely with confidence on my sincerity, and you shall never have cause to regret the kindness shown me. In returning to my native land, I beg you to receive the thanks of your grateful friend. Farewell!

"Ant°. Lopez de Santa Anna."

"Velasco, *June* 1, 1836."

But before the *Invincible* sailed, Gen. T. J. Green, with 230 volunteers, arrived from New Orleans on the steamer *Ocean.* A public meeting was held, violent speeches made, and great opposition expressed to the release of Santa Anna. "In this state of things," says Gen. Green, "President Burnet addressed me a note, requesting an interview, and asking my opinion in this emergency. I told him that, as to any violence being offered to him or his Cabinet, I pledged my honor to shield him and them with my life; but that I was of opinion that, in accordance with the overwhelming public will of the citizens of the country, he should remand the prisoner ashore, and await the public will to determine his fate. The President promptly replied that he would do so."

Santa Anna and suite were disembarked and again placed under guard.

Army supplies were short at Velasco and the want of provisions sorely vexed the volunteers.

An address was written, signed by officers and men, to the President, saying: "We shall not, however, address you in that spirit of irritation and indignation which pervades every one in this army, but in the tone which should ever characterize the *intercourse between the ruling parties* in a country." After setting forth their privations and want of provisions, they continue: "And to whom are we to charge these injuries? Surely to you, as the President of this republic! It was your duty to have paid particular attention to the army; to have inquired out their wants, and relieved them. It was surely your duty to have caused provisions, at least, to have been furnished, and to have dropped all other matters until this was done; and you will not be surprised to learn that the indignation and exasperation of the army is now very great at the total failure to pay attention to them, *and the consequences may be serious if redress is not had.* And we now *require* that this army be immediately furnished with a sufficiency of such provisions and clothes as the public may possess or can be procured. . . . . In conclusion," they said, "we repeat to you, General Santa Anna *must be safely secured*, and placed at the disposition of the coming Congress."

On receiving this address the President remonstrated. He reminded the citizens in the field, that "deeds of valor were not alone sufficient to establish the high character of an enlightened, patriotic, and Christian people—a scrupulous regard to the established and beneficent principles of morality were equally indispensable. Their country had but recently aspired to a standing among the nations of the earth; her character, only partially displayed at home, had not been developed abroad; and much of her future happiness and prosperity depended upon the moral qualities that should be unfolded to the world in the development of that character. The Government of Texas had deliberately entered into a treaty with the President, Santa Anna; that treaty might or might not be wise; be it what it might, it had been solemnly made, and the good faith of Texas was pledged for its consummation. The treaty had for its ultimate object a firm peace with Mexico, based upon the full recognition of Texan independence. The price to be paid for a blessing, great in the estimation of every good citizen and patriotic soldier, was the enlargement of the President, Santa Anna, and his restoration to Mexico.

"It was alleged, that Santa Anna was faithless and

unworthy of trust—that he was a prisoner, and incapable of treating—and a murderer, that ought to be executed. To this he replied that *the government had already treated* with him, and that *he had performed*, and *was daily performing*, part of his stipulations The treaty having been ratified by executory compliance on one part, was irrevocably and solemnly binding on the other. Besides, the government believed that Santa Anna's highest political interests would require the complete execution of the principal stipulation in his part of the treaty. 'Is there any man in Texas who does not believe that it is impossible for Mexico to subdue this country, and retain it as an integral part of the Mexican Republic? No man in Texas is more fully and impressively convinced of the impossibility than is the President, Santa Anna. He has learned the fact by sore experience, the best possible teacher of practical truths. Will he then be faithless to his own plain interests, and to the interests of his country?'

"It was objected that Santa Anna was a murderer, and ought to be tried and executed. He (President Burnet) had yet to learn the principle of international or civil law that would justify the courts, civil or military, of one belligerent nation in taking cognizance of the official military acts of the opposing commander-in-chief. But supposing the right of jurisdiction to exist, they were debarred from exercising it by the military convention agreed upon and ratified between General Houston and the Mexican chief, before the Government were apprised of his capture, in pursuance of which, General Filisola had agreed to evacuate their territory, and had already passed the Nueces, and was probably by that time crossing the Rio Grande, at the head of 5,000 men."

In conclusion he objected to having his duties prescribed by *an armed force*, which, if adopted as a precedent, might end in *military misrule.*

No doubt there was cause for complaint on the part of the troops, for if nothing to eat is not a good cause, what can be? But who could remove that cause? 'Tis strange—but 'tis true—*the horse marines* did it, in this way: Major I. W. Burton, with a company of Rangers, was commanded to scour the coast from Velasco to Copano, and discovering a vessel in the bay of Copano, signalled the same to send its boat ashore, when, in answer, a boat with five Mexicans landed who were immediately captured, and the boat manned by sixteen Rangers—these hastened back to the vessel, boarded and took it. With this vessel, which was called the *Watchman*, loaded with provisions for the Mexican army, Major Burton approached and captured two others—the *Comanche* and *Fanny Butler*, *both also freighted with provisions*, and the three sent into Velasco. Major Burton and his Rangers were called *horse marines*, and by these valuable cargoes relieved the wants of the troops.

Gen. Santa Anna, mortified, and no doubt extremely troubled at his longer detainment, on the 9th of June sent to President Burnet the following *Protest:*

"I protest against the violation of the faith engaged in the agreement made between me and the Government of Texas, signed the 14th of May ult. and commenced verbally with the general-in-chief of the army of Texas, Sam Houston, and T. J. Rusk, Secretary of War.

"1st. For having been treated more like an ordinary criminal than as a prisoner of war, the head of a respectable nation, even after the agreements had been commenced.

"2d. For the treatment as prisoner of war, and ill usage received by the Mexican general, Adrian Woll, who had come to the Texan camp with a flag of truce, under the safeguard and word of honor of Gen. Houston, and with the consent of the members of the Cabinet.

"3d. Against the non-fulfilment of the exchange of prisoners, stipulated in the 9th article, inasmuch as, up to the present time, not even one Mexican prisoner of war has been set at liberty, notwithstanding the liberty given to all the Texans in possession of the army under my command.

"4th. Because the *sine qua non* of the 10th article, as follows, has not been carried into effect: which is, that I shall be sent to Vera Cruz 'when the government shall deem it proper;' whereas the President himself, and the Cabinet of Texas, being convinced that I had punctually fulfilled all my engagements, viz., that the Mexican army, 4,000 strong, should retreat from the position it occupied on the Brazos to beyond the 'Rio Grande;' that all the property should be given up, also the prisoners of war—had determined on my embarking in the Texan schooner of war, the *Invincible*, in which I finally did embark on the 1st June instant, after addressing a short farewell to the Texans, wherein I thanked them for their generous behavior, and offered my eternal gratitude.

"5th. For the act of violence committed on my person, and abuse to which I have been exposed, in compelling me to come again ashore, on the 4th instant, merely because 130 volunteers, under the command of General Thomas J. Green, recently landed on the beach at Velasco from New Orleans, had, with tumults and with threats, requested that my person should be placed at their disposal.

"Finally, I protest against the violence kept up towards me, by being placed in a narrow prison, surrounded with sentinels, and suffering privations which absolutely render life insupportable, or tend to hasten death; and finally, for being uncertain in regard to my future fate, and that of the other prisoners, notwithstanding a solemn treaty."

To the protest of Santa Anna, President Burnet answered the next day, with "profound mortification," and *plead* the action of *the army*, or the troops at Velasco.

"But," he added, "the causes that have produced the constraint under which the government have acted are not unknown to you, and I should regret to believe that you were incapable of giving to them a just appreciation. The citizens, and the citizen soldiers of Texas, have felt, and do feel, a deep, intense, and righteous indignation at the many atrocities which have been perpetrated by the troops lately under your Excellency's command; and especially at the barbarous massacre of the brave Colonel Fannin and his gallant companions. How far your Excellency participated in that abominable and inglorious slaughter I am not disposed to conjecture; but it is both natural and true that the people of Texas impute it to your Excellency's special command.

"1st. I do not precisely comprehend the character of the treatment objected to, and would have been pleased to have had the specifications. If your Excellency alludes to the accommodations which have been assigned to you, I would reply that I have cheerfully subjected my own sick family to many hardships in order to render to your Excellency the best accommodations in our power. That we are at present destitute of the ordinary comforts of life is mainly attributable to your Excellency's visit to our new country; and on this account we feel less regret that you should partake of our privations.

"2d. Your second protest, relating to the treatment experienced by the Mexican general, Adrian Woll, involves some facts which I do sincerely deplore, but for which this government is not strictly responsible.

"Your Excellency is sensible that we have done all in our power to guarantee the safe return of Gen. Woll to the Mexican camp; but our orders have been contravened by the commander of the Texan army, at a remote distance from the seat of government. The reasons that have actuated that officer have not been fully detailed to us; but we are informed that they are predicated on some alleged imprudences of Gen. Woll, whose good discretion, we know, has not been very conspicuously manifested during his stay amongst us.

"3d. The third article of your protest is 'against the non-fulfilment of the exchange of prisoners stipulated in the ninth article, inasmuch as, up to the present time, not one Mexican prisoner of war has been set at liberty, notwithstanding the liberty given to all the Texans in possession of the army under my command.'

"Your Excellency seems to have a more minute intelligence on this subject than has come to my knowledge; for I have no official information of a single Texan prisoner having been given up under the treaty. Some of the intended victims, the companions of the murdered Fannin, have happily effected their escape, and safely arrived amongst us; but these cannot be considered as liberated in the sense of the treaty; whereas, this government has gratuitously discharged several Mexican captives, and defrayed their expenses to New Orleans, the destination which they solicited.

"4th. The fourth clause of your Excellency's protest has been antecedently answered in part. Your Excellency's recollection has betrayed you into an error, when you say, 'the President himself, and the Cabinet of Texas, being convinced that I had punctually fulfilled all my engagements,' etc.

"This government were convinced that your Excellency had complied with some of your stipulations, and this conviction aggravates the mortification which the late events have inflicted upon them. But they were not informed that 'all the property had been given up; or that any of the prisoners had been restored, as your Excellency erroneously imagines. On the contrary, we were advised that large herds of cattle had been driven in advance of the retreating army; and that a few only of the slaves that had been abducted were returned.

"It is due to your Excellency to say, that the government confidently believed that these restorations would be effected as early as a proper convenience would admit. But I am induced to advert to another fact, in relation to which it would be difficult to extend the same charitable exculpation to the officers of the Mexican army. It has been reported that the walls of the Alamo at Bexar have been prostrated, and that the valuable brass artillery attached to that fortress have been melted down and destroyed.

"There were many painful, and pleasing, and glorious reminiscences connected with that Alamo, which renders its wanton dilapidation peculiarly odious to every Texan spirit; and your Excellency needs not to be informed that the destruction of it was an infraction of the armistice, and a violation of the treaty.

"5th. In reply to your Excellency's fifth protestation, I remark, that the painful circumstances which induced the government to direct your debarkation have already been adverted to in a spirit of frankness and of self-humiliation, which a consciousness of error alone could extort. It were superfluous to repeat the causes which induced this Government to vary its discretion in regard to the time they should deem the departure of your Excellency to be proper. I am not sensible of any act of 'violence and abuse' to which you were exposed, that was not necessarily concomitant on your return to shore.

"To your final protest I reply, that while you are a prisoner ordinary precautions are inevitable. I have not been apprised of anything more; and your privations (as alleged) are those we suffer ourselves."

For being uncertain in regard to my future fate! Poor wretch! no doubt he was sincere in his protest, *and wanted to go home.*

But no man can put off the law of God which pervades the universe, and rewards or punishes every human action, making it *foolish to do evil*, and *wise to do good.*

Well might he exclaim, in the language of the poet:

"That high All-seer, which I dallied with,
Hath turned my feigned prayer on my head,
And given in earnest what I begg'd in jest.
Thus doth *He* force the swords of wicked men
To turn their own points on their masters' bosoms."

And thus a knowledge of the law of *retribution* should ever stay the evil-doers' hands, for

"Our acts our angels are, or good or ill,
Our fatal shadows that walk by us still!"

CHAPTER XI.

The Policy of the United States towards Texas.—Instructions to the District-Attorneys.—Sympathy of the people for Texans.—Austin's great success and letter to Houston.—Henry Clay speaks of Texas and San Jacinto.—Resolutions pass Congress, and Morfit sent to Texas.—Gorastiza and President Jackson.—Urrea supersedes Filisola in command of the Mexican army.—Santa Anna and Austin.—Efforts for Peace.—The Army.—Lamar appointed *Major-General.*—His Rejection by the Army.

THE government at Washington, D.C., gave no encouragement to the Texas revolutionists. Soon after the battle of Gonzales, the administration, at the instance of the Mexican representative at Washington, caused letters to be written and sent to the United States District-Attorneys on the frontier and Gulf coast, instructing them, as far as they could legally, to enforce the existing treaty with Mexico, and give neither aid nor comfort to her rebellious colonists.

But these colonists went from the United States to settle Texas, and left fathers, mothers, brothers, and sisters behind them, who listened with eagerness for news from their loved ones who were struggling for their new homes against such tremendous odds.

Austin and his associate commissioners were among them and spoke winged words that went home to their hearts, and brought forth tears from their eyes, and *fruits*—aid and comfort—to their needy kin-folks.

Yoakum says: "General Austin was particularly successful; his long services in Texas, and his known truthfulness and simplicity of character, gave great weight to what he said. Though not an orator, he spoke with clearness and judgment, and enforced his positions with facts that were irresistible. His address at Louisville, which was widely published, presented the claims of Texas upon the civilized world for sympathy and aid in such manner as to bring her both." "Austin is doing wonders among us for his country," says a sensible writer of Virginia; "he is a Franklin in patience and prudence."

Edward Conrad, another agent, wrote from New Orleans, April 30th, to Gen. Houston:

"News received here from every part of the United States is very cheering. The cruelty of the Mexicans and their disgraceful treachery have caused a general burst of indignation from North and South. Fifty men leave here to-day by way of Galveston. General Felix Huston leaves Natchez, on the 5th of May next, with from 500 to 700 men. He will be accompanied by Rezin P. Bowie, brother of Colonel Bowie who fell in the Alamo. They will march through lower Louisiana, directly to Harrisburg, or wherever your headquarters may be established. Fifty men have left Philadelphia; and, by the latest papers, I see that a county and town meeting has been called for the relief of Texas. A meeting has also been called in Baltimore. Men are gathering in Tennessee and Kentucky; and, in short, in every part of the United States the barbarity of the enemy has harrowed up the hearts of all Americans, and a storm is gathering, the thunders of which will reach the centre of Mexico. The whole American press is in our favor. . . . In case our arms are successful, I hope our soldiers will not allow their passions to urge them to acts of barbarity, and thus deprive us of the immense moral strength we now possess in the sympathy and respect of all civilized men. Such acts, on the part of the Mexicans, have injured them more than our arms could have done; and retaliation on our part, I fear, would be equally fatal to Texas. I am happy in assuring you that you possess many warm friends in the United States, and that the prudent course you have pursued has inspired universal confidence as to the eventual result of the war. It is sincerely wished that a doubtful engagement will not be risked by you, as a very short time must give you force enough to place the contest beyond hazard."

This letter was written before the writer had heard of the Texans' *feast of blood* at San Jacinto.

On the 18th of June, Mr. Austin wrote from New Orleans to Gen. Houston:

"I shall do all I can to procure the annexation of Texas to the United States, on just and fair principles. . . . . The first step is a recognition of our independence; that done, the way is clear and open. If *official* reports in manuscript of all the principal facts in regard to the political and military state of things in Texas had been sent by the executive government of Texas to their agents at Washington, I could now have had the recognition of our independence to take home. Nothing but the want of such *official documents* was wanted when I left Washington. I believe that a report from you, signed by yourself, would have been fully sufficient. There were no accounts of the battle of San Jacinto, except those in the newspapers.

"I am of opinion that our independence will be acknowledged, and that Texas will be admitted into these United States if they are regularly asked for."

On the 18th June, the great American orator, Henry Clay, chairman of the Senate's Committee on Foreign Relations, reported favorably to the recognition of the independence of Texas, *so soon as it should appear that she had in "successful operation, a civil government, capable of performing and fulfilling the obligations of an independent power."*

Speaking of the military struggle, he said:

"If the contest has been unequal, it has, nevertheless, been maintained by Texas with uncommon resolution, undaunted valor, and eminent success; and the recent splendid victory—in which that portion of the Mexican army which was commanded by Gen. Santa Anna, the President of the Mexican Government, in person, was entirely overthrown with unexampled slaughter, compared with the inconsiderable loss on the other side, put to flight and captured, including among the prisoners the President himself and staff—may be considered as decisive of the independence of Texas."

Mr. Clay's report was adopted, and resolutions passed both houses of Congress, under which President Jackson appointed Mr. Morfit commissioner to visit Texas, and report on its situation, population, and resources.

The Indians about this time becoming troublesome, the President ordered Gen. E. P. Gaines to attend to them.

When informing the Mexicans of this, he said:

"It is my duty to preserve neutrality; and with that view I have ordered Gen. Gaines to a position favorable to a speedy execution of the boundary treaty, and to prevent interference with the Indians."

When the subject of Texas was alluded to, and the *no-prisoner* policy of Santa Anna censured by *Old*

Hickory, Gorostiza alleged that it was necessary to the consolidation of the dictator's *liberal policy* that rebel blood should be sacrificed. Jackson replied that it was a sacrifice of American blood. "True, your Excellency," said the minister, "but among the candidates for land, we could not discriminate." "Well, well," answered the President, "Santa Anna, and all others, will find such immolations very unsavory and indigestible."

Never did the *hero of Chalmette* say truer words. Even the instruments of Santa Anna's cruelty shuddered at the execution of his decrees.

But Mexico still tenaciously clung to the idea of subjugating Texas. Filisola was superseded by the conqueror of Goliad, Gen. Urrea, who concentrated at Matamoras, in July, 4,000 troops.

But the poor children of Montezuma had no leader nor master-spirit to preside in their council.

Their house was divided, and, in the absence of their President-General, one of the people published a pamphlet, entitled, THE TRIAL OF SANTA ANNA, in which that distinguished individual is thus truthfully described:

"Don Antonio, like Icarus, in attempting to soar too high, was precipitated into the abyss below. We would ask, who is this protector of religion? A man loaded with vice in all its forms. The particular attribute of religion is charity; it knows not how to cause evil or pain to any one. Nevertheless, Don Antonio has shown himself vicious by instinct! He rose successively against Iturbide, Victoria, Bustamente, and Gomez Farias: no commotion occurred in which he did not take an active part. His aim was always disorder, and for no other purpose than the satisfaction of disturbing the public tranquillity. We have seen him at one time for the Yorkists, and at another for the Scotch. . . . The pretensions of this monster have caused the death of many citizens at Vera Cruz, Tolomé, Oajaca, El Palmar, Puebla, Posados, Casa Blanca, Otumba, Queretaro, Guanajuato, San Luis, Los Carmelos, Zacatecas, etc. At the time of the presumptuous campaign of Tampico, he put to death, without any cause, a number of Mexicans; and now, in Texas, he has given cause to horrible reprisals by his inhuman conduct. If it were possible to pile one upon the other the bodies of the dead whose untimely end has been promoted by Gen. Santa Anna, they would doubtless form a mountain higher than that of Popocatepetl!—and we would say to his flatterers, '*Behold a monument erected to humanity and the protector of religion!*'"

But bad as he was, Urrea and his Mexicans could do nothing without him.

According to Yoakum:

"Gen. Austin returned to Texas in the first days of July, and visited Santa Anna in Columbia (whither the latter had been taken). The prisoner now made another effort toward an adjustment of the difficulties between the two countries. He proposed to Austin the friendly mediation of the Government of the United States, and, with that view, addressed a letter to President Jackson. In this communication, after giving a pretty correct sketch of recent events, he stated that the home government of Mexico, not understanding matters, had displaced Filisola, and appointed Urrea to the command of the army, who had advanced, as was understood, as far as the Nueces, which had increased the excitement of the public mind in Texas, and the chance of further bloodshed, unless some powerful hand would interpose and cause the voice of reason to be heard; that in his opinion Jackson was the only man who could do good to humanity by acting as mediator in having the treaties carried out. He accordingly called upon him to act as such. At the same time he wrote a letter to Urrea, and gave it as his opinion that the war should at once cease, and that the existing differences should be settled by diplomacy; that Urrea should halt at some convenient place, and proceed no farther; "and then," continued Santa Anna, "I have not the least doubt that so soon as you officially say to the Texan commander that, 'so soon as my person will be in absolute liberty to join you, then you will retreat beyond the Rio Grande, and cease hostilities,' I shall effect my departure to join you, and proceed on my way to the capital." He further stated to Urrea that he need not regard the orders sent from Mexico; for that, as soon as he received his liberty and reached the capital, he would hold him harmless.

However, the Mexican Government had already notified the United States that the functions of their President-General were suspended, but President Jackson wrote to Santa Anna, that he very much desired peace between Mexico and Texas, and when Mexico desired it, the good offices of the United States should be devoted to a restoration of it.

In July, the army of Texas had increased to 2,300 soldiers, who were anxious for battle and burning for distinction.

They had come to gain glory and renown, as the poet hath it:

> "Full of strange oaths, and bearded like the pard,
> Jealous in honor, sudden and quick in quarrel,
> Seeking the bubble reputation
> Even in the cannon's mouth."

They had come for *business*, but there was nothing to do.

The army was

> "As idle as a painted ship
> Upon a painted ocean."

However, President Burnet, seeing their want of *business*, sent them a nut to crack.

About the 1st of July, 1836, he appointed Gen. *Mirabeau B. Lamar*, then *Secretary of War*, Major-General of the army, and his arrival at head-quarters, and introduction to office is thus described by Gen. Felix Houston:

"I arrived at the army on the 4th of July. I had no acquaintance with General Rusk, or any of the officers, except Adjutant-General Smith, Colonel Millard, and Captains Millroy and Wiggington, all of whom I had known but a day or two. I mention this to show that I was detached from the intrigues of the army, even were I capable of entering into the disgraceful contests for office, which are so often the bane of order and discipline.

"A few hours after my arrival I was waited on by an officer, who requested me to act as chairman of a meeting of officers convened for the purpose of determining on the reception of General Lamar. I accepted the appointment. At the meeting many suggestions were made, and I obtained much information that was new to me. All present appeared to estimate General Lamar highly, but were disposed to reject him as commander-in-chief, upon the grounds that the Cabinet had no right to supersede General Sam Houston, and because they would not consent to the destruction of General Rusk, which they deemed to be the object of the Cabinet in making the appoint ment. Seeing the disposition of the officers, and having a high opinion of General Lamar from character, I suggested the propriety of appointing a committee to draft resolutions, as respectful as possible to him. The suggestion was adopted, and I was added to the committee. When the committee met, I exerted my influence to have the resolutions so drawn that General Lamar's feelings should not be wounded; that he should see that the objections to his appointment were not personal to him, but that, on the contrary, all the officers esteemed him highly. The committee adopted my plan. . . . . General Rusk had no connection whatever with the meeting or resolutions.*

"When I ascertained that General Lamar was approaching the camp, I sent two officers to wait on

---

* "*Resolved*, That this meeting highly appreciate the gallantry and worth of General Lamar, and will be at all times ready to receive him with the cordiality and respect due to his personal and military acquirements.

"*Resolved*, That Colonel B. F. Smith and Colonel H. Millard be appointed a committee to wait on General Lemar, and tender him the respects of this meeting, and inform him that there being some question of the propriety him with the resolutions. Previous to their starting, General Rusk had ordered the usual salutes to be fired for his reception. On their returning and informing me that General Lamar acceded to the proposition, I countermanded the order for firing the salutes, without consulting General Rusk. When General Lamar arrived in camp, he was cordially received; and I hoped he would consult with the officers, and that the matter might be amicably settled: but I soon understood that he determined to lay the subject of his reception before the whole army, and take their vote. Accordingly, at his request, the army were paraded in the evening by General Rusk. After the square was formed, General Rusk presented him to the army in almost these words: "Fellow-soldiers, I have the honor to present to you Major-General Lamar, appointed by the Cabinet." General Lamar then addressed the army, and recounted his deeds in a glowing form. He stated that he had fought in the ranks, etc.; that he was about returning to the United States when the late news of the returning enemy—the Mexicans—reached him; that he

---

of his appointment by the President as major-general of the Texan army, by which he is directed to assume the chief command of the army, he is requested by the officers present not to act in his official capacity of major-general until the subject may be more maturely considered by the meeting of the officers of the army."

immediately determined to return to the army, when the Cabinet, unsolicited by him, had conferred on him the office of commander-in-chief; that, on his arrival in camp, he had learned that there were some objections, by some of the army, to his appointment; that he was not ambitious of the office—he did not desire to wear tinsel on his shoulders; that the voice of man made generals, but God made heroes, etc. And he repeatedly stated that if his appointment was not acceptable to the army, he would cheerfully go into the ranks and fight by their sides, and lead the van to victory, guided by the flash of his sword.

"From some remarks made by General Lamar, General Green appeared to think that some allusion was made to him! and he addressed the army in a short manner, stating that he thought that General Sam Houston was the proper commander-in-chief; and he said something about the impropriety of the Cabinet making the appointment over the head of General Rusk, who had the confidence of the army and the people. General Lamar replied, in an excited manner, that he did not disclaim the desire of being commander-in-chief; and made some remarks about some letters of General Rusk to the Cabinet, requesting a major-general to be appointed.

"After General Lamar concluded, General Rusk addressed the meeting, and complained that, when the army was reduced to 300 or 400 men, when it was dispirited by the loathsome office of gallanting a defeated enemy from the country, etc., he had written to the President, advising the appointment of a major-general, that the army should be increased, as the Mexicans were retiring, induced by their pay, and that the war was not at an end, etc. He said that his expectation then was to visit his family and to attend to his private affairs; but that, when the enemy were expected to return in force, when the army was increasing rapidly, and when it would be disgraceful for him to adandon his post, his letters, written under different circumstances, were used as the pretext for making the appointment, etc.

"After these speeches, there were a great many calls by the troops—a few '*Lamar!*' a number '*Rusk!*' and a great number '*Houston!*' Some few called out *particularly* for me. I advanced, and stated that I was aware that the great mass of the calls for '*Houston*' were intended for *Sam* Houston, the true 'commander-in-chief;' that I had no pretensions to the command, and, in a jocund manner, observed that the only gauntlet thrown which I would take up was the remark of one of the generals, that he would lead the van—that, so long as my name was *Felix* Houston, I would lead the van.

"Thus ended the speeches. After a little delay and some confusion, I applied to General Lamar, and asked him how he would have the question put; and told him I would put it to the army as he desired. He then stated the question, 'Were the army willing to receive him as commander-in-chief?' I ordered silence, and stationed two officers for the voters to form on, and put the question in these words: 'Those who are in favor of receiving General Lamar as commander-in-chief of the army will form on Major Ward, stationed on my right; and those opposed to receiving General Lamar as commander-in-chief of the army will form on Colonel Morehouse, stationed on my left.' When I stated the question, Major Handy, acting as aide to General Lamar, observed that he did not think the question was stated as General Lamar desired. I requested him to see General Lamar. He did so, and said that I was right. At that time another gentleman rode up, and said to me that General Lamar did not know whether it was understood in his speech that he would only hold the appointment temporarily, until the arrival of General Sam Houston, and wished I would so state, which I did, turning to the different parts of the army, repeating his request, and the question, and asking if they all understood me. I then gave the word '*March!*' The tellers whom I had appointed reported 179 votes for General Lamar; and as there appeared about 1,500 votes against him, I stated it was not worth while to count them.

"On the next day I was informed Lamar intended to insist on the command. I waited on him, in company with General Green. In the course of the conversation, General Lamar stated that General Sam Houston, by leaving Texas, had forfeited his station as commander-in-chief. General Green stated that he understood that he was absent on a furlough for three months. General Lamar said he was not aware of such being the case; and if so, he would have known it, as he was Secretary of War when General Sam Houston left. During the next day I understood that General Lamar had commenced acting as commander-in-chief, and had signed a furlough under that title. The camp was in great agitation: many persons commenced leaving it. I felt great uneasiness, and expressed a fear that serious difficulties might take place. This state of affairs lasted till General Lamar had a meeting of the officers called. He addressed them, and I understood him to refer it to them whether he should resign or not. After a pause, and some remarks of General Green and Major Miller, he signified his intention to retire. On the next day he left the army."

It can be readily imagined that such scenes as this

should cause men of genius, learning, and honor to despair of Texas and to withdraw from her army, for they had been taught in their youth:

> "Fling away ambition!
> By that sin fell the angels—
> Love thyself last!
> Still in thy right hand carry gentle peace,
> To silence envious tongues: be just and fear not
> *Let all the ends thou aim'st at be thy country's,*
> *Thy God's, and truth's!*"

CHAPTER XII.

Mexicans threaten Invasion.—The project of invading Mexico.—Houston opposes it.—Is elected President.—Santa Anna liberated and sent to Washington, D.C., and thence to Mexico.—His two letters.—Charles Compte de Farnesè, and his plan.—Poverty of Texas.—Scrip and Impressment.—Gov. McDuffie on Texas.—The President's Message.—Death of Zavala and Austin.

THE Mexican army remained inactive in Matamoras for months. Urrea was not supplied with the necessary appliances and means for the subjugation of Texas, so he moved not, while his commander-in-chief, General Bravo, at San Luis Potosi, by proclamation, thus abused the abominable Texans:

"Since the grand work of our independence was achieved," said the general, "our country never called upon its worthy sons in defence of a more sacred cause, nor to sustain a more just war. In that Texas, where there should only be found people friendly to the Mexicans, and grateful for the generous hospitality granted to them, you but meet with hordes of insolent adventurers, who, when our usurped lands are claimed from them, answer by raising the savage cry of war. A trifling success, which must be attributed to the contempt with which they were looked upon, and by no means to their own prowess, has filled them with vainglory."

The Mexicans not coming to Texas, it was proposed in the Texan army for the Texans to go to Mexico, but this was opposed by General Houston, who, in July, returned from New Orleans to Nacogdoches, to which place Gen. E. P. Gaines had ordered Col. Whistler with a portion of his regiment (including Lieut. R. E. Lee, afterwards distinguished as the great Confederate General), in order to look after the Indians.

Gen. Gaines was a friend of Texas, and not only by *words*, but in *writing* to that gentleman thus approved the policy of Gen. Houston:

"Your views, urging the propriety of concentration within supporting distance of the settled parts of Texas, and pointing out the inevitable and worse than useless risk of operations upon Matamoras, or upon any other part of your western frontier, without a superiority of naval force, evince an extent and a justness of reflection, comprehension, forecast, and military mind, which, if sustained, cannot but insure triumph—complete triumph—to the cause of Texas."

So the projected invasion of Mexico fell through; in the meanwhile the army took up the case of the President-General, who, in July, through the assistance of Bartholomew Pagés instigated by the Mexican consul at New Orleans, had attempted to escape.

A majority of the army favored his trial by a court-martial, and even sent after the august criminal to put him on trial, but when the officer and his company sent after him arrived at Columbia, whither Santa Anna had been removed from Velasco, he met the written protest of Gen. Houston.

Yoakum says: "The protest only reached Captain Patton, who had the captive in charge, in time to prevent his removal. Captain J. H. Sheppard, the bearer of the document, says the pleasant change of affairs filled Santa Anna with joy, and he embraced him as one who had saved his life."

Hearing of this affair, President Jackson, on the 4th of September, wrote to Gen. Houston: "I take the liberty of offering a remark or two upon a report which is current here, that Santa Anna is to be brought before a military court, to be tried and shot. Nothing now could tarnish the character of Texas more than such an act as this. Sound policy as well as humanity approved of the counsels which spared him his life. It gave possession of Goliad and the Alamo without blood, or the loss of any portion of your army. His person is still of much consequence to you. He is the pride of Mexican soldiers, and the favorite of the priesthood. While he is in your power, the difficulties of your enemy in raising another army will continue to be great. The soldiers of Mexico will not willingly march into Texas when they know that their advance may cost their favorite general his life. Let not his blood be shed, unless imperious necessity demands it as a retaliation for future Mexican massacres. Both wisdom and humanity enjoin this course in relation to Santa Anna."

Gen. Gaines, whose big heart was enthused in the cause of Texas, had, on the 3d of August, more than a month anterior, written to Gen. Houston as follows:

"No inconsiderable portion of your fame, resulting from your late campaign, the great victory of San Jacinto, will be found in the magnanimity and moral courage displayed by you in preserving the lives of your prisoners, and more especially the life of President Santa Anna, when taken in connection with the great provocation given in his previous conduct at the Alamo and at Goliad. The Government and infant Republic of Texas will derive imperishable fame from their and your forbearance and humanity in this case. All civilized and enlightened men, in all time and geographical space, will unite in filling the measure of glory and honor due for such magnanimity, forbearance, and humanity."

On the 23d of July, 1836, an election was ordered by the Provisional Government, to take place on the first Monday of September, in all the counties of the Republic, for President, Vice-President, and members of Congress, under the *new Constitution*, and the Government elected were ordered to meet on the first Monday in October for inauguration at Columbia.

Ex-Governor Smith, Gens. Lamar, Austin, and Houston were candidates.

The latter thus explains why he became a candidate: "After the capture of Santa Anna," says he, "I was compelled to go to New Orleans, in the month of May, for surgical as well as medical aid. On my arrival, I met a number of Texans there, and they requested me to become a candidate for the presidency. This I positively refused to do. From that time up to within fourteen days of the election, I refused to let my name be used, nor would I, if elected, consent to serve in the office. General Austin and Governor Smith were the candidates, and with these gentlemen my relations were most kind. It was not a desire to obtain the office of president which ultimately caused me to let my name be used; but there were two parties in Texas, which were known as the '*Austin*' and '*Wharton*' parties. I intend no disparagement to either of the distinguished gentlemen or either of their friends, but it is necessary thus to describe the condition of the political elements then in Texas. Governor Smith was the ostensible head of the 'Wharton' party. So far as I could judge, the parties were pretty equally balanced. In this posture of affairs, I was firmly impressed with a belief that, if either of the gentlemen should be elected, it would be next to impossible to organize and sustain a government; as, whoever he might be, he would be compelled to fill all the offices with his own friends, and those of opposite feelings would, of course, oppose the administration, which, in the then condition of the country, could only be sustained by the united efforts of the community. Not being identified with either of the parties, I believed I would be enabled so to consolidate the influence of both, by harmonizing them, as to form an administration which would triumph over all the difficulties attendant upon the outset of the constitutional Government of Texas."

Gens. Houston and Lamar were elected President and Vice-President of the Republic, and were installed into office on the 22d of October, 1836, the Congress, however, had assembled on the 3d of the same month.

They both made appropriate inaugural addresses to the Congress, for they were both excellent speakers. In learning no doubt Gen. Lamar was greatly Gen. Houston's superior, but in personal appearance, grace, and dignity of manners which tend powerfully *ad captandum vulgus*, Gen. Houston greatly excelled Lamar.

He delivered his inaugural with his sword on, but at its close he took it off and with memorable solemnity, handed it to the Speaker, saying: "It now becomes my duty to make a presentation of this sword, the emblem of my past office. I have worn it with some humble pretensions in defence of my country; and should the danger of my country again call for my services, I expect to resume it, and respond to that call, if needful, with my blood and my life."

Stephen F. Austin was appointed Secretary of State; Henry Smith, Treasurer; Gen. Rusk was taken into the new Cabinet; and Felix Huston succeeded to the command of the army.

And thus Texas began *to figure as a State*—not of the Mexican Union, but as one of the nations of the earth.

Soon the old municipalities were organized into Counties and Precincts. District Courts, County Courts, and Justices' Courts were established. Judges, sheriffs, justices of the peace, and constables succeeded the *political chiefs*, *alcaldes*, *commandantes*, etc., of the olden time, while the common law of England was adopted as the law of the land in all criminal cases, and partially in civil proceedings.

The old town of *Viesca* was renamed *Milam*, *Houston* was founded, and the steamers of Charles Morgan made regular trips from New Orleans to the Texas ports.

But the President-General still lingered in durance vile, yet cheered with the hope of once more revelling in the far-distant HALLS OF MONTEZUMA. Soon after handing the Speaker of the House his sabre, as before stated, President Houston visited the self-styled *Napoleon of the West* in his prison at *Orazimba*, and consoled him in his sore distress, no doubt promising, so soon as the troubled waters subsided, to rescue him from those *barbarians* who sought his blood, as the only worthy sacrifice they could make to the *manes* of the immortal heroes of the *Alamo*, and the loved but lost at *Goliad*.

What transpired between "*the hero of San Jacinto*" and "*the Napoleon of the West*" is not left to conjecture, and as it is good evidence to convict the wily Mexican of using more highly wrought and delicately polished hyperboles than that gay and festive but reverend gentleman, H. W. B . . . . , a letter written by Gen. Santa Anna on the eve of his liberation to President Houston is here inserted:

[TRANSLATION.]

"ORAZIMBA, *November* 5, 1836.

"*To His Excellency General* SAM HOUSTON.

"MY ESTEEMED SIR: Through the channel of your commissioners, and by my conversation with you on the 2d instant, I have manifested to you the importance of my visit to Washington City, to adopt the most effectual mode of terminating the Texan question; and, as time is passing, without any definite action, when it is most precious, I am desirous that you, who are so deeply interested in the welfare of this country, should expedite the final determination of this question—using, if you should deem it advisable, the following reasons:

"When the treaty of the 14th of May was entered into, it was based upon the principle that Texas should form an independent nation, and should acquire a legal existence by means of the acknowledgment of Mexico. But, as that basis has been changed by the recent declaration of the people of Texas in favor of annexation to the United States of the North, it appears to me that, by this declaration, the question is much simplified; because, in future, it will appertain to the Cabinet at Washington to regulate this matter, and with whom Mexico will not hesitate to enter into explanations, as a definite treaty is desired.

"The mode of effecting this important object, without loss of time, is what I hope to attain by my conference with the Cabinet at Washington, at the same time conciliating all interests. Convinced as I am that Texas will never reunite with Mexico, I am desirous, on my part, to improve the advantages which may offer, and avoid the sacrifices which will occur should an imprudent attempt be made to reconquer this country, which has hitherto proved more detrimental than beneficial: consequently reducing the Texan question to this single point—*the regulation of the limits between the United States and Mexico*, which, you are aware, has been pending many years, and may be fixed at the Nueces, del Norte, or any other boundary, as may be decided on at Washington. Thus, disagreeable discussions, which might delay the definite termination of this question, or cause a difference between two friendly nations will be avoided.

"This, in substance, is a plain, safe, and speedy mode of terminating this important matter; and, as all are interested, it becomes necessary that you facilitate my journey to Washington with the least possible delay.

"In regard to the stipulation in the secret treaty, that my journey should be direct to Vera Cruz, there will be no surprise when the reasons why I first go to Washington City are known; and, should I be sent the latter route, I would like that Messrs. Hockley, Patton, and Bee, should accompany me. Should it meet your approbation, you can commission them for that purpose.

"I conclude by repeating to you what I have said, both verbally and in writing—that my name, already known to the world, shall not be tarnished by any unworthy action. Gratitude is my characteristic: so you will have nothing, on your part, to repent. To you I owe my existence, and many favors of which I am deeply impressed; and these I will endeavor to reciprocate as they so justly deserve.

"I have the honor to remain

"Your most obedient servant,

"ANTONIO LOPEZ DE SANTA ANNA.

"P.S.—If you have no use for General Jackson's letter, I will thank you to return it by Major Patton.

"L. DE STA. ANNA."

Messrs. Hockley, Patton, and Bee, did accompany Santa Anna to Washington City, where they arrived on the 17th of January, 1837.

President Jackson received the President-General kindly, dined him, and had several private interviews with him, and after nine days' entertainment sent him home by a ship of war, the *Pioneer*.

Upon arriving in Mexico on the 20th of February,

1837, Santa Anna forthwith wrote to *the Minister of War*, thus:

"The *pleasure I feel* in again *treading upon my native land*, after the many outrages and tribulations I have endured; that pleasure, I say, was considerably diminished when I was informed that there were some individuals believing my disgrace was so much the greater because I had betrayed my country and compromised her independence. What! betray an object so dear to my heart? I who have so often fought to preserve her inviolable! Would it not be better that I should perish in the midst of my enemies than that I should be the mark of so serious and unjust an accusation coming from my own fellow-countrymen? In this case, as well as in many others, I have been the victim of calumny, and, in order to place myself beyond the power of those charges, I should protest to your Excellency, and in the face of the entire world, that I obtained my liberty without subscribing to any conditions whatever; that either before or since that conjuncture I have not made with any one, let him be who he may, any contract that might bring reproach upon the national independence or honor, or *place in jeopardy the integrity of the territory;* that I accordingly could have given no guarantees whatever to any individual or government relative to those pretended stipulations; *and before consenting, either willingly or through force, to any such conditions, I would have suffered a thousand deaths before subscribing to such terms.*

"Your Excellency will be pleased to make known all these facts to the President *ad interim*, and to felicitate him on account of the peace which reigns throughout the republic, under the auspices of the new fundamental laws which the nation has enacted through the medium of their representatives."

The first letter to Gen. Houston contradicts this to the Mexican Minister at War.

But he says: "The pleasure *I feel in again treading upon my native land.*" Was this pleasure feigned? Could one so cruel feel the divine inspiration of patriotism? Don Antonio has the benefit of a doubt, for the poet hath asked:

"Breathes there the man with soul so dead,
Who never to himself hath said,
This is my own, my native land!—
Whose heart had ne'er within him burned,
As home his footsteps he had turned,
From wandering on a foreign strand?"

Let us hope that his early education in Popery, priestcraft, and bull-fighting had not entirely effaced the love of country from his heart, and that this self-styled Napoleon could possibly appreciate the sentiment of the *Emperor* when he expressed the desire *to be buried on the banks of the Seine, in the midst of the French people whom he loved so well.*

There lives in St. Louis a beneficent, *magnanimous* old gentleman named Henry Shaw, who has planted a most lovely and beautiful GARDEN for the enjoyment of the public, which he has endowed and conveyed to trustees, so as to have it kept in good order perpetually.

Henry Shaw's greatest delight consists in making others happy, while Santa Anna's seems to consist in making others unhappy!

Now, when the dark-winged angel of Death comes for Don Antonio and Henry Shaw, which one will most dread, and be best prepared to enter

> "The undiscovered country, from whose bourn
> No traveller returns"?

The great Julian in his dying moments said:

"Friends and fellow-soldiers, the seasonable period of my departure is now arrived, and I discharge, with the cheerfulness of a ready debtor, the demands of nature. I have learned from philosophy how much the soul is more excellent than the body; and that the separation of the nobler substance should be the subject of joy, rather than of affliction. I have learned from religion that an early death has often been the reward of piety; and I accept as a favor of the gods, the mortal stroke that secures me from the danger of disgracing a character, which has hitherto been supported by virtue and fortitude.

"I die without remorse, as I have lived without guilt. I am pleased to reflect on the innocence of my private life; and I can affirm with confidence that the Supreme Authority, that emanation of the Divine Power, has been preserved in my hands pure and immaculate.

"Detesting the corrupt and destructive maxims of despotism, I have considered the happiness of the people as the end of government. Submitting my actions to the laws of prudence, of justice, and of moderation, I have trusted the event to the care of Providence."

It will be well for the present and future rulers of Texas to remember the noble Roman's dying words, and in their hands preserve the supreme authority *pure and immaculate!*

In the first year of President Houston's administration, the following letter was presented to OLD SAM (as he was and is familiarly called in Texas), by *Charles Compte de Farnesè:*

"VELASCO, *July* 11, 1837.

"*To His Excellency* SAM HOUSTON:

"DEAR SIR: This will be presented to you by the Count Farnesè. His object in visiting this republic is to offer his *fortune* and *personal influence* to the glorious Texan cause. His views are extensive, and, if fully consummated, will, no doubt, be of infinite service to this republic. They have been fully explained to Dr. Archer, General Green, and other influential gentlemen here, all of whom think highly of them. The count is, no doubt, a gentleman of high literary attainments, and seems to have his heart much set on the establishment of institutions of learning in this country. The proposition he makes, of opening at once (after seeing and consulting with you) a correspondence with the court of Rome, for the purpose of having established in this republic an independent bishopric, if successful, cannot fail to be productive of the most *beneficial effects.* It will not only place the Catholic citizens of this republic in a very different attitude, but will induce tens of thousands of other Catholics to emigrate to the country. . . . .

"Very sincerely yours,

"JOHN C. WILLIAMS."

'The count then represented to the President," says Yoakum, that, "having heard in Europe of the conquest of Texas, he had abandoned his country (where he enjoyed a fine fortune, was allied to several European courts, and had the prospect of a brilliant career), to offer his services and fortune tc Texas." After some preliminary remarks in relation to the protection given by European monarchs to religion, and the human heart and mind "which require to be cultivated like a young plant," he submitted to the President his "plan," which was, to treat, through his means, should the President think him worthy, with the court of Rome:

"1. To raise all Texas to an archbishopric. This step is the sure means of making peace with Mexico through the influence of the Roman court; it will break all communication with the Bishop of Monterey, under whose jurisdiction are the Catholics of Texas, and will remove all difficulty with other courts in acknowledging the independence of Texas."*

"6. To accord gratuitously, in all the cities and villages of Texas, a convenient place to build a church, house for curate, and school.

"7. In order that the archbishop, clergy, masters and mistresses of schools, may not become chargeable to government, to accord to them, without distinction, in their respective parishes, or the nearest district, twelve hundred and eighty acres of land."

"9. The churches, houses of clergy and schools will be built by the means of the church: consequently, the government will not have the power to

* 2, 3, 4, and 5, details as to archbishopric.

employ them for any other purpose, without the consent of the HOLY SEE.

"10. The religion Catholic Apostolic and ROMAN will be allowed to exercise freely her functions in all parts of Texas.

"11. She will enjoy the protection of government.

"12. She will observe strictly the rites and canons ROMAN."

What *Old Sam* said to Count Farnesè, *the Lieutenant* (Yoakum was 1st Lieutenant in Jack Hay's famous regiment of Texas Rangers) does not tell; but as he was raised up in Tennessee, had read "Fox's Martyrs," and had seen pictures in his boyhood "of the burning of Latimer and Ridley, John Rogers with nine children, and one at the breast,"—in the reign of Bloody Queen Mary, and had heard Popery denounced from his youth up, as having converted the noble Romans of the time of Cicero, Horace, Virgil and Cæsar into the poor, degraded macaroni, lazzaroni Italians of the present day—(may God aid them in their present struggle!)—it is presumable that, desiring the advancement, progress, and development of Texas; rather than its *decline and fall*, he rejected the magnificent offers of the Compte de Farnesè.

What a noble man the count must have been to come so far from his lazzaroni home to found institutions of Popery and superstition in Texas, in order to teach the children of the heroes of San Jacinto the *facilis descensus* travelled by the Cincinnatti, the Fabii, the Catos and Scipios of ancient Rome, to become the Borgias, Pios, Cencis, and poor *miserable* beggars of modern Italy!

But President Houston had other things than the establishment of Catholicism in Texas to attend to after he took the helm of state into his hands. Texas was not only devastated and poor, but in debt a million and a quarter of dollars, with a large army and without credit.

Five millions of dollars were voted to the government by the Congress, but this five millions was in scrip, and the scrip was hardly worth the paper it was written upon. Nobody would buy the scrip, so impressments were resorted to in order to keep things moving.

Even their friends in the United States turned against them. "Governor McDuffie, of South Carolina," says Kennedy, "in December, 1836, sent a message to the Legislature of the State, disapproving of the Texan revolution—enforcing the obligations of strict neutrality—deprecating recognition—and stating that, 'under whatever circumstances of adventure, speculation, honor, or infamy the insurgents of Texas had emigrated to that country, they had forfeited all claim to fraternal regard:" they having "left a land of freedom for a land of despotism, with their eyes open, deserved their destiny." Leading men in New York and Massachusetts coincided with Gov. McDuffie, and even the President of the United States in his Message to Congress on December 6th, 1836, says:

"*The known desire of the Texans to become a part of our system, although its gratification depends upon the reconcilement of various conflicting interests, necessarily a work of time, and uncertain in itself, is calculated to expose our conduct to misconstruction in the eyes of the world.* You will perceive by the accompanying documents that the extraordinary mission from Mexico has been terminated, on the sole grounds that the obligations of this government to itself and Mexico, under treaty stipulations, have compelled me to trust a discretionary authority to a high officer of our army, to advance into territory claimed as part of Texas, if necessary to protect our own or the neighboring frontier from Indian depredations. In the opinion of the Mexican functionary who has just left us, the honor of his country will be wounded by American soldiers entering, with the most amicable avowed purposes, upon ground from which the followers of his government have been expelled, and over which there is at present no certainty of a serious effort on its part being made to re-establish dominion. The departure of this minister was the more singular as he was apprised that the sufficiency of the causes assigned for the advance of our troops by the commanding general had been seriously doubted by me, and that there was every reason to suppose that the troops of the United States—their commander having had time to ascertain the truth or falsehood of the information upon which they had been marched to Nacogdoches—would be either there, in perfect accordance with the principles admitted to be just in his conference with the Secretary of State, by the Mexican minister himself, or were already withdrawn, in consequence of impressive warnings their commanding officer had received from the Department of War. It is hoped and believed that his government will take a more dispassionate and just view of this subject, and not be disposed to construe a measure of justifiable precaution, made necessary by its known inability, in execution of the stipulations of our treaty, to act upon the frontier, into an encroachment upon its rights, or a stain upon its honor.

"In the meantime the ancient complaints of injustice, made by our citizens, are disregarded, and new causes of dissatisfaction have arisen, some of them of a character requiring prompt remonstrance and ample immediate redress. I trust, however, by tempering firmness with courtesy, and acting with forbearance upon every incident that has occurred, or that may happen, to do and obtain justice, and thus avoid the necessity of again bringing this subject to the view of Congress."

In a subsequent part of the Message, the President stated, that

"At the date of the latest intelligence from Nacogdoches, the troops of the United States were at that station, but that the officer who had succeeded General Gaines had recently been advised that, from the facts known at the seat of government, there would seem to be no adequate cause for any longer maintaining that position, and he was accordingly instructed, in case the troops were not already withdrawn, under the discretionary powers before possessed by him, to give the requisite orders for that purpose on the receipt of the instructions, unless he should then have in his possession such information as should satisfy him that the maintenance of the post was essential to the protection of the frontier, and to the due execution of treaty stipulations as explained to him." *

* The following are the words of the treaty on which President Jackson justified the advance of General Gaines to Nacogdoches: "It is likewise agreed that the two contracting parties shall, by all the means in their power, maintain peace and harmony among the several Indian nations who

Here was a death-blow to the fondly cherished idea of annexation, *at least* for a time, and the Lone Star Republic must work out its own salvation.

To add to these misfortunes, Lorenzo de Zavala died on the 15th of November, and Stephen F. Austin on the 27th of December, 1836.

Of the former Yoakum says:

"His life had been eventful and useful. Providence had cast his lot in a land of revolutions and of blood, but at all times and under all circumstances he had been a constant and ardent lover of liberty and humanity. His remains lie in a free country, and his name will be remembered while that freedom endures."

The death of Mr. Austin was a national calamity *indeed*, for he was a safe counsellor, of sterling integrity, fine intellect, and *devoted* to Texas. Although elected *General* by the troops it was not on the bloody field—

---

inhabit the lands adjacent to the lines and rivers which form the boundaries of the two countries; and the better to obtain this object, both parties bind themselves expressly to restrain, *by force*, all hostilities and incursions on the part of the Indian nations living in their respective boundaries; so that the United States of America will not suffer their Indians to attack the citizens of the United Mexican States, nor the Mexican States the Indians residing within their territories to commit hostilities against the citizens of the United States of America, nor against the Indians residing within the limits of those States, in any manner whatever."

> "Where the battle wreck lies thickest
> And death's brief pang is quickest!"

—it was not where the warrior hurls his death-bearing missiles to wound and kill his brother man—it was not where men bleed and die, that Mr. Austin was in his proper element; but in *the social circle* at *the family hearth*, or *on the forum*, where mind meets mind in intellectual warfare, and by the charming, witching words of eloquence, chains the attention, convinces the understanding and enthuses the hearts of men with noble and generous impulse, that the amiable Austin was in his proper element.

He could not ride with pleasure over a field of battle strewn with the dead and dying, nor exult in the moment of victory gained by the death of beloved friends, but the appreciative laugh or applause of listening friends, or a spell-bound audience of his fellow-citizens, would cause his heart to swell and expand with delight.

"Let me be

> Great, not like Cæsar, stained with blood,
> But only great as I am good!'"

Or, "Let me

> 'Scatter plenty o'er a smiling land
> And read my history in a nation's eyes,'"

was rather his idea of excellence than

> "To wade through slaughter to a throne."

No one had a greater contempt for *the office-seeker* than he, nor appreciated more fully the great American idea, that "*office should seek men, not men office.*"

Texas has erected no monument to commemorate the fame of Stephen F. Austin. Nor has she voted monuments to any one of her heroes, but has very appropriately immortalized them by naming her counties and cities in honor of them; wherefore, so long as the lovely cities of Austin, Houston, Rusk, Sherman, McKinney, Crockett, Seguin, Bonham, and the beautiful counties of Milam, Lamar, Travis, Bowie, Fannin, Burleson, Wharton, Smith, Karnes, Zavala, Waller, Dimmit, Erath, Maverick, Chambers, Hunt and Ellis shall exist, so long will exist *the fame* of the daring men who rescued Texas from the domination of bull-fighting, prisoner-murdering, priest-ridden Mexicans.

While the philanthropist can but sympathize with the unfortunate children of Montezuma for their degrading lessons and early education in scenes of blood and priestcraft, introduced by their Spanish conquerors, which no doubt give a taste for shedding human blood, and have produced their unchristian habit of murdering their prisoners, their citizens and soldiers, and even their generals and *emperors*, he can but rejoice in the great gain to the cause of civilization and human progress accomplished by the heroes of Texas, whose honored names and chivalrous deeds will be fondly cherished and gratefully remembered until time shall be no more.

In the language of the poet:

> "Some, when they die, die all; their mould'ring clay
> Is but an emblem of their memories;
> The space quite closes up through which they passed;
> But these have lived, and leave a mark behind,
> To pluck the shining age from vulgar time,
> And give it whole to late posterity."

CHAPTER XIII.

Annexation and Anti-annexation.—Texas recognized by the United States.—Mission of Gen. Mermucan Hunt.—Annexation rejected by the United States.—Forsyth and Hunt.—Kennedy.

WHILE Gov. McDuffie, Mr. J. Q. Adams, Dr. Channing, and the Legislatures of New York, Ohio, Massachusetts and Vermont were opposed to Texas—or rather, in favor of letting *Texans who had left a land of Freedom and gone to one of Despotism, work out their own destiny*, there were other gentlemen who sympathized with their struggling kinsmen in their unequal contest with Mexico, and wished to throw over them the protecting *ægis* of the American Union.

Foremost among these were Gen. James Hamilton, Senators Preston and Calhoun, and Mr. Poinsett (formerly United States Minister to Mexico), of South Carolina, and Robert J. Walker, of Mississippi.

As chairman of the Senate's Committee on Foreign Relations, Gen. Hamilton, in a Report touching Texan affairs, said:

"The sequel of this deeply interesting drama must be left to the dispensations of a wise Providence, whom we are taught to believe orders everything for the best. There may be those who suppose that it will be neither the policy of the United States to recognize the independence of Texas nor to admit her into the Union. We do not desire to anticipate the vast considerations which enter into this subject. To such persons it might be said, that although both of these privileges might be denied, yet we cannot strike Texas from the map of the physical globe, nor from her territorial location. There she stands, as our neighbor, for good or for evil, touching our frontier at a point of intimate community with our most sensitive interests, and alluring, by her immense and boundless fertility of soil, a stream of emigration which is destined to make her a great state in our confederacy or a powerful separate empire."

In support of his views he said to the Senators of South Carolina:

"Would our refusal to recognize her independence, or admit her into the Union, in the language of the Report, 'strike her from the map of the physical globe?' Would it curse with an irreversible sterility the teeming fertility of her exuberant soil? Would it cover with a blight the cotton plant, which in that favored country grows almost with the perennial magnificence of a tropical production? Would our refusal check the current of her rivers in their journey to the ocean, freighted with the richest staples of the finest agricultural country probably in the habitable globe? Would, in one word, our refusal to receive her as a member of this confederacy check that disastrous stream of emigration that, without a reflux, is steadily setting west? No, not one jot. Let Texas once establish her independence, and a separate Republic, and throw open a series of free ports to the commerce of the world, and he would ask, whether the dangers of her competition would not be vastly augmented from the fact that, whilst her planters would make one-third more cotton to the acre than is produced on the richest Mississippi bottom, the exchanges on the commodities destined to purchase the staples of Texas, would come into that country burdened with 30 per cent. less of taxation?

"In this view the subject is scarcely less important and interesting to the merchant and manufacturer at the North. For what would become of their respective trades, with millions of untaxed British navigation crowding the ports of Texas, and millions of British manufactures introduced through Texas, flooding the vast valley of the Mississippi? These momentous considerations would have, he believed, to be presented one day or other, and that perhaps not very distant, to the deliberations of the American people. He trusted that their decision would add fresh stability and harmony to the Union." *

Mr. Poinsett, in supporting the motion, made the following observations:

"Ought we to imitate the conduct of the members of the British Parliament, who condemned them in unqualified terms, while they accused this government of fermenting the revolution of Texas, in order to acquire possession of that territory? Mr. Ward, who took the lead in that debate in the House of Commons on the 5th August last, from the circumstance of his having been the British Envoy in Mexico, asserted that the United States 'had long regarded Texas with covetous eyes, and that to obtain possession of that province had been the first object of its policy. Now this opinion is contradicted by the fact that Mr. Adams might, if it had been judged expedient to do so by Mr. Monroe's advisers, have obtained possession of it by treaty. There was no serious obstacle to his extending our boundary so as to embrace Texas, when he made the treaty of limits with Don Luis Onis. It was an error—of which he became afterwards fully convinced. Mr. Ward said, further, that he (Mr. Poinsett) had sought, during their mutual residence there, to acquire Texas for his

---

* *Columbia Telescope* of December 21st, 1836.

government, and had made proposals to purchase the territory for ten millions of dollars. This, too, is a great mistake. He did not doubt that Mr. Ward had been so informed; but the intelligence he received on that occasion was erroneous and unfounded. The American Government never made any overtures to Mexico for the purchase of Texas through him, nor during his residence there. Mr. Ward insinuated that these negotiations were conducted through the former Vice-President of Texas, Don Lorenzo de Zavala, of whom he took occasion to speak disparagingly—'a man of talents, certainly; but totally destitute of principle'—which simply means that he was not of the English party, but devotedly attached to republican principles—a devotion which he has displayed throughout all the trying scenes of the revolution in Mexico. In his youth he was immured four years in the dungeons of the castle of Ulloa, for having dared to murmur against the tyranny of Spain. Upon the adoption of the Constitution in that country in 1812, he was liberated and sent to Madrid by his countrymen, to plead for the liberties of Americans, which he did fearlessly and eloquently. When the revolution took place that separated Mexico from the mother country, he returned home and placed himself in the first rank of those who sought to give republican institutions to his country; and when the last change took place, he indignantly returned his commission of Minister to France to Santa Anna, and retired to his farm in Texas, declaring *that he had received the appointment from a free government, and would not serve a tyrant. He said*, in reply to Mr. Ward, *that the United States had maintained a strict neutrality in the controversy between Mexico and Texas, and had acted with the most perfect good faith towards both parties.*

"From what he had seen and known of the policy of our government in this particular, he thought South Carolina might repose upon the wisdom and prudence of their counsels. He presumed the same course would be pursued towards Texas that had been pursued towards the States of Spanish America. When a government *de facto* existed there, capable of maintaining its independence, it would, he presumed, be recognized by this country. Such an act could not be regarded as a cause of war by Mexico. It had not so been considered by Spain; and when we recognized her revolted colonies, the amicable relations between the two countries were not interrupted. . . . . If the annexation of Texas to these United States should become afterwards a question between us, and the proposal should come from them, he hoped it would be entertained by this country favorably. He believed that the best interests of this country would be consulted by the adoption of such a measure. If the time of the Senate permitted, and it were a question fitting to be entertained here, he thought he could prove conclusively, that the interests of the whole Union, and especially of the South, required that Texas, if once separated from Mexico, should be annexed to these United States.

"The result of the contest between Mexico and Texas was, as truly said in the Report, in the hands of Providence. He thought it too probable that the Texans might be driven from their homes by the overwhelming forces preparing to march against them, but the Mexicans cannot keep possession of that state—that government cannot maintain a large standing army at so great a distance from the capital. They would be compelled to withdraw it in a short time, and the Texans will reoccupy the country. To Mexico this is a perilous contest. Their retreating forces may be followed to the centre of their fertile fields. This danger is the more imminent as all the states north of Tamaulipas are essentially republican, and have submitted unwillingly to the repeal of their free institutions. Whatever reverses Texas is still destined to undergo, if that people continue firm and united, they must ultimately be free."

The vote of the United States Senate on the acknowledgment of the independence of Texas, was taken the 1st of March, 1837. It stood 23 to 22, and on the next day, upon a motion to reconsider, the vote was 24 to 24. On the succeeding day, President Jackson approved the resolution of Congress, and nominated Alcee Labranche as *chargé d'affaires* to *the Republic of Texas.*

Among the brave and daring spirits who left ease and comfort in the good old State of North Carolina, and came to Texas to slaughter Mexicans, and gain the great glory of a Lafayette or Kosciusko, was the celebrated Gen. Memucan Hunt, familiarly styled by his associates *Cousin Muke.*

Cousin Muke was one of those old-fashioned fellows who recognized no aristocracy but that of merit, and weighed men alone by the standard of virtue. He was as gentle as a lamb, but as brave as a lion. He brought with him an old rifle from North Carolina to Texas, the barrel of which became loose in the stock, but Cousin Muke tied a piece of twine or hickory bark round the stock and barrel to keep them together, put a new flint in the hammer, and when challenged one day for a mortal combat,* Cousin Muke took up this old flint and steel rifle, walked out on the field of honor, and with it—scorning all of Messrs. Walker

---

* About this time duelling was somewhat fashionable in Texas, and Gens. Felix Houston and Albert Sidney Johnson fought. After five rounds, Gen. Johnson was seriously wounded.

and Ely's double water-proof percussion caps, locks, or metallic cartridges—*shot his man.*

Within a few weeks after recognition, Cousin *Muke* was introduced to the President of the United States by the Secretary of State, Mr. Forsyth, as Envoy Extraordinary and Minister Plenipotentiary of the Republic of Texas to the United States—with the grand object of annexing Texas to the United States.

Not doubting his ability to accomplish this object, he addressed Mr. Forsyth a long letter containing a history of Texas from its discovery and settlement to that time: its soil, climate, riches, and the reasons why annexation should take place—that any delay might defeat it, as Texas was about forming treaties with foreign powers. In conclusion he said:

"The undersigned most respectfully represents to the Honorable the Secretary of State, that in this paper he does not presume to have presented all the inducements to the union of the two Republics. He has not thought it respectful to trespass upon the attention of the Honorable the Secretary of State, either by an extended detail of the resources of Texas, or of the mutual benefits involved in a treaty of annexation. The mineral wealth of the country, comprising valuable mines of silver and lead, immense strata of iron and coal, and salt springs in great abundance, has not been properly appreciated. Nor has the undersigned thought it necessary to allude to the immense fur trade which would be thrown into the lap of the enterprise of the United States by the annexation of Texas. The great aid and facilities which Texas, as an integral part of the Union, might render to the adventurous traders, who, in caravans, penetrate from Missouri to Santa Fé, and in general to the inland trade of the United States, with the countries bordering on the Pacific, have all been left unexplained; and the undersigned throws himself upon the courtesy of the Honorable the Secretary of State in desiring him to believe that, as he has not entered into any of the details of such a treaty of annexation as Texas might propose, but confined himself to the submission of the proposition itself, so he has not thought fit to discuss severally all the various interests involved, but merely has subjected them to a general, and, he trusts, a candid review.

"In closing this paper, the undersigned appeals to the Honorable the Secretary of State, and referring him to the details of the history of the Texan revolution herein set forth, asks, in the name of national honor, humanity, and justice, if a nation whose career has been marked, like that of Mexico, by a constant violation of the most solemn treaty obligations, by a series of the most licentious revolutions, by a most shameful prostitution of the lives, liberties, and the property of her people, and, in short, by every act of perfidy and cruelty recorded in the history of barbarians, has not thereby forfeited all claims to the respect of the governments of civilized nations? Look to her continued interruptions of the peaceful citizens of Texas, industriously engaged in the improvements of their estates and in the actual aggrandizement of the Mexican Empire; to her demolition by military force of the Constitution of 1824; to her bloody war of extermination under President Santa Anna; to her butchery of those gallant Texans who surrendered their arms under the sacred flag of a capitulation, in which their lives were guaranteed; and pronounce if the enormity of her misdeeds entitles her to be any longer considered, the undersigned will not say a nation of responsibility, but even humanity. The undersigned, however, forbears to continue this appeal, so irrelevant, and perhaps so unnecessary, to the due consideration of the subject under discussion. The world will do ample justice to the magnanimity of Texas in forbearing to visit upon the heads of the recreant tyrant and his captured host that retaliation which their offences against the laws of nations and the rights of mankind so signally deserved.

"In conclusion, the undersigned most respectfully begs leave to congratulate the Honorable Secretary of State upon the spectacle exhibited in this discussion, and which is so honorable a commentary upon the excellence of the government of this country, viz.: a sovereign, free, and warlike people, fresh from the fields of their own victories and glory, seeking to surrender their nationality as the price of a place among the United States, to become participants of the wisdom of its laws and the renown of its arms."

Mr. Forsyth answered Gen. Hunt's proposition by order of the President, Mr. Van Buren, with a prompt decisive negative, he wrote:

"Neither the duties nor *the settled policy of the United States* permit them to enter into an examination of the accuracy of the historical facts related by General Hunt. The United States were foremost in acknowledging the independence of Mexico. A sense of duty and a reverence for consistency, however, it was considered, left this government no alternative, and it therefore led the way in recognizing Texas. A hope was certainly entertained that this act, and the motives that conduced to it, even if no other considerations were to have influence, would point out to the Government of Texas the propriety not only of cherishing intimate and amicable relations with this country, but of abstaining from other connections abroad which might be detrimental to the United States.

"So long as Texas shall remain at war while the

United States are at peace with her adversary, the proposition of the Texan Minister Plenipotentiary necessarily involves the question of war with that adversary. The United States are bound to Mexico by a treaty of amity and commerce, which will be scrupulously observed on their part, so long as it can be reasonably hoped that Mexico will perform her duties and respect our rights under it. The United States might justly be suspected of a disregard of the friendly purposes of the compact, if the overture of General Hunt were to be even reserved for future consideration, as this would imply a disposition on our part to espouse the quarrel of Texas with Mexico; a disposition wholly at variance with the spirit of the treaty, with the uniform policy and the obvious welfare of the United States.

"The inducements mentioned by General Hunt for the United States to annex Texas to their territory, are duly appreciated; but powerful and weighty as certainly they are, they are light when opposed in the scale of reason to *treaty obligations* and respect for *that integrity of character* by which the United States have sought to distinguish themselves since the establishment of their right to claim a place in the great family of nations. It is presumed, however, that the motives by which Texas has been governed in making this overture, will have equal force in impelling her to preserve, as an independent power, the most liberal commercial relations with the United States. Such a disposition will be cheerfully met in a corresponding spirit by this government. If the answer which the undersigned has been directed to give to the proposition of General Hunt should unfortunately work such a change in the sentiments of that government as to induce an attempt to extend commercial relations elsewhere upon terms prejudicial to the United States, this government will be consoled by a consciousness of the rectitude of its intentions, and a certainty that although the hazard of transient losses may be incurred by a rigid adherence to just principles, no lasting prosperity can be secured when they are disregarded."

Mr. Forsyth's letter, of which but little is quoted, highly astounded Gen. Hunt. No doubt his indignation was great. "*Texas rejected! Why, Forsyth is crazy! I'll write him again*, and although he is a fool and—yet I'll not tell him so *in words*, but, like Bill Ransom after losing his money with Col. Hawkins at *seven-up, I'll insinuate.*"*

---

* After Mr. Ransom had lost his last ten dollar bill by the turning of a Jack by Col. Hawkins, he arose from the table and gave vent to his chagrin and vexation in these memorable words: "Col. Hawkins, the position you occupy in society, and the respectability of your family connections, forbid me to say that you would cheat at cards, but, sir, allow me to say, that *you*

So Gen. Hunt wrote again, from which I take the following extracts·

"The venerable ex-president, General Jackson, was so strongly impressed with a belief, at one time during his administration, that the negotiation then pending for the acquisition of Texas would be brought to a speedy and favorable issue, that he tendered the office of Governor of the Territory of Texas to the late Governor H. G. Burton, of North Carolina, to be entered upon so soon as the treaty of cession should be completed. (See a publication on the subject of Governor Burton's appointment.) The same principles, it appears to the undersigned, were involved in the negotiation for the acquisition of Texas from Mexico, previously to the recognition of the independence of the latter by Spain, which are now presented by the question of the annexation of Texas to the United States previously to the recognition of *her* independence by Mexico; and had his Excellency the President of the United States entertained any inclination to negotiate a treaty for the annexation of Texas—a hope which had been fondly cherished, as he had expressed a determination to carry out the measures and conform to the general policy of his venerable predecessor—it does appear to the undersigned, but

---

can turn more Jacks than any gentleman with whom I ever played cards in all my life!"

with distinguished deference to the Hon. Mr. Forsyth's opinions to the contrary, that neither a sense of duty nor the settled policy of this government, during the administration of the venerable ex-president would have prevented an examination into the accuracy of the historical facts accompanying the proposition. That brief compendium, which is believed to be correct, will show that there is as little prospect of the recovery of Texas by Mexico at this time as there was of the reconquest of Mexico by Spain at the time that General Jackson believed that the *chargé d'affaires* (Mr. Butler) of this government had succeeded in negotiating the acquisition of Texas. If the act of the annexation of Texas would involve the United States in a war with Mexico at this time, the undersigned is at a loss to perceive why a similar result was not anticipated with Spain in the event of a cession of Texas by Mexico. Texas asked nothing more of the United States, in proposing to negotiate for her annexation, than the United States had previously desired of Mexico, when General Jackson was at the head of this government—for Mexico was then as much at war with Spain as Texas now is with Mexico—and it is believed that as friendly treaty and commercial relations existed between Spain and the United States at that time as are now maintained between the United States and Mexico.

"In addition to the fact that this government, when administered by the sage of the Hermitage, proposed the acquisition of Texas by purchase from Mexico, many years before the recognition of her independence by Spain, the undersigned most respectfully invites the attention of the Hon. Secretary of State to the report of the House of Representatives of the State of Mississippi, contained in a newspaper which he herewith presents. That report, which is said to have been adopted unanimously, alludes in strong terms to the subject of the right of this government to admit Texas into its confederacy; and the undersigned refers to it thus particularly, that he may be sustained by high authority when he assures the Secretary of State of the United States, that, in submitting the proposition of annexation, it was far from his intention to ask the Government of the United States to accede to a measure which Mr. Forsyth was instructed to say was believed to involve unjust principles. *The undersigned assures the Secretary of State of the United States, that he could not knowingly consent to be the medium of presenting any proposition asking of the United States a disregard of just principles.*

"After the a surance of the Hon. Mr. Forsyth, that a sense of duty and a reverence for consistency left his government no alternative in leading the way in recognizing the independence of Texas, the undersigned confesses some surprise at the intimation of Mr Forsyth, that the circumstance of her having been *first* recognized by the United States should in any manner influence the foreign intercourse of Texas. However much the Government of Texas may be disposed to encourage the most friendly relations with the Government of the United States, the undersigned assures the Hon. Secretary of State, that the Government of Texas does not consider that any particular foreign policy was implied or made binding upon her by the circumstance of her independence having been first recognized by the Government of the United States. The representatives of Texas, in their interchanges with foreign powers, will not accept the recognition of her independence unless it is unconditional in this respect. In all their negotiations and treaties with foreign powers, the best interests of their own government and people will doubtless be consulted, and must indicate the policy which they will be directed to adopt With even the same permanent policy in its commercial interchanges with the United States, which may exist with the most favored nation, the undersigned cannot guarantee for his government that any advantage shall accrue therefrom to the manufacturing interest of the United States; for it is understood that great interest is mainly sustained in the United States by the protection afforded by high duties against the competition of similar interests in foreign nations, where labor and the facilities for manufacturing are more available, and at cheaper rates. Such being the case, it is apparent that, even should no detriment accrue to the manufacturing interest of the United States from the vicinity of Texas as an independent nation, certainly no advantages affecting that interest can be anticipated.

"*The apprehension of the Honorable Mr. Forsyth, that the refusal of this government to negotiate for a treaty of annexation, thereby declining all the commercial and other advantages which would be secured by that measure, may induce an attempt on the part of the Government of Texas to extend its commercial relations elsewhere on terms most favorable to its own welfare and prosperity, is perfectly natural;*" but the undersigned assures Mr. Forsyth that such endeavors will not proceed from any unkind feelings to the government and people of the United States; and he would take this occasion to reiterate the friendly disposition of the government and people of Texas towards the government and people of the United States, which he had the honor to communicate in his note of the 4th of August. Should, however, the foreign commercial and other relations of the Republic of Texas necessarily become such as seriously to affect the interests of the United States, or any portion thereof, the undersigned conceives that it would be unreasonable for the government and people who had been feeely proffered all she could bestow, and yet declined the offer, to complain of her on the ground of looking to her own interest primarily. Texas has generously offered to merge her national sovereignty in a domestic one, and to become a constituent part of this great confederacy. The refusal of this government to accept the overture must forever screen her from the imputation of wilfully injuring the great interests of the United States, should such a result accrue from any commercial or other regulations which she may find it necessary or expedient to enter into with foreign nations.

"Should it be found necessary or expedient hereafter, for the proper promotion of the interests of her own citizens, to lay high duties upon the cotton-bagging so extensively manufactured in the Western States, and upon the pork and beef and breadstuffs so abundantly produced in that region, such as would amount to an almost total prohibition of the introduction of those articles into the country, much as her government and people would regret the necessity of the adoption of such a policy, she would be exculpated from the slightest imputation of blame for taking care of her own welfare and prosperity after having been refused admission into this Union.

"The efforts which the government of the undersigned is making to open a commercial intercourse with Great Britain and France, it is believed, will succeed. Apart from the disposition of those two powers to avail themselves of the great advantages which must result to every nation with which Texas may form intimate commercial relations, it is believed that they, as well as the United States, cherish a liberal sympathy for a people who have encountered the most cruel treatment at the hands of Mexico.

"Reason would seem to indicate that the foreign policy of Texas will be dissimilar to that of the United States. Texas is now, and it is believed will continue to be, an almost purely agricultural country. The agricultural interest will claim the almost exclusive attention of the government: possibly from the circumstance of her climate and soil being so well adapted to the growth of hemp, and the great demand for rope and bagging in a cotton-growing country, the manufactures of these solitary articles may be encouraged at an early period; but with these single exceptions it is not apprehended that the capital and labor of the country can be so profitably employed in any other species of industry as in the planting interest. On the other hand, the interests of the United States are numerous and greatly diversified; and it is presumed that it was found necessary to establish such a foreign policy as would best reconcile them and redound to the advantage of each.

"With the most rigid adherence to whatever is just and right, the Government of Texas will naturally pursue such a course of policy, foreign and domestic, as will best conduce to the increase of her wealth and population, and thereby her national power and consideration. In its intercourse abroad, it will endeavor to find those markets where her agricultural products, cotton, sugar, rice, tobacco, etc., will obtain the highest prices, and where such articles as may be needed for home consumption may be procured at the lowest rates. If these advantages are presented in the commercial intercourse with the United States, the undersigned need not say that the warm predilection of the government and people of Texas for the government and people of the United States would render such an intercourse as agreeable to the former as it would doubtless be advantageous to both.

"The undersigned most respectfully assures the Honorable Mr. Forsyth, and through him his Excellency the President of the United States, that the prompt and decisive rejection of the proposition for the annexation of Texas to the United

States will not be imputed to an unfriendly spirit to the government and people of Texas."

So Gen. Hunt failed in his mission, and lost all his expenses while in Washington, for Texas had but precious little money in those days.

In April following, Mr. Jones, of Brazoria, introduced the following joint resolution into the Texas House of Representatives:

"Whereas, the citizens of the Republic of Texas, at their election of President and other officers in the year 1836, expressed an almost unamimous desire to become annexed to the United States of North America; in consequence of which expression, a proposition for annexation was made, through our Minister resident at the city of Washington, which proposition, after having been duly considered, has been distinctly and unconditionally refused by that government, and for reasons which it is impossible for time or circumstances to invalidate or alter; and whereas, it is believed that Texas, having interests at variance with those of a large portion of the United States, and having also demonstrated her ability for self-government, and for successfully resisting the efforts of her imbecile enemy to subjugate her, and now trusting, as a wise policy dictates, to her own strength and resources, no longer desires such annexation: and whereas, it is a fact that, pending this hopeless negotiation, the recognition of the independence of Texas by England and other powers, so essential to our welfare, is delayed or prevented;

"Be it resolved by the Senate and House of Representatives of Texas, in Congress assembled, that his Excellency the President be authorized and required, so soon as he may think proper, to instruct our Minister resident at Washington respectfully to inform the Government of the United States of North America, that the Government of Texas withdraws the proposition for the annexation of Texas to the said United States."

The resolution passed the House, but failed in the Senate.

The proposition of annexation was formally and absolutely withdrawn by Anson Jones (Texan Minister), in April, 1838, by order of President Houston.

Kennedy attributes the failure of annexation at this time to the stupidity and—"sheer jealousy of Northern politicians of augmenting the power of the South. Not content with this distrust of the South, opposition to Texas had been strengthened by a vile appeal to passion and fanaticism, and ministers of the gospel had been permitted to mount the pulpit and fulminate denunciations against Texas and the interests of the South. And what was the excuse? 'It was necessary to keep the Union together. Texas would have divided the Union.' Was not the period of separation fearfully accelerated by making Texas a sovereign and independent power, with such an ally as England?

"The question of Texan annexation or independence presented an embarrassing dilemma to those who wished, by means of *protective duties*, to secure a monopoly of the *home market for American manufactures.* If the United States extended their southern wing to the Rio Grande, the anti-tariff party would gain a preponderance most favorable to England. On the other hand, if Texas were independent, she might force the whole American continent into the *adoption of free trade principles*, which would be still more conducive to British aggrandizement, as it would "tranquillize her restless population by constant occupation, and, by receiving a superabundance of raw material in exchange for her fabrics, enable her to undersell the world."

CHAPTER XIV.

The Congress at Houston.—Message of President Houston.—Poor Condition of the Texan Treasury.—Capture of the *Independence*, *Champion*, and *Julius Cæsar*, with loss of the *Invincible*.—Comanches Raid on Texan Frontier.—Van Benthuyson and Miles defeated by Comanches.—J. O. Rice, William Ripley and Robert Beal.—The famous Fight of *the Bowies* with Indians.—Financial Condition of Texas.—Great Prosperity of Galveston and Houston.—Deaf Smith's Fight with Mexicans.—Col. Neill and Gen. Rusk engage the Comanches and Kickapoos.—Mexicans of Nacogdoches in arms.—Death of Col. Wharton and Judge Collingsworth.

THE second session of the first Congress of the Republic of Texas met at Houston on the 1st of May, 1837. In a little log cabin with two rooms only, one with puncheon-floor, the other of dirt, President Houston wrote his Message and held his levées.

His Message informed the Congress that the five millions of dollars voted to his administration were

"*Like the baseless fabric of a vision!*"

Not a dollar could be realized on that anticipated borrow!

The sale of land scrip had not succeeded, and that he had suspended their sale.

This Congress attempted to raise a revenue by imposts, direct taxes and the issue of promissory notes of the government, but it was not successful.

At the next session, in November, he informed the Congress that the extraordinary sum of five hundred dollars in specie had been paid into the treasury of the Republic during his administration! Not a dollar more nor less. During this session the famous ornithologist, Audubon, and a representative of Great Britain, Mr. Crawford, attended the levées of President Houston in his *palatial* residence.

The gallant achievements of Major Burton and his *horse marines* arrested the attention of the wily Mexicans, so, in 1837, they manned and sent out the *Libertador*, having sixteen eighteen-pounders and 140 men, the *Vincedor del Alamo*, armed with six twelve-pounders and one eighteen-pounder with 100 men, and the brig-of-war *Urrea.*

These vessels captured the Texan vessels *Champion*, *Julius Cæsar*, and *Independence*, and destroyed the favorite craft of the Texan navy, the *Invincible* (purchased from *McKinney & Williams*), after it had captured the *Alispa*, of eighty tons.

Wm. H. Wharton, Texas Commissioner to the United States, was captured on the *Independence*, taken to Matamoras and imprisoned.

Col. J. H. Wharton took thirty Mexican prisoners to

Matamoras to ransom his brother, but the gallant Mexicans cast him into prison for his temerity.

Resorting to bribery the Whartons *corrupted* (?) their guards and made their escape, thus making glad the hearts of their friends on old Caney and the Brazos. The Mexicans this year also incited the Indians to make war on the Texan settlements.

"Every day or two, during the year 1837," says Yoakum, "some murdered citizen or stolen property" attested Indian hostility and depredation upon the Texan frontier.

The head chief of the Comanches was Chiconie, a bold, dashing warrior, and when Major A. Le Grand, of the Texan army, was sent to treat with him, and having stated the object of his visit, Chiconie replied that "so long as he continued to see the gradual approach of the whites and their habitations to the hunting grounds of the Comanches, so long would he believe to be true what the Mexicans had told him, viz., that the ultimate intention of the white man was to deprive them of their country, and so long would he continue to be the enemy of the white race."

Whereupon the Texan Congress declared war against them, and authorized different persons to raise companies and attack them.

On the 7th October, 1837, Captain L. Lynch and William Eastland with sixty-eight men, started from

17

Fort Prairie, five miles below where Austin now stands, on the lookout for Indians.

On arriving at the sources of Pecan Bayou and the Clear Fork of the Brazos, a jealousy sprang up between the officers as to the right of command, when they partly divided, and Lieutenants Van Benthuyson and Miles, with sixteen men continued their Indian *hunt*, while Capts. Lynch and Eastland with the remainder returned to the fort.

Van Benthuyson, Miles & Co. soon fell in with a party of Keechies, attacked and defeated them, killing two of their warriors.

Emboldened by success, the little party pushed on to the head-waters of the Trinity, near "the knobs," called by the Indians "*the stone houses*;" on the 10th November they were surrounded and attacked by about 180 or 200 savage warriors.

The little band of eighteen men took position at the head of a ravine, near a forest of trees, but where the grass was abundant and their horses could eat while the fight lasted.

The battle was desperate, and for hours the Texans kept off the Indians, killing their chief among others, when they retired from the contest, elected another chief and renewed the struggle.

During the fight the Texans would pull off their hats, place them on the ends of their ramrods, raise them above the level of the walls of the ravine, and the Indians, mistaking the empty hats for hats with heads in them, would fire at them, sometimes putting as many as half a dozen balls through one hat, when immediately the Texans would rise, take aim and fire at the Indians.

At last the wily savages resorted to the expedient of setting the prairie on fire, and almost in an instant vast volumes of flames and smoke forced the little band to leave their advantageous position and seek safety in the woodland near by, to arrive at which point they must necessarily charge through the Indians as well as the flames.

Having lost three men already, the remaining fifteen left their horses, baggage, provisions, and dead, and at the word of command bounded off on their run for dear life.

In the charge through the Indians and run to the timber, a distance of about eighty yards, seven of the Rangers were killed, including Lieutenant Miles, and three wounded; in the engagement, ten of eighteen were killed and three of the survivors wounded, while the Indians, as they reported at a trading house, lost sixty-three killed and wounded.

Night coming on soon after the Texans gained the woods, under the friendly protection of its dark mantle, they retreated before the victorious savages and after much suffering and many hardships, going for two or three days without anything to eat, they finally struck the settlements and found rest for their weary limbs, and nourishing food for their empty stomachs, no doubt esteeming themselves fortunate in the possession of their scalps, and fully appreciating the language of the poet:

> "For he who fights and runs away
> May live to fight another day;
> But he who is in battle slain
> Can never rise and fight again."

One of these eight Rangers, J. O. Rice, verified the truth of this poetry, for, in 1842, only five years afterwards he joined the ill-fated expedition under General Somerville, and was wounded and captured.

Mr. Rice, with seven others, through the kind offices of H. L. Kinney, who happened to be in Mier at the time, and the expenditure of $500, bribed their guard to furnish them three guns, some ammunition and provisions for their flight into Texas.

On the night of the 20th of January, 1843, having all things ready, they left their prison and were piloted by an officer of the guard out of the city, and instructed when they crossed the river to go due northeast, whilst in his pursuit he would cross at Pilo Blanco fifteen miles above, and thus avoid them.

Becoming confused, the escaped wandered around until morning when they found themselves at the Pilo Blanco road, along which their pursuers were to come.

They took to the chaparral, and, as persons who have lost their reckoning often do, becoming confused they again, after wandering around, came back to the same road.

It being necessary to cross the road to Pilo Blanco, along which their pursuers were to travel by agreement, they were sorely puzzled until Mr. William Ripley, an Irishman, exclaimed: "Be the Howly Saint Patrick can't we jist walk across the road backwards, and make the divils think we are going the other way?"

The party acted on Ripley's suggestion, and when the Mexicans came up a few hours afterwards, they took the back track, and the poor wounded Texans were permitted to limp and hobble from the Rio Grande to San Antonio, subsisting alone on two mule-rabbits and two Mexican buzzards, besides what little they had started with.

On one occasion Robert Beal, who was shot through the right lung, fell down in the deep sandy road, gave up and said he could go no farther.

The little party halted for consultation and again Ripley's wit was of service. Speaking loud enough for Beal to hear him, he said: "It will niver do to lave the pore mon here to die of hunger and thirst, and thin be ate up by wild bastes. Not at all, at all! But as we can't afford to stay here and starve with him, we must shoot the poor fellow and put him out of his misery!"

This kind suggestion had a vivifying effect on Mr. Robert Beal, who immediately arose and continued his locomotion, and after a few more days of toil and suffering, arrived safely in San Antonio, no doubt perfectly satisfied with the

"Pride, pomp, and circumstance of glorious war."

The following graphic sketch of an Indian fight is from the pen of Rezin P. Bowie, brother of James Bowie, the hero of Concepcion and the Alamo, who was also in this contest, which took place on the San Saba, about four years before his death:

"Their number being so far greater than ours (164 to 11), it was agreed that Rezin P. Bowie should be sent out to talk with them, and endeavor to compromise rather than attempt a fight. He accordingly started, with David Buchanan in company, and walked up to within about forty yards of where they had halted, and requested them, in their own tongue, to send forward their chief, as he wanted to talk with him. Their answer was, 'How de do? how de do?'

in English, and a discharge of twelve shots at us, one of which broke Buchanan's leg. Bowie returned their salutation with the contents of a double-barrelled gun and a pistol. He then took Buchanan on his shoulder, and started back to the encampment. They then opened a heavy fire upon us, which wounded Buchanan in two more places, slightly, and piercing Bowie's hunting-shirt in several places without doing him any injury. When they found their shot failed to bring Bowie down, eight Indians, on foot, took after him with their tomahawks, and, when close upon him, were discovered by his party, who rushed out with their rifles, and brought down four of them—the other four retreating back to the main body. We then returned to our position, and all was still for about five minutes.

"We then discovered a hill to the northeast at the distance of sixty yards, red with Indians, who opened a heavy fire upon us with loud yells—their chief, on horseback, urging them in a loud and audible voice to the charge, walking his horse perfectly composed. When we first discovered him, our guns were all empty, with the exception of Mr. Hamm's. James Bowie cried out, 'Who is loaded?' Mr. Hamm answered, 'I am.' He was then told to shoot that Indian on horseback. He did so, and broke his leg, and killed his horse. We now discovered him hopping round his horse on one leg, with his shield on his arm to keep off the balls. By this time, four of our party, being reloaded, fired at the same instant, and all the balls took effect through the shield. He fell, and was immediately surrounded by six or eight of his tribe, who picked him up and bore him off. Several of these were shot by our party. The whole body then retreated back of the hill, out of sight, with the exception of a few Indians, who were running about from tree to tree, out of gunshot.

"They now covered the hill the second time, bringing up their bowmen, who had not been in action before, and commenced a heavy fire with balls and arrows, which we returned by a well-directed aim with our rifles. At this instant another chief appeared on horseback, near the spot where the last one fell. The same question of 'Who is loaded?' was asked. The answer was, 'Nobody;' when little Charles, the mulatto servant, came running up with Buchanan's rifle, which had not been discharged since he was wounded, and handed it to James Bowie, who instantly fired and brought him down from his horse. He was surrounded by six or eight of his tribe, as was the last, and borne off under our fire.

"During the time we were engaged in defending ourselves from the Indians on the hill, some fifteen or twenty of the Caddo tribe had succeeded in getting under the bank of the creek, in our rear, at about forty yards' distance, and opened a heavy fire upon us, which wounded Matthew Doyle, thè ball entering the left breast and coming out at the back. As soon as he cried out that he was wounded, Thomas M'Caslin hastened to the spot where he fell, and observed, 'Where is the Indian that shot Doyle?' He was told by a more experienced hand not to venture there, as, from the reports of their guns, they must be riflemen. At that instant he discovered an Indian, and, while in the act of raising his piece, was shot through the centre of the body, and expired. Robert Armstrong exclaimed, 'D—n the Indian that shot M'Caslin, where is he?' He was told not to venture there, as they must be riflemen; but, on discovering an Indian, and while bringing his gun up, he was fired at, and part of the stock of his gun cut off, and the ball lodged against the barrel. During this time our enemies had formed a complete circle round us, occupying the points of rocks, scattering trees, and bushes. The firing then became general from all quarters. Finding our situation too much exposed among the trees, we were obliged to leave them, and take to the thickets. The first thing necessary was to dislodge the riflemen from under the bank of the creek, who were within point-blank shot. This we soon succeeded in doing, by shooting the most of them through the head, as we had the advantage of seeing them when they could not see us.

"The road we had cut round the thicket the night previous gave us now an advantageous situation over that of our enemy, as we had a fair view of them in the prairie, while we were completely hid. We baffled their shots by moving six or eight feet the moment we had fired, as their only mark was the smoke of our guns. They would put twenty balls within the size of a pocket-handkerchief, where they had seen the smoke. In this manner we fought them two hours, and had one man wounded—James Corriell—who was shot through the arm, and the ball lodged in the side, first cutting away a small bush, which prevented it from penetrating deeper than the size of it.

"They now discovered that we were not to be dislodged from the thicket, and the uncertainty of killing us at random; they suffering very much from the fire of our rifles, which brought half a dozen down at every round. They now determined to resort to stratagem, by putting fire to the dry grass in the prairie, for the double purpose of routing us from our position, and, under cover of the smoke, to carry away their dead and wounded, which lay near us. The wind was now blowing from the west, and they placed the fire in that quarter, where it burned down all the grass to the creek, and then bore off to the right and left, leaving around our position a space of about five acres untouched by the fire. Under cover of this smoke they succeeded in carrying off a portion of their dead and wounded. In the meantime, our party was engaged in scraping away the dry grass and leaves from our wounded men and baggage, to prevent the fire from passing over them; and likewise in piling up rocks and bushes to answer the purpose of a breastwork. They now discovered they had failed in routing us by the fire, as they had anticipated. They then reoccupied the points of rocks and trees in the prairie, and commenced another attack. The firing continued for some time, when the wind suddenly shifted to the north, and blew very hard.

"We now discovered our dangerous situation, should the Indians succeed in putting fire to the small spot which we occupied, and kept a strict watch all around. The two servant-boys were employed in scraping away dry grass and leaves from around the baggage, and pulling up rocks and placing them around the wounded men. The point from which the wind now blew being favorable to fire our position, one of the Indians succeeded in crawling down the creek, and putting fire to the grass that had not been burnt; but, before he could retreat back to his party, he was killed by Robert Armstrong.

"At this time we saw no hopes of escape, as the fire was coming down rapidly before the wind, flaming ten feet high, and directly for the spot we occupied. What was to be done? We must either be burnt up alive, or driven into the prairie among the savages. This encouraged the Indians; and, to make it more awful, their shouts and yells rent the air—they, at the same time, firing upon us about twenty shots a minute. As soon as the smoke hid us from their view, we collected together and held a consultation as to what was best to be done. Our first impression was, that they might charge on us under cover of the smoke, as we could make but one effectual fire: the sparks were flying about so thickly that no man could open his powder-horn without running the risk of being blown up. However, we finally came to a determination, had they charged us, to give them one fire, place our backs together, draw our knives, and fight them as long as any one of us was left alive. The next question was, should they not charge us, and we retain our position, we must be burnt up. It was then decided that each man should take care of himself as well as he could until the fire arrived at the ring around our baggage and wounded men, and there it should be smothered with buffalo-robes, bear-skins, deer-skins, and blankets; which, after a great deal of exertion, we succeeded in doing.

"Our thicket being so much burnt and scorched that it afforded little or no shelter, we all got into the ring that was made around our wounded men and baggage, and commenced building our breastwork higher, with the loose rocks from the inside, and dirt dug up with our knives and sticks. During this last fire the Indians had succeeded in removing all their killed and wounded which lay near us. It was now sundown, and we had been warmly engaged with the Indians since sunrise; and they, seeing us still alive and ready for fight, drew off at a distance of three hundred yards, and encamped for the night."

No other attack was made upon the little party which remained on the field of battle eight days, when the Indians, who were Caddoes and Tehuacanas, having retired, they saddled up and returned to the settlements, with a loss of one man killed, three wounded, and five horses killed and three wounded, while the Indian loss, as reported to the Comanches, was eighty-two killed and wounded.

During the administration of President Houston, which extended from Oct. 22d, 1836, to Dec. 9th, 1838, crops were good and immigration and capital flowed into the country. Galveston and Houston grew amazingly, trade and commerce increased, and the gold and silver received for the cotton alone amounted to millions of dollars. This, with the money brought in by immigrants (which was estimated at about $1,000 per head), afforded something of a circulating medium, and when the cash notes, payable in cows and calves, were added to these, the people got on finely, and prospered much more than they ever did in the same period under Mexican Government.

Galveston, in 1836, hardly received into its harbor one vessel a month. In 1838, says Yoakum, "vessels were arriving daily, and the harbor presented the appearance of an Atlantic port. The merchants who had previously confined their trade to New Orleans were now extending their business to the Eastern cities.* With the demand from the interior grew up the traffic between Galveston and Houston. This trade was carried on by four steamboats; and the growth of the last-named town was equally rapid. For the first quarter of 1838, the imports at Galveston were over a quarter of a million, and the duties about $51,000."

The Treasurer's report showed a net revenue from imports, for the year ending September, 1838, of

* "*Telegraph*, February 17, 1838. A writer in that paper of June, 16, 1838, says that, twelve months previous to that time, there was but one building there, but at the time he wrote there were fifty or sixty elegant buildings, and fifteen or twenty vessels in the harbor."

$278,000; a circulation of $684,000 of promissory notes.; a funded debt of $427,000; unpaid audited claims, $775,000—exhibiting an indebtedness of $1,886,000. However, as it is unreasonable to suppose, as Lieut. Yoakum does, that the $278,000 was applied to the part payment of the public debt instead of to the government expenses, the debt of Texas at this time, September, 1838, was $2,164,000.

On the 16th of March, 1837, Deaf Smith, with twenty-one Rangers, was attacked five miles east of Laredo, on the Chançon, by forty Mexican cavalrymen, who, after an engagement of forty-five minutes, retired with a loss of ten killed and as many wounded. Col. J. N. Seguin and Captain Rodriguez, with companies of *Mexican Texans*, ranged the country between Matamoras and San Antonio. On the 25th of February, 1837, Col. Seguin, by order of his commander-in-chief, collected the ashes of the defenders of the Alamo under Travis, whose bodies had been burned by Santa Anna, and having placed them in a neat black coffin, buried them with the honors of war.

Col. Neill, in a bloody battle with the Comanches, on the 25th of October, 1838, at José Maria (Fort Graham), gained great *éclat* for himself and his command. The Indians, leaving many of their warriors dead, retired from the contest.

On the 16th of October, 1838, Gen. Rusk, at Kickapoo Town, near Fort Houston, on the Trinity, with 200 hastily levied men, defeated a large body of Indians, who fled, leaving eleven warriors dead on the field.

In August, 1838, the Mexican residents of Nacogdoches took up arms and concentrated on the Angelina, to the number of 150. President Houston issued a proclamation requiring them to disperse.

To this proclamation their leaders answered in the following letter:

"The citizens of Nacogdoches, being tired of unjust treatment, and of the usurpation of their rights, cannot do less than state that they are embodied, with arms in their hands, to sustain those rights and those of the nation to which they belong. They are ready to shed the last drop of their blood; and declare, as they have heretofore done, that they do not acknowledge the existing laws, through which they are offered guarantees (by the proclamation) for their lives and properties. They only ask that you will not molest their families, promising in good faith to do the same in regard to yours.

"VICENTE CORDOVA,	A. CORDA,
"NAT. NORRIS,	C. MORALES,
"J. ARRIOLA,	JOSHUA ROBERTSON,
"J. VICENTE MICHELI,	JUAN JOSE RODRIQUES,
"J. SANTOS COY,	and others.

"*August* 10, 1838."

Notwithstanding these brave words, on the approach of Gen. Rusk with troops, they fled and scattered.

Subsequent events will show that they were incited to this course by Mexican emissaries.

In 1838, Texas mourned the untimely death of "*the keenest blade of San Jacinto*," Col. John A. Wharton, and first Chief-Justice of Texas, James Collingsworth.

Although their loss was a public calamity, we know that

> "In the midst of life we are in death."

Yet in that of these two distinguished Texans, we can rejoice that while

> "Cowards die many times,
> These *heroes never* tasted death but once!"

CHAPTER XV.

Lamar and Burnet inaugurated President and Vice-President.—Extracts from Lamar's Inaugural Address.—His Indian Policy.—Expulsion of the Cherokees from Texas, and Death of their chief, Bolles.—Admiral Baudin takes Vera Cruz and visits Texas.—Treaty with France.—Texas' Minister to Mexico rejected.—War with the Comanches.—Death of Mrs. Coleman, her son, Jacob Burleson, and Edward Blakey.—Mrs. Blakey.—The Navy in 1839.—Austin selected as the Capital.—Surrounding Country.

THE September election resulted in the choice of Vice-President Lamar for President, and D. G. Burnet, the ex-provisional President, for Vice-President, who were inaugurated at Houston the 9th of December, 1838.

The *Houston Telegraph*, of the 12th of December, 1838, says of President Lamar's inaugural address:

"It was received with general approbation. It was pleasing to notice the remarkable degree of confidence and esteem that was everywhere manifested toward President Lamar. He is almost unanimously regarded as the pride and ornament of his country; and from his administration the most fortunate results are expected."

"The character of my administration," he said,

"may be anticipated in the domestic nature of our government and peaceful habits of the people. Looking upon agriculture, commerce, and the useful arts as the true basis of all national strength and glory, it will be my leading policy to awaken into vigorous activity the wealth, talent, and enterprise of the country; and, at the same time, to lay the foundation of those higher institutions for moral and mental culture, without which no government, on democratic principles, can prosper, nor the people long preserve their liberties. In the management of our foreign intercourse, I would recommend that we deal justly with all nations, aggressively to none; preserve friendly and amicable relations with such as may be disposed to reciprocate the policy. and, avoiding all protracted and perplexing negotiations, court free and unrestricted commerce wherever it may be the interest of our people to carry the national flag. Preferring peace, but not averse from war, I shall be ever ready to adjust all differences with our enemies by friendly discussion and arrangement, and at the same time be equally prompt to adopt either offensive or defensive operations, as their disposition and our own safety may render necessary."

Speaking of annexation, he said:

"Notwithstanding the almost undivided voice of my fellow-citizens at one time in favor of the measure, and notwithstanding the decision of the National Congress at its last session, inhibiting the chief magistrate from withdrawing the proposition of annexation to the United States, from the further consideration of that government, I have never been able myself to perceive the policy of the desired connection, or discover in it any advantage, either civil, political, or commercial, which could possibly result to Texas. But, on the contrary, a long train of consequences, of the most appalling character and magnitude, have never failed to present themselves whenever I have entertained the subject, and forced upon my mind the unwelcome conviction that the step once taken would produce a lasting regret, and ultimately prove as disastrous to our liberty and hopes as the triumphant sword of the enemy. And I say this from no irreverence to the character and institutions of my native country—whose welfare I have ever desired, and do still desire above my individual happiness—but a deep and abiding gratitude to the people of Texas, as well as a fervent devotion to those sacred principles of government whose defence invited me to this country, compel me to say, *that, however strong may be my attachment to the parent land, the land of my adoption must claim my highest allegiance and affection.*"

After referring to uncongenial communities on

account of slavery, *to free trade*, and to the *thraldom of tariff restrictions*, he said:

"When I reflect upon these vast and momentous consequences, so fatal to liberty on the one hand, and so fraught with happiness and glory on the other, *I cannot regard the annexation of Texas to the American Union in any other light than as the grave of all her hopes of happiness and greatness;* and if, contrary to the present aspect of affairs, the amalgamation shall ever hereafter take place, I shall feel that the blood of our martyred heroes had been shed in vain—that we had riven the chains of Mexican despotism only to fetter our country with indissoluble bonds, and that a young republic just rising into high distinction among the nations of the earth had been swallowed up and lost, like a proud bark in a devouring vortex.

"We have already laid the groundwork successfully and well, and it is only necessary now, that we pay proper attention to the strength and symmetry of the superstructure. As in the natural sciences, discoveries are daily being made, so in the art of good government, the great teacher, Time, is continually suggesting new and important changes, which, as a wise people, we should be ever ready advisedly to adopt, undeterred by the dread of innovation; and with conscious rectitude for our guide, move boldly onward in the rapid march of improvement, and keep pace with the progress of successful experiment. The American Constitution is certainly the highest effort of political wisdom, and approaches more nearly to perfection than any other social compact for the government of man; yet a fair trial of fifty years has detected in that sacred chart many serious and alarming errors, which if we will but wisely avoid, at the same time adopting its favorable features, and availing ourselves of all the lights of modern experience, we shall soon be able to devise and perfect a system of our own which shall surpass its model as far as that has excelled all others. To achieve this desirable end, we must turn to the great volume of History that lies open before us, and profit by the lessons it teaches. We may gather from its faithful records, not only a knowledge of what has been tested by other nations, and found to be practically beneficial or pernicious; but we may be taught the more solemn and important truth, that the instability of governments has not resulted from anything inherent in the nature of human institutions to flourish and decay, like the vegetable kingdom, but from the fact that all, with the exception of the American Constitution, have been the result of chance, vice, and rapacity, instead of being fashioned by reflection, and based upon the solid grounds of private integrity and public morals. The principles of virtue and justice are unchangeable and indestructible, and the government which shall be reared upon the one, and administered upon the other, cannot fail to be an eternal bulwark to the rights of man."

In another part of his Message he spoke of the border or *agricultural* Indians, of Eastern Texas, and denounced them as intruders and disturbers of the public peace.

Although the Cherokees, under Bolles, had settled on the Neches, a few miles north of Nacogdoches, in 1822, with the permission of the Mexicans and a promise of uninterrupted possession, which had been guaranteed to them by the CONSULTATION and the treaty made by Houston and Forbes in 1836, yet they were intruders, and should be removed.

Depredations and murders were frequent on the frontier, and when accused of doing them, the Cherokees laid the blame upon "*the wild Indians!*"

In order to guard the frontier as well as watch the Cherokees, Major Walters with two companies of troops were ordered to occupy the *Neches Saline*, which the Cherokees claimed as belonging to them.

Bolles notified Major Walters that the Cherokees would resist this occupation *by force and arms.*

Major Walters reported this fact to the Secretary

of War in November, 1839, but did not enter the ter ritory of the Cherokees.

Now, before this time, Manuel Flores, an agent of the Mexican Government, with some twenty-five men, passed between Seguin and San Antonio, where they murdered and robbed the defenceless, but were afterwards pursued, overtaken, and entirely defeated by Lieut. Jas. O. Rice on the San Gabriel fork of Little River, about fifteen miles from Austin. Rice captured 300 lbs. of powder, a like quantity of shot, balls, and bar-lead, and more than a hundred mules and horses. Flores was killed, and on his person were found papers and letters showing the grand strategy of the Mexican policy of arousing and inciting all the border Indians to aid them in their war with Texas. Flores had messages from General Canalizo, the successor of Filisola at Matamoras, to the chiefs of the Caddoes, Seminoles, Biloxies, Cherokees, Kickapoos, Brazos, Tehuacanas, and perhaps others, promising them the lands on which they had settled, and assuring them that they need "expect nothing from those greedy adventurers for land, who wish even to deprive the Indians of the sun that warms and vivifies them, and who would not cease to injure them while the grass grows and water runs."

By concert of action at the same time that the Mexican army marched into San Antonio, the Indians were to light up the whole frontier with the flames of Texan dwellings and cause the very air to resound with the cries of their women and children.

Whatever title the Cherokees had to their lands, and without doubt it was not far from a perfect one, they forfeited it by entering into the war with Mexico against Texas.

So upon receiving the notification of Bolles, through Major Walters, the Secretary of War, Gen. A. S. Johnston ordered Gen. Ed. Burleson with 400 men from the Colorado, Col. Landrum's regiment from Eastern Texas, and the Nacogdoches regiment under Gen. Rusk, to march into the Cherokee nation, and the entire force to act under the command of Gen. K. H. Douglas.

Commissioners preceded the troops and met the Indians in council, whom they promised to pay for their *improvements*, but required to surrender their gun-locks, and retire to the Cherokee nation of their brethren north of Red River, which the Indians refused to do, whereupon Gen. Douglas and troops attacked the poor Indians, and after two engagements, on the 15th and 16th of July, 1839, wherein the Indians were defeated with a loss of about 100 warriors, including their chief, Bolles (or Bowles—like Texan, Texian and Texas—use justifies either), while the whites lost eight killed and thirty wounded, drove them out of the country, burned their villages and made desolate their green fields.

In his report Gen. Douglas says:

"The Cherokees, Delawares, Shawnees, Caddoes, Kickapoos, Biloxies, Creeks, Ouchies, Muskogees, and some Seminoles, had established during the past spring and summer many villages, and cleared and planted extensive fields of corn, beans, peas, etc., preparing evidently for an efficient co-operation with the Mexicans in a war with this country."

In speaking of the territory of the Cherokees through which he marched, he says: "In point of richness of soil, and the beauty of situation, water, and productions, it would vie with the best portions of Texas."

This expulsion of the Indians from Texas was contrary to the advice and wishes of Gen. Houston, who spoke of it as an outrage, and in violation of treaty obligations and the public faith.

After a pursuit of ten days, the troops were marched back to the settlements, when they were disbanded and returned to their homes.

The Cherokees, having no home but the wilderness, thenceforth fed on wild game and revenge. "For eighteen months afterward," says Major John Wortham, a worthy officer in those engagements, "the Indians came back in small parties, and committed fearful depredations upon the lives and property of the people on the frontier."

During the early part of President Lamar's administration, the French, through Admiral Baudin, kept the Mexicans busy at home by blockading their ports.

On the 27th of November, 1838, Admiral Baudin, failing to bring them to terms, notified Gen. Rincon, the commandant of the castle of San Juan d'Ulloa, that unless satisfaction was immediately given for Mexican injuries to France that he should commence hostilities.

The commandant declining to give the desired satisfaction, the Admiral bombarded, and after an engagement of four hours took San Juan d'Ulloa, killing and wounding about 600 Mexicans. In March, 1839, Gen. Santa Anna, after attempting to drive the French from Vera Cruz and losing a leg for his pains, concluded a treaty with France, which being shortly afterwards ratified by Mexico, the Admiral left Mexico, and on his way home visited Galveston, where he was received and entertained with distinguished consideration as a most welcome guest of the city.

According to Kennedy: " An address of welcome, accompanied by the freedom of the city, was presented by the mayor and aldermen of Galveston to Admiral Baudin, who, in acknowledging the compliment, expressed himself gratified to find that what he had done in Mexico had proved beneficial to so just a cause as that of the Texan people. He hoped it would prove beneficial to the several nations who, either as friends or foes, had to deal with Mexico. Nothing could be more agreeable to his feelings, he said, than to be considered one of a community like theirs, whose industry and energy he so much admired. He assured them that he would greatly prefer being the humblest member of a well-regulated and thriving community like that of Galveston, than to move in the sphere of wealth and power in a corrupt and decaying society."

The friendship thus commenced between France and Texas was followed, on the 25th of September, 1839 (the same year), by a treaty of amity, navigation, and commerce, signed on the part of Texas by J. Pinckney Henderson, and on that of France by Marshal Soult, Duke of Dalmatia and President of the Council.

Having signed the treaty, the Marshal said: "*I am proud to have acted as the European godfather of Texas!*"

Great Britain followed on Nov. 16th, 1840, and thus enabled Col. Ashbel Smith to gain the reputation of a most skilful and consummate diplomatist while representing Texas at *the court of St. James.*

Some little trade having sprung up between the Mexicans of San Antonio, the Nueces and the Rio

Grande, President Lamar issued a proclamation for its encouragement, stating that Mexican goods might be carried over the Rio Grande into Texas *free* from Mexico, provided that those from Texas were permitted to pass into Mexico free from molestation.

In March, 1839, he appointed Barnard E. Bee Minister to Mexico, who arriving on the Mexican coast, notified the authorities of the country of his mission, but not receiving a favorable answer he returned.

The Vera Cruz *Censor* thus reflected upon Texans and their minister when he was off Sacrificios: "We do not know which most to admire, the audacity of those brigands in sending us their peddler to ask us to allow the peaceable possession of their robbery, or the answer the commandant-general gave to the individual who apprised him of the arrival of this quixotic ambassador. From the tenor of the reply, it appears that, if he lands, he will be accommodated with lodgings at the prison. Nevertheless, the Supreme Government will designate what ought definitely to be done. The commandant says he is not aware of the existence of a nation called the 'Republic of Texas;' but only of a horde of adventurers, in rebellion against the laws of the government of the republic."

On the 22d of February, 1839, Col. John H. Moore, W. P. Hardeman, Flacco, Castro and others, aggregating sixty-five whites and forty-one Lipans, mostly from La Grange and Bastrop, attacked the Comanches in their camp on Wallace's Creek, seven miles from San Saba, and completely surprised them, but failing to push their advantage, they lost their horses and marched home on foot, with the loss of one man accidentally killed and seven wounded.

The early history of Texas and a life on the frontier may be exemplified by the following incidents, the truth of which many living witnesses about Austin can prove:

Early in the spring of 1839, when the trees were covered with green leaves, and the earth with grass and variegated flowers, which perfumed the air with their fragrance; when the forest resounded with the "native wood-notes wild" of feathered songsters, and everything alive seemed to rejoice in existence, a band of 500 Indians attacked the settlements near Austin, just located in the hunting-ground of the Comanches.

They first attacked, about 10 o'clock A.M., the house of Mrs. Coleman, near the Colorado River, sixteen miles below Austin. She was in the garden at the time with her little son Thomas, aged about seven years, and on the approach of the savages she called her little boy and ran into the house. Mrs. Coleman, outrunning her son, arrived at the house first, when looking round for him, an Indian pierced her through the neck with an arrow; she then entered her house, and assisted another son, thirteen years old, in barring the door.

There were also in the house her two daughters, about nine and eleven years old; and an infant son, who took refuge under the bed.

After barring the door, Mrs. Coleman, with her maternal instinct of defending her young ones, seized a rifle, and seating herself in a chair, with the weapon on her knees, drew the deadly arrow from her neck, and almost immediately thereafter fell from the chair and expired, covering the floor with her blood.

The boy seized the gun, and as the Indians approached, first shot their chief, who fell dead on the door-steps, and then reloading, fired twice more, killing another Indian and wounding a third, when one of the savages thrust his spear through a hole in the side of the house, and pierced the brave boy through the body.

He fell near the bed where his sisters and brother lay concealed, when the eldest took his head in her lap; while bleeding to death he said to the poor little orphans:

"I will not groan to let them know I am wounded." Then, with his expiring breath he said to them

"Father is dead! Mother is dead! and I am dying! but something tells me that God will protect you!"

The Indians then broke open the door, but hearing voices under the bed, and fearing more deadly bullets, after piercing the dead bodies with their spears, by thrusting them through the door, retired, taking with them little Thomas, but leaving the other three defenceless children terribly frightened, but unharmed.

A few hours after, when relief came, they crawled from their place of concealment, and in giving their dear mother a farewell kiss, wet their clothes in her blood.

The Indians next attacked Dr. Joe Robertson's residence, about 350 yards from Mrs. Coleman's, and captured all but one of his negroes, but the Doctor was fortunately on a visit with his family, and thus escaped.

After robbing the premises, they next went to the place known afterwards as Well's Fort, where the three families of Mrs. Wells, John Walters, and G. W. Davis resided, but just before arriving at the houses, sixteen frontiersmen deployed in the front and stopped them, but retired before the Indians, taking the three families mounted behind them to Fort Wilbarger.

The Indians were on foot, and turning off from

the last place attacked, to Wilbarger Creek, camped for the night, and buried their dead, while the frontiersmen divided, a few remaining to watch the Indians, and the rest scattering as couriers over the country to raise men to fight them. By daylight eighty men had assembled at Wilbarger's, and Gen. Ed. Burleson, assuming command, marched to meet the Indians, leaving a detail of five men to guard the women and children.

Gen. Burleson came up with the Indians about one o'clock in the open prairie near Brushy Creek, about twenty miles northeast of Austin, when, dividing his men into two parties, one of which Capt. James Rogers led, and he the other, they charged the Indians, who took position in the bend of a ravine covered with scrubby elm and cactus.

The Indians at first retired before the galling fire of Burleson's men, but recovering, they charged and forced Burleson and his party back over the same ground. The contest lasted from one o'clock till night, when the Indians retired from the field of battle, beating their drums, rattling their shields, and singing their war songs, carrying with them their dead and wounded, supposed to be about eighty warriors.

Burleson lost four killed, viz., Jacob, his brother, Rev. James Gilleland, John Walters, Edward Blakey, and several wounded.

Jacob Burleson was killed in front, and his body fell into the temporary possession of the Indians, who cut off his hands, scalped him and cut out his heart, which they took off with them.

Wearied and exhausted from marching, fasting, and fighting, Burleson returned to Fort Wilbarger the next day after the battle, bearing the bodies of his dead, when a more painful scene was never witnessed; the bereaved wife wept for her lost husband, the mother for her only son, and brothers and sisters for their brothers.

One incident occurred, which equals or surpasses anything of the kind recorded in Grecian or Roman history.

On arriving at the fort, the bodies of the dead were laid out, preparatory to their funeral obsequies, in a room by themselves.

Mrs. Blakey, on starting into the room to take a last look at her son, was stopped and informed that he was shot in the face, and so mangled and disfigured that the sight would be so horrid and painful that she must not go in!

She claimed and demanded her right as mother to take a last look at her son. It was granted, and going into the room she kneeled down by his dead body, wiped the blood and brains oozing out from off his forehead, kissed him, and for a moment rested her head upon his manly breast, and then rising, pale and calm, she exclaimed with tearless dignity: "His father and brother died in defence of their country, now he is dead—my only remaining protector! But if I had a thousand sons, and my country needed them, I would cheerfully give them up."

God grant this mother and son the ineffable joys of paradise, and inspire all Texans with the same transcendent virtue and patriotic devotion!

In 1839, the Texan navy was increased by the addition of the steamship of war *Zavala*, the schooners *San Antonio*, *San Jacinto*, and *San Bernard*, and the brig *Colorado*, which, with the *Charleston* and *Potomac*, composed the navy of Texas, and cost the *republic* about $800,000 in government bonds.

On the 14th January, 1839, the Congress of Texas appointed Messrs. A. C. Horton, L. P. Cook, Wm. Menifee, J. Campbell, and the distinguished major of the HORSE MARINES, I. W. Burton, Commissioners to select a site for the capital of the republic, who made choice of the present location.

Judge Edwin Waller, in whose honor Waller County was named, surveyed and laid off the city into lots, selected sites for public buildings and erected them.

In selecting the site for the capitol, he was forcibly struck with the very remarkable resemblance between the landscape south of Capitol Hill in Austin and that in the same direction from the capitol in Washington, D. C.

Standing on top of Capitol Hill in Austin, and looking down Congress Avenue, he beheld the Colorado River and Heights, with the surrrounding scenery so strangely similar to Pennsylvania Avenue, the Potomac, Arlington Heights and the adjacent country, that, smitten with the singular coincidence, he thereupon instantly thrust his Jacob staff into the green sward, and (it is said) joyfully exclaimed, not in the famous word of the Indian chief on selecting the site of his camp, *Alabama!* but in the ever-memorable language of the Grecian sage: *Eureka.*

It has been said in praise of Texans that after their losses at the Alamo and Goliad, when the glorious victory of San Jacinto made them a free people, that they located the capital of their young republic on their extreme frontier amid the war-paths of the Indians, with the daring resolution of extending their settlements to and around it. That, imitating the Douglas when he threw the heart of Bruce in the midst of the Saracens towards the Holy Land, whither he had promised to take it, but with better success than the Scottish chief, they threw out the banner of the Lone Star beyond the outer wall of civilization among the hills overlooked by Mount Bonnel, in full view of Barton's lovely springs and the beautiful river and fertile valley of the Colorado; and that banner they have followed and defended.

Often has Austin suffered from the raids of the red man, still slowly, but firmly, that banner was fortified with happy homes, brave men and fair ladies, and now its gardens flourish and its fruits and flowers grow in hearing of steam engines and locomotives.

To give an idea of the country around Austin, I will relate the the following incident:

Several years ago, General Sam Houston and Judge Williamson, familiarly known in Texas as Three-legged Willie, together ascended Mount Bonnell, which overlooks Austin and all the surrounding country for miles. After looking around and surveying the beauties of nature spread out before them—the mountain-tops in the distance mingling with the sky; the thousands of horses, sheep, cattle, swine and goats, neighing, bleating, lowing, skipping and playing, as far as the eye could reach; the beautiful farms, the costly houses of the rich, and the humble but neat cottages of the poor; the lovely valley of the Colorado, and Barton's famous creek, dearer to Austinians than Pharpar and Abana to the people of Damascus—General Houston, filled with admiration at the transcendent loveliness and inspiring grandeur of the scenery, slapped his companion on the shoulder and exclaimed:

"'Pon my soul, Williamson, this must be the very identical spot where the devil took our Saviour to show and tempt Him with the riches and beauties of the world!"

"Yes, general," responded Judge Williamson; "and if Jesus Christ had been fallible, He would have accepted his satanic majesty's proposition!"

A distinguished sportsman of Austin thus writes to the *Turf, Field and Farm:*

"Though, like every ardent sportsman, a devoted lover of the beauties of Nature, animate and inanimate, yet it so happened that, shooting over the ground only in the autumn and winter, it had hardly occurred to me to imagine how lovely it looked in the pleasant spring-time.

"In approaching the spot where we intended to try our luck, you gradually ascend from the valley, until, at the end of two or three miles, you attain a considerable elevation, probably eight hundred feet or more above the level of the gulf, and reach the summit of a bold prairie ridge extending with occasional broken spurs three or four miles to your right and left. From this point, looking toward the north, the spires and domes of the lovely capital of Texas, twelve miles distant, shimmer in the sunlight; immediately beyond them Mount Bonnell, with its sum mit wreathed in a light mist, looks down upon the

ALL THESE WILL I GIVE THEE, IF THOU WILT FALL DOWN AND WORSHIP ME.—*Matt.* iv. 6.

city, while at the mountain's base the crystal waters of the Colorado leap over the Mormon Falls and hurry on to Matagorda Bay. To your left, the Pilot Knob is distinctly visible close at hand, covered from its base to its summit with a rich emerald carpet, interspersed here and there with immense beds of rich blue and scarlet flowers.

"Immediately in your front, in all its quiet pastoral beauty, lies the Valley of Onion Creek. The blue sky above is flecked with masses of light gulf clouds, driven northward by the wind. And such a breath of air nothing can surpass, and as I felt it playing upon my cheek I almost fancied I could hear the roar of the Mexican Gulf from whence it had come, and could not help thinking it was the very breeze that Bryant must have felt in all the pulses of his blood when he asked:

> . . . . "'Breezes of the South!
> Who toss the golden and the flame-like flowers,
> And pass the prairie hawk, that, poised on high,
> Flaps his broad wings, yet moves not; ye have played
> Among the palms of Mexico and vines of Texas,
> . . . . tell us,
> . . . have you fanned a lovelier scene than this?

"To the south, on the other side of this range of hills, stretches the lovely valley of the prairie stream, where we intended to fish."

CHAPTER XVI.

Comanches slaughtered in San Antonio and on the Colorado.—Santa Fé Expedition.—Houston's Second Term.—Foray of Vasques and Woll.—Meir Expedition.—Jack Hays, Tom Green, Ben. McCulloch, and others.—Indian Battles.—The Indian Chiefs Castro and Flacco.—The Archive War.—Death of Wm. Bell.—Heroism of Joseph Hornsby and Col. James Edmundson.—The Famous Retreat of John Wahrenburger.—Col. James Mayfield, Barton Sims, and Three-Legged Willie.—Congress Assembled at Washington.—Condition of the Country.—Navy in Ordinary.—Frontier Protection.—Friendly Offices of the *Great Powers*.—Armistice.—The Snively Expedition.—War of the Regulators and Moderators.—Annexation.

ON the 19th of March, 1840, twelve chiefs of the Comanches, with warriors, squaws, and children, amounting in all to sixty-five, while holding a treaty in San Antonio with the Texans, came to words, then to blows, and finally to fighting, which resulted in the killing of all the warriors, and the capture of their squaws and children, though the squaws fought like fury: one of them killed G. W. Casey, and another wounded Major Tom. Howard.

In order to avenge their loss on this occasion, on the 6th and 7th of August following, 400 Comanches attacked Victoria, and on the next day Linnville, killing fifteen whites at Victoria and seven at Linnville, as well as burning that place; but on the fifth day afterwards, the 12th of August, the whites, under Gens. Felix Huston and Ed. Burleson, Captains Bird, Caldwell, Jones, Wallace, Hardeman and McCulloch, attacked them on their retreat, at Plum Creek, killed about seventy, and captured much plunder and many horses.

Soon after, Col. John H. Moore with 102 men, followed the trail of the Comanches up the Colorado, about 300 miles above Austin, and on October 24, 1840, attacked their village, killing or drowning in the river 128, and capturing thirty-four Indians and 500 horses, with which he returned safely to the settlements, *with the loss of only one man.*

The ill-fated Santa Fé expedition, numbering 320 men, under the command of Brevet Brigadier-General *Hugh M'Leod*, a brother-in-law of President Lamar, set out from Austin on the 20th of June, 1841.

"The long train of wagons," says George Wilkins Kendall, in his very interesting sketch of this unfortunate expedition, "moving heavily forward, with the different companies of volunteers, all well mounted and well armed, and riding in double file, presented an imposing as well as an animating spectacle, causing every heart to beat high with the anticipation of exciting incidents on the boundless prairies."

Alas! that pain, suffering, and misfortune should

"Come when the *heart beats high* and warm!"

After marching nearly to their destination, having overcome many difficulties, and suffered from hunger, thirst and Indian hostilities, the members of the Santa Fé expedition, commanded by Brevet Brigadier-General Hugh M'Leod, surrendered at San Miguel on the 17th of September, 1841, without firing a gun, and were marched as prisoners into the interior of Mexico.

This expedition was not only without authority of law, at the wrong season of the year, without guides and provisions, but *very expensive.* Gen. Jackson said of it:

"The wild-goose campaign to Santa Fé was an ill-judged affair; and their surrender without the firing of a gun has lessened the prowess of the Texans in the minds of the Mexicans, and it will take another San Jacinto affair to restore their character."

The administration of President Lamar, after costing the republic millions of dollars—the Indian appropriation bills alone amounting to $2,552,319—terminated on the 13th of December, 1841, when Gen. Houston and Edward Burleson were inaugurated as President and Vice-President of the republic.

The Congress of 1842 rejected a loan negotiated from Belgium by Gen. James Hamilton, and commenced retrenchment, enacting a law which abolished many offices, and reduced the salaries of those retained.

Yoakum says: "A comparative statement of the officers employed at the seat of government, their grade and pay, during the years 1840, 1841, and 1842," made out by James B. Shaw, comptroller, on the 16th of December, 1842, is now before me, and shows the amount of salaries as follows:

1840	$174,200
1841	173,506
1842	32,800

Exchequer bills, receivable for customs alone, were issued, and served to pay the government officers, but fell to the value of twenty-five cents on the dollar, while Texas bonds, thrown by millions on the markets, sold for the enormous sums of three, five, and as high as ten cents *per* dollar.

Early in 1842, the Mexicans, under Gen. Vasquez, invaded Texas, captured San Antonio, but held it only two days, when they retired.

On September 11, 1842, the Mexicans, under Gen. Woll, while the district court was in session, and the presence of an enemy unsuspected, dashed into the city of San Antonio, and captured the city with the court in session.

After cutting up Dawson with his fifty-three comrades, the Mexicans fell in with Capt. Caldwell's com mand on the Salado, September 17, and after losing 120 killed and wounded, on the next morning retired with their booty and prisoners to the other side of the Rio Grande.

The foray of Vasquez caused the famous *archive* war, and the removal of the capital back to Houston, and afterwards to Washington, on the Brazos, while that of Woll caused the advance of an army of 750 Texans under Gen. Somerville to Laredo and Guerrero, which terminated in the disastrous *Mier expedition* in December of the same year, composed of about 300 men, who, after gallantly fighting on different occasions, surrendered to the enemy, were decimated at Salado for attempting to escape, and finally incarcerated in the dungeons of Perote, instead of "revelling," as some of them boasted, "*in the halls of the Montezumas, and hugging their yellow Jesuses* [as they styled the golden images of the Mexicans] *to their loving bosoms.*"

Many brave and gallant gentlemen left Texas in the unfortunate expeditions of Santa Fé and Mier, who never returned to their homes or families, while others gladdened the hearts of thousands by their return, two of whom, Gen. T. J. Green and G. W. Kendall, wrote histories of these expeditions, the former of the Mier and the latter of the Santa Fé expedition.

Sam Norvelle, a noted sport—who afterwards went to California—while several indictments for gaming were pending in the courts of Texas against him, and who wrote out, published in the *Alta Californian*, and sent back to all his friends, and most particularly the district-attorneys, an account of his death and burial, thereby causing a dismissal of prosecutions against him—was also of the Santa Fé expedition.

Hon. Alf. Thurmond, who used to amuse his fellow-prisoners at Perote, while working on the fortifications, by acting horse and running away with the wagon, was of the Mier expedition.

Capts. Fisher, Cameron, Eastland, Ryan, and Pierson were also members of this expedition; but Capt. John C. Hays, who was commonly called *Jack Hays*, returned from Guerrero with Gen. Somerville to San Antonio, and afterwards became famous as an Indian fighter, with an independent command, which ranged the frontier and did efficient service in protecting the settlements.

Generals Tom Green, Ben McCulloch, Sam Walker, Ad. Gillespie, W. W. Wallace (*Bigfoot*), Kit Acklin, Mike Chevalier, Henry McCulloch, Robert Neighbours, Jim Hudson (noted for his infinite wit and humor), besides many others since distinguished, did service on our frontier as officers or amateurs, who would visit Hays's camp in quest of adventure or amusement, and perform service without pay until they got tired, when they would return to the settlements and their different avocations.

Often around Hays's camp-fires were heard quotations from the original Greek and Latin, while many of them spoke French, Spanish, and German fluently.

Shortly after Capt. Hays commenced his distinguished career, the Comanches came down upon the settlements west of San Antonio, and after killing and robbing the defenceless inhabitants, started back with their booty to their prairie homes, when Hays, being informed of their raid, started in pursuit and came up with them on the Frio, west of San Antonio.

The Comanches numbered between 200 and 300, and when they saw the small number of their pursuers, who were but forty-two, they stopped, drew up in line of battle and waited to be attacked.

As the Rangers came up they commenced firing as they approached, and advanced without stopping to form in line.

Hays was riding a mule, and when the firing commenced was in the rear, but hastening to come up, he saw one of his men holding back his horse instead of letting him go ahead, as the horse wanted to do, when he exclaimed: "Why, d—n it, man, what do you mean? Why not let him go to the front?"

The soldier answered: "Captain, he wants to run

away with me!" "Then," said Hays, "let me ride your horse and you ride my mule."

The man eagerly agreed to the proposition, and they exchanged animals.

As soon as Hays mounted, he put spurs to the horse and was soon in the front, where the deadly balls and feathered messengers of death were flying thick and fast.

As he approached the line of Comanche warriors, all his efforts to curb the horse were unsuccessful, when, drawing his five-shooter, being joined by the Indian chief, Flacco, who rode a fleet charger, *the two*, yelling and firing, actually *went through* the enemy's line of battle!

The Comanches opened a way for them to pass, which they did amidst a shower of bullets, when the rest of the company, beholding the brilliant charge of their commander and one Indian, charged after them right in among the *redskins*, each armed with two five-shooters, and, firing with deadly precision, soon put them to flight.

Although Capt. Hays was a man of undoubted courage, this brilliant charge with the gallant Flacco was entirely attributable to the runaway horse.

Soon after this, Capt. Hayes with fifteen men, including Ad. Gillespie, Sam Walker, Sam Luckie, and the famous story-teller, Kit Acklin, fought his celebrated and most deparate battle with Yellow Wolf and eighty Comanche warriors at the Pinta trail crossing of the Guadalupe, between San Antonio and Fredericksburg; and, after a hand-to-hand contest and two charges, defeated them, killing and wounding about half their number, with a loss of one killed and three wounded, but without taking many spoils.

Hays's report of the efficiency of the five-shooters used in these battles caused Mr. Colt to produce the six-shooter and to engrave on the cylinder the Ranger on horse-back charging Indians.

Before or after this engagement a Ranger named James Dunn, whose hair was remarkably *red*, was captured by the Comanches and led away an hapless prisoner to their fearful camp. Strange to say, the murderous, blood-thirsty savages neither tortured, killed, nor ate him alive, which he imagined they would do, but actually took a fancy to him, treated him with great kindness, and, as *Jim* afterwards related, came within an ace of killing him with kindness, or, rather, drowning him in the Rio Frio while attempting to wash the red (paint) from his hair.

The Lipan chief, Flacco, was a large, fine-looking and symmetrically proportioned Indian, who lived mostly with the whites, and delighted to go with them on their raids into the Indian country. He was killed years ago and robbed of his horses near San Antonio by some blanketed, *thieving Mexicans.*

There were two chiefs of the Lipans named Castro, one of whom, in company with his squaws, visited President Lamar at his office, who, contrasting the age of Castro with that of his young squaws, said:

"These are your daughters, I suppose, Castro?"

"No, they are my wives," answered the old chief.

"But they are very young and you are an old man," exclaimed President Lamar.

"Yes," answered Castro, "an me telle you, ole woman, younge woman, any kind of woman is good for younge man, but younge woman is good for ole man."

In February, 1841, France, through her *chargé d'affaires*, M. De Saligny, suddenly broke off diplomatic relation with Texas and threatened to inflict on the Republic with her fleet what she had done to Mexico. The difficulty was caused as follows: M. De Saligny had a number of horses, which were fed with corn. Mr. Bullock's pigs intruded into the stables to pick up the corn the horses suffered to fall to the ground. One of M. De Saligny's servants killed some of the pigs. Mr. Bullock whipped the servant. M. De Saligny had Mr. Bullock arrested, and then came into Bullock's hotel and Mr. Bullock *put him out.* M. De Saligny demanded satisfaction of the government, and not getting it, left Texas abruptly. Anson Jones said: "It was understood that a French fleet was coming to the Gulf of Mexico to settle this affair; and the Texan *chargé* at Washington mentioned the subject to the American Secretary of State and to the British Minister in that city, both of whom promised to send their respective squadrons around there to look after the French. But when Houston came again into office, a kind letter was sent to France, which satisfied her wounded honor, and M. De Saligny returned to his post."

This Mr. Bullock venerated the late distinguished Justice of the Supreme Court, Hon. A. Lipscomb, who boarded with him and never failed to get his attention before all others, even almost using the Judge's name in his prayers or blessings before eating. Mr. Bullock's blessings were always the same, and in only one sentence, as follows: "*O Lord! make us thankful for what we are about to receive. Judge Lipscomb, will you have some beef?*"

As a general thing, war is a calamity, and we are rather disposed to admire a man like Jacob, who was the father of twelve sons, than one like Cain who slew his brother man.

Indeed the amiable and lovely character of the Saviour is so venerated that even the wicked sing:

"Oh, I would I were like Jesus,
So gentle, mild, and kind!"

But a bloodless war, like that of the *archives*, is an exception to the general rule, and the Austinians deserve praise rather than censure for their bloodless achievements in the *archive war*, which I will now give:

On the 5th of March, 1842, General Raphael Vasquez, with about 1,000 Mexicans, invaded Texas. He took and pillaged San Antonio, while other parties of God-and-liberty-loving greasers did the same thing for Goliad and Refugio, which so affected President Houston that he left Austin, the capital of the republic, went to Houston, and attempted—by ordering the archives, his cabinet, etc., there—to change the capital of Texas back to Houston, which, being named after him, was his favorite city.

The people of Austin, however, opposed this measure of the administration, looking upon it as a flagrant violation of the Constitution, and a heavy blow to the future development of their city. So when President Houston sent after the archives, to have them taken to Houston, they opposed it.

On the 29th of December, 1842, Captain Thomas I. Smith, with forty armed men, by order of the President, came to Austin with three wagons, and going up to the Land Office, of which Thos. W. Ward was the Commissioner, commenced loading the wagons with the records of the Land Office.

The Austinians having organized resistance and formally protested against the removal of the archives by Capt. Smith and his party, brought out an old howitzer, charged it with grape and fired just one discharge at Smith and his party, hitting the Land Office and knocking up considerable dust, but fortunately injuring no one.

Whereupon Capt. Smith and his party hastily retreated with as much of the archives as they had already in the wagons and got away with them in good order as far as Kinney's Fort on Brushy Creek, eighteen miles from Austin, where they were overtaken by about sixty Austinians under the command of Capt. Mark B. Lewis, and forced to carry back to Austin, in their own wagons, everything taken away and replace them in the Land Office.

The scene was a rich and rare one when the returning victors were met and welcomed by the ladies of Austin, who honored them not only with their smiles and embraces, but with their loudest huzzas of approbation, for they had returned safe and victorious, when horrid war and bloody death had been apprehended.

The archive warriors, as they have been styled, also took posession of the arsenal, formed a vigilance committee, and with arms in their hands retained and guarded the archives until the annexation convention assembled on the 4th of July, 1845, when they turned them over by agreement to the administration of President Anson Jones, on condition that the convention should meet in Austin.

Comptroller James B. Shaw and Judge B. F. Johnson, some time in 1843, came to Austin to get some forms and blanks from among the archives, but they went away without them, with the tails and manes of their horse and mule sheared, and with their mule's ears cropped.

From the 8th of March, 1842, to the 4th of July, 1845, the people of Austin had a hard time, for they were not only at war with their own people, but with the Mexicans and Indians.

An incident occurred on the third day after the bloodless "battle of the archives," which, from its rarity and unexampled dash and daring, has no equal that the writer ever heard or read of in either ancient or modern history.

On the evening of the 1st of January, 1834, after attending a public meeting in Austin, Capt. Alex. Coleman and William Bell started in their buggy for a ride, followed by Joseph Hornsby and James Edmonson on horseback.

Just as Hornsby and Edmonson mounted the spur of Robertson's Hill, east of Austin, where George L. Robertson now resides, they saw Coleman and Bell jump from their buggy, cross the fence and run for dear life across the field southeast of them, pursued by about thirty Indians.

They saw the Indians capture them both, kill Bell and about to kill Coleman, when, after a moment's consultation, they resolved, though unarmed save with one single-barrel pistol between the two, to stampede the Indians and rescue their friend Coleman or perish in the attempt.

In their flight Bell and Coleman had separated, and the pursuing Indians did the same, many of them leaving their horses at the fence when they entered the field, and it so happened that when Hornsby and Edmonson charged them at full speed, yelling terribly and discharging the single-barrel pistol in their midst, that they were frightened, left Coleman at liberty, but almost naked, and took to their heels, no doubt thinking that Hornsby and Edmonson would immediately be followed by more Texans.

Coleman did his best running back to town and raised the alarm, while his liberators hung on the rear of the retreating Indians for two and a half miles, yelling and hallooing until assistance joined them, when a little battle took place, wherein three savages were killed and their horses and accoutrements captured.

One night John Wahrenberger, a Switzer and gardener of Col. Louis P. Cook, Secretary of the

Navy, returning home with a bag of meal on his shoulder, fell in with a party of Indians at the head of the avenue, near the Alhambra. He fled and gained the residence of Col. Cook, who then lived where Col. A. H. Cook now resides, but received three arrows in his meal-sack and one in his arm.

As the poor fellow gained the door, he fell exhausted and fainted, while Col. Cook fired on his pursuers and wounded one so badly that their trail was easily traced the next day by the blood on the ground.

After recovering his senses, John Wahrenberger felt his wound, then looking round he exclaimed: "Mine Got! What a Texas!" Then casting his eyes around without any more ado, he earnestly inquired: "Where ish mine meal?" It was shown to him under his head, and taking it up he retired to his apartments.

One night, as Col. James S. Mayfield, Secretary of State, was returning home from a party with a young lady, Indians shot at and wounded him.

Once on a time, this same Col. Mayfield, Bart Sims, a large, powerful old Texan, and Judge R. M. Williamson, were in Swisher's hotel together, when the colonel taking umbrage at some remark of old Bart, so called by his acquaintances, drew his pistol and was about shooting him, to prevent which, Sims snatched up "Three Legs," as the judge was sometimes called, and holding him between himself and Col. Mayfield, exclaimed, "Shoot, damn you, shoot!" The judge, not liking his position, but unable to change it, alternately exercised his powers of eloquence and denunciation.

First, he earnestly appealed to the parties, saying: "Gentlemen, this matter can be settled amicably, there is no necessity for any bloodshed. For God's sake, Col. Mayfield, don't shoot!" Then, as Mayfield pointed his pistol at Sims, he said: "Mayfield, make a centre shot; for, damn you, I will kill you, sure, if my life is spared! Bart, damn your soul, let me down." From this appeal, or threat, or somehow else, Col. Mayfield's ire cooled down, and he didn't shoot. But he afterwards swore that Three-legged Willie saved old Bart's life on this occasion.

On Nov. 14th, 1842, Congress met at Washington, on the Brazos, when the President informed it that "*the country was without credit, without means, and millions of dollars in debt.*"

He attributed the misfortunes of the Mier expedition to "*a want of concert of action, and a disposition to proceed without means or orders.*"

The navy had not been able to enforce the blockade of the Mexican ports, and other nations complained of it, and asked its abolition. The *San Antonio* had been lost at sea, and the other vessels had been ordered to return to Galveston.

He advised, under the circumstances, the sale of the navy, which, in July, 1843, returned to Galveston and for want of funds was laid up in ordinary.

At this session he vetoed a bill for the protection of the frontier, the election of a major-general of militia, and appropriating $50,000 for that purpose, but the bill was passed over his veto, and Gen. T. J. Rusk made the major-general.

"He likewise," says the learned Yoakum, "gave an account of the trouble in regard to *the archives* and *the resistance opposed to their removal*; and also in regard to the steps that had been taken to conciliate the Indian tribes."

It can be said in great praise of President Houston that his Indian policy cost less money and less blood, but was more effective in protecting the frontier than his predecessor's. Comptroller James B. Shaw gives the Indian appropriations made by the republic as follows:

1837	Houston's first term.........	$20,000
1838		170,000
1839	Lamar's term..............	1,430,000
1840		1,027,319
1841		95,000

1842	Houston's second term........	$20,000
1843		66,950
1844		17,142
1845	..Jones's term..................	45,000

The raids of Vasquez, Woll, Sanchez, Garcia and others, together with the prisoner-murdering policy of the Mexicans, caused President Houston, on October 15th, 1842, to address the Great Powers who had acknowledged the independence of Texas an appeal, in which he said: "In view of the character of hostilities at present waged by Mexico against Texas, and of those principles which have been, in the opinion of this government, so frequently and so flagrantly violated by our enemy, the hope is confidently indulged by the President that the *direct interference* of nations mutually friendly *will be extended* to arrest a species of warfare unbecoming the age in which we live, and disgraceful to any people professing to be civilized."

Through the friendly offices of England, France, and the United States, Santa Anna, who was still at the head of the Mexican Government, on the 27th of May, 1843, agreed to an *armistice*, which was accepted and proclaimed by Texas on June 15th, 1843.

On the 25th of April of this year, the SNIVELY EXPEDITION, under the command of *Col. Jacob Snively* was organized at Georgetown, six miles from Preston, or Coffee's Station, about ten or twelve miles above the city of Denison, on Red River.

This expedition was authorized by the administration, but was to mount, equip, and provision itself, and yet to divide the spoils taken with the government. Its field of operations was to be between Santa Fé and the United States, and its object to capture Mexican caravans going and returning from Santa Fé to the United States.

Arriving at the head-waters of the Arkansas River, near the road from Independence, Mo., to Santa Fé, after innumerable vexations, trials, hardships, and sufferings in the wilderness, through the beautiful prairies, over the *glittering hills* and *sunlit summits* of the Wachita Mountains, no doubt often reflecting upon the truth of the poet, when he said,

> "'*Tis distance lends enchantment to the view,*
> *And robes the mountains in its azure hue,*"

they at last, on the 20th of June, fell in with a caravan, attacked, killed and captured the whole party—aggregating seventeen killed and eighty prisoners, of whom eighteen were wounded.

Now, this trade between Santa Fé and Independence, Mo., was *valuable* to the United States, and with the next caravan came an escort of 195 United

States dragoons with two pieces of artillery, commanded by Capt. *Philip St. George Cooke*, who claimed that Col. Snively was out of Texas, and in the United States, depredating upon its commerce.

Snively's command had been reduced to 107 men —seventy under command of Capt. Chandler having started home on the 29th. So, on the 30th, after Cooke had surrounded the remainder, lighted his port-fires, and threatened to cut them to pieces if they did not immediately stack their arms, they surrendered, were then given ten guns and permitted to return to Texas!

Snively started back, sent an express to Capt. Chandler and joined him on the 2d of July, when, after some delay, many wishing to remain and still attempt to carry out the grand object of the expedition, while others wanted to go home, *they returned*, losing sixty horses at one time by a stampede, and in return killing ten or fifteen Comanches. The Snively expedition was not a success! The greater portion of it *surrendered*, as did the members of the Santa Fé and Mier expeditions, neither of which added any sheen to the lustre of Texan arms.

During the years 1842, 1843, and 1844, in Shelby County, took place the famous war between the Regulators and Moderators, one of the prime causes of which was Charles W. Jackson, master and owner of a Red River steamer running between New Orleans and Shreveport, Louisiana, who, after some fighting and bloodshed at Shreveport, took refuge in Shelbyville, ran for Congress, was beaten, and then, for exposing some fraudulent headrights, was notified to leave the country or he would be killed. Capt. Charlie killed Mr. Joseph Goodbread, who served the notice on him, and was himself waylaid and killed near Logansport.

Wat. Moman, John E. Myrick, and others attacked Capt. Jackson's slayers, killed and captured some, hung two, and spared one.

Then, for revenge, and to stop Moman's career with his Regulators, the party called Moderators was organized, commanded first by John M. Bradley, who was killed immediately after divine service at a night meeting in San Augustine by Wat. Moman. This party was afterwards commanded by Alfred Truit and Sam Todd.

Col. O. T. Boulware (who, one morning before breakfast, killed Pete Whetstone, Barton, and Ward, in and near Marshall), with his party from Harrison County, including Alexander and Minor Davidson, joined the Regulators. War was declared, and the Regulators and Moderators met in battle at the Cowpens and the Church.

The first was a drawn battle between sixty-two Reg

ulators and 225 Moderators, in which several were wounded and one killed. The latter, the battle of the Church, resulted in the defeat of the 225 Moderators by 300 Regulators, with a loss of four killed and seven wounded; immediately after which the amiable landlord of the Colorado Valley, between Bastrop and Austin, Capt. Jack Nash, with others in command of the militia of the republic, ordered out by President Houston, appeared on the scene of action, arrested a few, who were required to give bail for their appearance at Shelbyville, and dispersed the rest.

But none of the offenders were ever tried, the prosecutions were dismissed, and the Mexican war coming on soon after, the Regulators and Moderators shook hands, formed companies, joined the same regiment, and vented on the unfortunate Mexicans the wrathful feelings formerly entertained for each other—thus ending the war between the Regulators and Moderators, which brought death upon about fifty Texans.

Col. M. T. Johnson and *Capt. Eph Daggett* (afterwards a distinguished officer in Hays's regiment, so famous in the Mexican war) were Regulators. At the Cowpens, Capt. Ephraim had a ball shot through his wardrobe, but fortunately the hero's life was spared, in order that he might bear aloft in victorious battle the glorious old star-spangled banner, even to the halls of the Montezumas.

The annexation of Texas to the United States may be compared to the courtship and marriage of a young couple, wherein John Bull, Brother Jonathan, and Louis Phillipe were suitors to the fair maiden of *the Lone Star*, which, though not a suppliant, but rather coy and coquettish, gave not only her hand but her heart to Brother Jonathan.

President Tyler, Mr. Dallas, Gen. Jackson, and James K. Polk, in whose honor the present lovely cities of Tyler and Dallas, and the fair counties of Jackson and Polk were named, favored annexation, and by preparing the public mind of the United States for it, did most to bring it about.

As early as July, 1842, President Tyler openly favored it:

"I am anxious for it," said he, "and wish most sincerely I could conclude it at once."

Gen. J. P. Henderson and Mr. Isaac Van Zandt, with great zeal and distinguished ability, represented Texas at Washington City during this interesting period of her history—in whose honor, Henderson, the county seat of Rusk County, and Van Zandt County were named. Gen. Houston did all he could, and yet wrote:

"I am as cool as a shoemaker's lapstone in an open shop at Christmas," yet at the same time cautioning Texans "*not to* evince too much anxiety—it would be *regarded as importunity, and the voice of supplication in such cases seldom commanded great respect.*"

On the 8th of June, 1844, the Senate of the United States, by a vote of 35 to 16, rejected the annexation of Texas, but the canvass of that year for President involved the question; Polk and Dallas, the Democratic candidates, were for annexation, while the Whig ticket, headed by Henry Clay, was against it.

Mr. Clay was defeated and the question settled. The people of the American Union coolly and deliberately expressed their desire that Texas should be annexed to the United States.

Before this, Texas had expressed the same desire; indeed, the people of Texas were mostly emigrants from the United States—their manners, habits, customs, language, and laws were similar—*they were the same people!*

So it required but little diplomacy to bring about annexation after the elections in 1844.

Although the French had first extended the right hand of fellowship to Texans, they long ago had done the same thing to their forefathers when contending against the tremendous power of Old England.

The gallant Lafayette, Savannah, Yorktown, nor *La Belle France* were forgotten!

Nor was the great nation which spoke the language of the victors of Agincourt, Poictiers and Cressy—

whose sons had wept over the Talbot heroes of the immortal bard of Avon, forgotten!

It was not because Texas loved France and England *less, but because she loved the United States more.*

On the 25th of February, 1845, the House of Representatives of the United States Congress passed the annexation resolutions by a vote of 120 to 98; in the Senate they passed by a vote of 27 to 25 on the 1st day of March, and were approved on the same day by President Tyler.

In the fall of 1844, Dr. Anson Jones and Col. K. L. Anderson were elected President and Vice-President of Texas, and inaugurated as such December 9th, 1844. On the 15th of May, 1845, President Jones called a Convention of the people of Texas, to meet on the 4th of July, and an extra session of Congress to meet on the 16th of June, 1845.

The Convention and Congress both approved annexation, and the Convention also framed a Constitution, which, with the resolutions, were submitted to a direct vote of the people and by them ratified, after which, in December, 1845, this Constitution was approved by Congress, and thus the Republic of Texas expired, and her *Lone Star* at that memorable epoch was added to the more brilliant and glorious constellation of the American Union.

CHAPTER XVII.

The Mexican War.—Sale of Santa Fé to the United States.—Public Buildings.—Railroads.—The Civil War.—The Soldiers' Return.—Military and Carpet-bag Rule.—The Administration of Govs. Hamilton, Pease, and Davis.—Peace and Development.—Union Sentiment in Texas.—Texas Pacific Railroad.—Governors of Texas.

THE annexation of Texas brought on the Mexican war, wherein Gov. J. P. Henderson and thousands of Texans participated, and gained great glory at Palo Alto, Resaca de la Palma, Buena Vista, Cerro Gordo, Molina del Rey, Cherubusco, and other famous victories of Gens. Scott and Taylor, which culminated in the capture of the city of Mexico, and were followed by the treaty of Guadalupe-Hidalgo, February 2, 1848, and the annexation of California as well as Texas to the American Union. Of the gallant men who took part in these brilliant victories were those of Col. Jack Hays's celebrated regiment, of which Sam Walker was lieutenant-colonel, Mike Chevallie major, and Tom Green, Ben McCulloch, Claib C. Herbert, J. B. McCown, Kit Acklin, S. L. Ballew, Eli Chandler, Frank Early, and R. A. and James Gillespie, were captains. Most all these gallant soldiers, after distinguished careers, sleep with the dead; but I will conclude this paragraph with the prayer of one of them, Capt. J. B. McCown, just before the storming of Monterey: "O Lord, we are about to join battle with vastly superior numbers of the enemy, and, Heavenly Father, we would mightily like for you to be on our side and help us; but if you can't do it, for Christ's sake don't go over to the Mexicans, but just lie low and keep dark, and you will see one of the d—dest fights you ever saw in all your born days."

Had all Mexico been annexed to the Union, it would, in all probability, have given peace and development to the revolutionary-loving children of Montezuma and rendered entirely unnecessary the sad fate of the amiable Maximilian and the downfall of the Mexican Empire. It might also have afforded an outlet for the negroes of the South, and possibly thereby prevented the late civil war; but Providence decreed otherwise.

In 1850, Texas sold to the United States a portion of its northwestern territory, including Santa Fé, for the sum of ten millions of dollars. With this money the State paid its debts, erected its public buildings, founded asylums for the deaf, dumb, and blind, as well as sanctuaries for poor, unfortunate lunatics, whom sorrow or misfortune had rendered incapable of taking care of themselves.

Two millions of dollars were set aside as a common

school fund, and six thousand dollars per mile were loaned to railroad companies, in order to facilitate their construction.

The Southern Pacific, Houston and Texas Central, and Galveston, Houston and Henderson Railroad Companies, etc., were chartered. Immigration and capital flowed into the State to such an extent that in 1860 its population was 604,215.

In 1861, selfish politicians, party spirit, and sectional animosity (engendered by the agitation of the slavery question) placed Texas with her sister Southern States in the late deplorable and unfortunate, but ever-memorable civil war between Americans.

The venerable ex-president, Gen. Sam Houston, was the governor of Texas at this time, and opposed the secession of the State, yet respectfully declined 50,000 Federal troops tendered him by President Lincoln to control his people, when, refusing to take *the oath* to support the Confederacy, he was deposed, or, as he himself used to say, *decapitated.*

So greatly was the secession feeling predominant in Texas that he was unable to direct his own family—even his dearly beloved son Sam was a Secessionist, and coming into the governor's office one day just before his deposition, wearing a secession rosette on his breast, the governor asked him:

"What is that, Sam, on the lapel of your coat?"

"It is a secession rosette, father," answered young Sam.

"Why, Sammy, haven't you got it in the wrong place?" said the governor.

"Where should I wear it, father," asked Sam, "if not over my heart?"

"I think, Sammy, it would be more appropriate for you to wear it pinned to the inside of your coat-tail!" answered the governor.

The Old Hero himself soon laid aside his opposition, and being invited to drill the Bayland Guards gratified that company, and when putting them through, gave his commands as follows:

"Bayland Guards! eyes right! Do you see Louis T. Wigfall?" There being no response, he continued: "Eyes left! Do you see Williamson S. Oldham?" There being no response to this inquiry, he went on with his commands: "Eyes front! Do you see either of them?" when some one answered, "No." "No," said he, "and you never will!"

Gen. Wigfall and Judge Oldham were his political opponents and violent Secessionists.

When his son Sam got ready to start for the Confederate army and came to bid his father farewell, the Old Hero straightened himself up to his majestic height and gave the young gentleman his benediction, saying: "My son, *do your duty* as a soldier! Bring no discredit upon the family! May God Almighty bless you!"

Young Sam did do his duty, and shed his blood for the Confederacy, though he was not killed.

In Virginia, Maryland, and Pennsylvania, as well as in Arkansas, Missouri, and all intervening States, Texans poured out their blood like water, and for four long years fought, bled, and died, until the dark clouds of adversity gathered over their heads, shutting out all hope of successfully continuing the struggle, when they furled forever at Appomatox their cross of St. Andrew, and, with sad hearts and weary limbs, many brave and gallant soldiers who had contended with impetuous valor at Manassas, Shiloh, Fredericksburg, and in the Wilderness, against vastly superior numbers, returned to the once lovely homes which they had left, thoughtfully saying:

> "Oh, weep not, dearest! weep not,
> If in the cause I fall!
> Oh, weep not, dearest! weep not,
> *It is my Country's call!*"

and found them abandoned, desolate, or in ruins!

The world has ranked Gens. Robt. E. Lee, Stonewall Jackson, Leonidas Polk, and Albert Sidney Johnston, as noble and gallant gentlemen; but it may be truly said, that the brave soldiers who fought under these distinguished generals and survive the many bloody battles of our late unhappy civil war, were animated by the same conscientious sense of duty which actuated their beloved commanders.

Among those who fought on the Southern side were many citizens who, born and reared in the North, had emigrated to the South.

The statistics of Johnson's Island, where Confederate officers were imprisoned during the war, show that the majority of officers, in proportion to numbers, who took the oath of allegiance or neutrality when tendered by the government and returned home exempt from military duty thereafter during the war, *was in favor of the South.*

I have often heard of a Boston mother who visited her son at this place, who was a Confederate officer, and said to him:

"My son, I have come for you and brought money and clothing. Your brother officers of the South are taking the oath and going home; I wish you to take it and go home with me."

He answered: "Mother, I have taken an oath to support the Confederate States. Do you wish me to perjure myself? I may be exchanged in a few days, and be ordered to my command. Shall I disgrace my Puritan ancestors by deserting the cause which I have sworn to support?"

"No, my son," she answered, "do your duty! I

would rather weep over the honored grave of my son, than see him alive dishonored! I go home without you, and while I shall pray to God for the success of the Union arms, I shall daily and nightly appeal to Him to shield and protect you! Oh, my son! may the great, wise, and most merciful God bless you!"

That Boston mother returned home, but her son remained, and through the whole war did his duty as a Confederate, and was surrendered by his heroic general only *after his cause was lost.*

During the war all internal improvements ceased, immigration stopped, railroads were run in the interest of the Confederacy, farms were abandoned, and those who cultivated them sent to the front, while their fields and gardens grew up in weeds and thistles.

In 1865, after "grim-visaged war had smoothed his wrinkled front,"

> "Peace began her victories
> No less renowned than war."

Old fences and houses were repaired, new houses were built, new fields were inclosed, new farms opened, and Northern immigration and capital, with labor-saving machinery and industrious habits, came to Texas, and were received with open-armed welcome hospitality and kindness, because those Texans who had been born and reared in the North had endeared themselves to the others by their fidelity and devotion to the State of their adoption.

It is a noted fact that no Confederate soldiers fought braver nor died more gallantly than those born and reared in the North, and it should be fervently hoped by all true patriots that the late unhappy struggle will be looked upon by the good people of both sections as a little quarrel and fight between brothers—to be regretted and hereafter forever, by both, to be forgiven, and remembered only to prevent a repetition of such a deplorable calamity.

Indeed, as a Texan and a citizen of the American Union, I can truly say, in the language of the poet:

> "I do not know that American alive
> With whom my soul is any jot at odds,
> More than the infant that is born to-night."

True, the military and carpet-bag administrations of the state government since 1865 have been very grievous, and are justly odious, while the colored troops *who fought so nobly*, and were afterwards stationed in many cities of the South, as if to show the Southern people, in the language of those odoriferous gentlemen, that *the bottom rail was on top*, have often caused the Southron's blood to boil, and incited him to denounce his victorious Northern brothers as foul

20

invaders of their native land, and the successful robbers of their less powerful Southern kinsmen.

From 1865, after the flight of Gov. P. Murrah to Mexico, where he died, in 1866, the military government of A. J. Hamilton was mild and conservative.

In 1866 J. W. Throckmorton was elected over Gov. E. M. Pease by a large majority, but after an administration of one year, which gave general satisfaction to the people, he was adjudged an impediment to reconstruction, and was superseded by the appointment and installation of Ex-Gov. E. M. Pease, whose administration was gentle, mild, and just, but not *de jure.*

In 1869 Gov. Pease resigned, and Gen. E. J. Davis was appointed in his stead; then came the Constitutional Convention and the *notorious* election of Gov. Davis over Ex-Gov. A. J. Hamilton, who, it is generally understood and believed by the people of Texas, received more votes than Davis, yet was *counted out,* while Davis was *counted in.*

With the administration of Gov. Davis came the militia bill, the police bill, printing law, school law, and all the leading radical measures of the odious 12th Legislature, which culminated in martial law for Hill, Walker, Limestone, and Freestone Counties—and the murder of Godley, House, Mitchell, Applewhite and others by negro policemen.

For more than four long years, by the exercise of patience, fortitude, and endurance, the people of Texas bore up under the heavy weight of this most odious, unjust, and corrupt of all their governments, either state or national.

But to cap the climax of an unenviable notoriety: at the meeting of the 14th Legislature, after a fair election ordered by himself, in which he was a candidate for re-election and was overwhelmingly beaten, Gov. Davis organized armed resistance to the inauguration of his successful competitor, Gov. Richard Coke, and actually, with about 200 armed men, for several days after his term had expired, held forcible possession of the basement of the Texas capitol, while he telegraphed to President Grant *about the insurrection of Texans, the great danger of his life, and begged for the nation's arms to sustain him* in his usurpation.

President Grant justly declined to sustain the tenacious office-holder, by which he caused the smashing all to flinders of the glass which covered *his picture* in the governor's mansion, the snatching of *his picture* from the frame, and the consignment of *his picture* to the flames of the executive kitchen!

The cost of the military and carpet-bag adminstration under the reign of Gov. E. J. Davis and the notorious 12th and 13th Legislatures, increased from a half million of dollars per annum to ten times that sum; and to give an idea of how, after more than four years of despotic rule over Texas, Governor Davis is estimated, the following incident, which took place towards the end of his eign, is very *apropos:* In Corpus Christi or some other Western town, there lived a certain man named Montgomery, who did all he could to elect Davis's candidate for the Legislature, and after the election came up to Austin, when Gov ernor Davis, true to his promise, gave him an office.

Montgomery started home, but at Lockhart, hearing some one abusing his friend, Governor Davis, and calling him very hard names, he struck the abuser, and after a very severe fight, whipped him.

At Victoria the same thing happened with a similar result, but a little harder fight.

Arriving at home, Montgomery was installed into his office and commenced the duties thereof, when, a third time, hearing Governor Davis very severely abused, he again essayed to whip his abuser. But this time his opponent, although rather a small man, was well skilled in the noble art of self-defence, and after a long and well-contested struggle, Montgomery sung out "Enough!" after which, feeling unable to fight Governor Davis's abusers any further, he sent in his resignation, stating his experience and the cause of his resignation, whereupon Davis declined to receive his resignation, at the same time ordering his appointee to stop fighting, with the very pertinent remark:

"Were I to fight every Texan who speaks ill of me, I should want many regiments at my back."

The wise policy of the present administration of the National Government in permitting Texans to enjoy the invaluable blessings of self-government without Federal interference is fast wiping out, to my great joy and satisfaction, all bitterness of feeling existing in the Southern heart consequent upon a long and bloody as well as an unsuccessful war, and will cause our people to look upon their Northern brothers, not as conquerors or victorious adversaries, but as joint heirs with themselves of the inestimable inheritance of constitutional liberty handed down to Americans by their illustrious Revolutionary ancestors.

It can be truly said that the great body of the people of Texas desire nothing so much as the peace, prosperity, advancement and glory of the great American Union.

They see in this their own progress, but in another war with the North, even were they the victors,* they see demoralization, credit mobilier, bribery, corruption and individual as well as *national decay.*

---

* It took four long years for the North, with the aid of mercenary troops from Europe, to take Richmond, while the Prussians took Paris in less than one year; and yet the French had often overcome Prussia *and Austria.*

Their interest and inclination is to protect and defend the beautiful and glorious fabric of constitutional liberty! They wish not to see it in ruins, like the Colosseum and the Parthenon.

They would not have the government of their ancestors pointed at by the nations of the world as a sad and mournful vestige of departed greatness and power, nor do they wish that Washington, Jefferson, Adams, Franklin, Madison and their compatriots, the revered founders of liberty in America, should have lived and struggled in vain!

Long before Gen. Lee said he thought his allegiance was first due to Virginia, the Chief Magistrate of Texas said *his was first due to Texas, the land of his adoption.*

A monument might well be erected to the Confederate dead, with the inscription similar in words and as true in fact as that placed over the heroes of Thermopylæ:

"*Tell it in the South, O stranger! that we died here in obedience to her laws!*"

Yet, instead of this, it has been attempted by some of their Northern brethren to make their memory odious by prohibiting the decoration of their graves by their surviving comrades and friends!

Oh, that *the gentlemen of the press* of Columbia, inspired by the heavenly goddess, instead of "going to bed at night and rising in the morning" with their columns *polluted* with personal scandal, would turn from such unworthy work and see to the preservation and advancement of the liberties of America, for *a house divided against itself shall not stand!* *

Since the abolition of slavery, which Texans generally look upon as a blessing in disguise, and would not re-establish to-morrow had they the power, the money formerly expended by the planters "to buy more negroes to raise more cotton" is seeking another channel of investment. The purchase and improvement of real estate and the construction of railroads are now drawing this surplus capital.

And notwithstanding the maladministration of E. J. Davis, the H. and T. C. R. R. was extended through the State to Red River and to the cities of Austin and Waco; the International was built from Rockdale to Longview; the Great Northern from Houston to Palestine and Minneola; the Gulf, Western Texas and Pacific from Indianola to Cuero; and the Point Isabel and Brownsville Railroad now connects those towns;

---

* The New York *Sun* of Sept. 23, pleading the cause of poor Louisiana, *to free her from harpies who steal as they sting*, condescendingly says of her noble and chivalrous sons: "For the sin which they committed they have paid the debt in punishment, and yet they linger on in a misery which no people have ever known on our continent with whom the English language was a mother tongue and British liberty an inheritance."

the B. B., B. and W. T. R. R. has been extended west from Columbus towards San Antonio as far as Luling; while the Texas Pacific was extended from Marshall to Dallas and Texarkana, connecting Sherman and Bonham, and getting within eight miles of Paris.

This road, notwithstanding the late financial crisis and the great stringency in the money market, even without the aid of the National Government in guaranteeing the interest on its bonds, is slowly progressing westward.

The government aided the Northern Pacific by guaranteeing its bonds and interest to the amount of $88,400,000.

When the Texas Pacific asked Congress to aid it by the guarantee of the interest on its bonds, *with perfect security*, it was denied! The Northern Pacific asked much, and it was granted; the Texas Pacific asked but little, yet that little was refused, although the latter is a much better road for government purposes than the former! However, it is to be hoped that Congress will take a sober second thought on this subject, and grant the aid asked for this great national road.

The leading Republican journal of Kentucky, the *Louisville Commercial*, thus speaks of the national advantages to accrue from the completion of this road:

"In the first place, it will give competition, causing a

decline in rates of freights and passage, as the Texas Pacific can afford to carry at less rates than upper lines. It will form a reliable line between the East and the West, which can never be interrupted by snow blockades, to which the Union and Central Pacific are yearly liable, and will command the greater part of the through passenger travel during the winter months.

"The new line will develop a rich field for American trade and enterprise in Northern Mexico, and open up mineral fields of fabulous richness in all that section. The saving to the government in the transportation of troops, munitions of war, and the mails will more than equal, annually, the amount of interest guaranteed, even if the company never paid back one dollar. The line will form a perfect protection against the ravages of the Indians in Northern and Western Texas and Southern California.

"The State of Texas has recently passed a bill to organize seven companies of minute men, which will actually cost the state at least $500,000 to perform a duty which should devolve on the general government. All this will be saved by the completion of this great enterprise. It will attract across its line much of the commerce of the Orient, as the length of rail from San Diego to the Atlantic at Charleston and Savannah is about two-thirds of the distance from

San Francisco to New York, and, owing to differences in grades and curvatures, practically but one-half. From San Diego to Galveston the distance is but 1,767 miles, against 3,315 by the Union and Central Pacific. It will direct a stream of immigration to the South, from the piny woods of the Carolinas to the prairies of Texas, and infuse new life into the entire railroad system of the South. It will give vitality to the now inert and sluggish current of Southern commerce, and bind the entire country together with closer and more fraternal ties. Towns and cities will spring up along their lines, and the cotton will be manufactured where produced, and exported over this great thoroughfare to China, Japan, and India. The immense mineral resources of the South in iron and coal will be utilized, and new life and vigor infused both North and South."

Since annexation, Texas has had the following governors:

J. P. Henderson, from 1846 to 1847.

George T. Wood, from 1847 to 1849.

P. H. Bell, from 1849 to 1853.

E. M. Pease, from 1853 to 1857.

H. R. Runnels, from 1857 to 1859.

Sam Houston, from 1859 to 1861.

Edward Clark, from March 18, 1861, to end of the year.

THE PRESENT GOVERNOR AND PUBLIC OFFICERS OF TEXAS.

F. R. Lubbock, from 1861 to 1863.

P. Murrah, from 1863 to 1865.

A. J. Hamilton, from 1865 to 1866.

J. W. Throckmorton, from 1866 to 1867.

E. M. Pease, from 1867 to 1869.

E. J. Davis, from 1869 to 1874.

Richard Coke, from 1874 to ——.

CHAPTER XVIII.

TEXAS LAND TITLES.

THE earliest titles to land in Texas emanated from the kings of Spain, who, being good Catholics, claimed through the Pope of Rome, who, as the successor of St. Peter and vicegerent of the Son of God on earth, derived his title from the Almighty; hence the old Spanish titles or *testimonios* for *labors*, *leagues*, one-third and one-fourth of a *league*, and *eleven leagues*, issued prior to the 13th of November, 1835, either by the Spanish or Mexican Government, being of divine origin, have been generally held by the courts of Texas to be good, but titles issued between the 13th of November, 1835 (when the Consultation closed the land offices), and the 14th December, 1837, have beeen adjudged worthless.

On the 13th of December, 1837, the Congress of the Republic of Texas passed the act establishing a *General Land Office*, which was immediately vetoed by President Houston, but on the next day passed over his veto by constitutional majorities of both houses, and became the law of the land—and from this office have issued all titles to lands in Texas since the 14th of December, 1837.

By ordinances and decrees of the *Consultation* at San Felipe, passed the 24th of November and the 5th and 11th of December, 1835, every noncommissioned officer, private, drummer, and fifer of the *regular* and *volunteer* armies of Texas, were granted bounties of 640 acres, or one mile square of land each, which, in case of death or disability in the service, was to descend to their heirs or legal representatives.

By acts of the Convention and Congress, the bounty to soldiers was increased to 1920 acres for all who volunteered or enlisted for during the war, while volunteers for three months were granted 320, for six months 640, for nine months 960, and for twelve months and upwards 1280 *acres.*

The acts of December 5 and 10, 1836, and June 12, 1837, for frontier protection, extended the same bounties to the Rangers.

On the 4th of December, 1837, the Congress of Texas granted to each living hero of San Jacinto, San Antonio, Goliad, and the Alamo, and the heirs of the dead, one mile square of land.

A joint resolution of December 10, 1841, granted to the soldiers enlisted under the act approved December 21, 1838, for frontier protection, a bounty of 240 acres each, and on the 11th of February, 1852, the

State of Texas granted a bounty of 320 acres of land each to the members of a company of Rangers com manded by Capt. Wm. Becknell in 1836.

These *bounty* land claims came before the Secretary of War and the Adjutant-General, who, upon the presentation of regular discharges signed by company officers and countersigned by some field officer or commander of a post, issued the *bounty land warrants.*

By the Constitution of the Republic, section ten, general provisions, adopted March 17, 1836, every head of a family then living in Texas, who had not received his portion of land as a colonist, was entitled to one league and one labor of land, and every single man of the age of seventeen and upwards was entitled to the third of a league.

Orphans of those entitled to land under the colonization laws of Mexico were entitled to all the rights of their parents at the time of their death.

The twenty-ninth section of the act of the 14th of December, 1837, entitled every head of a family who arrived in Texas after the declaration of independence, but previous to the 1st of October, 1837, to 1280, and all single men to 640 acres: and if they married before the 1st of October, 1837, they were entitled to an additional 640 acres, upon condition that they should reside three years in Texas, "and do and perform all the duties required of other like citizens."

The twenty-third section of the same act entitled all single men who were by the Constitution entitled to a third of a league, to two-thirds of a league additional, on condition of getting married within the next twelve months thereafter.

Under these wise and salutary provisions, which passed the Senate unanimously, the morals as well as fortunes of the early immigrants improved. Young men quit playing poker on Sundays and went to church; barbers, tailors, and dancing-masters were employed; horse-racing and cock-fighting were neglected, and our gay and festive bachelors *capered nimbly with sporting tricks before their amorous looking-glasses!*

Camp-meetings in the wilderness were frequent; balls and parties became fashionable.

> There was a sound of revelry by night,
> And our Texan parlors gathered then
> Their beauty and their chivalry, and bright
> The lamps shone over fair women and brave men;
> A thousand hearts beat happily; and when
> Music arose with its voluptuous swell,
> Soft eyes looked love to eyes which spoke again,
> And all went merry with the marriage-bell.

It has been said that a minister stood on one side of

the Brazos, and, the river being up, with no means of crossing it, actually *married a couple standing on the opposite bank.*

Even General Houston was heard to exclaim in one of his public speeches,

> "The world was sad—the garden was a wild;
> And man, the hermit, sighed—till woman smiled."

Heaven was propitious, or if a little Homeric fancy might be excused, the gods and goddesses of high Olympus gave their approving nod,

> "And coming events cast their shadows before;"

while apron-strings reminded, poetically, the ex-bachelors

> "Of linked sweetness long drawn out."

Indeed the population increased, and Texas flourished under this benign legislation of the early Solons of the Republic.

The act of January 4, 1839, granted to heads of families who might immigrate before January 1, 1840, 640 acres, and to single men of the age of seventeen and upwards 320 acres, conditioned on a permanent residence of three years, and performing all the duties of citizens for that term.

Seeing the splendid and beneficent effect of these *headright grants,* the great and good men who composed the Congress of Texas, on the 16th of January, 1843, extended the time of these grants to immigrants from the 1st of January, 1840, to the 1st of January, 1842.

The law of December 14, 1837, creating the General Land Office, also provided for the election, by joint vote of both houses of Congress, of a *Board of Land Commissioners* for each county, composed of a president and two associates, for the purpose of investigating all claims on the government for headrights to lands, and granting *certificates* to all persons by law entitled to them.

This law was superseded by the act of January 26, 1839, which made the chief justices of counties, the associate justices, and the county clerks, boards of land commissioners for their respective counties, subject to the same laws prescribed for the action of the former boards.

By the act of May 13, 1846, county courts were invested with all the powers of land commissioners.

The acts of January 15, 1841, and January 16, 1843, extended the authority of the chief justice and associate justices to issue certificates of headrights to immigrants.

The act of February 7, 1853, provided that the functions of the various boards of land commissioners should cease December 31, 1853, but they were again revived by the act of February 4, 1854, and by the law of January 8, 1862, the county courts were required to take proofs and forward former reports on unconditional certificates, where, from neglect or other causes, they had not been entered and reported to the General Land Office.

An appeal was allowed from the county court, as it had been from the boards of land commissioners, to the district court, hence many headright certificates were issued by the district courts of the various counties on appeal, as well as under the act of February 4, 1841, which gave them original jurisdiction for hearing cases and granting headright certificates to all persons by law entitled to them, who had not received them or who held certificates *not recommended* by the board of land commissioners appointed to detect fraudulent certificates. The acts of August 1, 1856, January 16, 1858, February 16, 1858, and February 7, 1860, gave the Commissioner of Land Claims the power to grant certificates to all persons entitled to them by law, who had not received them.

The old Texans often bought and sold their homes, lands, and *land certificates*, and from the value of the latter, wicked men who delight in evil deeds forged or caused the issuance of *fraudulent certificates*, and sold or located them. When detected, these rascals expiated their crimes by serving in the penitentiary for a time not less than two nor more than five years. In order to checkmate these villains, *the Travelling Boards* of Land Commissioners to detect fraudulent land certificates were created January 29, 1840, whose duty it was to inspect the records of the various county boards of land commissioners, and from satisfactory evidence ascertain and report all genuine certificates to the General Land Office. This was done, and all the old genuine certificates and patented lands are now contained in printed books taken from the records of the General Land Office, including titles issued by the governments of Spain and Mexico, headrights issued by the district and supreme courts, by special laws, by the commissioner of claims, and bounty and donation warrants issued by the Secretary of War and Adjutant-General.

By laws passed December 6 and 10, 1836, June 9, December 3, 9, and 14, 1837, *land scrip* was issued for hundreds of thousands of acres of land, and patents authorized to be issued for the same.

An act of January 26, 1839, granted three leagues of land to each county for the purpose of establishing a primary school or academy in every county in the republic. This act was repealed illegally by the present Constitution of the State.

By acts of January 22, 1845, February 10, 1852, and February 7, 1853, pre-emptions of 320 acres were granted to actual settlers on the public domain, who had resided on and cultivated the same for three years.

The 320 acres were reduced, by act of February 13, 1854, to 160 acres, which, by the law of August 12, 1870, is still granted to heads of families, and 80 acres to single men twenty-one years old, upon condition that they select, locate, and occupy the same for three years.

By law lands were granted to colonists introduced by Peters, Castro, Fisher & Miller, 640 acres to heads of families, and 320 acres to single men.

The act of December 15, 1863, encouraged the erection of manufacturing establishments of iron, cotton, wool, fire-arms, nitre, sulphur, powder, paper, salt, oil, etc., granting 320 acres of land for every $1,000 so invested.

For the encouragement of railroads to aid and facilitate the development of the vast resources of Texas lying dormant in her immense forests and prairies, the Legislatures of 1854 and 1856 granted 10,240 acres of land per mile, and loaned $6,000 per mile, in money, at six per cent. interest per annum, for every mile of railroad to be constructed in the State.

Since then grants of lands to railroad companies have been increased to 20 sections, or 12,800 acres per mile.

By the act of the 14th of December, 1837, each

surveyor was required, as soon as practicable, to make out or procure *a map* of his county, on which plats of all the granted lands in each county should be made, so as to make a fair showing of the same. The acts of February 4 and 5, 1840, and May 11, 1846, more completely enforced this provision. Titles to land in Texas also emanate from sheriffs and tax-collectors.

Unpaid judgments and taxes are liens upon the lands of persons owning them, but a judgment to bind land outside of the county where the judgment is obtained must be recorded in the county where the land lies if in a State court, but if in a United States court it binds only within the jurisdiction of the court. However, judgment liens become dormant unless executions issue within twelve months from the date of judgments.

So, notwithstanding, the amount of titled land and the various tenures by which it is held, the *records* of the district courts of the different countins of the State, wherein deeds of all kinds to land are required to be recorded in order to make liens or titles valid, the records of the United States courts in Texas, and the records of the General Land Office, whence all *patents* emanate, afford very good evidence of good or bad titles to land in Texas.

CHAPTER XIX.

Mina, Bastrop.—The Colorado Valley.—Jones Rivers and Phil Claiborne.—Brenham—with descriptions of Bastrop, Fayette, Washington, Nacogdoches, San Augustine, Sabine, Shelby, Panola and Harrison Counties.—Scenes and Incidents.—Sam Graves, Tom Ochiltree, etc.

BASTROP is a pleasant little village nearly halfway between Austin and La Grange, on the Colorado River, containing about 1,000 or 1,500 inhabitants.

It was first called Mina, but was afterwards renamed Bastrop, in honor of Baron de Bastrop, who gave to the corporation four leagues of land.

The valley of the Colorado above and below Bastrop is exceedingly rich and productive. The old stage route from Austin to La Grange crosses the river four times, and after travelling it and beholding the bounties of nature spread out before me, I have esteemed it as beautiful and as attractive as any other portion of Texas, abounding in fish and game, and flowing with milk and honey.

In Bastrop resides the ancient friend and companion of the celebrated Jones Rivers, renowned Phil Claiborne, who, as landlord and lawyer, as well as the beloved associate of Col. Rivers, commands historic attention.

Many interesting stories are told of them, two of which are as follows:

One morning, while at Georgetown attending court, they, with others, met in the hotel parlor, when Phil asked his friend: "How are you this morning, Jones?"

Col. Rivers, putting on a solemn countenance, answered:

"Very well, I thank you, Phil; but I had a very strange dream last night. I dreamed that I was dead and in heaven, and, to my astonishment, I saw you enter the heavenly kingdom."

Phil exhibited great astonishment at this information, and earnestly requested his friend to tell him how he acted on the occasion.

"Well, sir," answered Rivers, "you came in just about as you did into this parlor a moment ago, stepped up to Mr. Clay, and shaking him warmly by the hand, you said: 'Why, Henry Clay, how do you do?'

"Then you shook Mr. Webster by the hand, saying: 'Why, Daniel Webster, how do you do?'

"Then with equal familiarity you shook hands with John C. Calhoun, Gen. Jackson, George Washington, and finally, pushing Gens. Houston and Rusk out of the way, saying, 'Sam! Tom! let me pass,' you stepped up to the Saviour of the world, and, slapping him on the shoulder, exclaimed: 'Why, Jesus Christ, ole fel, how do you do? I heard of you when I was a boy!'"

A loud peal of his inimitable laughter was Phil's only answer to this story of Col. Rivers.

Phil Claiborne never received a classical education, and it is said Col. Rivers used to amuse himself and the crowd by relating such stories as the following: "A party of us, including Henry Clay, Madam Le Vert, Mark Antony and his wife Susan B., left New Orleans by steamer for St. Louis. Everything went on very pleasantly—laughing, talking and playing whist until we got to Vicksburg, when Julius Cæsar, Cleopatra, and old Tom Benton got on board, soon after which, old Tom, Mark Antony, Julius Cæsar and myself went to playing seven-up for the whiskey and cigars.

"We were playing the fourth game when Mark Antony, looking toward the ladies' cabin, exclaimed, pointing his finger in that direction, 'Great Jove! look, Julius!'

"Cæsar and all of us looked and beheld Henry Clay with his arm around Cleopatra, waltzing about the cabin in fine style; and, Phil, it would have done you good to see the fire flash in old Cæsar's eyes, for he was jealous and powerful fond of Cleopatra.

"In jumping to his feet, he overturned the table and made for Mr. Clay furiously, but as he entered the ladies' cabin, Madam Le Vert, with one of her irresistible smiles, motioned Cæsar to take a seat by her side. He did so; and, Phil, I never saw the superiority of our American women over the ladies of Rome more fully displayed than on this occasion! Actually, sir, Madam Le Vert fascinated the whole party, and even caused Henry Clay to divide his attention between her and Cleopatra, which made the wily Egyptian bite her lips in mortification and chagrin.

"At Memphis, Daniel Webster and Mrs. Hemans came aboard, and I tell you what, Phil, there was more hugging and kissing and fun and frolic on the whole trip than I ever saw before."

Here Phil interrupted his friend and wanted to know if Mrs. Hemans, the poetess, either kissed or hugged any one on the trip, and being informed that she was seen frequently to kiss and fall lovingly into the arms of Mr. Webster, he remarked earnestly:

"Well, Jones, I have a copy of Mrs. Hemans's poems at home, and my wife and children have been reading it, but as soon as I get back, you may bet your bottom dollar I shall burn it up."

Thus would Col. Rivers mingle ancient and modern historical celebrities in his stories for the amusement of his less erudite friend.

Col. Claiborne is a true believer in the Bible and Christianity, and it is said of him that, once on a time, being in the congregation of the faithful, he was called upon to exhort, when, drawing from his pocket a small Bible of about two by three inches in size, he read from the Sermon on the Mount: "Whatsoever ye would that men should do unto you, do you even so unto them." Then holding the Scriptures up before the audience and turning over its sacred pages, he spoke as follows:

"This book, my dying friends, is the Bible, and these are the words of Jesus Christ, who wrote as no man ever wrote and spoke as no man ever spoke, and I pledge you my word and honor as a gentleman, the Bible is a good egg and Jesus Christ is no sardine!

"He went about the world, not like a roaring lion seeking whom he might devour, but doing good—healing the wounded, curing the sick, consoling the unfortunate, changing water into wine, and commanding us poor, erring mortals to drink it in remembrance of Him—God bless Him!—and that we should inherit eternal life!

"Now, my friends, let us reason together. Suppose you lose all your property, you can work for more; if you lose your wives you might marry again! Were you to lose your children, you might get more:

PHIL CLAIBORNE HOLDING FORTH.

but if you lose your immortal souls, up the spout you go!"

Shortly after this exhibition of his piety, Phil met with some friends down-town, and after drinking hot Scotches and Tom and Jerries, he started home loaded down to the guards; but on the way, becoming weary of his burden, he braced himself up against a horse-rack, and was throwing overboard his unhealthy cargo, when a passing friend came up and inquired:

"Phil, are you sick?"

Straightening himself up to his full height, he very contemptuously answered:

"You must be a d——d fool! do you suppose I'm puking for fun?"

Arriving at his room he became deathly sick, when, moved by his abiding faith in the efficacy of prayer, he fell upon his knees and besought the Lord to spare his life and heal him, promising most solemnly never to get drunk again; at which moment the prayer of Jones Rivers from the next room came very distinctly to his ears, and was in effect that the Lord should not hearken to Phil Claiborne's petition and spare his life—if He did, Phil would be drunk again in less than a week, and would finally die in his sins! "Take him now, O Lord!" prayed Rivers, "while the boon most dear to Heaven, the first tear of the repentant sinner, is in his eyes, or Phil Claiborne may be irrevocably lost!"

But as he once said to Judge Devine in behalf of this same friend, it is human to err and divine to forgive, the prayer of Col. Rivers ascended not higher than his head, and Phil Claiborne is still a living monument of God's mercy and compassion.

BRENHAM AND WASHINGTON COUNTY.

Washington, on the Brazos, once the capital of Texas, twenty miles northeast of Brenham, was the first county-seat of Washington County; Mount Vernon, five miles west of Brenham, was the second county-seat; and Brenham, named in honor of Dr. Brenham, one of the unfortunate Texans who lost their lives in the ill-fated Mier expedition, was made the third, and laid off into a town in January, 1844.

It is beautifully located on sandy soil in the heart of one of the richest bodies of land in Texas, ninety-three miles east of Austin, and twenty-one miles west of Hempstead, on the western branch of the Houston and Texas Central Railroad. It contains about 4,000 inhabitants, and although it has been nearly burnt up five times since the war, the first time by order of Lieut. G. W. Smith, commander of the post in 1866, yet it is now steadily improving.

In 1846, in the District Court of Washington County, Hon. R. E. Baylor presiding, the celebrated case of Coles *vs.* Kelsey was being tried, when Judge Baylor said to Three-Legged Willie, who was somewhat under the influence of inspiring bold John Barleycorn and annoying to the court:

"Mr. Williamson, take your seat, sir!"

Three Legs straightened himself up, and looking defiantly at Judge Baylor, said indignantly: "I sha'n't do it, sir!"

Judge Baylor calmly took up his pen and was in the act of imposing a fine for contempt, when Willie said:

"Ah, sir! I beg pardon of the court! and as the court has ordered me to sit down I will do so, with the express understanding that I shall get up again!" Then sitting down he exclaimed: "Now I'm down!" and immediately rising, he exclaimed: "Now I'm up!"

The inimitable acting of the man caused the Judge to smile and the crowded court-house to roar with laughter.

Nacogdoches, once the largest town in Texas, is pleasantly situated on sandy soil in the fork of the Lananas, two beautiful streams with gravelly beds, which, after uniting, flow into the Angelina.

At present it contains about 1,500 inhabitants and is the county-seat of Nacogdoches County, one-half of which, the famous red land, is quite productive and well timbered, and is watered by the Carissa, Atascosa, Mast and Bear Creeks, which afford fine water-power, and upon which a few mills have been erected.

Nacogdoches was settled about 1714, which the date on the old stone house attests, was depopulated in 1819 during the invasion led by Gen. James Long,* and suffered much from the Fredonian war of 1827,† yet in 1835 it numbered 3,500 inhabitants.

Here resided Generals Houston and Rusk, Henry Raguet, and the lamented Col. James Reiley, who fell in battle at Franklin, Louisiana, nobly struggling for Southern rights.

---

* Dr. James Long, of Natchez, with seventy-five followers, set out for Texas on the 17th June, 1819, was joined on the way by others, and on arriving at Nacogdoches his force was 300 men, with whom he took possession of Nacogdoches and the surrounding country, proclaimed Texas free and organized a government. He visited Lafitte at Galveston and tried to get him to unite their forces. Lafitte declined. Long's forces were soon after attacked, defeated and expelled from the country, while he himself was captured, taken to the city of Mexico, and put to death. Thus ended this inglorious attempt to make a republic of Texas.

† In the Fredonian war "*one man was killed and ten or twelve wounded.* It consisted in the very slight resistance of the empresario, Hayden Edwards, to his expulsion from Texas by Gov. Blanco. Edwards tried to unite with the Indians but failed, and left the country. His contract was abrogated, and the territory embraced in it was divided between David G. Burnet and Joseph Vehlin, as empresarios."

Here, in 1836, the pure-hearted, noble-minded, and dearly-beloved Southern hero, Robert E. Lee, was stationed with his regiment of United States regulars, and here he was promoted from the rank of second to that of first lieutenant.

The writer frequently met Gen. Lee while in San Antonio, and for some time ate at the same table with him while he was lieutenant-colonel, and was forcibly struck with the purity of his manners and the dignity of his bearing.

After the war, his efforts to restore harmony and good-will between Americans so exalted him in the estimation of the Northern people, as to draw from a leading journal of New York City the very truthful compliment:

"Never did mother give birth to a nobler son."

San Augustine, Sabine, and Shelby Counties, lying east of Nacogdoches County, partake of the same character of soil and timber to be found in the latter, the timber consisting principally in pine, oak, and hickory. They are watered by the Attoyac, Patrone, Towash, Flat Fork, Caney, and other rippling perennial streams.

Panola and Harrison Counties, lying north of Shelby, are also fine farming and cotton-growing sections, but Carthage, the county-seat of Panola, is not quite so populous as its namesake, the old rival of Rome, was, nor is Marshall, formerly styled the Athens of Texas, so large as Jefferson, fifteen miles north of it, although the great eastern depot and machine-shop of the Texas Pacific Railroad has been located there.

But Marshall *is* a distinguished place, for here Governors Henderson, Clark, and Murrah, Wigfall, Ochiltree, Jennings, Mills, Hill, Frazier, Adams, Mahone, Poag, Pope, and other distinguished members of the Texas bar once lived, and on the rostrum and from the press eloquently uttered

> " Thoughts that breathe, and words that burn."
> " Their tongues
> Dropt manna, and could make the worse appea
> The better reason, to perplex and dash
> Maturest counsels."

Here took place the celebrated game of poker between his Honor John T. Mills and Governor Henderson, wherein several hundred dollars and a new trial in the Snowdon case were said to have been lost and won on the same hand.

At any rate, in the morning, after taking his seat on the bench, the first order made by his Honor, and that, too, withont solicitation from any one, was for a new trial in the Snowdon case.

In Marshall still resides that amiable associate, good citizen, and indulgent father, Judge George B. Ad kins, a fair sample of *the old Texas gentleman*, who, many years ago, while holding court up-stairs, was annoyed by a game of faro going on down-stairs. After ordering the sheriff to stop the game, and being informed of the refusal of the sportsmen to obey his order, he adjourned his court for fifteen minutes, and being experienced in the game, commenced betting, and within the fifteen minutes broke the bank and again opened his court, which thereafter was not disturbed by the broken gamblers.

Here I first met that *rara avis in terris*, the golden-haired hero and most celebrated and inimitable story teller, Tom Ochiltree, whose name is familiar not only in Texas and the United States, but also in England, France, Germany, and the other great nations of the world. When but a boy, Tom gave promise of his future grand financial ideas in dealing faro from an old sardine-box to his associate urchins, and refusing to turn for less than a dime.

"Who put that ar five-center down there?" he indignantly inquired.

"I put it there, Tom," answered one of the little fellows.

"Well, you take it up," rejoined Tom, "for I sha'n't turn for less nor a dime!"

It is said that Major Ochiltree killed more men and went through more close places than almost any other officer of the lost cause. I have heard him speak

> "Of most disastrous chances,
> Of moving accidents, by flood and field,
> Of hair-breadth 'scapes, i' the imminent deadly breach;"

how he had two horses killed under him at Val Verde, and was blown forty feet in the air, but came down unharmed, lit upon his feet, mounted another horse, and charged home to victory! how, in one of the battles 'round Richmond, he had slaughtered thirty-eight Yanks that he got, besides cutting off with his sword a wagon-load of arms and ears; how he punched Stonewall Jackson in the ribs with his sabre, and waking him up, inquired: "Ole hoss, where is Gen. Jackson?" And then how small he felt when Stonewall exclaimed: "I am Gen. Jackson, what do you wish?"

Everybody has heard his story of the Arkansas girl who listened with tearful eyes to his touching account of the death of her dear brother who died in his arms, and with his dying breath spoke of his mother and sister in Arkansas—and how, when she inquired his name and he answered: "Major Ochiltree," she exclaimed in astonishment: "What! Tom Ochiltree!" and then upon his answering her affirmatively, how she smiled, wiped away her tears and pleasantly said: "Well, if you are Tom Ochiltree, it's all right! My brother is still alive"—so I will not repeat it.

It is reported that he was bearer of despatches from Gen. Sibley to Richmond, giving accounts of the battles of Val Verde, Glorietta, and other engagements, and after an audience with Mr. Davis, at which Gen. Wigfall was present, when Tom retired, Mr. Davis inquired of Wigfall:

"Who is he?" Wigfall answered: "Major Ochiltree." Mr. Davis rejoined: "I know that as well as you do. But he's from your state. Who is Major Ochiltree?"

"Well, sir," answered Wigfall, "he is a man who would tell a story on credit rather than tell the truth for cash."

"But what I wish to know of you, Gen. Wigfall, is, is he a reliable man?" again asked Mr. Davis.

"Reliable! Yes, sir!" answered Wigfall, "he can outlie and *out*relie any man you ever saw."

Major Ochiltree's amiable manners and very interesting conversational powers have made him friends everywhere, including Gen. Grant, whose appointment of him to be United States marshal was not at all distasteful to the good people of Eastern Texas.

As an ordinary sample of his story-telling, a recent instance is here inserted from the *New York Herald:*

"SARATOGA, *July* 30, 1874.

"Said Mr. James Valentine to Dr. Quackenbos on the quarter-stretch to-day:

"'It is just fifty years since Eclipse and Henry ran their great four-mile race on Long Island. It was a Tuesday in May. I crossed the East River on a tread-mill boat, worked by a mule in harness.' 'Yes,' said Dr. Quackenbos, 'there was not a steam-vessel on the water. I went over in a periauger.'

"'I went over on a raft,' said Tom Ochiltree, of Texas. 'I had to run off from school to see the race. Society has changed very much since.'

'You,' said all, 'why, how old are you, Tom?'

"'Threescore and ten,' exclaimed the United States marshal in question.

"Valentine drew a long sigh. 'Well,' said he, looking at Tom profoundly, 'I'm afraid I wasn't there.'"

For the information of parents and guardians who may wish to cure their children and wards of stretching the blanket too thin, I will relate how Mrs. Graves, a venerable Christian mother, who lived twenty miles from Marshall, on the road to Shreveport, cured her son Sam.

After Sam married and had become the father of three or four children, he took up his gun one day, and going through the woods, a mile or two from his residence, to his father's house, killed several squir-

TOM OCHILTREE GOING TO THE RACES.

rels, and, in giving an account of his hunt to his mother, said that he had seen at least one hundred squirrels upon one tree.

After dinner Sam retired to his old dormitory, and was soon sound asleep, when his mother came in with ropes and very gently, but unbeknowenst to Sammy, tied both hands and feet to the bed-posts; then with a whip she came down on Sam with all her might.

Sam begged and implored, but his mother kept on whipping him, once in a while exclaiming: "A hundred squirrels upon one tree, Sammy!"

"'Fore God, mother, there were at least fifty!"

"Too many my son!" exclaimed Mrs. Graves, as she continued the flogging.

Sam next fell to twenty-five. "Too many, my boy!" said his mother, and her castigation continued until Samivel came down to "at least three or four, mother," when she stopped and untied him.

Mrs. Graves then informed the gentleman that, being her only son, she had neglected to correct him too long and too often! Her conscience smote her for it, and that what she had done was from a sense of imperative duty to bring about his reformation and eternal salvation.

Mrs. Graves' plan worked like a charm, and Sam Graves became one of the most truthful and reliable men in Harrison County.

As the providence of God has deprived Major Ochiltree of both father and mother, it is to be hoped that, like the pious monks of old, he will administer to himself the castigation necessary for his reformation, and thus gladden the hearts of his numerous friends and secure his own everlasting happiness.

CHAPTER XX.

Galveston, Brazoria, Matagorda, Wharton and Fort Bend.—Houston, Jefferson, San Antonio, Austin, Dallas, Hempstead, Plantersville, Waller, Graines, Montgomery and Walker Counties.—Ike Baker, Jim Pinkston, Joe Bates, the Bell-men, etc.

GALVESTON, the great port of entry and largest city in Texas, containing some 35,000 or 40,000 inhabitants, the fourth cotton depot in the South—New Orleans, Savannah, and Charleston only excelling it—is situated on the east end of the island of the same name, which is about twenty-seven miles long, and where the city stands is about one mile wide.

This "beautiful isle of the sea" was selected and fortified by the notorious pirate Lafitte as his stronghold, to which he fled for safety when attacked by superior numbers, and whither he carried the vessels, cargoes and prisoners captured on the main. How many beautiful captive maidens were here forced to live and endure the horrid companionship of rude pirates, far away from the parental roof! And how often the poor victims sighed for the realization of the poet's ideal of earthly happiness when he sung:

"There is a bliss beyond all that the minstrel has told,
  When two that are linked in one heavenly tie,
With heart never changing and brow never cold,
  Love on through all ills, and love on till they die!
One hour of a passion so sacred is worth
  Whole ages of heartless and wondering bliss;
And, oh! if there be an Elysium on earth,
  It is this! it is this!"

may be rather imagined than described.

Lafitte was represented as a tall, symmetrically formed man, with pleasant address and agreeable manners. Just before the battle of New Orleans, on the 8th of January, 1815, he was offered £30,000 sterling, a post-captaincy, with the command of a frigate in the British navy, if he would join Lord Packenham on that famous occasion.

Lafitte declined the offer of the British Government, enclosed the written proposition to Gov. Claiborne, of Louisiana, with whom he was then at variance, offering his services to the United States, in consideration of a pardon and amnesty for himself and followers for all past offences, which proposition was accepted, when he joined Gen. Jackson in the defence of New Orleans, and participated in the glorious victory of American valor achieved over British discipline on the plains of Chalmette.

But *his habits were formed*, and no angel gave either to him or his followers that *wondrous potency* to change their abandoned, odious, sensual, and piratical lives, and although for his services against the British his past crimes were overlooked, he and his followers, with the pardon of the President of the United States in their pockets, again returned to piracy on the high seas, were detected, and ordered, in 1821, to leave Galveston Island, which they forever abandoned in that year.

After the departure of Lafitte, the island was occupied by the Tonkaway Indians for fishing purposes, when tired of eating buffalo, Comanche, and other animal food.

From 1821 to the Texas revolution, the island was mostly thus occupied, when the God-and-liberty-loving Mexicans established thereon a custom-house, and called the place Galveston, in honor of a distinguished Greaser named Galvez.

Velasco, at the mouth of the Brazos, and Anahuac, at the head of the bay, had fairer prospects at first of being the great port of Texas, than Galveston.

It was only after the victorious Texans, under Gen. Houston, had made the plains of San Jacinto immortal, and avenged the Alamo and Goliad, that fame trumpeted abroad, in terms of the highest praise, the beauty, fertility and productiveness of the soil and the salubrity of the climate—then Galveston commenced growing.

Young men of daring and enterprise came from Massachusetts, Vermont, New York, Connecticut, and even the State of New Jersey gave to Galveston several very good citizens, David and D. The. Ayres, among them. From Democratic Connecticut alone came E. S. Wood, Joe and William Hendley, George and Albert Ball, Ashbel Smith, Munson Hitchcock, Stephen Southwick, and that accomplished jurist and ripe scholar, laughter-loving Frank Merriman. The Nestorian Dr. Levi, the Hon. J. B. and Jeff. Jones—the amiable editors and publishers of the *News and Civilian*, Hamilton Stuart and Willard Richardson—the Ballengers, Jacks, R. and D. G. Mills, the great bankers of Texas, and thousands of others, soon made Galveston a sober, industrious, and orderly city, exporting produce amounting to more than $25,000,000 annually.

It is amusing to hear old Texans relate little incidents which took place at an early day, and hoping to give the reader cause for a smile, I will relate one on Frank Merriman, in which Uncle Stephen Southwick and Judge Swett were actors.

Frank had just arrived from pious, God-fearing New England, and was perfectly ignorant of "draw poker," but having learned never to trump his partner's ace, and being a first-rate "seven-up" player when Southwick and Swett insisted on a game of "draw," he assented, and asked to be shown how the game was played.

After being informed that the higher cards beat the lower cards, and that pairs of higher cards beat pairs of lower cards, and so on, the game commenced, and Frank was soon piling up and taking down, and enjoying himself hugely, when finally he got four aces. Swett held four "trays." Frank, after betting right sharply, "called" Swett, who, showing his hand, said: "Well, Mr. Merriman, I guess I've got you this time! I have four trays."

Whereupon Frank threw down his four aces, exclaiming, "Confound the luck, when I have ones or twos somebody else has threes or fours!"

Swett quietly raked down the money, and the game went on.

In the Rev. Doctor Eaton's church the next day Uncle Stephen went to sleep, and when the baskets were passed around for contributions, the collector partially waked him, and held out the basket, when Uncle Stephen, not fully aroused, spoke out loud enough for the whole congregation to hear him, "Oh, Swett, I pass, I do!"

On one occasion Mr. Southwick ran for the mayoralty of Galveston, and after going to every voter, all of whom he knew, and asking their votes, he expressed himself as perfectly confident of his election by a majority of 350 votes.

However, when the votes were counted out, Uncle Stephen lacked just that number of being elected, and being laughed at by his friends, exclaimed:

"Well, I've got the satisfaction of knowing 350 d—d liars! sure as my name is Stephen Southwick!"

During the late civil war, Galveston was attacked and captured twice, one time by the Federals, the other by the Confederates, wherein a father and son fought on opposing sides; the son, Lieut. Lee, was killed on the *Harriet Lane*, and the grief-stricken father, who was a graduate of West Point, participated in his funeral obsequies—possibly slew his own son!

God shield our country forever from another civil war!

West of Galveston are the great sugar counties of Texas, Brazoria, Matagorda, Fort Bend, and Wharton, watered by the Brazos, Old Caney, San Bernard, Colorado and other streams.

The land of these counties is very rich and productive, but not so valuable now as before the war, as they were then made productive by the forced labor of the sable-colored sons of injured Africa, who since their emancipation are, in many instances, opposed to regular labor or continued physical exertion.

In Brazoria, Mr. S. F. Austin lived and died, and here lives Capt. Robt. J. Calder, who was at San Jacinto, and as sheriff of Brazoria arrested the notorious Monroe Edwards.

On Old Caney lives the venerable Capt. John Duncan, an eighty-year-old Texan, and his estimable neighbor, John Rugely. The gallant Erasmus Smith lived and died in Richmond, where now survive the genial-hearted, amiable and accomplished Dr. G. A. Feris, Randolph Foster, the oldest living Texan, and T. J. Smith, of Fannin's command, spared because he was a blacksmith.

The section of country embraced within these four counties is destined within a few years to be *one of the garden spots of the world.*

HOUSTON.

Houston, the second city in size and importance in Texas, and famous for its notable, as well as very distinguished and highly creditable STATE FAIRS, was surveyed and laid off into lots by John K. and A. C. Allen in 1836, soon after the battle of San Jacinto, and named after Gen. Sam Houston.

It is the great railroad centre of Texas, and is connected by rail with Galveston, Columbia on the Brazos, Columbus on the Colorado, Luling, Waco, Dallas, Denison, Austin, Palestine, Marshall, Jefferson, and all intermediate cities and towns, many of considerable mercantile importance.

The *Bayou City*, as it is frequently called, is situated on Buffalo Bayou, about fifty miles northwest of Galveston, has about twenty thousand inhabitants, and besides its very creditable schools and churches can justly be proud of its two very successful manufacturing establishments of cotton and woollen goods, the *Eureka* and *City* mills.

The merchants of Houston do considerable business with interior merchants, and calculate when they complete the *ship* channel, so that ocean steamers can come up to Houston as easy as they can enter Galveston Bay, which scientific engineers say can be done, to compete with Galveston as to future growth and commercial importance.

It was here during the war that Gen. Magruder established his head-quarters, cast cannon, and organized his famous attack and capture of Galveston.

From Houston Gen. Tom Green and his gallant soldiers sailed on their frail little boat down the bayou, in sight of San Jacinto, through the bay, up to the *Harriet Lane*, boarded and captured her! and thus Galveston.

As the little vessel passed the memorable battle-ground, and the lamented hero beheld the plain whereon, twenty-seven years before, he and his comrades, manfully contending against superior numbers, had gained a glorious victory and made the Republic of Texas an independent nation—thought he of the fearful battle-cry of the Texans: "*Remember the Alamo!*" or of the appealing shriek of the poor defeated Mexicans: "*Me no Alamo!*" or of the dear ones at home, who were soon to lose dear brother, kind father, and tender husband?

Alas, that one so useful, beloved and needed by friends, country, and family, should be killed in the moment of victory!

The reader will pardon this passing tribute of respect to one of the bravest soldiers and most accomplished officers who fought and died for the *lost cause*, and I will relate the following Houstonian anecdote:

During our late civil war, which Gen. Houston opposed, many of his old friends, among them the genial hearted Frank Lubbock, and other good Confederates, did not speak kindly of the old hero, but in order to counteract his influence against the harmony and union of Texans in support of the Southern Confederacy, said things which excited his wrath and brought forth the following evidence of his sarcastic powers.

Coming up one night on the steamer *Diana* from Galveston to Houston, he called to the steward several times and asked, when the boat stopped:

"What place is this, steward?"

On arriving at the Bayou City, when the boat stopped, not knowing where he was, he repeated his inquiry, and was answered: "Houston."

"Houston!" said the old general, "Houston! Oh yes, I recollect now. I raised some pups in Houston—they have grown to be big dogs, and now when I walk out, they bark at me!"

JEFFERSON.

The sixth city of Texas, numbering more than 8,000 inbabitants, is Jefferson, situated on Cypress Bayou, at the head of navigation.

Jefferson, since the war, was almost entirely burned, but has been rebuilt with more substantial and elegant structures—more than 150 new brick stores have been erected in the place of the wooden ones consumed by the fire.

In 1869 Jefferson shipped to New Orleans about eighty thousand bales of cotton, besides an immense quantity of wool, hides, tallow, beeswax, etc., etc.

The whole of *Northern Texas*, from Dallas on the Trinity to Fulton, Arkansas, traded with Jefferson, bringing down cotton, flour, pork, wool, hides, beeves, etc., etc., and carrying back in their *wagons* supplies of clothing, machinery, farming utensils, and other articles of merchandise.

The people of Jefferson *aided* in the construction of the Texas and Pacific Railroad from Longview to Texarkana, but this road and the Central now supply the vast country with merchandise, which was formerly *tributary to Jefferson*, the trade of which has in consequence decreased immensely.

> "So the struck eagle, stretched upon the plain,
> No more through rolling clouds to soar again,
> Viewed his own feather on the fatal dart,
> And winged the shaft that quivered in his heart."

The country near Jefferson abounds in iron ore of the finest quality, of which very fine stoves and ploughs, as well as all manner of castings, are made. As the great source of wealth to the people of Marion County, this inexhaustible supply of ore should be properly and immediately appropriated, so as to supply all Texas with home-made iron goods.

A few miles from Jefferson on Soda Lake, through which the Cypresses flow into Red River, is the famous promontory jutting out into the lake, overlooking the surrounding country for miles, called Potter's Point, in honor of the celebrated Robert Potter, Secretary of the Texas Navy, who, from its dense forest abounding in game and cool fountains of pure water and splendid facilities for fishing and ducking, selected it as his home. Here he hunted, fished, and killed ducks to his heart's content, and then retired to his library and indulged his fondness for reading.

He was a rare genius—gifted and eloquent. No other member of the Texas Congress did Gen. Houston fear so much as Col. Potter, who had all the English poets at his tongue's end, was an expert logician, quick at repartee, fluent, and at the same time a fine actor.

The story of his death runs as follows:

For some time there had been war between himself and his followers, and Capt. Wm. P. Rose and his friends.

One morning after daylight, but before sunrise, Col. Potter and his party galloped up to Rose's house, and surrounding it expected to capture him. On searching the house, they found the bed still warm where he had slept during the night, but Capt. Rose was gone! He was an early riser and was out in the *new ground* with the negroes *clearing*, and seeing his enemies approach, he laid down on the ground and ordered his slaves to cover him all over with brush, and in order to prevent any suspicion of his presence, *to set the heap on fire*, which they did, and as Potter and his party approached seeing no place of concealment except the burning *brush heap*, they went away, when although somewhat scorched, he crawled out from his hiding-place, mounted his horse, hastily summoned his partisans, and next morning attacking Potter, surrounded him in his house.

Col. Potter aroused and conscious of his danger broke through his enemies, plunged headlong into the lake, dived and swam for dear life, but as he raised his head above the water to get breath, it was riddled with bullets.*

Thus perished Col. Robert Potter! but Potter's Point still remains, and is one of the most pleasant resorts for fishing, hunting, and ducking in all Texas.

SAN ANTONIO.

In 1682, the same year that Wm. Penn and his

---

* Dickens, in his "American Notes," thus quotes the tragedy:

"TERRIBLE DEATH OF ROBERT POTTER.—From the *Caddo Gazette* of the 12th inst. we learn the frightful death of Col. Robert Potter. . . . . He was beset in his house by an enemy, named Rose. He sprang from his couch, seized his gun, and in his night-clothes rushed from the house. For about two hundred yards his speed seemed to defy his pursuers; but, getting entangled in a thicket, he was captured. Rose told him that *he intended to act a generous part*, and give him a chance for his life. He then told Potter he might run, and he should not be interrupted till he reached a certain distance. Potter started at the word of command, and before a gun was fired he had reached the lake. His first impulse was to jump in the water and dive for it, which he did. Rose was close behind him, and formed his men on the bank ready to shoot him as he rose. In a few seconds he came up to breathe; and scarce had his head reached the surface of the water when it was completely riddled with the shot of their guns, and he sank to rise no more."

Quaker followers laid out the beautiful site of Phila delphia, between the Delaware and Schuylkill Rivers, about fifty Spanish families from the Philippine Islands, headed by the Navarros, Garzas, Leals, Rodriguezes, Perezes, Manchacas and others, landed upon the coast of Texas, and, wending their way up the country, were captivated by two beautiful streams, between which they settled, calling one the San Antonio and the other San Pedro, where they laid out a city into lots with very irregular streets, and named it San Antonio, which to day is the third city in size in Texas, containing about eighteen thousand persons.

San Antonio has five streams of water running through it, and is a remarkably healthy and flourishing city; its colleges, schools, and churches bear evidence that its citizens are great lovers of learning and morality.

Near the heart of the city stands that antique but memorable structure, known in history as the *Alamo*, where Crockett, Bowie, and their heroic followers fought their last fight, and gave to Texas historians the right to record truthfully:

> "Thermopylæ had its messenger,
> The Alamo had none!"

No monument marks their tomb. They were denied sepulture. Their bodies were burned and their ashes scattered to the winds of heaven, but their names will live in history and song as the bravest of the brave, so long as Americans continue to love deeds of noble daring and heroic achievement, or so long as the beautiful San Antonio River with arrowy swiftness shall continue to flow by the Alamo and Goliad, and mingle its waters with those of the Gulf.

Below San Antonio on the river are the celebrated Missions of *Espada*, *San Juan*, *San Jose*, and *Concepcion*, erected more than a century ago, which from their ancient style of sculpture, structure, and architecture never fail to repay the strangers' visit. These missions were built by pious Spanish priests, in which to fight as well as pray; to Christianize the wild savages, and to be used as forts when attacked.

After railroad communication is established between San Antonio and the rest of the world, its commerce, trade, population, and wealth must necessarily increase; wherefore San Antonians should aid and encourage the speedy completion of the International and Mexican Gulf Railroads, with all their might, amity, and resources.

AUSTIN.

Austin, the capital of Texas, contains about twelve thousand inhabitants, is beautifully situated on the

Colorado River, was surveyed in 1839, and made the seat of government in 1840, when the Indians in the neighboring mountains were as thick as leaves in Valambrosa.

It has more hills than the Eternal City, and hence its cognomen City of Hills, high above all of which Mount Bonnell rears its lofty head, looking down with complacent grandeur and dignity upon the sparkling waters of the river at its base.

The following legend of the Colorado Valley was related to me years ago by that reliable gentleman, good citizen, and gallant soldier, George L. Robertson:

"Mount Bonnell was called by the early settlers of Colorado Valley Antonette's Leap, which was given to it in consequence of the self-immolation on that picturesque spot, at an early day, of a most lovely and accomplished young senorita, who came over from Spain at the first settlement of the Missions of San Jose, San Juan, Espada, and the Alamo.

"The fame of Antonette's beauty and intellectual charms was spread abroad through the settlements, and even extended to the hunting-ground and camp-fires of the red men of the forest, till it came to the ears and inflamed the passions of Cibolo, the chief of the Comanches, who selected a band of his favorite warriors, made a raid upon the settlements, captured the beautiful Antonette, and carried her far away to his camp in the wilderness, on the head-waters of the Colorado.

"The parents and friends of the unfortunate senorita mourned her as lost forever, except Don Leal Navarro Rodriquez, her betrothed lover, a brave and elegantly educated young Spanish caballero, of fine personal appearance and honorable, as well as brave to a fault, who determined to follow the murderous Indians to their home and rescue his beloved Antonette, or perish in the attempt.

"Don Leal mounted his favorite steed, and, well armed, started from the Alamo alone in pursuit of the Indians, and after many hair-breadth escapes, *undiscovered*, descried the camp of the savages, and selecting a dark night, he entered it, and by imitating the mocking-bird, of which Antonette was very fond, and whose singing they could both imitate to perfection, he soon discovered what spot inside the encampment she was, then came into the very tent which she occupied, and found her tied securely to prevent her escape.

"In an instant the lover severed the bonds which confined the dear idol of his heart and with her cautiously returned to where he had left his horse when he entered the Comanche camp; then quickly mounting and taking Antonette up behind him, he started to regain the Mission of the Alamo.

"The fury of Cibolo in the morning, when he discovered the escape of his fascinating captive, knew no bounds. He raved and blasphemed terribly; then sounding the alarm, with an hundred chosen warriors, he hastily started in pursuit, leaving the main body of his tribe to await his return.

"For several days Don Leal and his beloved Antonette made good speed towards the settlements, subsisting most bountifully upon game, which was easily obtained through Don Leal's rifle, and at night sleeping under the forest trees; but on the seventh day, leaving the prairie land, they became entangled in the mountains bordering the Colorado, and early in the morning of the eighth day the lovers discovered themselves surrounded upon all sides by the cruel savages and all attempts at further flight entirely hopeless.

"The wrathful Cibolo, with cow horns on his head and face horribly painted, advanced in all the pride of power to where they had fled as a last refuge, but when about fifty yards off, Don Leal, who had firmly resolved to fight and die rather than surrender, raised his rifle to his shoulder, and taking deliberate aim, fired! In an instant the savage chief bounded into the air and then fell to the ground a corpse; but in another instant at least twenty arrows pierced his own body, and he too fell to the earth and expired without a groan.

"After surveying the situation, and revolving in her mind the miserable fate awaiting her from the merciless Comanches, the emptiness and vanity of human life compared with the ineffable joys of Paradise, the poor, unfortunate girl bent over the prostrate and lifeless form of her lover, kissed his dear lips, and then rising, with her eyes toward heaven and murmuring her last prayer to God, she plunged headlong down the precipice and struck the rocks beneath, mangled, bleeding, and dead!

"For a long time the place where these rare, devoted but most unfortunate lovers met their sad and untimely fate was called 'Antonette's Leap,' but years ago a wandering Bohemian, who happened to pass a few days in Austin, ambitious of fame or notoriety as Herostratus, or emulating the example of Americus Vespucius, whose presumptuous vanity cheated Columbus out of his just glory, blotted it out and substituted his own, and now Antonette's Leap is Mount Bonnell just as certainly as Columbia is America."

As an evidence of the abundance of game formerly on the Colorado, I will relate an incident in the early history of Austin:

One morning an emigrant, answering to the familiar name of Adams, walked into the most popular hotel of the place, then kept by Capt. Swisher, the father of that amiable gentleman, good citizen, and well-known Austinian, Col. Milt Swisher, and engaged board by the month, agreeing to pay for it in turkeys, at fifty cents each—making the contract and eating his dinner he walked up the valley of the river and being very expert at throwing rocks, in that way killed six wild turkeys, which he brought home and turned over to his landlord.

In the morning he went out again and about dinner time returned with seven which he had killed in the same way. At night he returned with another load, when Capt. Swisher said to him:

"Mr. Adams, you have overstocked me with turkeys. Don't kill any more for a few days."

Mr. Adams paid his board regularly in wild turkeys, and ever afterwards went by the soubriquet of *Turkey Adams.*

For some time after the capital was removed to Austin the Indians were very troublesome, making frequent raids on the settlements, killing and robbing without mercy.

On one occasion Capt. Billy Wilson, with a party of young men, including Col. Jack Baylor, who relates the story, pursued them for three days, without rest or food, and overtook them on the head-waters of the Yegua, near Austin.

Just before the Indians, who were retreating at their utmost speed, reached the timber, one of them, to facilitate his speed and escape death, being left behind, cut loose a large piece of raw meat, and letting it fall to the ground continued his flight. Col. Baylor and his companions saw this operation, and being exceedingly hungry, stopped, lighted a fire, cooked and commenced eating the captured meat.

When Capt. Wilson, who rode a safe rather than a swift horse, and was behind, came up, and saw them devouring the captured property, he being hungry himself, exclaimed:

"Great God! that meat is poisoned! you'll all be dead in fifteen minutes! Run down to the creek and drink just as much water as you can, to kill the poison!"

Baylor and his young Indian hunters heard and obeyed their chief, but as they returned to the spot they beheld their commander as he was swallowing the last particle of the captured meat, who, wiping his mouth with his sleeve, exclaimed, with a cunning smile: "Well, boys, we'll all die together! I have *histed in* what you left!"

DALLAS.

No city in Texas or the south has grown so fast in the last year as Dallas, which is beautifully situated on the Trinity River, at the junction of the Texas Pacific Railroad with the Houston and Texas Central.

This city was settled in 1842, by Colonel John Neely Bryan, and named in honor of Commodore Dallas, of the United States Navy, while the county was named after George M. Dallas.

In 1846 the Legislature made it the temporary county-seat, and in 1850 it became permanently so by the vote of the people.

In 1846, when the writer passed round it, there were but about thirty or forty inhabitants, but in a few years afterwards, when it became the permanent county-seat, many houses and much improvement were added to it.

In 1860 all the business portion of the city was burned, and the war coming on after, there was a stand-still, while the fierce and bloody strife between Americans called many of its citizens to the tented field and the soldier's grave.

Not until 1868 and 1869 did Dallas again commence to improve, but in July, 1872, the Houston and Texas Central reached it, followed, in August, 1873, by the Texas Pacific, and then came the era of improvement and progress.

Many large, fine brick stores and residences have sprung up like magic, while a second bridge, for the Texas and Pacific Railroad, will soon span the river. A court-house has been built of stone at a cost of about one hundred thousand dollars, and the population to-day seems to be not less than ten thousand souls, and is rapidly increasing, while Dallas County, with its springs of pure, clear water, rich and productive lands, is gaining population and wealth daily.

As the city of Dallas is about the centre of one of the finest wheat, cotton and corn growing counties of Texas, of which about one-third is timber and two-thirds prairie land, capable of producing a bale of cotton, or from twenty-five to thirty bushels of wheat, or from thirty-five to fifty bushels of corn, or from forty to sixty bushels of oats to the acre; as it is soon to have two more railroads, one to intersect the Great Northern at Palestine, and the other the Trans-continental in Tarrant County, and the Denver City Railroad in Clay County, it bids fair to be one of the largest inland cities in the State of Texas.

The old streets of Dallas are broad and at right angles; their names, such as Latimer, Burford, Record, Cochran, Ochiltree, Bryan, McCoy, etc., call up in the minds of old Texans many pleasing reminiscences of past and by-gone days.

Latimer Street was named in honor of the late J. W. Latimer, who, in 1849, founded *The Dallas Herald*, and edited it with distinguished ability until the day of his death in 1859. Mr. Latimer was a fine writer, and through the columns of *The Herald*, like a vigilant sentinel from the watchtower of liberty, sounded the alarm at the stealthy approach of the enemies of freedom and progress. In the prime of his life and usefulness, at the early age of about thirty-three, regretted by all who knew him, he passed away, leaving to his partner, Mr. J. W. Swindells, the control of *The Herald*, under whose management it has, from a weekly, become one of the leading and most useful daily journals in the state.

Record Street was named after the late J. K. P. Record, and Burford Street after the Hon. Nat. M. Burford, who still defies the destroying effects of time, and makes glad the hearts of his friends by his genial smile and great magnanimity.

Judge Burford has been called "Magnanimous Nat," from the following incident:

Several years ago Mr. George Laws, himself and Jim Record (as the late Senator J. K. P. Record was familiarly called by his friends) went fishing, carrying with them a few bottles wherewith to enliven their day's sport and as an antidote for snake-bites.

Now it so happened, from a rise in the river, not catching any fish, drinking too much whiskey, or some other cause, that these gentlemen found themselves in their flatboat without poles or oars, gliding down the turbid waters of the Trinity River, when Record appealed to his friend, and said:

"Great God, Nat., what will become of us? We

will be carried away, and lost in the Gulf of Mexico!"

Whereupon magnanimous Nat arose, and assuring his friends of his ability to save them, took up the log-chain attached to the end of the flatboat, and putting it around his neck, fastened the hook into one of the links of the heavy chain, and plunging into the swollen stream essayed to swim ashore and carry the boat and his friends to safety.

After one lusty stroke as a swimmer he went under, when Record and Laws seized the chain, and pulling him up from under the water thus saved his life, and soon after, by catching the limbs of overhanging trees, got the boat to bank, and returned to Dallas, wetter and more fatigued, if not as sober as when they sallied forth in the morning on their famous excursion.

Another true story of Judge Burford is as follows:

One night, at Lancaster, Georgetown, or some other place, in consequence of the crowded condition of the hotel where he had stopped, he was placed in the same bed with an Irishman, whereupon he pleasantly remarked:

"Well, Pat, I reckon you'd have lived a long time in old Ireland before you'd have slept with a judge."

"Yes, yer honor," rejoined Pat, "but the likes of ye might have lived longer in ould Ireland before yes become a judge."

Nightcaps followed this rejoinder, and Judge Burford tucked the drapery of his couch on one side of him, and with Pat Maloney on the other, laid down to pleasant dreams, which the great, wise, and most merciful God always sends to the pure hearted and magnanimous.

In Dallas I heard the following laughable story:

Billy Harlan, a noted character, was indicted a good many years ago for stealing a pair of hames, was tried, convicted and sentenced to receive thirty-nine lashes, without a scintilla of testimony being introduced to sustain the charge.

Tom Jones, one of the jurors, being asked how, under his oath, he could bring in a verdict of guilty upon the evidence adduced, answered:

"Why, didn't he steal old Mrs. Lovejoy's apple dumplings out of the pot while it was boiling; he ought to have a thousand lashes instead of thirty-nine."

The next morning, on the opening of court, Billy's attorney made an application for a new trial, on account of the absence of any testimony to warrant the finding of the jury. Immediately after the adjournment of court on the previous evening, the sheriff took Billy out, made him fast to a tree, and in genuine frontier style administered the sentence of the court.

When Billy was informed of the application for a

new trial, he ran into the court-house, interrupted his lawyer, G. A. Everts, by pulling his coat-tail, and saying, "Stop that, they have already whipped me."

The attorney withdrew his motion for a new trial, but the court, Hon. Nat. M. Burford presiding, satisfied that there was no testimony to warrant the verdict, against Billy's desire, granted a new trial; but before his rearrest, Billy, not wishing to be rewhipped, broke out of the court-house and fled to parts unknown.

If, in the course of his promiscuous reading, these few lines should ever fall under his observation, it may be well for Billy Harlan to remember that the record in his memorable case is still in a state of preservation.

HEMPSTEAD,

The county-seat of Waller County, is at the junction of the western branch of the Houston and Texas Central Railroad, with the main trunk, about fifty miles above Houston, and not more than three or four miles from the Brazos River. It is pleasantly located on sandy soil in the prairie, surrounded by the timbered lands of Clear Creek and the Brazos.

By the Legislature of 1873, Waller County was created out of Austin and Grimes Counties, and Hempstead made a court-house town. This had often been attempted before, but had as often been defeated by the citizens of Austin County living west of the Brazos. Hempstead has about 1,000 or 1,500 inhabitants, is rapidly improving, and is sustained by a rich and productive surrounding country, abounding in all kinds of game and fish.

I have passed some the most pleasant moments of my life in and around this town, and will relate a little incident which occurred there but a few weeks ago:

Meeting with my old friends, Judge W. S. Day, Major J. B. McCown, and others, we were indulging in pleasing reminiscences of the past, when we were interrupted in our enjoyment by two drunken men, one of whom, as he sat down by my side, repeated the following lines of the poet:

> "Oh, ever thus from childhood's hour
> I've seen my fondest hopes decay,
> I never loved a tree or flower
> But what 'twas sure to fade away!"

Somewhat annoyed by the intruder, I slapped him on the shoulder, and, intending to be severely ironical, thus addressed him:

"Sir, nature intended you for a great poet! Had you not gone back on nature, the immortal Homer, Shakspeare, Milton, Pope, Byron, Burns, Scott, and all the poetic stars of ancient and modern times, would have paled into insignificance before your brilliant genius, as the smaller luminaries do before the sun."

At this remark the person addressed hung his head, while his drunken companion thus addressed me:

"Lookee here, stranger, you're mistaken about Bill. Nature intended Bill for a damn fool, and he haint gone back on nature, nary inch! He fills the bill to a fraction."

Amid the smiles of the party our little social re-union broke up, and we left Bill and his companion alone in their glory.

In its earlier days, Hempstead was a great place for pistols and bowie-knives. I have seen dead men there, but will only relate two incidents which come to my recollection from local association:

A. B., the editor of a newspaper, assailed, in a very bitter editorial, Mr. C. D.

C. D. took no notice of the editorial, and Mr. A. B. challenged him.

C. D. paid no attention to the challenge, whereupon A. B. took a stand on the street, and as C. D. came along, bounced him and commenced fighting. C. D., who was a large, powerful man, received three or four blows before he became angry, then exclaiming, "Why, great God, man, you are fighting," and in an instant knocked the editor down, and beat him until he cried "enough!"

The next morning an editorial appeared in Mr. A. B.'s *Journal*, stating that the difficulty between the editor and C. D. had been satisfactorily *settled*.

On another occasion J. Brown remarked, under the excitement of the moment, to Mr. Smith, that he could knock a half-dozen of Smith's teeth down his throat at one lick.

Smith, being rather a small man, quietly retired, but suddenly returned with his double-barrel shot-gun presented, and exclaimed:

"You are my meat!"

Whereupon Brown, seeing murder in Smith's eyes, and his own death imminent, smilingly and eloquently rejoined:

"Smith, my dear friend, hold on! We have often drank together, but if you shoot and kill me, we can never drink together again, and you will have to be tried for murder! You know how the lawyers talk about hanging and the penitentiary on a murder trial! Look here, old fel! Let's go take another drink and quit this foolishness!"

The appeal was irresistible, and Messrs. Smith and Brown again imbibed, after which all animosity between them was buried in oblivion, and the two were as one.

Twenty-five miles north of Hempstead is Plantersville, a very lovely little village of a few hundred inhabitants. Several years ago, two men from Indiana came to Texas, with a wagon-load of bells, and after selling them, together with their wagon and team, started home on foot from the interior of Texas, by way of Plantersville and Houston.

Having heard many stories of robbery and murder in Texas, and having all their wealth, consisting of six or seven hundred dollars in silver, on their persons, the hoosiers were wide-awake, and on the lookout for attacks from whatever source they might come.

Now it so happened that as they were walking quietly along the public road near Plantersville, three gentlemen, Messrs. Ike Baker, Jim Pinkston, and Joe Bates, were out hunting, one of whom, Mr. Bates, coming out of the woods into the road with his gun in his hands, and meeting the hoosiers, rather surprised them; but after mutual questions and answers, the bell men went on their way, and Joe Bates wishing to know the whereabouts of Ike Baker and Jim Pinkston, sounded his horn, which was answered by those of Baker and Pinkston in front of the travellers, who, as they advanced, supposing themselves surrounded by robbers and about to be attacked, killed and robbed of their money, drew their pistols and commenced their defence by firing at Baker and Pinkston from behind trees.

Mr. Ike Baker and Jim Pinkston received the fire

of the bell-men, and not liking the liberty taken by the strangers with their wardrobes, returned the fire, and seven buckshot floored one hoosier, while five more perforated the body of the other.

As Baker and Pinkston went up to their assailants, they threw before them their silver and exclaimed: "Take our money, but spare our lives!"

After learning the mistake of the bell-men, the hunters went for a doctor and a wagon to take the wounded men to shelter and medical attendance. But when the hunters returned, the bell-men had fled, still believing them to be robbers.

Bloodhounds were put on the track of the bell-men, and after a chase of two or three miles they were caught, their wounds dressed, and they were carried to Mr. Baker's residence and kindly cared for until their wounds were well.

The money was found on the ground where it was thrown, and returned to its owners.

After the unfortunate hoosiers got well, Mr. Baker sent them in his carriage to Montgomery, whence they took stage for Houston.

Several years afterwards, Ike Baker met one of the unfortunates in the theatre at Galveston, and after a friendly greeting, he said: "I never related the affair in Indiana, and for God's sake don't let the story get out on us!"

A railroad is contemplated to connect Hempstead, Huntsville, Montgomery and Plantersville; it would run through a beautiful, well watered and finely timbered section of country. The lumber alone from the immense forest of pine through which the road would run, together with the cotton, would surely pay the expense of running it, and add greatly to the development of one of the most sparsely settled but very desirable portions of the State.

CHAPTER XXI.

Georgetown.—Williamson County.—Sam Houston.—Salado.—Sterling Robertson.—Waco and surrounding country.—Limestone and Freestone Counties.—Trinity College, Fairfield, Groesbeck, Sister Jane, Joe McDonald, Anderson, Smith, Rains, and Hunt Counties.—Palestine, Tyler, Dr. Jowers, Hardin Hart, etc.

GEORGETOWN, the county seat of Williamson county, was named in honor of *George* W. Glasscock, a native of Kentucky, who was a partner in business of the late Abraham Lincoln, and one of the famous storming party which captured San Antonio, December 10, 1835. He died in Travis county, February 28, 1868, full of years and honors, leaving several sons and daughters, among them the prosperous and very responsible lawyer and land-agent, George W. Glasscock of Austin.

Georgetown is pleasantly situated on the South San Gabriel, twenty-five miles north of Austin, about the centre of Williamson county (named after Judge Williamson, *alias* three-legged Willie), through which Indian creek and eleven other lovely streams—named Salado, Donohoe, Dyers, Williamson, Mustang, Willis, Opossum, Battleground, Brushy, North, South, and

Main San Gabriel—flow, and is surrounded by most beautiful, rich and productive lands.

It was laid off and settled in 1848, and the first district court was held in the open air over a pile of logs.

Here Jones Rivers came to practise law, and died *with as little regret as he could have died anywhere else,* so he said when dying; here also may be seen to this day, the grave of Phil Claiborne which Col. Rivers caused to be dug in anticipation that the Lord would answer his prayer on a certain occasion and take Phil to himself, while in repentance, peradventure Philip might backslide and be irrevocably lost.

Here also reside the eldest son and daughter of the hero of San Jacinto, Mrs. Nannie Morrow, and young Sam Houston, one of the bravest boys who fought to sustain the lost cause, and who was shot down on the battlefield of Shiloh, and so terribly wounded that the surgeon who first examined him pronounced his case hopeless, and advised poor Sam to talk quick and fast to God, as his hour had come when his soul must wing its way to the mansions of everlasting life and eternal felicity, or go down the easy descent to the dark and gloomy regions where dwell those poor, erring, sinful mortals who hate "the pure, the beautiful, and the good," and "love darkness rather than light."

He says he felt mighty bad when the surgeon told

him his wounds were mortal, and left him; but still he hoped to get well, and live, and enjoy himself, and luxuriate in the bright smiles and inestimable love of some fair Texan maid.

While thus hoping and helplessly lying, with his bones broken and his life's blood oozing gently from his wounds, the minister, sent to him by the surgeon, came to his side, and bending down upon his knees, commenced an appeal to the throne of Grace on behalf of Sam's immortal soul, which Sam interrupted with these words:

"My friend, if you will stop talking to God, and will stanch my blood, and dress my wounds, I think I will get well."

The pious man stopped praying, and asked:

"Young man, what is your name?"

"My name," said the wounded boy, "is Sam Houston."

"Are you related to Gen. Sam Houston of Texas?" asked the minister.

"I have been taught since infancy to look upon him as my father," rejoined young Sam.

"Well, gracious goodness alive!" exclaimed the preacher, "I know your father well! he is my friend! and, God permitting, you shall not die!"

Whereupon he had poor Sam carried upon a litter to his house, and kindly attended on him until his bones had knitted together and his wounds were healed, when the youthful hero bid farewell to his preserver, and again joined that brave and noble-hearted army of Southern patriots who contended so long and so gallantly against the inexhaustible resources and overwhelming numbers of the enemy—but, alas! in vain.

I love a brave man on any part of the ground, and no one can see and talk with Sam Houston without recognizing the virtue of bravery united with a cultivated mind, a fine person, and most agreeable manners.

Georgetown is a very healthy and delightful place to live in, and no better locality could have been selected for the Texas Methodist University, which is an honor to as well as the pride of the citizens of Georgetown, who donated for its establishment $175,000. This University at present contains accommodations for 300 students, and is in a flourishing condition.

North of Georgetown, about half-way between Austin and Waco, is the fair and thriving town of SALADO, noted for its fine schools and beautiful spring.

Here settled, in 1853, that sterling old Texan, sterling soldier and sterling gentleman, Col. *Sterling Robertson*, son of the old empresario, Sterling C. Robertson, whose colony embraced all the territory north of the Camino del Rey, from San Antonio to

Nacogdoches, included between the Navasota and Col orado rivers, where said Camino del Rey, or *King's highway*, crosses them. It embraced many counties east and west of the Brazos, but that part west of the Brazos, including the counties of Williamson, Bell, Milam, Burnett, Lampasas, Bosque, Coryell, Hamilton, Erath, Hood, Comanche, Brown, Eastland, etc., at the first Congress of the Republic was re-christened, re-baptized and re-named *Milam County*—before that time it had been called the municipality of *Viesca.* The name of the town, as well as of the municipality, was thus changed.

This territory is rich, productive and settling up very fast. Within six miles of Salado there are six grist mills run by water-power. In 1859, there was but one family in Salado; now there are 250. Nine miles north of Salado is the county seat, Belton, which has a fine court-house, jail, a bank, two wholesale and fifteen retail stores, with a thrifty population of several hundred persons.

To the west of Bell are the counties of Lampasas and San Saba, famous for their beautiful streams of mineral waters, whose health-giving qualities draw thousands of visitors yearly. The Lampasas springs are becoming quite a fashionable watering-place.

The city of Waco, formerly Waco village, and the home of the Waco Indians, is beautifully located on the Brazos river, about 100 miles north of Austin, and about the same distance south of Dallas, containing about six or eight thousand inhabitants, and rapidly increasing in houses, wealth, and population.

The country round about Waco is one of the richest and most attractive in the world, producing excellent qualities of wheat, corn, cotton, rye, barley, and all other productions of the climate.

A few miles above the city, the Brazos de Dios (the arms of God) affectionately embraces the clear and beautiful Bosque; and a few miles below, lovingly takes to its bosom the less beautiful Indian-named stream, the Tehuacana; and between these two branches, about a mile apart, run directly to it, through the city, while several lovely fountains of water run on its southern bank, with which the amiable Wacoes are wont to water their whiskey, and wash their linen.

Capt. S. P. Ross and T. H. Barron, in 1849, built the first houses in Waco, and the first sale of city lots took place in the spring of 1850, soon after which time it was made the county seat of McLennan county, and flourished so finely that, in 1856, the first Democratic State Convention ever called in Texas—which nominated H. R. Runnels, who beat Gen. Houston for governor—was held in Waco.

The population is composed almost entirely of

adventurous persons who emigrated from the older States of the Union, and their children born within the last twenty years, and is excelled in intelligence, industry, enterprise, refinement, and morality, by that of no city of equal size in the State.

The Wacoes have a railroad tapping the H. & T. C., at Bremond; they have a magnificent suspension bridge across the Brazos; a university; a female college; several fine schools, and a very goodly number of churches, wherein their true believers congregate for worship, and their "fair women and brave men" often meet and sing, laugh and talk—and with

> "Soft eyes look love to eyes which speak again."

In these same churches—

> "In life's morning march, when my bosom was young,"
> I have luxuriated "with rapture-smitten frame" in
> "—— the smiles from partial beauty won,"

and passed many delightful moments in Waco;

> "But now Memory looks o'er the sad review
> Of joys that faded like the morning dew."

A family named Beck formerly lived in Waco, of which I have heard the following story; but—

> "I say the tale as 'twas told to me."

"Theodore Beck, like many other persons born and reared in New England, at early manhood came to Texas, went to work, and made a fortune.

"But having made his fortune, Theodore sighed once more to look upon his native hills, and to behold again the familiar faces of beloved but long unseen relatives and friends.

"Theodore went back to New England; his pious friends inquired and listened, while Theodore told his marvellous adventures and thrilling stories of blood and murder in our western wilds.

"Finally, his uncle William, a venerable old Puritan, looked Theodore full in the face, and said:

"'I hope, Theodore, it has never been your misfortune to kill a fellow-man.'

"'Well, uncle William,' said Theodore, 'I am sorry to say that it has!'

"The venerable old gentleman heaved a sigh, and rejoined: 'Well, Theodore, I hope to God you did it in self-defence, and that your conscience is easy about it! But pray, tell me how you happened to do it.'

"'Well, uncle,' answered Theodore, 'I will tell you all about it. Tom Jones was the best friend I ever had. He was brave, generous and noble-hearted. We had run together for years, and had fought Indians side by side many times. Now, on one occasion, while we were on the frontier, hunting Indians, our provisions gave out, and we had nothing to eat for two or three days, when one of the party brought into camp a fine fat venison, which we all cut up and commenced broiling, with our ramrods on the fire. Now, it so happened that the wind changed while we were cooking our meat, and Jones, in order to keep the smoke out of his eyes, jumped across the fire and knocked my piece of meat into the ashes. My six-shooter was by my side, and in a moment I drew it, fired, and poor Tom fell, shot through the head!'

"His uncle William exclaimed: 'Why, gracious goodness, Theodore, I hope you didn't shoot him just for knocking your meat into the ashes!'

"'Yes I did, uncle William,' said Theodore; 'and I'd shoot anybody for such a thing! But poor Tom died mighty hard. I shot him an inch or so too low, and all I regretted about it was, that I didn't shoot him in the right place, for he did die powerful hard.'"

By this story, Theodore amused himself and his friends, but gave a very incorrect idea of our Texas frontiersmen, for I have often heard Latin, Greek, Spanish, French, and German spoken at the same camp fire.

Many times I have heard very apt quotations from Shakspeare, Burns, Byron, Milton, Moore, and other immortal English bards, while no people on the face of the earth are more hospitable, kind and generous than the old Texans.

The old followers of Jack Hays, Tom Green, Mike Chevalier, Henry and Ben McCulloch, Gotch Hardeman, Alf Thurmond, John Torrey, George Neal, George Barnard, Bob Neighbours, Geo. Frath, John Tom, Sam Walker, Ad Gillespie, John Henry Brown, and many others, whose names are written on the brightest pages of Texas history, would laugh at this story of Mr. Beck as a good joke.

In one of the finest and most substantial private residences in Waco, containing a billiard table for the amusement of his guests, resides a famous sport by the name of Telephus Johnson, who (in *ante bellum* days, when our sable-colored fellow-citizens and legislators were bought, sold, and bet on horse-races) planked up two thousand dollars and his favorite boy Jake against the same amount and a negro boy owned by his competitor, Bob Porter.

Telephus bribed Porter's rider to hold back Porter's horse and let his come out ahead, while Porter paid two hundred dollars for the same purpose to the rider of Telephus.

Telephus was beaten, and went home carrying Jake, whom he solemnly promised to return back to his master as soon as he arrived home, which he failed to do.

He wrote, however, to Porter, that Jake was very

sick, and wrote again soon after that he was dead, enclosing a doctor's bill and funeral expenses, and collected a thousand dollars for the same, while Jake was at work sound and hearty.

This is the same person who, just after the "break up," bet the Federal officer who was collecting rebel property, twenty dollars that he could prove by negro testimony that the spurs worn by the officer were not the officer's, but the property of himself.

Calling up Jake, he inquired of him:

"Whose spurs are those?"

After examining them closely, never having seen them before in his life, Jake responded:

"Dey ar' your spurs, master; I seed you buy um from Mr. House, in Houston."

The officer pulled off the spurs, handed them to Telephus with the twenty dollars, and departed; giving up all further claim to about fifty mules then in his possession, which the officer claimed and could fully prove, by negro testimony, was the property of the United States as victors over the Confederate States.

The section of country embracing Limestone and Freestone counties is finely watered by the Navasota, Trinity, Tehuacana, Richland, Keechi, Caney, Steele, Christmas, and other beautiful streams. It is one of the finest agricultural portions of the State, and being mostly settled by Georgians, Alabamians, Tennesseans and Floridans, contains a population of intelligent, moral and industrious yeomanry, among whom the immigrant seeking a home in Texas can find good neighbors and fine society.

The soil is a sandy loam, exceedingly rich and productive, covered alternately by the meadowy grass of the prairie and forest trees, among which the post oak predominates.

Groesbeck, the county seat of Limestone county, named in honor of Mr. A. Groesbeck, vice-president of the Houston and Texas Central Railway Company, is on the Central Railway, half way between Kosse and Mexia.

Groesbeck contains a few hundred inhabitants, but will, in time, doubtless contain a few thousand.

Fairfield was laid off in 1851, when Freestone county was severed from Limestone, and organized; it contains about 800 inhabitants, is a beautiful, healthy little town, and may justly feel proud of its excellent female college, where the fair daughters of Texas seize and use the golden moments as they fly by and join the irrevocable past, in the improvement of their minds and manners, as well as in the acquisition of learning and those gentle, winning, witching ways which please, fascinate and enslave the hearts of men.

In this section is also located Trinity College, one of the best in the State, wherein the Cumberland Presbyterians educate their children and teach them the lovely precepts of Divine revelation, the folly of sin, the wisdom of virtue, and the sublime principle of *faith*.

And here, for the edification of the reader, I will relate the story of Sister Jane and the enthusiastic young preacher.

"Sister Jane was a very pious, good Christian, who, one day, while discussing the idea of faith with the preacher, said she had faith, and sometimes she felt as if she could fly.

"The preacher asserted that if she had faith and believed she could fly—that without a doubt *she could fly;* and insisted on Sister Jane's making the trial of her faith.

"Sister Jane consented—a table was placed out in the yard, Sister Jane mounted the table, clapped her hands and jumped off, striking the air with her arms as a bird in flight does with its wings.

"Sister Jane came to the ground with greater speed than grace, when the enthusiastic minister, while aiding her to rise, said to her:

"You were mistaken, sister! You haven't faith; if you had, you could have flown through the air as a dove.'

"Sister Jane answered: 'I have faith, brother, and I still believe I can fly, but I didn't get the right flop.'"

The early settlers of Limestone county, who built their houses in the wilderness and although often troubled by the Indians, converted it into green fields and happy homes, were truly men of faith!

Indeed, if success is any evidence of merit, and getting the right flop leads on to fortune, it may be said of the pioneer settlers of this magnificent farming country, "They got the right flop!"

They not only converted a wilderness into *green fields* and *happy homes*, but they built school-houses, colleges and churches. Nor did they stop here, but, led by an *abiding* faith in God, who had so long defended them against the tomahawk of the cruel, bloodthirsty savages, they joined hands and hearts, formed bands more numerous than that of Gideon, and made the wilderness resound with the songs and shouts of their glorious, old time-honored *camp meetings*.

I have attended camp meetings and listened with delight to songs similar to the following:

"I want to go, I want to go,
I want to go there too;
Where solid joy fills the soul,
I want to go there too!"

Once on a time a very amiable old Texan named

Joe McDonald, after getting on the outside of as much whiskey as he could conveniently carry, went to one of these camp meetings with a bottle in his pocket.

The minister gave out a hymn, which was sung by the congregation and followed by prayer, during which Joe, while on his knees, imbibed from his bottle, which so affected him that when the congregation, after prayer, again commenced singing, Joe arose from his seat, and after exclaiming: "Brethren, stop that song! it would freeze h—l over a foot thick in a minute and a quarter; let me sing!" He sang in a loud musical voice, *solo*, the following beautiful lines of the poet:

"Oft in the stilly night,
Ere slumber's chain hath bound me,
Fond memory brings the light
Of other days around me."

The effect of his song may be more easily imagined than described. Joe was taken out from the congregation of the faithful—some laughing and others smiling, while the rigidly righteous frowned their rebuke and indignation in angry looks at poor Joe's ungodly condition and impious conduct.

At one of these camp meetings, on Mill creek, Guadalupe county, in Western Texas, where stock-raising is followed as a business, and the branding of animals by the owner is required by law, and they gather them in pens, brand and turn them out again, Gen. Henry McCulloch was converted to a knowledge of the Lord, and becoming enthused in the cause of his new Master, he appealed to his old soldiers who had followed him in his numerous battles with Indians and Mexicans, to lay aside their love for the vain and empty pleasures of this wicked world, and follow him in his new expedition, the grand object of which was to avoid the pains and penalties of hell and damnation, and, after a safe passage of the river Jordan and victorious assault upon the fortifications of Zion, was to end in everlasting life and eternal happiness.

The general's appeal took like wildfire, and in a moment or two the little sanctuary was filled, and the preacher exhorted the new converts to stand back and not crowd in so fast.

This exhortation of the preacher was followed by the loud command of one of the newly converted cow-boys: "Brand 'em and turn 'em out."

Soon after this occurrence there was a lull of almost a perfect calm, which was ended by three loud resounding yells from a shouting sister, when one of the cow-boys inquired of his chum:

"*Say, Jim, what you reckon the sister is hollerin for?*"

"Don't know, Jack," answered the other, "thout the sister's on her transit, got to Jordan, and is a hollerin for the ferryman to come and cross her over the river."

On another occasion a famous old Texan, Jack Cryer, of Colorado, at the earnest entreaties of converted friends, manfully walked up to the altar and anchored himself on the anxious seat, to be prayed for.

The prayers of the faithful were answered, and Jack was brought to a knowledge of the Lord, and became a member of the church.

Two or three days afterwards, a young lady, after conversion, fell into a trance; a doctor and two or three preachers, after examination, expressed the opinion that the patient was not dangerously sick, and would be all right in a few hours, when Mr. Cryer took the hand of the young lady in his, and finding no pulse, solemnly exclaimed: "I'll be d——d if she don't seem to me might'ly like she's dead!"

Jack Cryer's faith was *simon pure*, and no doubt the recording angel, after entering this oath of Jack's, let fall a tear on the record and blotted it out, for it was uttered *unbeknownest* to himself, and owing alone to his deplorable habit of profane swearing.

East of Freestone is Anderson county, through the fertile valleys of which flow the Trinity and Nachez rivers. Palestine, the county seat, was laid off in 1846, and is a pleasant, healthy, and thriving town of about 2,500 or 3,000 inhabitants. Here resides Hon. John H. Reagan, his partner Col. Thos. B. Greenwood, Gen. T. J. Word, Col. A. T. Rainey, and that distinguished gentlemen, Dr. W. G. W. Jowers, who was one of the number who once suffered in a little game of cards, in consequence of the Hon. Hardin Hart's conscientious scruples about gambling on Sunday, as will appear from the following reminiscence:

Many years ago, in Austin, at a little outhouse belonging to Captain James Swisher, near the Treasury building, Forbes Britton, Doctor Jowers, Gen. Tarrant, and the learned Justice Hardin, engaged in a game known among sportsmen as poker. Now, it so happened that it was Saturday night, and that Hardin was lucky, and when the clock struck twelve, having won from the party about five hundred dollars, he arose from the table from which he had raked and pocketed his winnings, and pointing to the clock, with pious solemnity covering his venerable countenance, said: "Gentlemen, you see it's now twelve o'clock; ef we play eny longer we'll be violatin' the Sabbath! My conscience checks me, an' I won't play another *curd* to-night!"

With this classic remark, according to Forbes Britton's account of it, Hardin jumped the game!

Nearly north of Palestine, about fifty miles, is the fair city of Tyler, county seat of the finely timbered and productive county of *Smith*, named in honor of the immortal Deaf Smith, or some other member of that illustrious family.

A branch of the District Court of the United States is held at Tyler, but in a little rented building, the Government not having either the money or the inclination to erect a court-house in Texas.

The Supreme Court of the State is also held in Tyler, which, as it is surrounded by a very healthy and finely watered country, producing the most delightful apples, peaches, pears, and grapes, bids fair to flourish and advance from its present population of three thousand to ten or twenty thousand inhabitants in a very short time.

Rains and Hunt counties, watered by the Sabine and its tributaries, which extend even to Collin county, are also rich, fertile, and productive, as well as settling up rapidly.

It was in the flourishing town of McKinney, which was named in honor of Collin McKinney, as was Collin county, the richest in the State also, that in 1868 I first beheld Judge Hardin Hart on the bench.

I did try, as follows, to describe Hardin as he appeared when I entered the temple of justice, with his drawers hanging at least two inches below his pants, over a pair of rough brogans, showing his skin to the observer, and his shirt, none of the whitest, exposed between his vest and pants for about three inches. His honor wore a blue coat (said to have been won from a Federal soldier), not after the style of "old Father Grimes," which was long-tailed, but more after that of Bones, the dancing negro in the Olympic.

After sitting erect for a few moments Hardin rested his elbows on the plank which served him as a desk, and then rested his head upon his hands, occasionally running one of his fists as far into his mouth as he could get it.—"Them is my idees of what the law ar," he said, when enunciating a decision.

The judge was reported to have bought a new shirt and paper collar lately at Bonham, but I am informed that the rumor is false—he having on the same one he wore at Sherman a few weeks ago.

He walked into a crowd of lawyers and citizens the other day, and hearing one say: "Well, President Johnson will be deposed, that is certain," Judge Hart remarked with a joyous countenance: "Yes, and I reckon his fall will be as great as that of Michael *wus!*" One of the gentlemen asked him: "What about Michael? How and where did Michael fall from?" "Why, don't you know," said Judge Hart, "that the angel Michael wus flung clean over the battlements of heaven?" "I don't know it, judge;

where do you get your information from?" "Why, from the Bible, to be sure!"

In an action of debt the other day, on a question involving the statute of limitations, Hardin, in deciding the point at issue, said: "Gen. Maxey, you 'stood pat' on your note. Sam Roberts 'saw' you, for the widow and children, on the plea of intervention; but Capt. Brown 'has seed' you both, and 'raised' you on the statute of limitations, and as the case now stands, Capt. Brown is entitled to the pot, and it is so decided. Mr. Sheriff, adjourn court until to-morrow mornin'."

In another case Col. Sam Roberts declined to amend after exceptions to his pleadings had been sustained, but afterwards, when going to trial, asked leave to amend, when Judge Hart said:

"Col. Roberts, you stood pat! you can't draw now! you must play your hand for what it's worth."

From these decisions it would appear that in addition to the legal learning which Judge Hart has acquired by the *lucubrationes viginti annorum*, he has also acquired some knowledge of card playing.

Had Cervantes known his Honor, Sancho Panza, the Governor of the Island of Barataria, would have been a richer character than he is.

While Hardin was in Austin as a legislator, he was standing one morning before Swisher's hotel on the edge of the ditch, and by his attitude, which was that of a man just about to jump, drew the attention of Jones Rivers, who stopped, and after looking at him for a while, yelled out:

"Jump! damn you, *jump!*"

His Honor turned on Col. Rivers, and said very indignantly:

"I don't want to jump! I ain't a gwien to jump, and I'll be d—d if you can make me jump!"

Whereupon Jones smiled, and in his peculiar way, which caused the crowd to laugh, said:

"Well, sir, don't get excited; I thought you were going to let out your last link and jump your level best, and was waiting to see you jump, but if you don't wish to jump, you needn't to jump, narry time!"

After the inauguration of Gov. Coke, while the Davis administration was claiming to be the *de jure* government of Texas, Judge Hart sent in his resignation to both Govs. Coke and Davis, remarking to his friend, E. G. Bower, of Dallas: "If this ain't enough to kiver the case, I'll send 'em duplicates."

Judge Hart is kindly spoken of in his district as one of the best judges who ever served them, for it is said he did his best to give justice.

On one occasion, a jury brought in a verdict contrary to his instructions, when Hardin solemnly said: "Gentlemen of the jury, you are discharged! Mr.

Sheriff, you will summon another jury, but if you get another set of as blasted rascals as compose this one, *I raise you a bean!*"

With Judge Hart I also met in McKinney, Judge G. A. Everts, known familiarly over Northern Texas as "Old Bustamente," and always associated in my recollection with bull nettles and centipedes, from the fact that once on a time he came running into a room at night in Bonham, where I was enjoying an innocent game of "draw," holding his pantaloons with both hands, and fright and terror speaking from his whole aspect, and exclaimed: "Bit by a centipede! dead in fifteen minutes, by G—d!" It turned out that the judge had mistaken a bunch of bull nettles for a centipede.

CHAPTER XXII.

Northern Texas.—Jonesborough, Travis, and George Wright.—Kiowa Indians kill Hon. G. N. Martin, his Son Mat.—Gen. Leavenworth.—Clarksville, Paris, Honey Grove, Bonham, Sherman, Ennis, Denison, Jones Rivers, etc.

BOWIE, Red River, Lamar, Fannin, Grayson and Cook counties, on Red river, as well as Denton, Collin, Hunt and Hopkins counties, lying south of them, contain magnificent lands, on which, in the same field, grow, most luxuriantly, wheat, corn, cotton, potatoes, cabbage, rye, oats, barley, tobacco, and all other productions of the climate, while the many streams which flow through them abound in fish, and the forests in game.

No portion of the South presents greater inducements to the farmer, mechanic, or professional man, than this, and yet, in old Red River county, where the town of Jonesborough,* containing two thousand inhabitants, once stood, now grow splendid crops of corn and cotton!

Jonesborough once outnumbered Galveston, Hous-

---

* This 2,000 is given by Almonté, Kennedy and Yoakum, but I learned from the Wright brothers and Doss family who lived there, that Jonesborough never contained more than 500 inhabitants.

ton, Jefferson and Dallas, all put together! Now, the site of the once flourishing and promising city—the metropolis of Northern Texas, where its merchants, traders and husbandmen most did congregate—is fenced in, plowed and cultivated!

Like many Mr. Joneses, Smiths, Johnsons, Jacksons and Browns, Jonesborough started out in life with very promising prospects of becoming famous; but as—

"A flower that does with op'ning morn arise,
And, flourishing the day, at evening dies!"

Jonesborough put forth the tender leaves of Hope, bloomed, and then was nipped by a killing frost! Like Palmyra, Persepolis, Illium and San Filipe de Austin, but not like Herculanæum nor Pompeii, Jonesborough *was!* but, "as the baseless fabric of a vision," Jonesborough is gone!

"Alas, the uncertainty and insecurity of all earthly things!"

"The stoutest vessel manned by brave hearts and skillful hands may founder in a hurricane, while the frail bark which owns no mastery in building, may be gently wafted into its destined harbor!"

"Well—well, the world must turn upon its axis,
And all mankind turn with it, heads or tails,
And live and die, make love and pay our taxes
And as the veering wind shifts, shift our sails."

In the days of the Republic of Texas, there lived in Red River county, two brothers named Travis G. and George W. Wright, the former of whom served as a legislator of Arkansas, while at the same time the latter served as a member of the Texas Congress.

Arkansas still claims a portion of land west of the river which should be added to Bowie or Red River county, but at an early day the boundary line was not known, and Texans and Arkansawyers thus fraternized.

The Wright brothers settled on Red River about 1816—fine specimens of the old Texan—and are, indeed, *par nobile fratrum*, whose ancestors fought under the immortal Washington in the glorious struggle which resulted in American Independence, and whose children lately bore aloft in battle the cross of St. Andrew.

I have heard them tell of their early lives in Texas —how, after the labor of the day and eating their suppers, they would take their blankets, go to the woods, and by the sides of logs enjoy that refreshing sleep and security which their house, on account of the nocturnal attacks of the Indians, did not afford.

In May, 1834, the Kiowa Indians made a descent upon the settlements of Northern Texas on Glass's Creek, killed Judge Gabriel N. Martin, the brother-in-law of T. G. and G. W. Wright, and carried away to their stronghold in the Wichita mountains his little son, Mat W. Martin, then eight years old.

After burying the husband of his only sister, who was almost distracted by his death, Capt. T. G. Wright, with three volunteers, John Ragsdale, Thos. McCown, and Hardy, a negro who had lived with the Kiowas and spoke their language, bid good-by to their friends, and struck out over the boundless prairie to hunt the murderers of Judge Martin, rescue little Mat and return him to his grief-stricken mother.

It was arranged that when the little party should find the camp of the Indians, Capt. Wright, with Ragsdale and McCown, should conceal themselves in a thicket, while Hardy should enter alone the camp of his old associates, and, while pretending to rejoin them, find the little boy, and, when opportunity offered, with him leave the camp of the Kiowas, seek the hiding place of his friends, and with them and little Mat return as best they could to the settlements.

For days and weeks they traversed the prairies and cross timbers, but before they neared the village of the Kiowas, these bold and death-daring frontiersmen most fortunately fell in with Gen. Leavenworth of the United States Army, who, with detachments of infantry and cavalry, was seeking these same Indians, by order of the Government, to treat with them for the delivery of other captives then held by them.

Capt. Wright and his party joined the command of Gen. Leavenworth, and all of them being good woodsmen, were of great service in finding lost horses and killing game.

The weather was hot, the prairies all dry and water very scarce, while the Indians fled before and hung around their rear, refusing to stop even for a white flag or to hold any communication whatever with them.

From bad water, exposure, anxiety of mind, or some other cause, Gen. Leavenworth sickened and died, when Capt. Wright and his party, with twelve soldiers, were detailed to carry back his body to Fort Washita, from whence it was afterwards taken for final interment to Delhi, New York.

As a soldier and officer Gen. Leavenworth was admired for his many excellent qualities, and his untimely death was sincerely mourned by his whole command.

Capt. Wright and his party returned from Fort Washita to the little army then under command of the next senior officer, Capt. Dean, with which he and his party passed through the cross timbers, suffering much—often pressing the juice from wild grapes to quench their thirst, which not only relieved them, but had an exhilarating effect similar to wine.

After much suffering and hardship they came to a country abounding in water and game, when they luxuriated upon roast turkey, venison and buffalo steaks, besides a variety of fresh-water fish, and honey found abundantly in the hollow trees.

But it was some time before they found the village of the Kiowas: in the course of time, however, after scouring the country all round where the trail disappeared, they discovered an Indian on the prairie, when two select men on swift horses were ordered to catch him. The race was short, for when the Indian saw his pursuers gaining on him and lost all hope of escape, he dismounted, and levelled his gun at them; whereupon they also dismounted and advanced upon him without presenting their guns, but making signs to him not to shoot, which he did not do, and the two horsemen came up to him without harm and induced him to visit their camp.

The Kiowas had been at war with the Osage Indians, and when this Kiowa entered the camp of the white men, to his great joy and astonishment, *his only sister* (who had been captured by the Osages in one of their battles with the Kiowas, and had been ransomed or purchased by the United States, in order to present her as a token of friendship to her tribe) ran up to him, and falling upon his neck, wept for joy.

The objects of the expedition having been explained to this Indian, he piloted Dean's command to the place where the trail or path gave out on the bank of a creek, up that creek several hundred yards through the water to a plain road on the opposite bank, which led to their village, where a treaty was soon concluded and many liberated captives ran to the open arms of their kindred and friends.

Little Mat Martin again made glad the heart of a fond mother and other relations and friends, while Capt. Travis G. Wright still lives and enjoys that sweetest and most exquisite pleasure which always comes home to the hearts of those who delight to make others happy.

The Hon. George W. Wright often speaks of the six changes of governments under which he has lived.

1st. Under the United States, by cession from France in 1803; 2d. Under Spain, by cession from the United States, in 1819 to 1824; 3d. Under the United States of Mexico, from 1824 to 1836; 4th. Under the Republic of Texas, from 1836 to 1846; 5th. The United States again, from 1846 to 1861; 6th. The Confederate States, from 1861 to 1865; 7th. The United States again, which he don't count as the 7th government, has not yet changed, *and it is fervently hoped, never will!*

The Wright brothers also told me of the good old times of the cash-note system, payable in cows and calves, when every Texan's credit was good for what he wished to buy, unless he was a notorious character, and then how they used to swing up these notorious characters to the limbs of trees.

Page's tree, at Clarksville, and Bighorn Smith's, at Bonham, stand to this day as living witnesses to the swift and certain punishment meted out to the wrong-doer by the old Texans. No games of seven-up were then played by jurors in order to agree on a verdict, but when crime was found out its punishment followed.

This certainty of punishment for crime prevents its often occurrence, and it might be well for our State and National legislators, in view of the great demoralization of the times, to lay aside their sickly sentimentality about reforming thieves, robbers, and murderers in penitentiaries, and by inflicting certain, full and speedy punishment upon them, thus make crime odious, perilous, and less frequent. If they will not listen to the voice of wisdom, the aspect of terror may arrest their wicked resolves.

If, as we learned from Webster's old spelling-book, they will not listen to kind words, nor heed harmless turfs of grass, then let fly at them bone-breaking *death-bearing* stones.

When the gentle words of peace and love are scoffed at by the careless, *hardened* villain, then

"*Cry* HAVOC, *and let slip the dogs of war*"

on the hopeless, unrepentant wretch, and thereby protect society and throw over the innocent and defenceless the shield of terror.

In 1846, while riding alone about dusk, on the national road cut through the dense forest of the Red River bottom, between Pine Bluffs and where the Kiamitia flows into that stream, near the place where three men had been hung for murder or robbery, I saw approaching me a terrible-looking man, who, from his staggering, was either drunk or acting the drunkard.

I was entirely unarmed, and the idea occurred to me that the individual might attempt to rob me. When he approached, and after shaking me warmly by my right hand with his, suddenly he changed his grasp of my hand from his right hand to his left, and thrust his right hand into his bosom!

Blood and murder! my hair stood on end, and elevated my hat! Was he going to draw a pistol or bowie-knife? Should I pop both spurs into my horse's side and thus try to escape, or bounce on him from the saddle for a death struggle?

In a moment, which seemed a mighty long time, he drew forth his hand from his bosom, holding in it neither pistol nor knife, but a bottle of *Dexter's double rectified*, and exclaimed:

"Take a drink, stranger! take a drink!"

Never was my surprise and astonishment so great, so agreeable, or so sudden!

I have often been in danger, have seen many shells explode, and have been shot at when only a few feet from my enemy, but I never felt half so much scared in all my life as I did when this highwayman, who proved to be an honest, good citizen, thrust his hand in his bosom.

Paris, Bonham, Sherman, and Clarksville are beautiful and flourishing towns, — each surrounded by rich lands, fine farms, and a prosperous people.

Sherman was at one time as large as Dallas, but the Texas Pacific, when it connected the latter with Shreveport and Texarkana, while the Transcontinental failed to connect Sherman even with Paris, precipitated the growth of Dallas.

Denison, sixteen miles north of Sherman, at the junction of the Central railroad with the M. K. and T., ships thousands of beeves to St. Louis annually, and has the largest flour mill in Texas.* It is but

---

* In this I may be mistaken, for Mr. Joseph Mulhall, of St. Louis, the famous stockyard man, has recently erected a very fine flouring mill at the very prosperous city of Ennis, in the midst of rich and very productive

THE AGREEABLE SURPRISE.

three miles from the Indian Territory, and daily the red men with their wives and pappooses throng its streets.

Denison has one of the most elegant institutions of learning in the State, and bids fair to increase in wealth and importance. It now numbers several thousand inhabitants, although but little more than two years old.

About midway between Paris and Bonham is the lovely little village of Honey Grove, in the midst of a very rich, beautiful and productive country—here the hero, Davy Crockett, stopped and rested when he first came to Texas, and finding bees and honey in the trees, named the place *Honey Grove.*

The Transcontinental railroad, a branch of the Texas and Pacific, runs by this place.

Soon their old mode of transportation, by horse and ox-wagon, will be a thing of the past, and the old North Texan can smile as the locomotive carries him pleasantly over iron rails his old day's journey in an hour.

But never will the old Texans forget the long weary miles, over boggy roads and hog-wallow prairie,

---

fields of wheat, corn, cotton, etc. Ennis is in Ellis County, east of Waxahachie, the county seat; is beautifully located on the Houston and Texas Central Railroad, thirty-three miles south of Dallas, and is certain to become a city of considerable trade and importance.

to market, and how they used to ask: "Stranger, how far is it to town?" and how, sometimes, *the stranger* would not do as Jones Rivers did, lessen, but increase the distance.

Jones being asked this question, answered: "Well, sir, your team appears fatigued, you look very thirsty, and the road is bad, so I'll let you have it at twelve miles, but I'll be d—d if anybody else should have it for less than fifteen."

Col. Rivers was indeed a man of infinite wit and humor, and I will relate with what ease and pleasantry, in his expiring moments, he "folded the drapery of his couch around him, and laid down to pleasant dreams!"

Cæsar's *et tu, Brute!* Napoleon's *tête d'Armée!* and Mr. Webster's exclamation, *I still live!* are history.

"Socrates died like a philosopher, but Jesus Christ died like a God!" is familiar to the school-boy.

Jones Rivers died as he had lived, with wit on his lips and a smile on his face.

In his expiring moments, while gasping for breath, a lady attendant asked: "Col. Rivers, will you have a little air?"

"No, madam," he answered, "no more heirs for me. Too late! Excuse me, if you please."

May you, dear reader, without regard to your race,

nation or language, when the dark-winged angel of death shakes his sable banner before your closing eyes, die as carelessly, as pleasantly and with as little regret as did Jones Rivers, and with him, Phil Claiborne, and all other good men, who love the pure, the beautiful and the good, and whose greatest pleasure comes from wiping tears from the eyes of suffering humanity and pouring the balm of consolation into a wounded spirit—after crossing over the river, meet in the great Beyond, where

> "God gives the milk, the honey and the wine,
> And pleasure never dies."

CHAPTER XXIII.

Agriculture, Farming, Stock Raising, Wool Growing, Fishing and Hunting in Texas.—Manufactures, Wine Growing, Minerals, Financial Condition, Educational Advantages and Advances illustrated.—An Address.—A Novel.—The Conclusion.

AGRICULTURE is the grand pursuit of Texans, and cotton the great staple or chief article of produce for exportation.

Wheat, corn, oats, rye, potatoes, tomatoes, etc., have rarely been exported.

The estimated receipts of cotton at Galveston alone for this year, is 400,000 bales, worth, at sixteen cents per pound, $32,000,000.

Many thousands of beeves are also raised and exported. In the month of January, 1873, the Morgan line of steamers transported to New Orleans *via* Brashear, 5,300 head. But the great market for Texas beeves is St. Louis, although Memphis is receiving some by way of Little Rock.

Wool, hides, tallow, and bees-wax are annually exported to the value of millions of dollars.

Many persons in Western and South Western Texas are engaged exclusively in cattle raising, others in raising sheep and wool-growing.

The latter was the pleasing avocation of the late George Wilkins Kendall, who settled on the Guadalupe river, about forty miles north of San Antonio, who once on a time amused me by relating the manner of his life in one day's experience as follows:

"At four o'clock in the morning I arose, saddled my pony, and, with my gun and fishing tackle, rode to the Guadalupe, a mile and a half from my residence. I had baited a particular spot for fishing, and in a short time I caught twenty-six pounds of perch, trout and cat. The last one broke my three hooks, after which I took out my knife and filed the blunt end of the least broken hook, so that it would penetrate, baited it well and threw it in the water. In a moment it was swallowed, and I could tell by the heavy pulling that it was by a large fish, so in order to let him exhaust himself, and avoid breaking the hook again, I gave him the line and let him struggle round and round for a good while, then drawing him in quietly I landed him on *terra firma*. It was a magnificent trout weighing six pounds and a quarter. Just as I had fastened him on the string with the others, I heard a turkey gobble about three hundred yards from me on the other side of the river. Taking out my 'yelper,' I talked turkey to him, and could plainly see him on his roost turning his head sideways and looking for me. Finally he stretched out his wings, jumped from his perch, and after flying across the river, walked up in a gallant style, no doubt expecting to meet and woo and win a fair and lovely turkey hen. As he came up sideways, strutting, now and then gobbling and striking haughtily the earth with his huge wings, I did indeed admire him. At forty yards from my 'blind,' he fell a bleeding victim to misplaced confidence. Oh! he was an imperial fellow, weighing eighteen and three-quarter pounds.

"Barely had the beautiful visions of hope faded in the imperial mind of the majestic gobbler, when I heard a noise resembling the snort of a buck. Turning round, there stood before me a large deer, just fifty yards off. In an instant, nine buckshot from my trusty double-barrel pierced him through the neck, and he was added to my morning's trophies, making in all one hundred and fifty pounds of venison, turkey and fish, which I tied to the limb of a tree and left on the river bank until I returned home, got my breakfast and sent a cart for.

"After my morning's sport, I wrote a letter, of a column, for the *Picayune*, went out among my sheep, dined, and in the evening, after reading that pastoral of Virgil, commencing

"'Tityre, tu patulæ recubans sub tegmine fagi,'

indulged in reflections upon the times of Virgil com pared with the present, and the great superiority of our Constitutional Republican Government over the imperial despotism of Rome.

"When Virgil wrote the above line, Augustus had confiscated the lands and homes of all the inhabitants of his section of the empire, for having sided against his party in the civil war, which had just terminated, leaving him in possession of supreme power.

"The clemency of the Government of the United States has left us our homes, our property and institutions, except our peculiar one of negro slavery, the abolition of which Southerners now look upon as a real blessing.

"With reflections such as these, and meditating upon the future greatness and glory of the American people, about nine o'clock I retired for the calm sleep and pleasant dreams which always repay the laborer for his toil."

In this account of one day's life of a distinguished Texan, most accomplished gentleman and beloved friend, I have confined myself to the words as they fell from his lips, to the best of my recollection.

But he says nothing of wild ducks, geese, cranes, plover, quail, squirrels, rabbits, etc., which are abundant.

Sportsmen have killed as many as two and three hundred ducks in a day, but the geese and cranes (esteemed by epicures as superior to the turkey) fly higher, and are not so easily killed.

Curlew are killed by the thousand, as they come and go in great numbers.

Having been brought up in the country myself, I am not ignorant of the pleasures of hunting, fishing and farming. Indeed, when fortune smiles upon my efforts and blesses me with a few thousand dollars, I intend to buy me a farm on the Trinity, Brazos, Colorado, Guadalupe, or some one of the many beautiful streams of the Lone Star State, in which the fisherman can delight himself in catching bass, trout, perch, rock, sheepshead, flounder, cat, and king fish, besides many others too tedious to mention, and where with but little labor I can raise an abundant supply of provisions, and have most of my time for hunting, fishing and literary enjoyment. There are thousands of Texans now living in this way.

Col. Tom Scott, after visiting Texas, thus speaks of it:

"For the past two or three weeks, in company with Colonel Forney and General Dodge, I have been making a tour through Northeastern Texas, which is the location of that line intended to be built from the eastern line of the State of Texas, through to the

Pacific coast. In making this visit to Texas, the first time in my life that I have ever been in that region, I may state to you, very briefly, the impression made upon my mind in relation to that country for productions and for the extension of railroad facilities. We found in Texas, very much to our surprise, a country capable of producing all your great staples, to a degree that is remarkable. We found there, within a circle of a few miles, as good wheat, good corn, good cotton, good tobacco, good oats, all grown on the same soil, as I have ever seen standing on the ground in any part of the world. I believe that the country can produce—that the State of Texas will produce—more of those great staples than are produced to-day in the balance of the United States."

The *Patriot*, of Harrisburg, Pennsylvania, years ago, truthfully said:

"Texas has, beyond all question, superior advantages over every other State in the Union. Its soil not only yields a larger return of sugar and cotton than any other portion of the United States, but for the raising of the cereals it far outstrips the heaviest productions of the Genesee valley. Not only is Texas most prolific in the production of cotton, sugar, grain, fruits and vegetables, but it far excels all other portions of the habitable globe for the breeding of cattle. Texas is an empire within itself, embracing every variety of soil and climate. There are millions of dollars in prospective to enterprising men, and pleasant homes and a competency for all who may venture within her borders."

The Washington *Chronicle*, corroborating the statement of the *Patriot*, also very truthfully says:

"Texas possesses the advantages of a salubrious climate, a soil unsurpassed in fertility—adapted to the growth of all the cereals; produces the very finest short staple as well as sea-island cotton, and possesses inexhaustible mineral wealth. The rich grazing fields of Northern Texas, known as the 'black waxy land,' produce not only fine crops of wheat, oats, rye, barley and corn, but are also well adapted to cotton. The lands of Middle and Northern Texas produce on an average 600 pounds of ginned cotton to the acre. One man can easily cultivate ten acres in corn and ten in cotton. The corn alone will pay the expense of cultivating and gathering the entire crop, and leaves the farmer the net profit of, say at least 5,000 pounds of cotton, which at present prices would be worth $1,150, currency. These same lands produce all kinds of fruits, except the strictly tropical, to which may be added the great advantage of free pasturage, whereby a thrifty farmer can, in a few years, sell from one to three thousand dollars' worth of stock, wool and hides, making a net profit for one man of from one to four thousand dollars per year, which certainly cannot be excelled in any country. Texas *is* emphatically the country for industrious poor men.'"

Many crops of cotton and corn have been raised without more subsistence to either man or beast than the abundance of game and grass to be found in the glades and prairies.

Manufactures do not flourish in Texas.

Its beautiful rivers with arrowy swiftness still flow through vast regions of rich and productive lands, and mingle with the waters of the Gulf, without turning machinery of one-millionth part of their capacity.

In San Antonio and Austin, many years ago, the machinery of the mills was run by wheels propelled by the natural swiftness and force of the San Antonio and Colorado rivers, without any dams whatever.

Houston, Waco, New Braunfels and Hempstead have taken the lead in erecting manufacturing establishments.

By the laws of Texas 320 acres of land are granted to the introducer for every $1,000 worth of machinery introduced and operated in Texas, yet but few persons or companies have engaged in the business.

Texans buy sugar, rice, molasses, shoes, hats, clothing of all kinds, saddlery, waggons, carriages, and almost all their wooden ware, besides farming implements, household and kitchen furniture, from a distance. True, it would save expenses of transportation, tariffs, and intermediate profits were they to manufacture their own articles of consumption, but they are not a manufacturing people.

Shall I go farther and inform strangers that Texans buy and consume many thousands of dollars' worth of concentrated milk, as well as butter, pickles, canned goods and preserves put up in and transported from Boston, Mass.?

I doubt not, in the course of time, when New England capitalists learn that the manufacture of all kinds of cotton and woollen goods in Texas will pay better than in New England, that some of them may voluntarily go down to Texas and invest their capital and skill in the development of our unrivalled capacities as a manufacturing state.

Peaches, apples, and grapes are very abundant in Texas. I have never seen larger or finer apples and peaches grown anywhere than in Texas, and as for the grapes, they grow wild and in great abundance.

I have known many persons to make several barrels of wine yearly just from the wild grapes gathered in the woods.

I have sometimes gathered a quantity of wild

grapes in the forest, and, after eating them, felt an exhilarating effect similar to that produced by drinking wine.

With a few exceptions, however, Texans pay no attention to the cultivation of the vine, the growth of the grape, or the filling of their cellars.

When a few emigrants from France and Germany shall have planted their vineyards in Texas and made wine from our cultivated native grapes, I doubt not that it will be unsurpassed by the famous brands of Verzeney, Heidseick, Mound Vineyard, Napoleon, or even the renowned Johannisberg.

But Texans are even behind Californians as to the cultivation of the vine, the growth of grapes and the making of wine.

They seem to forget that the first miracle of our Saviour was to change water into wine, and that His last command to erring mortals was to drink it in remembrance of Him.

Never did I hear one of them repeat, *In vino veritas*, but often such legends as the following:

"After the expulsion of Adam and Eve from the garden of Paradise, Adam planted the vine, which, as Satan beheld in passing by, his majesty was pleased with and took under his especial care.

"He first caught a little lamb, and killing it, poured its blood upon the roots of the plant which grew luxuriantly; next he captured a lion, and after slaying it, poured its blood also on the roots of the vine and it grew amazingly. On visiting his favorite the third time, his satanic majesty brought the hog, slaughtered and poured its blood upon the roots of the vine, when it grew wonderfully and brought forth fruit which, strange to say, when made into wine gives to the descendants of Adam, when taken, the characteristic disposition of these three animals.

"When taken moderately, wine causes a man to feel gentle and playful like the lamb; when taken immoderately, it makes him fierce and bloody like the lion; and when taken to the *extreme*, gives him the disposition of the hog to wallow in the mire."

Camp-meeting songs are often heard in the hamlets of the poor and the fine residences of the rich, at a late hour of the night; but that familiar old song of—

> "Landlord, fill the flowing bowl,
> Until it doth run over!
> For to-night we'll merry be, merry be,
> For to-night we'll merry be, merry be,
> For to-night we'll merry be, merry be,
> To-morrow we'll get sober!"

is never heard.

The following sample of logic from the irreligious pen of an old wine-bibber would be considered by the good people of the Lone Star State as infamous and horrible :

"Good wine makes good blood,
Good blood causeth good humors,
Good humors cause good thoughts,
Good thoughts bring forth good works,
Good works carry a man to heaven;
ergo
Good wine carrieth a man to heaven."

Without a doubt the following lines, from a popular song of the boys at West Point when out on a "tear," would be anathematized:

"Here's a health to General Jackson,
God bless the old hero!
May he rest upon his laurels
And never know of woe;
May he rest upon his laurels,
And never know of woe;
And drink his whiskey every night,
At Benny Haven's, O.

"The commentators tell us all,
That when above we go
We'll follow that same handicraft
We followed here below.
If this be true philosophy—
The preachers say so too—
Then, oh! what days and nights we'll have
At Benny Haven's, O."

Old Applejack and Peach brandy might be manufactured to any extent, and become a source of immense revenue to the state, but these, as well as Bourbon and Rye whiskeys, are almost entirely imported from Cincinnati, New Orleans, and New York.

Thus Texans piously aid in building up and sustaining the manufacturing establishments of the older states, and let the capacities and resources of their own state lie dormant and undeveloped.

Although fortunes have been made, and are now being made in Texas, by planting cotton, making sugar, growing wheat, and stock-raising, I am of the opinion that any one skilled in vine-growing and wine-making might go there and not only accumulate a fortune, but gain distinguished consideration and great glory, by turning the attention of Texans to the great but hitherto unproductive mine of wealth which now lies idle, dormant, and undeveloped in the midst of their forests and wild woods, serving only as food for wild beasts and the birds of the air—not sour grapes by any means, but pleasant to the eye and taste.

The mineral wealth of Texas, consisting in unlimited deposits of coal, iron, copper, zinc, lead, gold, silver, salt, oil, manganese, cobalt, nickel, and bismuth, in a large portion of the country, lies just in the same condition it did when the great Jehovah first called it into existence.

A correspondent of the Cleburne *Chronicle*, giving an account of the discovery of coal in Johnson County, exultingly ends his communication in these words: "So you can see that it seems to be well scattered on the border of the rich prairie lands, and settlers thereon can have no fear of freezing, for ere long these beds will be opened, and millions will be made to our country otherwise than by the superabundant crops of corn, cotton and wheat."

"Yet gold all is not, that doth golden seem,"

Or, as Shakespeare hath it:

"All that glisters is not gold."

And although coal may exist elsewhere, it would be rather hard to make Capt. Scogin believe now that Travis County has much of it.

A correspondent of the *Turf, Field and Farm* thus tells how the captain was sold:

"Do you know Capt. Wm. D. Scogin, head drummer for the well-known hardware house of Samuel Roosevelt & Co.? I will introduce you to him. Bill, as he is familiarly called by his friends, is one-eyed, a swift talker, has been to California, and knows every hog-path in Arkansas and Texas.

"Taking Capt. Billy up one hill and down another, 'he is a regular brick.'

"He was in Austin a month or two ago, and struck *ile*, or rather got oil-struck.

"Some everlasting reprobate about our town bought a gallon of oil, carried it out to a deep ravine about two miles from our city, and poured it out on the ground.

"After this he told of discovering oil, and thousands of people immediately congregated 'thar or thara-abouts.'

"Captain Scogin came, he saw, he conquered, that is, he had travelled, he knew what was what, and forthwith invested a few hundred dollars: a company was immediately organized and boring commenced.

"At first the indications were favorable, then more favorable; oil and cannel coal. I met Bill on his return from the mine, when, slapping me on the shoulder he said: 'Well, ole fel, I've made a ten strike at last! There's no use talking. By the everlasting gods, heathen mythology and Scandinavian history, I've struck ile.

"'Now won't I have a gay time in New York when the drumming season commences?

"'Won't I ask the boys up to drink champagne, when they come around to the Metropolitan Hotel?

"'Won't I tell 'em about having been poor once myself?

"'Why, bless your soul! I'm going to buy me four

or five acres of brown stone fronts on Fifth Avenue. But, Colonel, won't my wife feel happy? Won't Mary feel joyous? I am going to settle a million on her and the children immediately, so in case of accident she'll always be independent.

"'Colonel, I reckon I've got the best wife in the world. Won't she be glad?'

"After he had run on thusly for a while, I intimated something about his *dividing with his friends.*

"He went on:

"'I wrote to Mr. Roosevelt that he might come in with me—half interest! Sam Roosevelt is a mighty good man! There's enough for both of us, so I am going to let him in, but nobody else need apply.

"'Colonel, come, let's go and take a drink! Whoop pee! ole fel; did you ever feel rich? You bet I'm going to lead a gay and festive life—

"'Gay and happy, gay and happy;
We'll be gay and happy still.'

"Thus Capt. Billy carried on for hours, but finally the boring ceased; the truth leaked out; there was neither oil nor coal, and away went the captain's brown-stone fronts like 'the baseless fabric of a vision.'"

The financial condition of Texas is a source of pleasant reflection to its citizens.

Gov. Coke's Message of the 10th of February, 1874, which is based upon the reports of the comptroller and treasurer, shows the public debt of Texas, including interest to the 1st of September, 1874, to be $2,248,831.75.

Gov. Coke says: "The revenues which have been paid by the people, and should have prevented the accumulation of debt, have been squandered and filched by those whom a cruel fortune placed in her offices of trust."

His Message also shows the taxable property of Texas, for 1874, to be $240,420,000, and he very justly says: "With her vast resources and rapidly increasing taxable values, the public debt of Texas is as nothing."

Whether by a reduction of the salaries of state officers or by the issue of state warrants drawing interest from date till paid, or how this debt is to be paid or its increase stopped, are questions for the consideration of our legislators.

No state of the Union has shown a greater desire for the advancement of learning than Texas.

The Constitution of 1836 made it "the duty of Congress, as soon as circumstances would admit, to provide, by law, a general system of education."

In 1839, the Texas Congress gave 50 leagues of land for the endowment of a University, and three leagues (which were increased in 1840 to four leagues) for school purposes.

The Constitution of 1845 made it the duty of the Legislature to provide for free schools, and in 1854, $2,000,000, paid by the government in the purchase of Sante Fé, was given to the common school fund, the interest only to be expended, while the principal was loaned to railroads.

In 1860, 104,447 pupils were taught in the common schools of Texas, at the cost of $104,447, but in 1861, and during the days of the late Confederate States, they were deserted by the boys and girls for the field and fireside; while *the boys* made *history* at Bull Run, Manassas, Gains' Mill, Malvern Heights, Sharpsburg, Oak Hills, Mansfield, Fredericksburg, in the Wilderness, and on many other sad and mournful battle-fields, which their children and their children's children may read with admiration of their impetuous valor,—the girls used the cards and spinning-wheels, the loom and their needles, to supply them with clothing.

Since the war, the present Constitution of Texas has given to the public schools all the proceeds from the sale of public lands, one-fourth of the state revenue, and the poll-tax of one dollar on every citizen of the state.

The last annual report of the comptroller shows

that $690,762.04 were paid by the state for public schools, in which 227,615 pupils were taught by 3,687 teachers, during the last year.

It is very much to be regretted that the University exists only on the records of the state, but it is earnestly hoped that ere long suitable buildings will be erected, a library and scientific apparatus purchased, qualified teachers employed, and its career as a first-class institution of learning *commenced.*

The Agricultural College near the fair and prosperous city of Bryan, although a state institution, and the finest college building in Texas, and very creditable to the state, should not do away with the *University.*

Yet schools and colleges, public and private, have been established in many cities and towns of Texas, in which the minds of the youth are learned to think, reason, and reflect, and their powers of thought (*the grand object of education*) trained, strengthened, and developed, while their memories are stored with useful information and the wisdom of ages.

In order to give an idea of the advancement of two students at Austin, I here insert an address of one before a debating club, upon oratory, and a burlesque on the yellow-backed literature and trashy novels of the day, by another.

They are as follows, and explain themselves :

ORATORY.

GENTLEMEN:—The power of arresting and fixing the attention of an audience upon any subject, and so discussing it as to excite the passions and convince the understanding, has always been held in the highest repute among the most civilized nations of the old and new world.

Indeed, the accomplishment of so addressing an audience on any given subject as to make it feel as you feel, think as you think, and act as you would have it act, is one of the rarest and most difficult things for you to acquire in this life.

Greece had but one Demosthenes, Rome but one Cicero, England but one Fox, France but one Mirabeau, and America but one Patrick Henry. Yet the first named should give you encouragement that oratory is not a natural gift, but an accomplishment, which may be acquired by labor and perseverance, for the impediment in his speech and his awkward manner of action while speaking, are known to the schoolboy.

In order to develop his voice, he spoke to the roaring sea; to acquire distinct enunciation, he spoke with pebbles under his tongue; and to obtain that grace or *suaviter in modo*, so pleasing to an audience, he spoke under the sharp point of a sword suspended over his shoulder. Then, again, his great preparation before delivering his orations—shaving one side of his head so that he could not go out into society until his hair grew out again, but would be compelled to stay in his room and thus have all his time for labor, should not escape your attention. As his orations are most excellent, we may conclude that in their preparation he laid down his major and minor premises clearly, before he said *therefore*, and drew his conclusion. So, without doubt, Demosthenes had studied logic—or syllogistic reasoning. And when we see how appropriately and elegantly he used the climax, simile, metaphor and trope—how replete his orations are with allusions, personifications, and allegories, artfully interwoven so as to please, dazzle, and fascinate his hearers, we may believe that he had often burned the midnight lamp over the pages of rhetoric. So you may conclude, that were you to ask me by what means you can soonest become good debaters, I should recommend the studies of logic and rhetoric.

The beautiful and masterly oration of Cicero in defence of Milo is the plain syllogism. Any one who kills another in self-defence is justifiable. Milo killed Claudius in self-defence, therefore Milo was justifiable. However, these will be of little use without practice and the continued use of the rules therein laid down. So necessary is practice to debaters, that they have been known, in the absence of hearers, to speak before looking-glasses. I have often heard it said that a poor thing well spoken was more effective than a good thing poorly spoken; indeed, the orator has been accused of making the worst appear the better cause.

Æschines, who was the competitor of Demosthenes after his banishment, taught a school of rhetoric, and on one occasion delivered to his class the oration of Demosthenes on the crown, and was highly applauded, when he remarked: "Could you have heard Demosthenes himself deliver his oration, your applause would have been much greater."

There is a tone of voice and a manner of acting what one says, which are frequently more eloquent than the things said. Often actors, on the stage, so pathetically act their parts in the play as to bring tears into the eyes of observers and hearers, who might read the play in their rooms with ordinary emotions.

Shakespeare, in his celebrated play of Hamlet, gives the following advice to actors, which is, like all things produced by that great man, most excellent: "Speak the speech, I pray you, as I pronounced it to you, trippingly on the tongue; but if you mouth it, as many of our players do, I had as lief the town-crier spoke my lines. Nor do not saw the air too much with your hand, thus; but use all gently, for in the very torrent, tempest, and (as I may say) whirlwind of your passion, you must acquire and beget a temperance that may give it smoothness. Oh, it offends me to the soul to hear a robustious, periwig-pated fellow tear a passion to tatters, to very rags, to split the ears of the groundlings; who, for the most part, are capable of nothing but inexplicable dumb shows and noise. I would have such a fellow whipped for o'erdoing Termagant; it out-herods Herod; pray you, avoid it. Be not too tame neither, but let your discretion be your tutor; suit the action to the word, the word to the action; with this special observance, that you o'er-step not the modesty of nature, for anything so over-done is from the purpose of playing, whose end, both at the first and now, was and is to hold as 'twere the mirror up to nature; to show virtue her own feature, scorn her own image, and the very age and body of the time his form and pressure. Now, this overdone, or come tardy off, though it make the unskilful laugh, cannot but make the judicious grieve; the censure of which one must, in your allowance, o'erweigh a whole theatre of others. Oh, there be players that I have seen play, and heard others praise, and that highly,—not to speak it profanely, that neither having the accent of Christians, nor the gait of Christian, pagan, nor man, have so strutted and bellowed, that I have thought some of nature's journeymen had made men, and not made them well, they imitated humanity so abominably."

But, besides the study of logic, rhetoric and acting, any one desirous of excelling as a speaker should not be unacquainted with history and poetry.

When Patrick Henry exclaimed: "Cæsar had his Brutus, Charles I. had his Cromwell, and George III. —may he profit by their example!" he made the fact known that he was not ignorant either of ancient or modern history. When Mr. Webster, in his famous speech on the Constitution, spoke of State rights, individual security, and public prosperity, he illustrated his subject by allusions to the *Colosseum* and the *Parthenon*—Greece and Rome. The great Irish orator, Phillips, in contrasting our western world with the departed glory of oriental empires, alludes to the ancient glory but present decay of Palmyra and Persepolis. Cicero, in one of his orations, alludes to the impropriety of a man sick with fever drinking copiously of cold water to allay it, when the opposite effect is generally produced. From which fact we may conclude that Cicero had some knowledge of medicine. Indeed, what Dr. Johnson says of the poet may well be said of the orator, who, like the editor of a newspaper, is supposed, at least by some, to be ignorant of nothing, but should be acquainted with all the arts and sciences, and draw his illustrations from Esculapius and Archimedes as well as from Homer and Herodotus—and as soon as they are invented of a safe character, be as well able to navigate the air in aerial vehicles as the ocean in steamships.

Lord Byron said that to be a good poet one must commence writing verses in his youth, and keep it up to old age; so it is with oratory and all things appertaining to poor, frail humanity—they must be cultivated, increased and developed by practice, labor and perseverance! You must practise it, labor at it, and persevere in it.

It was once my good fortune to hear the Rev. Henry Ward Beecher preach a most excellent sermon on the development of the religious principle in the human heart. He asserted that as the blacksmith, by constantly wielding the sledge-hammer, caused the muscles and strength of his arm to increase; as the speed of the swift-footed race-horse may be increased by training, so the religious principle, by conversation and association with pious people, the study of the Bible and other religious books, may be increased and greatly strengthened in the hearts of men.

The greatest man of this age was the great novelist, poet and orator, Bulwer, who, throughout his works, but nowhere more forcibly or more beautifully than in his character of Claude Melnotte, in the Lady of Lyons, holds out the grand idea of self-cultivation and development.

The gardener's son, by study, application, and perseverance, makes himself superior in all those accomplishments which dignify and ennoble mortals, to the titled aristocrats with whom he came in contact.

But there is no royal nor easy road to the proud eminence on which the orator stands—from which he may look back

> "And scorn the base degrees by which he did ascend."

No one better than he can exclaim with sincerity:

> "Ah! who can tell how hard it is to climb
> The steep where Fame's proud temple shines afar?"

THE BLUE ROBBER OF THE PINK MOUNTAIN.

Near the close of the thirteenth century, Sir Hildebrand Hiltersplit, covered with a complete panoply of neuter verbs and relative pronouns, commenced his ascent of Mount Paphros, that lies in the Gutta Percha Range. Arriving at the summit, he beheld, stretched out before his excited imagination, the beautiful valley of Neuralgia. There he saw the seahorse and the crocodile sporting side by side, the reindeer and the humming-bird flitting from flower to flower, and the melodious watermelon and the isingglass growing upon the same vine.

Upon the banks of an umbrageous stream that ran careering from the mountain-side, and nestled in a small Alpine grove, reposed the tent of the ancient Barbacon—the grand Clam-sloop of the country. At about the hour of half-past four o'clock in the afternoon—his daughter, the fair Sarsaparilla, clad in chloroform, and waving her nascent and sporadic sceptre, entered the presence of the ancient Barbacon her father, bearing in her left hand a small dish of stewed parasangs and fried conostrophies, on which her ancient sire made his evening repast. And seating herself on the asteroids of public grief in one corner of the pavilion, she poured forth her native gypsum in the most delightful strains, as she swept the cords of her light bandana.

Attracted by this wonderful operatic copologo, Sir Hildebrand Hiltersplit entered the apartment, and throwing himself at her feet doled out his love-ditty in the most mellifluous and oleaginous cadences.

Scarcely had he risen from his recumbent position when the Blue Robber of the Pink Mountains broke into the apartment. At sight of this horrid monster, clad in the form of an obese fandango, the fair Sarsaparilla shrieked, and uttered a cry so piercing that Sir Hildebrand Hiltersplit shrank into the interior of the ottoman. With the most audacious strides the robber approached the fair Sarsaparilla, and with his left arm encircled her waist, whilst with his right hand he seized a small catapult of silver she wore suspended from her neck by a bill of lading.

Agonizing with grief and unbounded rage, Sir Hildebrand Hiltersplit darted from his place of concealment and seizing a boot-jack, that lay "floating on the floor," stabbed the monster to the heart, and left the fair Sarsaparilla like an illuminating light standing upon the binnacle of her own expectability, from which exalted position she looked down with mingled scorn and contempt upon her baffled pursuer.

And now, dear reader, I close this work, with a feeling akin to that which one feels on parting with a beloved friend.

May your future path be strewn with flowers, and while ever ascending the hill of prosperity, may you never meet a friend!

In the language of the poet:

> "Farewell! a word that must be, and hath been—
> A sound which makes us linger;—yet—farewell."

INDEX.

T.

www.ingramcontent.com/pod-product-compliance
Lightning Source LLC
LaVergne TN
LVHW021100110826
845150LV00001B/132

9781425566128